Storming the Gates

STORMING THE GATES

*Protest Politics and the
Republican Revival*

Dan Balz and
Ronald Brownstein

Little, Brown and Company

Boston   New York   Toronto   London

FIRST EDITION

ISBN 0-316-08038-1
Library of Congress Catalog Card Number
95-81725

1 3 5 7 9 10 8 6 4 2
HAD
Published simultaneously in Canada by Little, Brown & Company (Canada) Limited

Printed in the United States of America

To our families —
Nancy and John;
Nina, Taylor, and Daniel

Contents

Storming the Gates

Introduction

AS THE SUMMER OF 1995 turned toward fall, almost everything in American politics appeared up for grabs at once.

In Washington, resurgent Republicans pressed their assault to limit the size of government by beginning to dismantle half a century of social programs underpinning the New Deal and the Great Society. On September 19, the Senate voted 87–12 for a welfare reform bill that ended sixty years of federal policy guaranteeing aid to the poor. "We are not only fixing welfare," Senate Majority Leader Robert J. Dole of Kansas said. "We're revolutionizing it."

Two days later, on the other side of the Capitol, the House Ways and Means Committee erupted in a partisan shouting match over Republican proposals to slash the growth of Medicare by $270 billion over the next seven years. Democratic Representative Sam Gibbons of Florida wadded up a bunch of papers, tossed them on the table, and stormed out of the committee. "You're a bunch of dictators, that's who you are," he yelled. In the corridor outside the committee room, Gibbons and Representative Charles Rangel of New York verbally collided with Republicans Jim Nussle of Iowa and William Thomas of California, and before it was over, Gibbons had grabbed Thomas by the necktie to punctuate his unhappiness. The next day the House Commerce Committee approved a Republican plan to cut the growth of Medicaid spending by $182 billion over seven years and give states enormous power to manage the program. One Republican called it the "beginning of a new chapter based on federalism, not paternalism," but Democratic Representative Henry Waxman of California, the architect of much of the modern Medicaid system, described it as "a breathtakingly heartless, radical, extreme proposal." Outside the Capitol, police arrested twenty senior citizens wearing T-shirts emblazoned with the word "Shame" in red letters. On September 29, 1995, the Senate Finance Committee approved legislation that encompassed the GOP reforms of both Medicare and Medicaid, and on October 19, 1995, after a contentious debate, the entire House approved the Medicare restructuring plan. Then, on successive days in late October, the House and Senate approved legislation putting the country on a path toward a balanced budget by the year 2002.

The events in Washington captured only part of the political turmoil at the time. In the midst of the legislative debate, Ross Perot returned to *Larry King Live* to declare his intention to form a new Independence Party, which he said would give disaffected voters a new vehicle to register their unhappiness with the two parties that have not faced a serious competitor in this century. First in California and then elsewhere, Perot supporters set up tables at shopping malls and on street corners to gather the signatures to qualify the new party on ballots across the country in 1996. He quickly cleared the biggest hurdle by beating a tight deadline to qualify for the California ballot. "Democrats and Republicans are the same," said Betty Montgomery, a South Carolina United We Stand leader who went to California to help. "They're in bed with special interests. They're not listening to the American people." As the Perot movement geared up, another political phenomenon grabbed the country's attention. Retired Joint Chiefs Chairman Colin L. Powell published his autobiography, which became one of the fastest-selling nonfiction books in history, and his book tour took on the trappings of a presidential exploratory committee. Thousands of Americans disillusioned with their elected leaders stood in long lines to have Powell autograph his book and to encourage him to run for President, as Republican, Democrat, or None of the Above. On November 8, Powell announced that he would not seek the presidency in 1996, a decision that left many Americans deeply disappointed and still searching for an alternative to the traditional choices. A day earlier, disappointing results for the GOP in the few state and local elections at stake in 1995 suggested that many voters retained doubts about the Republican revolution under way on Capitol Hill.

All of these events underscored the unsettled nature of American politics. The legislative struggles in Washington represented the aftermath of a historic partisan shift triggered by the 1994 Republican victory, which in turn set off a fierce and fundamental debate about the role of government in this country — and raised the prospect of an era of Republican political dominance that could rival the Democratic preeminence in the decades after Franklin Roosevelt assembled the New Deal. And the agitation around Powell and Perot provided two more markers of public disenchantment with politicians of all stripes and raised the specter of radical political change that could present *both* parties with their most fundamental challenges in more than a century.

Both stories wind through this book. The principal narrative in *Storming the Gates* follows the revival of the Republican Party after George Bush's landslide rejection in 1992, and the party's reconfiguration after the twelve years Bush and Ronald Reagan held the White House. Republicans today, as House Speaker Newt Gingrich often says, stand on Reagan's shoulders. But they are more than renovated Reaganites. The core of the Republican Party is more conservative, more populist, and even more antigovernment today than it was a decade ago. The party's success in 1994 depended heavily on its ability to marshal the frustrations of armies of Americans fed up with Washington. Who are these Republicans and how did they come to the brink of total power so quickly after losing the White House in 1992? What explained their remarkable victory? Who shaped and will continue to guide their revolution? Was 1994 just one more jolt of instability in a decaying political order or what political scientists call a "realigning" election that will trigger a stable new era of conservative governance? These are the questions we explore in the chapters ahead.

This is not a comprehensive accounting of the Republican Party over its 142-year history. Instead it is a contemporary examination of a political system, and two political parties, in transition. The book divides into three broad sections. The first focuses on the dramatic Republican advance in 1994 and the breakdown of President Clinton's effort to renew the Democratic Party over his first two years in office — a failure that opened the door to the Republican success. The second section highlights the critical forces that have transformed the GOP over the past decade and created the modern Republican Party: the rise of the aggressive young conservatives in the House of Representatives that we call the "Gingrich generation"; the power of the grassroots, conservative populist movement that pulses through talk radio and groups like the National Rifle Association, the Christian Coalition, and antitax and term limits activists; the Republican takeover of the South that has sent platoons of new conservative voices to Washington and redrawn the geographic balance within the party; and the intellectual realignment that has lurched the GOP's domestic policy agenda sharply to the right after Bush's search for a "kinder and gentler" America. The final section looks forward, to examine the fissures within the GOP electoral coalition created by the ascent of the religious conservative and Perot movements, and the difficulty either party will face in securing lasting allegiance from a majority of voters.

THE backdrop for the partisan story that we recount is the much larger pattern of social and political upheaval that has alienated Americans from their political leadership — and created an environment in which rapid, unpredictable, political change has become increasingly commonplace. Turmoil is the defining characteristic of American politics in the 1990s. Just two years before Republicans routed the Democrats in the 1994 election, voters repudiated Republican President George Bush in near-record numbers; from his initial victory in 1988 to his rejection in 1992, Bush suffered the fourth-largest decline in his share of the vote ever for an incumbent President. Just two years before that, in 1990, the percentage of the vote won by congressional incumbents in both parties declined — a simultaneous vote of no confidence rare in American electoral history.

Accompanying these sharp swings between the parties has been a growing interest in alternatives to both of them. In 1992, Ross Perot attracted nearly twenty million votes in his independent presidential bid — the strongest showing for a third-party candidate since 1912 and the third best ever. For 1996, more than half a dozen political leaders — topped by Colin Powell — talked about or were touted for independent presidential bids of their own. Perot's effort to create a new party makes another significant independent candidacy all the more likely in 1996.

Behind this political turbulence is the most destabilizing force in American politics today: uncertainty about the nation's direction and concern about the future. Optimism about the future has been a defining characteristic of American history; now, America appears tangled in an age of anxiety, as rapid economic and social change undermines assumptions on which we have built our lives — from the security of lifetime employment in major corporations to the primacy of the two-parent family. "People feel like there is nothing they can depend on, there is nothing certain," says Stanley B. Greenberg, a leading Democratic political pollster.

It may be too strong to say America is in "a funk," as President Clinton suggested in September 1995. But surveys leave little doubt that Americans are uneasy about the nation's fundamental trajectory. The most basic question pollsters ask is whether Americans believe the nation is moving on the right track or is headed off in the wrong direction. For the past decade, in times of strong and slow economic growth, under Republican and Democratic Presidents, and now under both a Democratic and Republican Congress, most Americans have said they consider the nation on the wrong track — a finding that amounts to a persistent fever, a warning that something in the system is not quite right. Looking forward, Americans are even more edgy. If the American Dream has an operative definition, it is that each generation will live better than its parents. Most Americans, in fact, tell pollsters that they believe they are living better than their own parents. But people express doubt that their children will continue to advance. In one recent survey conducted by Frank Luntz, a Republican pollster who worked for Ross Perot in 1992, just one-third of Americans said they expected the next generation to live better than this one — the lowest figure, Luntz noted, pollsters have ever recorded on that question. Other surveys have found somewhat less gloomy responses, and these numbers vary in response to current events. But there is no doubt that a form of intergenerational anxiety unusual in our history has crept into the American consciousness.

THREE broad trends — economic stagnation, cultural fragmentation, and political alienation — intertwine at the core of this anxiety.

Together they are shaping the underlying terms of the political struggle between Democrats and Republicans that we explore in this book.

The first trend represents public concern about the economy's ability to generate upward mobility. For the first quarter century after World War II, Americans enjoyed a period of almost uninterrupted economic stability and prosperity. Industries jump-started by the war — chemicals and electronics, appliances and airlines — created millions of new jobs. American manufacturers, reading the commandments of mass production laid down by General Motors' Alfred P. Sloan, became the assembly line for the world. Above all, living standards for the mass of the American public rose dependably year after year. From 1947 through 1973 the median family income doubled. But since then the median income has been virtually stagnant; at the current rate of growth, it will not double again for centuries, the President's Council of Economic Advisers recently calculated.

In retrospect it is clear that the early 1970s marked the pivot from an era of secure prosperity to a new era of economic uncertainty. In the past two decades, a combination of forces has threatened the reliable upward mobility that Americans long considered a birthright. Most important has been the restructuring of the economy under the combined pressure of advancing technology and integrating global markets, which has forced companies to reexamine their most basic operations and diminished the return for workers without advanced skills. Once it was not unusual for a young man to graduate from high school and move on to a job at the assembly line in Chrysler or Ford that paid enough to allow him to support his family while his wife stayed at home and raised their children. But, as the nation continues its shift toward an information-based economy, the average hourly wages for men with only a high school degree has dropped by 20 percent over the past twenty years; for high school dropouts the decline has been even greater. More recently, hourly wages have eroded slightly even for men with college degrees, though not nearly as much as for those without advanced education. Women college graduates have continued to gain ground, though modestly, in recent years.

In this complex new environment, the experience of American workers simultaneously diverges and converges. On the one hand, the income gaps between the skilled and unskilled, between the most affluent 20 percent and the rest of society, even between the top 1 percent and the rest of the top 10 percent, are widening; on the other, all workers in the economy — from the shop floor to the boardroom — now find themselves at increased risk of economic reversal in an era of corporate downsizing, global production, and the contingent workforce. This pattern is generating pervasive economic anxiety despite steady overall economic growth, low inflation, and relatively low unemployment. "While the economy may experience growth in general, more individuals are now left behind, and all suffer enhanced job insecurity," writes Anthony Carnevale, the chairman of the congressionally chartered National Commission for Employment Policy.

Economists can come to blows over exactly what is happening to average families in this new economy. Some point to figures — such as growth in per person national product, or in total compensation to workers, which includes fringe benefits like health care and pensions — that offer somewhat more optimistic portrayals of the past two decades. The best evidence suggests that the heart of the middle class, which both parties praise, court, and fear, is not uniformly losing ground, as the most critical analysts sometimes imply. But the middle-class experience is fragmenting: Some families (especially those headed by workers with four-year college degrees) are moving ahead, though not as quickly as in the past; many others are merely treading water; and more are falling back than in the quarter century after World War II. One recent government study following individual families with workers in their prime earning years — between age twenty-two and fifty-eight — found that fully one-third earned less money at the end of the 1980s than at the beginning; that compared to only about one-fifth who lost ground during the 1970s. Especially hard hit have been those workers without a college education: Among men with only a high school education, more than four in ten suffered an income decline during the 1980s.

This economic change has had enormous social implications by increasing pressure on women to work outside the home. The only type of family that saw its median income rise in the two decades after 1973 were married couples with both partners in the workforce, according to calculations by Lawrence Mishel of the Economic Policy Institute in Washington. Many women, of course, have sought careers outside the home; but the decline in men's wages has forced into the workforce many other women who would like to remain home with their children, and left both partners straining to juggle the demands of work and parenthood in a world where time now often seems the most precious commodity.

That dynamic has generated increased discontent for the past decade, leading young families to talk of being stuck on a "treadmill" — running faster and faster without seeming to gain much ground. The new dimension is that economic unease is no longer confined to working families caught on the treadmill — much less those struggling on the ledge between sufficiency and poverty. Over the past decade, economic anxiety has spread in ever widening circles, reaching even into affluent neighborhoods where the relative merits of Lexus and BMW can be knowledgeably debated. In the 1980s, the image that conveyed economic insecurity was a middle-aged auto- or steelworker in the Midwest whose factory had failed in the face of foreign competition. But now, more white-collar Americans are caught in the same squeeze as computer and communications advances render obsolete the layers of middle-management bureaucracy fattened during the years of prosperity. In the early 1980s, about 60 percent of all Americans who permanently lost their jobs were blue collar. But as corporate downsizing rains pink slips on suburban cul de sacs that once considered themselves immune to economic reversal, white-collar workers now comprise a majority of Americans permanently displaced from their jobs. "People are trying to find their moorings," says John Challenger, the executive vice president of a Chicago-based firm that works with restructuring companies. "If you can't anchor yourself in a large company for a long time, where do you find your anchor?" As the past several elections have demonstrated, workers without anchors are voters without patience.

THE second large source of anxiety about the nation's direction is concern about cultural fragmentation — the fear that society is both Balkanizing into antagonistic ethnic enclaves and losing the capacity to transmit a set of commonly accepted values from one generation to the next. These concerns ricochet through the political system in many directions. With immigration running at its highest level in a century, the flood of new arrivals has generated a backlash in several states along the Mexican border, particularly California. More broadly across America, suspicion and misunderstanding between blacks and whites now seem at their highest point in decades — as vividly demonstrated by the stark racial division over the acquittal of O. J. Simpson in October 1995 on charges that he murdered his former wife and her friend. At this moment of demographic change and economic uncertainty, almost everyone feels unsteady, aggrieved. Blacks, Latinos, and other minorities are frustrated that they remain on the fringes of power; yet among white males, there is a deepening fear that their social dominance is passing if not passed. Thus, close behind the publication of a book that heralds the rage of middle-class blacks came this cover of *Business Week*: "White, Male & Worried." This racial polarization presents an intense problem for Democrats, whose success depends on building a bi-racial coalition of blacks and middle-class whites — both of whom increasingly seem to share the suspicion that there is no common interest that binds them.

Reinforcing these ethnic and racial tensions is a new form of social division separating America: the increasing gap in opportunity and experience between children raised in the traditional two-parent family and those growing up with only one parent, almost always a mother. From 1960 through 1993, the share of children under eighteen living with only one parent rose from about one in eleven to just under one in three. In recent years, the divorce rate has declined slightly (though it remains double the level of 1960), but out-of-wedlock births have increased to the point where in 1991 about three in every ten children were born outside of marriage, up from just one in twenty in 1960. Among African-Americans, two of every three children were born out of wedlock in 1991. Though some recent evidence suggests the growth in illegitimacy may be slowing, sociologists have estimated that by the end of the century four of every ten American children are likely to be born to a mother who is not married.

These trends in family structure amount to a mass abandonment of the two-parent model for raising children that societies have employed throughout world history. So far the early returns on the experiment are not promising. Many single parents provide loving, secure homes, but research shows that children growing up with only one parent are far more likely to be poor and to have emotional problems, drop out of school, become unwed parents themselves, and encounter trouble with the law. It is that final association — the link between an absent father and crime — that has politically electrified the concern about family breakdown. Many Americans see the enormous rise in violent crime over the past generation — particularly the increase in juvenile crime symbolized by gang violence in the racially segregated urban cores of cities from New York to Los Angeles — as the bitter fruit of the collapse in family and an erosion of moral standards. Through crime, the breakdown in family structure becomes a problem that generates anxiety in all corners of society. That gnawing concern, as we shall show, has opened voters to conservative arguments about illegitimacy, the poor, and welfare reform that were beyond the pale of respectable political discussion only a few years ago.

IF fears of economic and cultural decline are the first two forces clouding perceptions about the future, the third is a collapse of faith in government and the political system itself, partly for its failure to reverse these other worrisome trends. Perhaps the single most powerful shift in public opinion over the past thirty-five years has been the relentless increase in alienation from Washington. In 1960, when John F. Kennedy in his inaugural address told Americans to "ask not what your country can do for you — ask what you can do for your country," he spoke on behalf of a government that within the living memory of every one of his voters had defeated the Nazis, educated the returning soldiers with the GI bill, and linked the nation through the interstate highway system.

That legacy translated into a reservoir of public goodwill on which public officials could draw: In 1958, in a University of Michigan poll, 73 percent of Americans said the "government in Washington" could be trusted "to do what is right" most or all of the time. By 1964, as Lyndon Johnson launched the Great Society, the percentage of Americans who trusted Washington most or all of the time increased to just over three-fourths. But over the next fifteen years, confidence in government plummeted, in several discrete steps, like a rock bouncing from ledge to ledge down a mountainside. The University of Michigan surveys, conducted every two years, recorded the change. After the first wave of urban race riots in 1965, the percentage of Americans expressing a high degree of confidence in government dropped to 65 percent; in the wake of widening social tensions over Vietnam and race relations, that number fell to just over half in 1970. After the Watergate scandal, only about one-third of the public expressed a high level of trust in government; by 1980, after the energy and inflation shocks of Jimmy Carter's presidency, just one-fourth of Americans said government could be trusted most of the time.

Ironically, attitudes toward government improved slightly under Ronald Reagan — who rode to Washington on a message that "government is the problem" — but by the end of the decade perceptions about Washington soured again. After a series of congressional scandals through the early 1990s, George Bush's abandonment of his "read my lips, no new taxes" pledge, the continued pressure on living standards, and disappointment over Bill Clinton's first two years as President, the percentage of Americans who said Washington could be trusted to do what is right most of the time shriveled in 1994 to just one in five — the lowest number ever recorded.

As Republican pollster Fred Steeper found in a 1995 analysis, discontent about government now runs down two powerful streams. On the one hand, the vast majority of Americans subscribe to a populist critique that assails Washington as wasteful, ineffective, in thrall to special interests, and crowded with duplicitous self-serving politicians who will say anything to be elected. (This populist alienation from government is strongest among working-class white voters — the same group that has faced the most economic pressure over the past two decades.) From a second front, a smaller, but still substantial number of Americans indict government on ideological grounds — as an overreaching behemoth that is eroding individual liberty and self-reliance, discouraging religion, and favoring minorities and the poor. This distrust of Washington has proven a huge hurdle for Democratic efforts to assemble support behind new government initiatives — even those aimed at combating economic insecurity through expanded job training or guaranteed health care. Hostility toward Washington is now as much a part of American culture as reverence for the flag.

THE competition between the two established parties now largely revolves around their explanations and proposed responses to these three entrenched and complex dynamics.

In his 1992 campaign, Bill Clinton spoke more directly about eroding cultural values and the strain on middle-class incomes than any Democratic presidential candidate before him. In the address announcing his candidacy he declared he was seeking the White House because he refused "to stand by and let our children become part of the first generation to do worse than their parents." Clinton acknowledged the power of public discontent with government, but he insisted that government could be reformed — "reinvent[ed] to deliver new services in different ways" — to launch fresh offensives against these cultural and economic problems and regain the public's faith. With a policy agenda that he called a "third way" between traditional liberal and conservative approaches, Clinton's goal was to create a new language and a new political synthesis: one that reached out to the anxious middle class with a broad program of economic uplift grounded in the idea of reciprocal responsibility — that notion that government would work to increase opportunity for those who displayed responsibility in their own lives. Clinton's blueprint offered a promising path for Democrats to rebuild faith in government at a time when Americans had lost confidence in traditional liberal solutions. But as we shall show in chapter 2, in office Clinton could not implement his design — leaving open the door for Republicans to advance a competing explanation for the nation's difficulties.

The key to the Republican revival since 1992 has been the party's success at blaming government for the nation's cultural and economic dilemmas — and identifying itself as the antigovernment, anti-Washington party. At least for now, each of these three basic trends is tending to increase the audience for conservative messages. Economic stagnation opens working- and middle-class voters to Republican attacks on taxes, immigration, and affirmative action. Fears of moral decline amplify conservative calls for a reaffirmation of "virtue" and self-reliance, and retrenchment of a welfare state that is said to breed "dependency" and encourage illegitimacy. And alienation from Washington furrows the ground for the neo-Reaganite appeals of GOP leaders who condemn "career politicians" and proclaim government not the solution to our problems, but itself the problem. From each of these angles, the modern Republican agenda has fused the populist and ideological critiques of government into a single battering ram aimed at Washington. In the midst of a broad-based uprising against the national government, Republicans have gained the upper hand over the Democrats by leaping the moat and joining the army storming the castle.

At the end of the Cold War many analysts speculated that conservatives would splinter without the unifying principle of opposition to communism. The "Cold War's end deprived [conservatives] of common purpose," wrote the liberal analyst John B. Judis. Instead, opposition to Washington has succeeded opposition to communism as the unifying focus for the Right. "Washington has replaced communism as the glue for conservatives," said Don Fierce, the director of strategic planning at the Republican National Committee. "Washington is financially and morally bankrupt and because of that it is the glue that binds economic and social conservatives. These are people that love their country but hate their federal government. Where is the evil empire? The evil empire is in Washington."

THE story of the GOP over the past decade — the principal story of this book — is the rise of the forces within the party committed to the most uncompromising assault on Washington, forces that we call the antigovernment coalition. The antigovernment coalition is a constellation of interests that includes grassroots populist groups like the National Rifle Association, the National Federation of Independent Business, and the Christian Coalition; the network of conservative talk radio hosts led by Rush Limbaugh; conservative intellectuals such as former Education Secretary William J. Bennett and social theorist Charles Murray; and the young conservatives in Congress, many of them embodying the growing Republican political dominance in the South, who march under the banner of House Speaker Newt Gingrich. Their rise amounts to an intellectual, institutional, regional, and generational transition of power within the GOP.

Though the antigovernment coalition's control is not complete — as demonstrated by resistance in 1995 to many of its initiatives from Republican moderates in the Senate and declining public support for key parts of the GOP agenda — it is now the preeminent force in the party, and likely will grow more dominant over time as generational change replaces older congressional moderates with younger conservatives inspired by both Reagan and Gingrich. Today, these ambitious young conservatives dream of a retrenchment of federal power — an unwinding of the New Deal and Great Society and even the Progressive Era — that greatly exceeds Reagan's hopes of shrinking the state. As Grover G. Norquist, a leading strategist in the antigovernment coalition, puts it, "Gingrich is Reaganism at warp speed."

This militant, antigovernment message has brought the GOP to the brink of control over national politics. As we shall explore, many of the underlying trends in American political life point toward the GOP as a new majority party that will control government into the next century. But first it must overcome the same forces of economic anxiety, cultural unease, and alienation from government that battered Clinton — and fight against its own image as a party insensitive to the most vulnerable in society but in thrall with those who have money, whether individuals or corporations. By focusing voter anger at Washington, the Republicans routed the Democrats in 1994. But if the Republican assault on government cannot resolve the broader economic and cultural concerns the party rode to power, the second half of the decade could see even greater political turmoil than the first half — and perhaps even a serious challenge to the two major parties that have dominated American politics since the Civil War.

The Republican resurgence in just the three years since Bush's collapse has allowed the party to dream of a new period of conservative dominance; but the tremors of alienation and discontent reshaping the political landscape show no signs of abating. Our story begins with the revival of the Republicans but concludes by looking forward into an era in which both parties may find the ground shifting suddenly and unpredictably beneath their feet.

★★★

I

Rise and Fall

★★★

1
———

The Whirlwind

T**HE FIRST RETURNS** reached Washington soon after the polls closed in Kentucky on the evening of May 24, 1994, and in the cream-colored, brick building on First Street in southeast Washington, an explosion of cheers erupted. The Republicans were anticipating a long night of counting, and a few of the stalwarts from the House had assembled with the campaign staff at party headquarters to await the outcome. In the annals of American politics, the contest that held their interest seemed insignificant, just another special election for a vacant House seat in a mostly rural congressional district in Kentucky. But the Republicans knew this was no ordinary election, and now the early numbers looked far better than anyone expected.

Six months later, they would look back on the Kentucky election as the first volley in the revolution of 1994, but if there was anything notable to most of the country about the contest that night, it was the event that had precipitated the election: the death two months earlier of the man who had held the seat for more than forty years. Democrat William H. Natcher had come to Washington in 1953, the next-to-last year the Republicans controlled the House of Representatives. After four decades in Congress, the courtly and courteous Kentucky gentleman was an institution within the institution. He rose to the chairmanship of the powerful House Appropriations Committee and established an astonishing attendance record by casting 18,401 consecutive roll-call votes — the last four from a gurney rolled onto the House floor — before his ailing body finally rebelled and prevented him from leaving the hospital, where a few weeks later he died. Natcher's long career neatly encompassed the forty-year era in which the Democrats had controlled the House and, in a very real sense, controlled Washington itself. Through five Republican Presidents and six years of a Republican Senate, the House remained in Democratic hands, a bulwark against conservative insurgents and the central nervous system that maintained and nurtured the tight web of relationships and interests that defined official Washington.

Kentucky's Second Congressional District long had contributed to Democratic dominance in the House. Home to both Fort Knox and Abraham Lincoln's birthplace, the Second District had been in Democratic hands since 1865, and even in 1994, 68 percent of voters registered as Democrats. Over the years, however, the voters in the Second District, which spreads from the Louisville suburbs west along the Ohio River and south toward the Tennessee border, had regularly cast their ballots for Republican presidential candidates. George Bush carried the district by twenty percentage points in 1988 and even in the Republican debacle of 1992, when Bill Clinton was winning Kentucky on his way to the White House, Bush still managed narrowly to capture the Second District. On paper at least, the Republicans should have been able to win the Second District. But that was the case with scores of districts around the country. On paper, they always looked good. It was finding the right candidate and honing the message and raising the money and building the coalition and all the other elements of a good campaign that so often seemed to elude the Republicans.

So much had escaped from them below the level of the White House. After controlling the presidency for twelve years with Ronald Reagan and George Bush, Republicans held fewer seats in Congress than when Reagan took office. During the Reagan-Bush years, the National Republican Congressional Committee (NRCC) had spent $260 million trying to win back the House, but they managed to reduce the GOP numbers from 192 in 1981 to 176 when Clinton took office. The GOP's position in the Senate was similarly shaky: After Bush's defeat Republicans held just forty-three seats, ten fewer than after Reagan's election. In the states, things looked no better. When

Clinton took the oath of office in January 1993, just seventeen of the fifty governors were Republicans; the GOP had not held a majority of governors since 1970. As a party, Republicans appeared demoralized over the loss of the White House, confused about how to combat the new President and struggling to find a unifying symbol to replace the devil of communism that had bound them throughout the Cold War. In the summer of 1993, Newt Gingrich, then the Republican whip in the House, groused that the party's image was that of "a negative, out-of-touch, country club party that failed." At that point, it was far from clear that the party could summon the will or the unity to revive itself.

But by the spring of 1994, Republicans had begun to sense extraordinary opportunities, and some of the more astute Democratic operatives glumly agreed. Among them was David Dixon, the political director of the Democratic Congressional Campaign Committee, who quietly called in reporters and independent analysts like Charles Cook and Stuart Rothenberg to point out to them in striking detail the Democrats' predicament in district after district. Dixon hoped that, through them, he could shake the incumbent Democrats from their electoral complacency.

Beginning a few weeks after Clinton's election in 1992, Republicans had won a string of elections, including contests to fill Senate seats in Georgia and Texas, governorships in Virginia and New Jersey, and mayoral offices in the nation's two largest cities, New York and Los Angeles. Retirements in the House and Senate had created unexpected openings for the Republicans, and for the first time in the postwar era, the round of redistricting that followed the 1990 census had erased many of the advantages Democrats earlier had enjoyed, thanks to a massive legal and political effort coordinated out of the Republican National Committee during Bush's presidency. With all their other problems, Democratic candidates now faced district boundaries far more evenly balanced between the parties than in prior years. In addition, Republicans reported a banner year in recruitment of candidates and actually expected to field more candidates for the House than the Democrats. With Clinton's legislative agenda — particularly health care, the crown jewel of Clinton's presidency — stalling in Congress, and with the President's popularity sinking in the polls, Republican leaders like Gingrich, then–Senate Minority Leader Bob

Dole, and Republican National Committee Chairman Haley Barbour expressed increasing optimism about the fall elections — and were beginning to believe their own pumped-up rhetoric.

The party that lost its way in 1992 once again had begun to act like a political party with a unified message and internal discipline. Over the eighteen months since Bush's defeat, Republicans had eagerly returned to the anti-Washington themes that had resonated from Republican candidates since Barry Goldwater's 1964 campaign but that had become increasingly muted throughout the Bush presidency. Recasting themselves as the vehicle for the swell of anger rising up around the country, Republicans sought to energize a growing anti-government grassroots army of gun owners, term limits advocates, religious conservatives, small-business owners, taxpayer activists, and followers of Ross Perot. With the help of sympathetic talk radio hosts around the country, the Republicans systematically stoked the populist resentment toward Washington — or simply allowed themselves to be swept along in its wake. In the process, they tried to change their own image. "We had to change the definition of who we were," said Don Fierce, who directed the RNC's office of strategic planning and maintained the party's links with the grassroots organizations. To most Americans, Fierce said, Republicans were still the party of "rich, white, fat guys not connected to the people. What we were trying to do was to become a populist party."

KENTUCKY'S Second District appeared to be the ideal laboratory to test the limits of this appeal. Two weeks earlier, the Republicans had won another special election, this one in a longtime Democratic district that stretched from Oklahoma City west into the Oklahoma Panhandle. The Republican candidate, a farmer and rancher named Frank Lucas, had pummeled his Democratic opponent, Dan Webber Jr., as a creature of the liberal Washington establishment. Even though Webber worked for popular Oklahoma Senator David Boren, a conservative Democrat who frequently frustrated the Clinton White House, he might as well have been part of Ted Kennedy's inner circle the way the Republicans portrayed him. Lucas, who farmed land his family had owned for a century, attacked Webber in television ads for having a home in the capital but not in Oklahoma and for "Washington values" that were by implication antithetical to those in the district. On the ground in Oklahoma, an antigovernment army mobilized support behind Lucas: U.S. Term Limits sent out fifty thousand pieces of mail and aired radio ads; the Oklahoma Taxpayer's Union spent $30,000 on a radio campaign; and the Christian Coalition passed out eighty thousand "voter guides" favorable to Lucas. With all these forces behind him, Lucas raced to an easy victory. On the night of Lucas's victory, Gingrich turned to John Morgan, one of the GOP's leading analysts of congressional districts, and asked, "Can we win Kentucky?" "I've had my eye on it for thirty years," Morgan said.

Despite the euphoria over Oklahoma, the contest in Kentucky looked like a terrible mismatch for the Republicans. The Democratic candidate, Joe Prather, was well known, having served as state party chairman and for a decade as the Democratic leader in the Kentucky state Senate. The Republican candidate was a little-known minister named Ron Lewis, who operated a Christian bookstore and had not run for office in more than twenty years. But well before the Oklahoma election, Kentucky Senator Mitch McConnell had tipped Gingrich and the chairman of the National Republican Congressional Committee, Representative Bill Paxon of New York, to the possibility of an upset in his home state. Flying to Richard Nixon's funeral in late April, McConnell pulled Gingrich aside and assured him that, despite Lewis's light credentials, he could win the race against Prather — if the party made a maximum financial commitment to his campaign.

The campaign committee earlier had commissioned a poll of the Kentucky district, and a few days after Nixon's funeral, the results came back. Conducted by the firm of Richard Wirthlin, who was Reagan's pollster, the survey showed Prather with a fifteen-point lead over Lewis, which was far from insurmountable in a low-profile special election. Even more promising were the results on Clinton, which demonstrated the President's abysmal standing in the district. Only 30 percent thought he deserved reelection in 1996, while 56 percent — including almost half the Democrats surveyed — agreed that voting Republican would be a good way to send a message of dissatisfaction with Clinton and the Democrats. The poll results dictated the Republican strategy. "We're going after Clinton," Paxon told his NRCC staff.

Republican leaders agreed on one other element of strategy: The only way they could win was with a stealth campaign that caught the

Democrats napping. Even though the campaign committee was broke, Gingrich and Paxon ordered the staff to prepare a full-scale campaign plan, then called Lewis and quietly advised him to keep organizing but hold on to his money. To reinforce the message, the state Republican committee sent in a staff member to take control of the Lewis campaign's checkbook, knowing that every cent available would be needed for a last-minute television blitz. Meanwhile, back in Washington, GOP leaders threw up a wall of disinformation. "We kept sending out the word around town that we can't win this race; we're not even going to try," Paxon said. "We've got the wrong candidate, we have the wrong district, it ain't going to happen." It was not a tough sell. Maria Cino, Paxon's aide, who was executive director of the campaign committee, received a telephone call from a friend one Saturday morning proposing an afternoon golf game. Cino begged off, saying she had to work on the Lewis race. "I'll give you Oklahoma," the friend, who happened to come from Kentucky, told Cino. "But there is just no way to ever win Kentucky. You're wasting your time."

At the Republican National Committee, Haley Barbour also remained a skeptic, despite McConnell's pleadings for financial help for Lewis. "Mitch just blistered me over the phone," Barbour said. Before he would agree to commit the RNC's money, Barbour demanded something in return. First, McConnell had to agree to help raise a substantial amount of money too; and second, Barbour wanted Terry Carmack, the Republican Party chairman in Kentucky, to take direct control of Lewis's campaign. Carmack later slipped out of his office without alerting reporters to his temporary deployment. Shortly after the Oklahoma victory, Paxon met with Gingrich at the Georgia congressman's Capitol office for one last, agonizing meeting about money. Their House colleagues had pitched in to help finance the Lucas victory in Oklahoma, but it took them six weeks to raise the money. The GOP needed an even larger effort for Lewis, but had a few days to do it. Gingrich and Paxon knew energy already was building for 1994. If they made an all-out effort in Kentucky and then fell short, would that blunt their momentum? But Gingrich lived to take risks. "The polling was clear," Paxon said. "People were pissed at Clinton, so let's take a shot at it."

True to their mandate, the NRCC staff had prepared a wickedly effective campaign plan built around a single, visually stunning televi-

sion commercial quickly dubbed "the morph ad." The morph ad came to symbolize the GOP strategy for 1994. "If you like Bill Clinton, you'll love Joe Prather," an announcer's voice intoned, while on the screen Prather's face magically dissolved into Clinton's. The ad, which represented an ingenious technique for linking every Democratic candidate to the unpopular President, was the brainchild of Dan Leonard, the NRCC communications director. Leonard had begged Cino for the money to produce the ad, and a colleague found a computer firm in downtown Washington to create the digitized images for only $2,000. Armed with the ad, the staff convinced Lewis to scrap a planned series of biographical spots and hit Prather head on with the morph ad. "I wanted to get it out as soon as we could," Lewis said. On Friday, May 13, the Lewis campaign suddenly surfaced across the Second District with a saturation-level television buy. "Send a message to Bill Clinton," the announcer concluded in the ad, reading straight out of the Wirthlin poll. "Send Ron Lewis to Congress." When Gingrich and Paxon showed their colleagues the commercial during a caucus early the next week, they went wild, cheering, stomping, standing on chairs, and applauding.

Overnight, the morph ad reshaped the Kentucky contest. Prather, once so confident that he had been searching out housing in Washington, suddenly found himself on the defensive, unable to respond to the digital pummeling. Democratic leaders in Washington begged him to fight back aggressively, but he seemed frozen in the headlights by the Republican assault. Meanwhile, Lewis continued to press his newfound advantage. Bob Dole came in to fly around the district with Lewis. It was the first time Lewis's wife had ever been on an airplane. On the ground, as in Oklahoma, a storm of direct mail, voter guides, and other pro-Lewis material rained down on the voters from populist, grassroots groups like the National Rifle Association, the Christian Coalition, Americans for Tax Reform, and United We Stand. The Democrats protested that these "independent expenditures" smelled of collusion with the Republican Party and Lewis's campaign; the same media-buying firm, they noted, was purchasing commercial time for both Lewis and Americans for Tax Reform. But the Republicans simply brushed aside the complaint and kept firing.

The polls closed at 6 P.M. on May 24. Within an hour, a friend of Lewis's, analyzing precinct returns from the district, told the

Republican he was on his way to Congress. In Washington, NRCC analysts came to the same conclusion a short time later, and word spread quickly to the row of House office buildings lining Independence Avenue, bringing Gingrich and a stream of Republicans to the NRCC offices on the second floor of the party headquarters. They found a celebration that looked like a fraternity keg party already well lubricated. The giddy members toasted one another with beers and high fives, and someone called Barbour in Israel with the news of Lewis's 55–45 percent win. Republicans knew the Kentucky race represented a turning point of enormous significance. "You could almost just feel that dam burst," Paxon said.

Lewis's victory gave sudden credibility to Republican claims that a tidal wave of resentment threatened to sweep away forty years of Democratic control of the House. Republican incumbents who had spent their careers in the minority began to believe that what once was only a dream might actually be possible, that they might hold the gavels and sit in the majority. They had found in Clinton the glue to unify their voter coalition. The next day, speaking of the television commercial that torpedoed Prather's campaign, Gingrich said, "I wouldn't be surprised to see that ad in two hundred districts this fall." To which Clinton pollster Stanley B. Greenberg replied, "I hope so. I think people will vote for change rather than negativism and a return to the Reagan-Bush years."

THE FIRE OUT THERE

The Kentucky election instantly and dramatically changed the complexion of 1994, despite days of denial by the Democrats. Democratic leaders tried to pin the defeat on the inadequacy of their candidate rather than the weakness of their President, but most people knew better. Whatever Prather's weaknesses, the loss of confidence in Clinton's leadership and the intensity of voter frustration with Washington created a climate for Democrats that had all the stability of a Mason jar full of nitroglycerin. "Even under the best of circumstances, this would be a tough year for us," Geoffrey Garin, a Democratic pollster, said one day in the summer. "But frankly, this isn't even close to the best of circumstances."

The evidence of volatility was unmistakable, and yet no one could

be certain how the voters would express their wrath with politicians in Washington. It was like a power line blown down in a storm, charged with electricity and pulsing randomly along the road. Much of the anger was aimed at the Clinton administration. One voter, a participant in a Republican focus group during the summer of 1994, complained that in watching the administration, it was impossible to know if he was watching "a bad rerun of *The Little Rascals* or *The Keystone Cops*. Is it a bunch of kids playing games, or are they totally clueless?" But an equal amount of venom spewed forth toward the Congress. In mid-1994, a *Washington Post*–ABC News Poll found that six in ten Americans disapproved of the 103rd Congress, a level of disapproval double that of twenty years earlier, and the more they knew the less they liked. Voters saw Congress as a distant institution where perks and privilege passed for public representation: Four of five voters said members of Congress cared more about keeping power than caring for the country, while three in four said candidates made promises with no intention of keeping them. "I think Democrats and Republicans both are clones of their own systems and neither of the two groups really seems to care about the needs, the desires, the concerns of average Americans," Rik Sawyer, an antiques dealer from Maine, said.

Why shouldn't people believe that? Over the previous decade, congressional scandals, not great legislative accomplishments, had captured the public's attention: Jim Wright's resignation as Speaker of the House in 1989, which came after a long ethics investigation; the midnight pay raise that looked like grand larceny to a cynical electorate; the revelation that the House bank had routinely allowed members to cash checks running into the thousands of dollars without demanding the money in their accounts to cover them; reports that some congressmen had traded in their official office stamp allowance for cash at the House post office. The post office scandal produced the indictment of one of the most powerful men in Congress, Dan Rostenkowski, the burly Chicago pol who chaired the House Ways and Means Committee. Rostenkowski's legal troubles literally turned him into a poster boy for the term limits movement. Republicans, led by Newt Gingrich, had done much to amplify those scandals and as a result to undermine public confidence in the institution, confident that the fallout would harm Democrats much more than themselves. But the cynicism toward Washington, expressed in everything from focus groups of voters to the opening monologues of Leno and Letterman, permeated the campaign-year atmosphere like a morning fog on the freeway, threatening to engulf Republicans and Democrats alike in a major pileup.

"The American electorate is angry, self-absorbed and politically unanchored," the Times Mirror Center for The People & The Press reported in a major survey issued in September of 1994. "Thousands of interviews with American voters this summer find no clear direction in the public's political thinking other than frustration with the current system and an eager responsiveness to alternative political solutions and appeals." The report went on to warn that the "discontent with Washington that gained momentum in the late 1980s is even greater now than it was in 1992." A computer bulletin board message sent to Perot followers earlier in the summer gave a more pungent taste of what awaited the politicians in the fall. The Internet message read: "Never give in, never give in, never, never, never!!! We will remember in November!!! Oh yes, we will remember!!!"

Equally powerful was a parallel current of anger toward big government and a noticeable tilt toward the right among voters who saw the rising crime and illegitimacy, declining schools, and movies and rap lyrics saturated with sex and violence as symptoms of a broader breakdown in traditional values that threatened not only their own families but society at large. These social concerns, rather than the economic anxieties that dominated the campaign of 1992, stood at record levels, and the Times Mirror Center reported voter attitudes "punctuated by increased indifference to the problems of blacks and poor people" along with growing "resentment toward immigrants." The Republican National Committee conducted a massive survey of Republicans in 1993 and found that 93 percent believed the federal government "no longer represents the intent of the Founding Fathers." Even more startling was another finding, which showed that 63 percent of Republicans saw the government as "an adversary to be avoided rather than a positive force for helping people solve their problems."

All the dots stood out in bas-relief on the canvasses of political forecasters. The only trouble was, no one knew quite how to connect them. Would they line up to topple incumbents of both parties in a collective gesture of anti-incumbency? Would they strike principally at the Democrats who now held both the White House and Congress? Or, might the vibrations of disaffection shake, but not fundamentally upend, the status quo? The Kentucky and Oklahoma special elections suggested the answer to the riddle: The Republicans were coming back. The real questions were how far and how fast.

REBUILDING THE PARTY

Hindsight is the most reliable lens of all for viewing American politics, for, as the old saying goes, "The only certainty of political campaigns is surprise." In the haze of summer 1994, most experts were cautious with their predictions; in retrospect, what should have been clear by then was the degree to which the Republicans had rejuvenated themselves after the demoralizing defeat of 1992, recast themselves once again as the guardians of conservatism, restored a sense of unity and purpose, and begun to think anew of becoming the majority party in America. That alone was not enough to guarantee a majority in the fall, but it represented a considerable first step.

Many people could claim part of the credit for the GOP's revival, including Bill Clinton himself, who doubtless would have refused the honor. But three people stood above all the others: Newt Gingrich, Bob Dole, and Haley Barbour. Each had contributed, at key moments in 1993 and 1994, the combination of leadership and discipline essential to the success of a political party. All shared a belief that the Republicans once again had to stand for the conservative principles that had defined the Reagan presidency. But they were equally united in the strategy of opposing Clinton at every turn and finding legislative vehicles to restore their connections to their conservative, grassroots supporters.

Barbour was the least well known of the trio, but no less indispensable to the party's resurrection than Gingrich or Dole. A good-natured, wisecracking Mississippian with a rich southern drawl, Barbour, with the exception of a losing run for the Senate in 1982, had spent his career as a Republican operative. He worked in Richard Nixon's campaign in 1968, directed the Mississippi Republican Party in the 1970s, attached himself to John B. Connally's failed presidential campaign in 1980, served as political director in the Reagan White House from

1985 to 1986, and acted as a troubleshooter for the Bush campaign in 1988. After that he settled into a comfortable life as a Washington lobbyist and political commentator.

Barbour looked deceptively like an aging southern fraternity boy, all lacquered hair and calculated bonhomie. But he had firm ideas about the road to revival, a keen strategic sense of how to implement them, and a knack for putting them in language voters understood. "Compromising with the Democrats," he once said, "is like paying the cannibals to eat you last." With Bush's defeat, he blossomed into one of the party's most effective chairmen, ranking with Ray Bliss, who guided the party back to life after Barry Goldwater's defeat in 1964, and William Brock, the former Tennessee senator who led the party during major victories after the Watergate debacle of 1974 and Jimmy Carter's victory over Gerald Ford in 1976. Barbour had been known mostly as a self-deprecating, nuts-and-bolts operative. But within days of Clinton's victory in 1992, another Barbour began to emerge, a philosophical hard-liner interested in ideas and public policy and determined to steer the party back to the principles that were at the heart of Reagan's successes in 1980 and 1984. To Barbour, the lesson of 1992 was clear: Bush had foolishly reneged on his "no new taxes" pledge, tacked toward the center on other domestic policies, and blurred the distinctions between Republicans and Democrats. Barbour told Republican governors at a meeting in Lake Geneva, Wisconsin, "Our problem was the people felt we had repudiated our own principles by not acting in accordance with them." Shortly after Clinton's inauguration, Barbour was elected chairman of the Republican National Committee in a five-way contest.

Barbour wanted to reenergize the party's conservative coalition. He wanted to polarize the debate in Washington and the electorate in the country along conservative-liberal lines. He wanted to reestablish Republicans as the party of lower taxes and smaller government. And he wanted to find a common enemy around which Republicans and independents could unite. That enemy was the federal government. "We've got to quit being so Washington-oriented," he told the Republican officials in his first speech as chairman.

He believed in the power of ideas and the importance of a consistent message, and he began to build an infrastructure to meld the two into a powerful weapon that would, if nothing else, recharge the energies of Republican true believers who had gone flat in the final years of the Bush presidency. He hired a first-rate staff that included Chief of Staff Scott Reed, a former adviser to Jack Kemp; Charles Greener, part of a family of Republican operatives, as communications director; and Don Fierce, his former business partner, to act as a liaison with congressional leaders and grassroots organizations. He rapidly built a communications empire that included a think tank, a glossy magazine, and a weekly television program (housed in state-of-the-art facilities paid for with a $2.5 million donation from the Amway Corporation) in which he acted as the genial host serving up powder-puff questions to Republican officials. To influence political insiders, he papered Washington with faxes and dispensed his wisdom through "Haley's Comments," attacking Clinton every time the President even glanced to his left. Barbour began clubbing Clinton the day the President delivered his economic plan before a joint session of Congress. The plan called for $500 billion in deficit reduction through a combination of spending cuts, increased taxes on the rich, and a broad-based energy tax. "Clinton ran on the promise to 'put people first,'" Barbour said. "Tonight his plan is to put government first." As much as anything, Barbour displayed a willingness to attack Clinton even when it appeared risky to do so. "We just hammered him," Barbour said of Clinton. "I'll be honest. I had not anticipated we'd be able to go on the offensive that early, because Presidents get honeymoons, and I knew it was not the right thing to do to go out and attack him on personal grounds or anything like that. I actually thought he would move in his early phases like a new Democrat. He didn't."

The RNC also fanned the prairie fire of talk radio programs, providing talk shows with background information, RNC talking points, and encouragement to bash the Democrats. Talk radio hosts provided Americans with an outlet for their frustration, and, like field commanders, often directed the citizen assaults that gridlocked switchboards at the Capitol or the White House. No medium had a greater effect on establishing the climate of the 1994 elections than talk radio, and no one played a more prominent role in stirring up conservatives than the cherubic but devastating Rush Limbaugh, the irreverent and indomitable conservative who fused the sensibilities of Ed Meese and John Belushi into three hours of relentless Clinton-bashing every day. Limbaugh's program — a mixture of conservative monologue and antic satire, or as he calls it, "America the way it ought to be" — broadcast on 660 stations, reaching some twenty million listeners every week, more than four million at any given time. Before the inaugural reviewing stand had been dismantled out front of the White House, Limbaugh had begun to batter the new administration as the reincarnation of the flower children of the 1960s.

Barbour's RNC reinforced that angry message to the Republican core constituency through a blizzard of direct mail to potential donors, and in the process rebuilt the party's fund-raising base, which had atrophied after twelve years of Republican control of the White House. To run the finance department, Barbour stole Albert Mitchler, a great bear of a man with a walrus mustache, from Senator Phil Gramm and the National Republican Senatorial Campaign Committee. At the RNC, Mitchler instantly quadrupled the number of direct mail appeals to 1.2 million a week and revved up the RNC's telemarketing operation — and the money began to pour in. From the beginning, the message of the fund-raising appeals was, as Scott Reed put it, "red meat . . . one hundred percent anti-Clinton." Positive appeals bombed, reducing the RNC strategy to a mantra of, as Mitchler described it, "Clinton bad, Republican good." One letter said, "In Bill Clinton's eyes, if you worked hard and succeeded — you're the enemy." Another attacked the Clintons for supporting "far-out social concepts of diversity, multi-culturism and political correctness." The responses built throughout 1993 and 1994; one day, about a month before the election, the postal service delivered 134,000 contribution letters to the RNC offices.

As he wooed conservative contributors, Barbour also stroked the conservative activists, from gun owners and antitax protesters to westerners inflamed over Clinton's proposal to increase fees for grazing on public lands. He was particularly solicitous of the religious conservatives, who had been roundly criticized in some quarters for turning the 1992 national convention in Houston into a public display of intolerance. Barbour believed Christian conservatives represented a critical constituency, and he looked for opportunities to display his fealty to them. When Representative Vic Fazio of California, chairman of the Democratic Congressional Campaign Committee, attacked religious conservatives in the summer of 1994, Barbour quickly rushed to their defense. "We wanted Christians to know that we weren't going to run from them," said the RNC's Don Fierce. But first, Barbour called Jerry Falwell and Pat Robertson, the movement's best-known leaders, and asked them to hold their fire. Republican leaders did not want either Falwell or Robertson, both divisive figures, to respond personally to the attacks. They wanted this fight to be Republicans against Democrats, not Democrats against two evangelical lightning rods.

BOB Dole provided a different kind of boost to the Republicans in 1993, with cutting humor, relentless partisanship, and the tactical skills that made him the foremost legislative leader of his time. Clinton had barely awakened in Little Rock on the morning after his election when Dole, noting that 57 percent of the voters had preferred someone other than Clinton as President, declared that he would be the representative in Washington of that anti-Clinton majority coalition. With Bush fallen, Dole became the party's de facto leader and most visible foil to a White House that sometimes seemed to lack adult supervision. Dole proved to be both the principal spokesman for the opposition and an experienced, tenacious, legislative adversary at a time when the party desperately needed leadership.

In the spring of 1993, Clinton attempted to push his economic stimulus through the Senate with a set of parliamentary maneuvers that prevented Republicans even from offering amendments. Devised by Robert Byrd, the white-haired Democratic philosopher-tactician who had served in the Senate since 1958, the rules of debate outraged Republican moderates who had sent signals of possible compromise to the White House. Dole immediately mounted a filibuster against the stimulus package, a small but symbolic piece of Clinton's overall economic plan. Almost instantly the partisan lines hardened like epoxy on a piece of wood. Although Democrats held a majority in the Senate, Clinton could not move without sixty votes to choke off the filibuster. Clinton sought a way out of the legislative stalemate, but Dole refused to budge. Yielding to the obvious, Clinton eventually withdrew the package, handing the Republicans not just a substantive victory but a huge psychological boost: The GOP had drawn first blood.

Dole's leadership on the stimulus fight not only earned him the gratitude of Republicans desperate for any scrap of self-assurance, but vaulted him atop the rapidly growing field of possible challengers to Clinton in 1996. That was an astonishing reversal in fortunes for a man whose two previous presidential campaigns were remembered only for ineptitude. Dole was so convinced that his White House hopes had expired that he gave serious thought to retiring from the Senate in 1992. Now he was toasted by Republicans as a genuine war hero who embodied the American Dream. Once seen as a wily but often mean-spirited political hatchetman, he now drew the approval of columnists who dubbed him a mature statesman. With one eye on the presidency and another on a Senate Republican caucus growing steadily more conservative, Dole continued to pull back farther and farther from a posture of potential cooperation with the White House into outright and total opposition. Nowhere was that shift more significant — nor more politically inspired — than in Dole's stance on Clinton's health care program: He began by promising to work with the administration and ended up leading a unified Republican opposition that helped kill the plan and cripple Clinton and the Democrats.

Throughout 1993 and 1994, Republicans offered a host of alternatives to the Clinton agenda, from the budget to health care to welfare reform. But the most effective tool leaders like Barbour and Dole found in rebuilding the Republican Party and energizing their conservative constituencies was the politics of "no" — "no" to Clinton, "no" to the Democrats, and "no" to bipartisanship. Clinton provided Republicans a common target, and the Republicans gave the antigovernment forces in the country a vehicle for their protests.

A PLAN OF ATTACK

Whatever contributions Dole and Barbour made to the revitalization of the Republican Party, no one played a more central role in shaping the election of 1994 than Newt Gingrich. Gingrich represented a paradoxical — and controversial — figure in Washington. The bulky, white-thatched Georgia congressman was a mercurial, impulsive personality; a brilliant visionary one moment, a petulant, uncontrollable four-year-old the next.

Gingrich had built his career by tearing down — Democrats, Washington, Congress itself. And yet, no Republican had done more to instill a sense of unity and purpose in his party. Nor had anyone preached more tirelessly the importance of Republicans offering the American people a positive blueprint of how conservatives would govern if given power. Looking ahead to the 1996 elections during the summer of 1993, Gingrich told us,

> There are two sentences that describe all of modern American political history from 1968 to the present: The Democrats under Johnson and McGovern went too far to the left and never came back; [and] the Republicans rejected successfully for a quarter of a century every effort of the American people to make them a majority. Now a Republican Party which doesn't communicate its vision and its beliefs in a hundred-day program, and a Republican Party which doesn't campaign on what it seriously intends to do, and a Republican Party which doesn't arrive in office in the House, the Senate and the White House and ram through in the first one hundred days exactly what it promised, is a Republican Party that will just continue the stasis of American politics.

A few weeks after the Republican victory in Kentucky, Gingrich summoned House Republican leaders to Room H-227 in the Capitol, which sits along a corridor closed to tourists a few steps off the huge, central Rotunda. Like many rooms in the Capitol, H-227 combined the ornate and the ordinary, as gilded mirrors, a marble fireplace, and intricate, hand-painted ceilings coexisted with utilitarian conference tables laid end to end and covered by a dingy, felt tablecloth that would have been an embarrassment even in a church basement. A few weeks earlier, buoyed by the Lewis victory, Gingrich had asked his closest political adviser, Joseph Gaylord, to prepare a battle plan for the fall campaign, one that described everything that Republicans would have to do to turn the fall elections into the watershed Gingrich believed they could be. Now they were prepared to share with their colleagues the scope of the challenge ahead.

Gingrich had been planning for a Republican majority for two decades. Elected to Congress in 1978, he came to Washington a month before his swearing-in to meet with Guy Vander Jagt, then a Michigan congressman and chairman of the NRCC. For three hours, the brash freshman-to-be bombarded Vander Jagt with ideas, hoping to convince him that the NRCC needed a committee to plot the path to majority status. "In those three hours, he absolutely boggled my mind," Vander Jagt said. "Totally boggled my mind. I said, 'I'll tell you what, I'll make you the chairman of the NRCC task force to plan for a

Republican majority.' I'm not sure anybody could be that brash. . . . I skipped him over 155 sitting Republicans to do it."

Gaylord, a tall, slender, perpetually tanned operative, drafted the outlines of a memo on a pair of long plane rides between Washington and Alaska, where he was conducting a campaign training workshop for the party, and with Gingrich's help had revised it several times since. Like Gingrich, Gaylord was an enduring optimist about the party's aspirations to become the majority in the House, but as the director of the NRCC in the mid-1980s had seen those hopes — and his own predictions — constantly frustrated. He was convinced 1994 would be different, and the cover of his twenty-page memo underscored just how confident he felt. In capital letters, the document's cover said: "The Plan: Create a Solid GOP Majority in the House of Representatives of 231 members." The memo described with remarkable prescience the components needed to reach the target. At the time, the conventional wisdom in Washington projected a Republican gain of about 20 to 25 seats, enough to put the Republicans around 200, but still short of the 218 needed for a majority. Gaylord's plan envisioned a 51-seat gain (although 7 of those seats were to come from party switches by Democrats after the election), which turned out to be the most accurate forecast of the year.

Among those in the room that day were Jim Nussle of Iowa, a young House Republican who was part of Gingrich's informal team of activists. He remembers being overwhelmed by what Gaylord and Gingrich put before the group — not simply the notion that Republicans might actually be able to win a majority in November, but what it would take to get there. Nussle was a believer, but he knew what Gaylord had laid out would require more than the energy of a dozen or so committed activists. "Getting one hundred eighty [people] to help you paint the fence was another task entirely," he said. Gaylord recommended task forces for practically everything: message, media, training, money. But at its heart, the plan described three broad challenges. The first called for Republicans to develop a positive governing agenda and to communicate their vision in language voters could understand. The second called for derailing Clinton's agenda for the rest of the year and then framing the election around his failures as President. "We must maximize Clinton's weaknesses and turn '94 into a referendum on his policies," the memo stated. The third challenge underscored the critical importance of money and of finding the means to assure that no viable Republican candidate lost because of lack of resources. The first part became the House Republican Contract With America; the second produced a legislative strategy to guarantee that Clinton would receive no political boost from the final months of the 103rd Congress; and the third triggered an unprecedented effort to raise and dispense money.

NEWT AND THE CONTRACT

Gingrich's life was an endless round of meetings, and one of the informal groups he regularly convened was called The Round Table. That gathering constituted the GOP leadership-in-waiting and included Dick Armey of Texas, then chairman of the House Republican Conference; Tom DeLay of Texas, then chairman of the House Republican Study Committee; Robert Walker of Pennsylvania, a longtime ally of Gingrich's and then chief deputy whip; and Bill Paxon, the chairman of the NRCC.

In 1980, Gingrich had helped to plan a campaign event on the Capitol steps that featured Ronald Reagan and Republican candidates posing for photographers and promising to cut taxes and increase defense spending if they were elected. Gingrich long had wanted to re-create the event and had talked often of the need for Republicans to develop their own governing agenda to accompany it. In 1992, the Bush campaign rebuffed those efforts, but early in 1994, free to chart his own course, he began planning anew. What Gingrich proposed was a vision statement writ large and converted into a campaign document that he hoped would nationalize the fall elections. From those outlines sprang the Contract With America, the ten-point platform issued by Republicans in the fall of 1994 that not only helped to unify Republican candidates around a sweeping set of policy proposals but also energized some of the party's key constituencies for the fall campaign. But Gingrich understood the Contract's value if Republicans took power: The Contract would establish their agenda for the 104th Congress and give House Republicans a head start over their Senate colleagues in defining the Republican revolution.

From the outset, Gingrich stipulated two things: First, the document would contain ten items, because, as one aide said later, Gingrich believed in the "mythic power" of the number ten. Second, after consulting with a long-range weather forecaster in Georgia, Gingrich decreed that the event would be held on September 27, 1994, because the forecaster had assured him it would not rain that day. He also said Republicans should promise to bring all the items in the Contract to a vote in the House during the first ninety days of the new Congress. When his colleagues protested, he rounded it off to one hundred days.

Construction of the Contract involved two major enterprises: developing the agenda of issues and determining how to make it attractive to voters. Gingrich put Armey in charge of the substance, and Armey in turn delegated the day-to-day responsibility to his chief of staff, Kerry Knott, and to his press secretary, Ed Gillespie. Some issues were obvious: Given the climate of distrust with career politicians and the federal government, term limits and the Balanced Budget Amendment to the Constitution had to be included, despite strong opposition from many Republican incumbents to term limits. The rest had to fall under Gingrich's definition of "60 percent issues": issues that in their blandest form at least had popular appeal. Republican leaders also insisted that the issues not divide the Republican caucus in the House and, if possible, that they be tailored to appeal to conservative, grassroots constituencies — and they actively solicited those constituencies to help them shape the Contract. Having learned the lessons of the Kentucky special election, the Republicans wanted the fall campaign to be a contest between an aroused conservative movement and a lethargic Democratic base.

The leadership's guidelines quickly eliminated any mention of abortion in the Contract, but school prayer proved to be more controversial. Gingrich and Armey clashed fiercely over whether to include it, particularly with abortion off the table. Armey believed school prayer had to be included to excite religious conservatives. At a meeting with religious conservatives to discuss the Contract, Gingrich portrayed the prayer amendment almost as a contagion that could imperil the entire effort. "If I put school prayer in, just think of the kind of column Al Hunt [of the *Wall Street Journal*] will write," Gingrich said, according to one lobbyist. "He'll call the Contract a religious Right agenda." But led by Representative Ernest Istook of Oklahoma, conservatives continued to press Armey. "We have a big fight here," a Republican staffer told pollster Frank Luntz. The issue resolved itself not by a meeting of the minds, but by the Realpolitik that Gingrich was in charge. "I didn't relent, I got beat," Armey said. "I still to this day think it was a mistake. The omission of school prayer in the Contract had a domino effect and made the tax provisions tougher and more imperative. Made the welfare provisions tougher and more imperative because we had a very, very important, significant part of our base already disappointed." Ultimately, the Contract embraced a $500 per child tax credit largely because it was among the Christian Coalition's top priorities, not because it was sound economic policy.

Some issues were simply too big to include, such as Armey's proposal to scrap the current federal income tax and replace it with a flat tax, because Congress could not draft it, debate it, and pass it in one hundred days. Republicans also opted not to include health care reform because at the time they began work, no one knew whether Clinton's or a compromise plan would pass the Congress later in the year. But other items were naturals: welfare reform; tougher measures on crime; the line-item veto; regulatory reform; measures to stimulate economic growth. Republicans also agreed to change the rules of the House and force Congress to live under the same laws as everyone else. Throughout the spring and summer, under Kerry Knott's direction, the Republicans built the planks of the Contract through outside consultation with their conservative allies, long debates among themselves about the provisions (the welfare debate raged until the morning the Contract was unveiled), and hours and hours of drafting legislative language to back up the generalities of the Contract itself.

THE selling of the Contract began in a bar in Annapolis, Maryland, one night in early March 1994. Senate Republicans had come to Annapolis for a political retreat, with both Barbour and Gingrich in attendance. Long into the late-night conversation, Gingrich asked Barbour for a favor: Would the RNC be willing to pay for a political ad in *TV Guide* later in the fall? Barbour had by that time consumed a considerable amount of whiskey and he wasn't about to begin a long discussion about Gingrich's latest scheme. Gingrich always had some revolutionary new enterprise in mind, and it wasn't always worth trying to keep up with the details. Without bothering to press for specifics, Barbour agreed to underwrite the cost of the ad (about $265,000) in what may have been the most casual and expensive conversation party leaders had all year about how to package and promote their hundred-day plan of attack. It was some time before Barbour knew what he had agreed to finance.

The marketing of the Contract involved polling, focus groups, dummy commercials, and multiple mockups of the *TV Guide* ad, all aimed at squeezing the maximum political advantage from the plan. But at no time did the Republicans survey the public to determine which issues to include, nor was there a poll proving that the Contract had wide support. As the scope of the Contract event mushroomed, House Republican leaders prevailed on Barbour to set up a Contract "war room" at the RNC offices. Under the direction of Barry Jackson, a young adviser to Representative John Boehner of Ohio, the war room directed preparations for the Contract's unveiling and supervised the marketing research that continued from early July into September. The first survey was conducted by Frank Luntz, an ambitious, young Republican pollster who had bounced from the presidential campaign of Patrick J. Buchanan to the candidacy of Ross Perot in 1992 and who reveled in attracting publicity for himself. He asked Republican incumbents and Republican candidates around the country to identify their priorities from a list of sixty-seven items in twelve categories. Republican leaders had an ulterior motive for commissioning the poll: They believed that the Republican candidates first running for office would be more radical in their priorities than the incumbents back in Washington, and they wanted ammunition for the intra-party debate over what to include in the Contract. They knew, for example, that the newcomers would force incumbents to include term limits in the document. "We wanted to err on the side of more bold, not less," said Armey's press secretary, Ed Gillespie.

The next phase involved three focus groups in mid-July in Raleigh, North Carolina. Republicans hoped to begin testing possible messages for the fall campaign, but their confidence was shaken by the stark expressions of distrust toward both parties that the forty-five participants exhibited. The three focus groups, directed by The Tarrance Group, a Republican polling firm, began with a set of dummy television commercials, using members of Congress reading prepared scripts. The attendees were given hand-held devices that allowed them to register their impression of various words and phrases. Their combined responses were then condensed into a single graph that was later

superimposed over the commercial, and it moved like a conveyor belt across the screen in sync with the words and pictures, providing almost instant visual feedback of the commercial's power. The Republicans found plenty of hot buttons — lower taxes, big government, welfare reform — but they were caught short by the vehemence of the reaction to any suggestion in the ads that the fastest way to change the country was to "vote Republican." The swing voters in the Raleigh focus groups held no brief for either party; every time one of the ads suggested that the Republicans enjoyed divine wisdom, the line on the graph plunged downward in disapproval. "Remember, you're Americans," one woman said in disgust. "The hell with the party. There's too much emphasis put on Republicans and Democrats."

The responses stunned Republican officials; several feared that, with the electorate so cynical toward political promises, a Capitol steps event that simply produced another list of proposals would die like grass seed on an asphalt driveway. By the time of the third focus group, the moderator began to probe the audience about another approach: Would they be more receptive to a *contract* with the voters, rather than an unsecured promise of change? Heads bobbed in agreement. In a memo written to party leaders after the focus groups were completed, Tarrance Group president Ed Goeas said, "The most important concept revealed in the focus groups was accountability. Respondents felt that government and Congress are no longer held accountable for their actions. The hope of the Contract is that it will offer some method of accountability — if only in the short run."

In August, the party commissioned Luntz to test specific language for the Contract and the *TV Guide* ad. He first took a poll of one thousand people, and for each of the ten items in the Contract, asked them to choose between two wordings. Luntz specifically wanted to see how former Perot voters in the sample responded to the choices. In some cases, one version was significantly more popular than the other, but if there ever was a doubt about which language to choose, Luntz recommended using the version the Perot supporters preferred.

A few weeks later, Luntz convened a focus group of Perot voters in Denver. Armed with multiple versions of the front and back pages of the *TV Guide* ad, he tried to coax from the group some sense of which versions most appealed to them. Luntz later reported in a memo to Republican leaders, "They were literally the most negative, hostile

voters I have ever assembled." After about forty minutes of discouraging attempts to prompt a discussion, Luntz called for a break and walked back into the viewing room, ready to cancel the rest of the session. But Barry Jackson and Don Fierce, two Republican officials watching from behind one-way glass, fortified him, and he returned to try again. This time, he pressed the group on the issue of accountability. Finally he received the first glimmer of a positive response from the caustic Perot voters when he read a proposed line for the ad: "If we break this contract, throw us out. We mean it." The group also expressed near unanimous support for the mock-up of the ad's front page that said simply: "A campaign promise is one thing. A signed contract is quite another." Like the three focus groups in Raleigh, the Perot group hated partisan labels; that convinced GOP leaders not to call their document a "Republican contract." Reporting back to Republican leaders on his findings, Luntz wrote in a memo: "The Contract is our best hope of winning back Perot voters, disgruntled Republicans and conservative Democrats."

On September 27, more than three hundred Republicans gathered on the West Front of the Capitol beneath an intense autumn sun to launch their revolution. Gingrich's weather guru proved accurate, but not by much. It had rained until 2 A.M. that morning. Earlier, all but 5 of the 157 incumbents seeking reelection had signed the document, and with martial music blaring on the public-address system, 185 Republican challengers trooped forward to sign for the cameras. Gingrich described the ceremony as a "historic event" that marked the coming-out party of a new GOP. "For all those who are tired of negative attacks, smear campaigns, for all those who have asked political parties to get together and be a responsible team, for all those who said we have to deal in a positive way with the challenges of America's future, I hope that you listened to each of our candidates as they outlined each of the ten bills that we have committed in our contract to bring to the floor," he said. And then, he launched into an attack on the Washington press corps, which already was beginning to critique the Contract, as the "praetorian Guard of the Left." Out of sight of the cameras, standing in the back rows on the West Front, a number of Republican incumbents snickered at all the extravagant language being heaped on the Contract by their leaders. Many incumbents hated the idea of the Contract. As Representative Steve Gunderson of

Wisconsin later admitted, "We didn't take it seriously." But Democrats did, and they were poised for attack. After months on the defensive, Democrats saw the Contract as their last opportunity to shift the focus of the campaign from Clinton's failures to the Republicans' agenda — and for once they expressed gratitude toward Gingrich. Don Sweitzer, the political director of the Democratic National Committee, said, "Newt gave us back our manhood."

THE FIELD OF BATTLE

On the Sunday before Republicans unveiled their contract, Senator Dianne Feinstein sat in the coffee shop at the Beverly Hilton Hotel in Los Angeles. She had just finished speaking at a fund-raising brunch, and now, with her husband and members of her political team, was pausing for lunch before resuming her campaign schedule. Two years earlier, the former San Francisco mayor had won election to the Senate in a landslide; now the polls showed that she was in a virtual dead heat with her Republican challenger, Michael Huffington. Huffington was a lightly regarded conservative congressman best known for his bank account and his ambitious wife, Arianna. He had spent millions of his personal fortune on a television assault against Feinstein's vote for Clinton's 1993 budget, which he portrayed as the biggest tax increase in history. The ads sent Feinstein's popularity plummeting and unexpectedly plunged her into one of the closest Senate races in the country.

Feinstein seemed dazed. "Want to know something that's frustrating?" she said. "I feel very good when I'm out there. The crowds are big, they are enthusiastic, the response is good. It is very hard for me to understand it." But Feinstein knew how illusory such indicators could be, and she was plainly worried about a Republican legislative strategy designed "to stop any [bill] at all [in order] to impugn this President" and undermine further the public's eroding confidence in government's ability to solve problems. "I think basically what it is, is a very stressed electorate, very worried," she said. "Schools are overcrowded, kids aren't learning, streets aren't safe, and most importantly, people are working harder for less. And into this there's all this fuel being thrown to raise the level of anxiety instead of being able to stabilize it."

In fact the Republicans had done everything possible to put the electorate on overload, and Democrats were paying the price. Feinstein was just one in an army of dazed Democrats. In Massachusetts, Senator Ted Kennedy faced his most difficult challenge in thirty years. In Virginia, Senator Charles S. Robb, damaged by revelations about his personal life, struggled to fend off another flawed candidate, Republican Oliver L. North, a central actor in the Iran-contra scandal. In New York, Governor Mario Cuomo struggled for survival against George Pataki, a state senator whose best attribute was his anonymity. In Texas, Governor Ann Richards tried to hold back George W. Bush, the son of the former President, while in Florida, another Bush son, Jeb, appeared on the brink of unseating Governor Lawton Chiles. There were nine open Senate seats around the country; all six of the seats held by the Democrats appeared in jeopardy. In California, with Feinstein treading water, fellow Democrat Kathleen Brown was slowly sinking in her race against Governor Pete Wilson, a man who had been so unpopular only a year before that he briefly considered not running for reelection. In the House, strategists for both parties estimated that at least 150 races could break either way, a staggering number far higher than anyone could remember.

The Republicans may have touted the Contract as a positive vision for America, but on television, the voters heard something entirely different: a GOP message that was almost completely negative. In state after state, Republican candidates battered their Democratic opponents on issues of social and moral decay by fusing Reagan's "government is the problem" with a Perot-like populism that said "politicians are the enemy." Bill Frist, a Republican surgeon seeking a Senate seat in Tennessee, distilled the whole Republican message to a single phrase in a television commercial in which he promised to seek "term limits for career politicians and the death penalty for career criminals."

In Illinois, Governor Jim Edgar put away his opponent, Dawn Clark Netsch, with a withering attack on her opposition to the death penalty, although Netsch had done plenty to kill her own campaign by calling for higher taxes during the Democratic primary. Wilson had used the same soft-on-the-death-penalty message to overtake Kathleen Brown, and then followed up with another line of attack against her for opposing Proposition 187, the anti-immigration ballot initia-

tive that he championed. In Michigan, Spencer Abraham, who had
served as an aide to Vice President Dan Quayle, promised to fight
crime "with punishment, not more welfare," and warned that the
"moral crisis" in America could be solved only by changing Washing-
ton. In Texas, George W. Bush talked about welfare reform and juve-
nile justice, urging the state to get tough with minors, while his
brother ran against Chiles from a location even farther right along the
political spectrum, showing that "kinder and gentler" did not neces-
sarily flow in the genes of the Bush family. In a year of disaffection
from Washington, Republicans cast themselves as Carrie Nations who
would end the capital's long, drunken bout with the demon rum of tax-
ing and spending. Fred Thompson, a Watergate committee lawyer
from Tennessee and part-time actor, campaigned as an antigovern-
ment populist, trading his lawyer's pinstripes for a red pickup truck
and a flannel shirt. In scrambling to fend off the attacks, Democrats
sometimes sounded like Republicans themselves. Kennedy aired ads
touting his bona fides as a crime fighter, while Jim Sasser ran commer-
cials about traditional values that highlighted his support for school
prayer and warned of the threat of illegal immigration to Tennessee,
not previously known for its proximity to Mexico.

Back in Washington, the 103rd Congress neared adjournment in
an ugly, partisan meltdown. In the face of united Republican opposi-
tion and deepening division within their own ranks, Clinton and Dem-
ocratic congressional leaders pulled the plug on their health care
reform plan without bringing it to a vote. To some voters, the failure
on health care represented a breakdown in the entire political system;
to others it symbolized Clinton's abiding and misguided love affair
with liberal, activist government. A post-election analysis by Clinton
pollster Stanley B. Greenberg identified the health care plan as the
single item that most directly linked Clinton with big government.
But if health care was the big disappointment, the battle over the $33
billion crime bill in the summer of 1994 may have left the deepest im-
pression of government in disarray on the voters. What initially
seemed like an election-year triumph for Democrats turned into a
Democratic disaster. Republicans first blocked the bill from coming to
the House floor and then relentlessly redefined it as a pork barrel give-
away to liberal constituencies. A few days after House Democrats lost
a key procedural vote, preventing the House from beginning debate

on the bill, Democratic Representative Bill Richardson of New Mexico, the chief deputy whip in the House, shook his head at the predicament in which Clinton and his party found themselves. "We have to find a way to pass it, otherwise we're going to be history," he said. "We will have achieved the ultimate act of gridlock."

Congress eventually approved a compromise crime bill, but Richardson's description proved accurate. Democrats were damaged in two ways. First, the ban on assault weapons mobilized a revolt by gun owners and the National Rifle Association. But more devastating perhaps, the wrangle over the crime bill appeared to transform the simmering frustration with Congress into laser-directed anger at the Democrats. "It crystallized the idea that it just wasn't working," said Democratic pollster Geoffrey Garin, who noted, perhaps coincidentally, that "the roof fell in" on Jim Sasser in Tennessee the weekend after the House had failed to pass the rule on the crime bill.

From there the spiral spun downward for the Democrats. A GOP filibuster in the Senate killed campaign finance reform. An uprising in the House led by Gingrich and fanned by Rush Limbaugh, the Christian Coalition, and other conservative groups interred a bill to reform the rules governing lobbying — even though the House had already approved the bill. The 103rd Congress did not so much conclude as collapse. The final act came directly out of the GOP's fall campaign script, denying Clinton a record of accomplishment that he could promote; dividing and demoralizing Democratic constituencies; and rallying conservatives to depose Democrats on election day.

THE COLOR OF MONEY

With the Contract launched and the Democratic Congress crashed, Republicans turned their attention to fund-raising, the third pillar of their strategy for control. Earlier in the summer, Republican leaders concluded that, with 150 or more competitive House races, their opportunities far exceeded their resources. The choice was stark: Either raise millions more in contributions or abandon as many as seventy competitive candidates for lack of funding.

Barbour moved first, deciding in June that he would increase the RNC budget by $12 million and pour $10 million of the new money directly into campaigns. Having decided to spend the money, he then had to find it. Barbour recruited Dole and Gingrich to commit to a late-summer fund-raising blitz, and then unveiled the new financial plan at the RNC's summer meeting in Los Angeles in July as part of a conscious plan to heighten expectations. To demonstrate his confidence that Republicans could produce major gains in November, Barbour announced that he would borrow $5 million of the total. His gambit had the desired effect: The political community concluded for the first time that Republicans believed their own spin. To reinforce that belief, Barbour ordered his staff to borrow the $5 million before the end of August so that it would show up on campaign finance reports in the early fall, even though they did not then need the money. With the help of the Barbour-Dole-Gingrich blitz, the RNC eventually pumped a total of $20.2 million directly into campaigns in the fall, far surpassing its previous record of $9 million in 1982.

Under the frenetic direction of Senator Phil Gramm of Texas, the Senate campaign committee continued to raise money at a prodigious pace. But throughout much of 1993 and 1994, the House campaign committee continually flirted with bankruptcy. Eighteen years of control by the former chairman, Guy Vander Jagt, had left the committee $4.5 million in debt. Barbour finally stepped in and, in essence, assumed control of the committee. Barbour and Scott Reed, the RNC chief of staff, dispatched Joe Gaylord, Gingrich's alter ego, to oversee operations. "We lent them three hundred grand to get the direct mail started, but they had to change everything," Reed said. "And Gaylord had to be the de facto executive director, and he reported [to] me." Reed and Barbour wanted Gaylord there for another reason other than his expertise. "We knew Newt was the future," he said, "and if we were ever going to cement ourselves with Newt and make this really work, we needed to have Newt's guy kind of bought into the solution."

The financial crisis at the NRCC forced drastic changes in the committee's operation. Ironically these resulted in unprecedented teamwork among House Republican incumbents. When Paxon and Maria Cino, the NRCC director, slashed the staff, Republican House members personally pitched in, recruiting candidates, raising money, even sometimes opening the committee's mail. And when Gingrich and Paxon decreed that none of the committee's money would be funneled to incumbents, the members responded by raising a record sum for their own campaigns. This represented a revolution in committee financing. Under Vander Jagt, every incumbent could count on a $5,000 check from the NRCC, regardless of need. Now it was just the opposite. No one received any money unless a peer review committee approved, and even then incumbents could draw only on a pool of funds other incumbents had raised. It was as if new management had taken over a small-town bank and called in all the sweetheart loans to the directors. Gingrich and Paxon established a dues structure for incumbents: $2,500 for freshman members; $5,000 for longer-term incumbents; $7,500 for leaders or those with top committee assignments. Like the unwelcome chairman of the parish finance committee, Paxon passed out pledge cards to the members, who laughed at the audacity of the eager, young congressman from Buffalo. Eventually, the members pitched in $1.1 million, twenty times the amount they had raised for the committee in 1991–92.

But the incumbent-protection money represented only a fraction of what the committee needed to fund all the competitive races. In mid-July, Republicans in the House received a letter from Gingrich with a thirteen-page plan attached that read: "14 Weeks To Change The House." Gingrich asked for "an unprecedented commitment from members" and outlined a series of options, from contributing $148,000 directly from their own campaign accounts to other Republican candidates to agreeing to raise at least $50,000 for the committee through their own networks of contributors. The plan was an ingenious device to funnel incumbent-raised money into nonincumbent races and in the end raised another $5 million to $6 million for challengers.

The first two respondents, John Boehner of Ohio and Susan Molinari of New York, both bidding for leadership posts, agreed to do both. Bob Livingston of Louisiana, who eventually jumped over several more senior members to become chairman of the Appropriations Committee, instantly contributed the $148,000. Gingrich pressured senior Republicans to use their clout with the business community to raise far more than the minimum asked; in case solidarity wasn't enough, Gingrich appealed to self-interest, reminding his targets that if the Republicans won the House, committee chairmanships would be determined in part on the basis of how they responded. That was language the legislators understood: Thomas Bliley of Virginia, in line to take over the powerful Energy and Commerce Committee, raised half a million dollars. Jack Fields, whose position on the Commerce Committee's Telecommunications Subcommittee gave him entree into the giant telecommunications companies, which desperately wanted freedom from government regulation, raised several hundred thousand dollars, as did Tom DeLay, running for Republican whip, John Kasich, in line to take over the Budget Committee, and Pat Roberts, the ranking member on Agriculture. Bill Archer, the ranking Republican on the House Ways and Means Committee, responded more slowly — until Gingrich sent him a tart note pointing out that no member of Congress had more to gain from a Republican majority than he did. Archer got the message and eventually raised about half a million dollars.

Meanwhile, Gingrich, Gramm, and other Republicans called in political action committee managers and browbeat them into giving more money to Republican challengers. Gingrich was seeking to reverse a pattern that had hardened into place in the 1980s, when Tony Coelho, then the chairman of the Democratic Congressional Campaign Committee, convinced the PACs to put aside their philosophical differences with the Democrats with an argument of crass simplicity: Business needed friends with power; the Democrats held power and they were not likely to give it up anytime soon. His success at wooing business dollars with that argument made it a self-fulfilling prophecy. Stick in hand, Gingrich came with a different message. "This is the year to change who's in the room, rather than to try to get access to the room," he told them. "Don't come in later, after trying to prop up people who oppose your values and tell us you were secretly with us." At one meeting, according to the weekly *Roll Call*, he warned those who refused to help, "It's going to be the two coldest years in Washington."

The unprecedented fund-raising mobilization brought in enough money to assure Republican challengers, who often found themselves short of funds near the end of their campaign, the resources to compete against their Democratic opponents. Money poured in from PACs ($5.5 million to challengers and open-seat candidates compared to just $1.7 million to their Democratic counterparts), from individual donors, and from other Republicans. The top staffers at the RNC and the House and Senate campaign committees spent their days on the phone, begging PAC managers and other contributors for more money and offering lists of candidates who needed help. For the last month of the campaign, the RNC's Scott Reed said, "I was a money manager."

PLAYING THE ANGLES

By Labor Day, even the rankest amateur could smell a big Republican year coming, but few people in the middle of the campaign maelstrom had ever seen or experienced a tidal wave in the making. The range of predicted Republican gains became laughable.

In early September, Bill Paxon, the NRCC chairman, estimated at a press conference that Republicans would gain two dozen seats in the House. It was a safely conservative forecast, and reflected both Paxon's desire to lower GOP expectations and his own doubt that they could win a majority before 1996. But Gingrich wanted no public pessimism; the GOP game plan depended on convincing their conservative army to make the maximum possible effort in November. When he heard what Paxon had said, Gingrich exploded. "Find Paxon," he told aides. Gingrich ordered the NRCC chairman to sit down with John Morgan, an expert on congressional districts, for several hours of reeducation. But even Gingrich needed reassurance. A few weeks after the Paxon press conference, he boarded a private plane at Washington's National Airport to begin a long campaign swing. With him were Joe Gaylord, Dan Meyer, his chief of staff, and Steve Hanzer, an old friend. Meyer was along for transition planning, and Gingrich wondered whether they were planning for him to become Speaker or minority leader. "You should be planning to become Speaker," Gaylord told them. Gingrich implicitly trusted Gaylord, but now he wanted to see the evidence. As the small plane churned westward, the four men began to review the electoral map, starting in Maine and moving across to California. Gaylord's best estimate added up to a gain of fifty-one seats.

At the White House, the President's advisers were looking at other evidence and describing a different picture. Shortly after Congress adjourned, White House Chief of Staff Leon Panetta sat at the small conference table in his corner office in the West Wing and offered his own rather rosy forecast. Neither the House nor the Senate was in jeopardy, he declared confidently, although he conceded that losses in the House might be large enough to cost Clinton his working majority. His mission that day was to talk up the Democrats' chances and, he hoped, diminish the sense of doom that surrounded the party and its constituencies. But as the conversation progressed, his certainty wavered. "What we underestimated," he admitted, "was the ability of Republicans to . . . control their message to the American people, build on the anger that was out there, and then implement that by basically blocking a lot of legislation we wanted to pass." And then, like Feinstein a month earlier, he expressed near disbelief that the voters were angry with Clinton and the Democrats. "I honestly do not think that the American people are so angry and so mad that they're not willing to listen to what is responsible government and what is responsible representation," he said.

By that time, other Democrats had privately concluded the opposite, and were convinced not only that the Senate was gone but that their House losses would be greater than predicted. Representative Vic Fazio of California, chairman of the Democratic Congressional Campaign Committee, had been one of the lonely voices in warning his colleagues of the coming upheaval. The spin from the White House ill-served the party and demonstrated that the Democrats were fighting an old war at a time when the country had changed. Instead of listening to the country, the Democrats complained that the voters did not appreciate them enough. Still Panetta had at least some slivers of evidence upon which to construct his upbeat forecasts: In a year of disappointments, mid-October provided the Democrats with their one brief moment of hope. Kennedy had snapped back to life in Massachusetts, while in California, Feinstein opened up some distance from Michael Huffington. Clinton's free fall had ended, and the GOP advantage in the closely watched "generic ballot" indicator in the polls, which measured whether voters had a predilection to vote Republican or Democratic in House races, had narrowed slightly — although it remained at a historically high level for the Republicans.

The Democratic moment began ironically when the Republicans unveiled the Contract With America. The first ten days were, in the description of one Republican party official, "terrible." The initial revolt came from Republican consultants, who saw the Contract as an unwelcome diversion at best, a dead weight around candidates' necks at worst. Most Republican consultants preferred that candidates continue their relentless attack against Clinton — a strategy that coincided with advice that Richard Nixon had given to Barbour a year earlier when he urged a campaign built on the GOP's 1946 slogan of "Had Enough?" After the consultant complaints came a flood of nervous calls from Republican candidates desperately seeking advice on how to fend off their Democratic opponents. For the first time in the campaign, Democrats had seized the offensive by attacking the Contract. "They all got home and the missiles just kept coming," said Barry Jackson, who quickly converted his war room operation at the RNC into a rapid response team.

The Democratic attack was both predictable and unsettling. Democrats accused Republicans of wanting to slash Social Security and Medicare; of offering tax cuts for the rich; of wanting to bring back trickle-down economics; of advocating policies that in the aggregate would balloon the deficit. Democrats also attacked Republican challengers as clones of Newt Gingrich who had signed away their independence by coming to Washington and pledging their support for the Gingrich agenda. Jackson's team volleyed back a barrage of faxes: talking points; specific answers to Democratic attacks; facts and statistics; favorable editorials. When one campaign encountered turbulence, Jackson's team devised a response and then zapped it around the country to help other candidates inoculate themselves. Gaylord, traveling constantly with Gingrich now, spent part of his time at pay phones patiently explaining to campaign managers how to counter the Democratic counteroffensive. When all else failed, Jackson recommended in an October 1 memo, go back to basics by attacking the President. One message used effectively by several campaigns, he wrote, was "Clinton and Congress — out of step and out of touch."

The Democrats' overall strategy had a clear but limited objective. Polls showed that the only enthusiastic voters in the country were Republicans. Democrats needed something to energize their own forces — minorities, working women, senior citizens — and they carefully combed through the Contract for outrages that could be used to excite their own base. Clinton's advisers produced a series of television commercials attacking the Contract, although they clashed over advice from Stan Greenberg, the President's pollster, to link the Contract to Ronald Reagan and Reaganomics. To some Democratic advisers, offering voters a choice between Reagan and Clinton was, in the climate of 1994, suicidal. But Greenberg argued that many swing voters still believed Reaganomics had hurt them. The dispute was resolved by producing four different ads and letting state party officials decide which ones to use. But none had much effect, particularly after a memo from White House budget director Alice Rivlin, outlining budget options for Clinton that included many of the same things for which Democrats were attacking the Republicans, surfaced in October. Gingrich, campaigning in Connecticut in mid-October, boasted that Democrats had fallen into a GOP trap by elevating the Contract in importance. "The Contract is working perfectly," he said over breakfast at a Holiday Inn in New London. "It is nationalizing the election in a manner I'm shocked to see the Democrats fall into."

No one disputes that the Contract gave Republican candidates a positive platform upon which to campaign and a series of proposals that, individually, were highly popular with many voters. But it was the Democrats, not the Republicans, who made the most frequent use of the Contract in their television commercials; far more Democrats spent money attacking the Contract than Republicans did in promoting it. For all the debate the Contract provoked within the political community, fewer than a third of all voters said they had even heard about the Contract by the end of the campaign. Gingrich's claim that the Contract itself had nationalized the election overstated its impact. The remorseless bashing of Bill Clinton in state after state did as much as the Contract to create a national message for the Republicans. The Contract's real impact would come after the election.

DISAPPOINTMENT with Clinton and disgust with Congress continued to drag down Democratic candidates, and many of them looked for ways to put distance between themselves and the President. David Mann, a Democratic House member from Ohio, ran a television commercial proudly noting how he had voted against "Clinton's tax increase" and "Clinton's pork barrel program." Oklahoma Representative Dave McCurdy, who had campaigned avidly for Clinton in 1992 and was now seeking a Senate seat, repeatedly criticized Clinton for straying from the themes of his presidential campaign and said he was determined not to let Republicans "wrap the President's unpopularity around my neck." When Clinton traveled to Michigan for a campaign event with auto workers, Representative Bob Carr, who was running for the Senate, chose to sit in the audience rather than share the stage with the President.

With his domestic agenda in ruins, Clinton had one only card to play: commander in chief. In mid-October, he flew to the Middle East to witness the signing of the Israeli-Jordanian peace agreement and then to the Persian Gulf to visit U.S. troops who had been ordered there a few weeks earlier when U.S. intelligence analysts warned that Iraqi President Saddam Hussein might be planning another invasion of Kuwait. The White House naturally denied any political motives for the trip, but both parties knew that Clinton pollster Stan Greenberg had calculated that every percentage point rise in Clinton's approval rating could save two House seats. On the eve of Clinton's departure, Republican pollster Bill McInturff offered the President a parting grenade: "At least when he gets overseas," McInturff said, "he can be pretty sure someone will meet the plane."

Clinton returned from the Middle East to a debate among his advisers over how he should close the campaign. Some wanted him to stay above the fray with a series of major speeches; others said he was needed in states with close races to rally the Democratic base. For Clinton the inveterate campaigner, the choice was easy; after a brief rest, he plunged back onto the trail, with one of his first stops Pennsylvania. There, Democrats were fighting to save Senator Harris Wofford, whose 1991 victory in a special election had signaled the depths of Bush's problems. They were trying also to hold the seat of the retiring Democratic governor, Bob Casey. Hours after Clinton left the state, the Republicans moved in to take a quick snapshot of the President's impact on the races. Astonishingly, both their candidates, Representative Rick Santorum in the Senate race and Representative Tom Ridge, who was running for governor, had risen several points. Republicans quickly realized that Clinton's return, rather than energizing the Democratic base, actually was sending one last jolt of electricity through the entire conservative coalition. Clinton's return once again nationalized the election around a choice between his way and another way. Republicans decided the last days of the campaign would be relentlessly anti-Clinton from coast to coast. "If he had stayed in the Middle East," the RNC's Don Fierce said, "I don't know how we would have closed."

THE ELECTION DAY DELUGE

Election Day produced an unprecedented wave of Republican support and a political transformation not seen in forty years. Disappointment with Clinton's presidency and the chaotic performance of the Democratic Congress, a resurgence of anti-Washington conservatism, a debate nationalized more around Democratic governance than the Contract With America, and a skillful Republican campaign plan added up to the biggest midterm-to-midterm increase in votes for one party in American history. Almost thirty-seven million people voted Republican, about nine million more than in 1990. The torrent of Republican votes produced an upheaval reminiscent of the Democratic sweep in 1930 that foreshadowed the coming of Franklin Roosevelt and the New Deal two years later. In the South alone, where voters long had supported Republican presidential candidates but had been more stingy in their support of Republican congressional candidates, the GOP received 3.8 million more votes than in 1990.

No superlative or metaphor seemed large enough to encompass the results. Republicans gained 52 seats in the House, the biggest midterm gain by either party since 1946, to give them a 230-seat majority. They captured eight Senate seats by winning all six of the Democratic open seats and defeating two incumbents, Wofford in Pennsylvania and Sasser in Tennessee, and gained another the morning after the election, when Alabama's Richard Shelby switched parties. They added eleven more governors to give them a total of thirty, and now held the governor's office in eight of the nine largest states. Incumbent governors like Bill Weld of Massachusetts, Tommy Thompson of Wisconsin, John Engler of Michigan, George Voinovich of Ohio, Jim Edgar of Illinois, Stephen Merrill of New Hampshire, and even embattled Pete Wilson in California enjoyed landslides ranging from 55 percent to 72 percent. In the states, Republicans gained an additional 484 legislative seats, giving them control of fifty legislative chambers. Perhaps most remarkable of all, in a year of deep dissatisfaction with government, not a single incumbent Republican governor, senator, or member of the House was defeated in the general election.

A few notable Democrats survived: Kennedy in Massachusetts; Feinstein in California; Robb in Virginia; Chiles in Florida. But some of their biggest names and most glamorous symbols fell beneath the

Republican onslaught: Speaker Thomas S. Foley in Washington, who had dared to take the term limits movement to court; House Ways and Means Committee Chairman Dan Rostenkowski in Illinois, crippled by scandal; Governors Ann Richards in Texas and Mario Cuomo in New York, lashed to liberalism in the year of conservatives. Surveying the wreckage, Democratic National Committee Chairman David Wilhelm said curtly, "We got our butts kicked."

The experts would spend months analyzing the exit polls and the post-election surveys to find clues to the real meaning of 1994. Some facts were clear from the beginning. The results signaled a vote of "no confidence" in government's performance under the Democrats, with an overwhelming majority agreeing that government should do less, not more. But out of the post-election work came more precise conclusions. One focused on ideological polarization. Republicans benefited from an enormous surge of conservative votes, urged on by the angry diatribes of talk radio hosts and mobilized by the likes of the Christian Coalition, which distributed thirty-three million voter guides, and the National Rifle Association, which poured $3.4 million into targeted campaigns. Not only did voters who called themselves conservative constitute a larger share of the electorate than in 1992, but far more of them voted Republican than in past congressional elections. "The voters perceived Republicans as representing a conservative direction and Democrats as representing a liberal direction and chose accordingly," wrote Republican pollster Fred Steeper. Cultural and social issues like crime, welfare reform, and immigration, more than economic issues, helped shape those perceptions and power the Republican victory.

Second, the "change" vote that had swept Bush out of office in 1992 now reversed course, trapping the hapless Democrats in its path. Almost four in five voters said they disapproved of Congress, and they voted strongly for Republican candidates. So-called angry voters who had narrowly backed Democratic House candidates in 1992 voted strongly for Republicans in 1994. Perot voters, who also gave Democrats a small majority in 1992, heeded the advice of their leader and cast two-thirds of their votes for GOP candidates.

A group of Democratic analysts argued that class more than ideology shaped the result. They noted that the Republican vote among less-educated voters surged in 1994, and they attributed this to the fact that this group faced the greatest pressure on their living standards and had seen little improvement under Clinton. Only a quarter of all voters believed their economic circumstance had brightened. From 1992 to 1994, support for Democratic congressional candidates among white men with only a high school education dropped by twenty percentage points. White voters, even those with lower incomes, were as likely to prefer Reagan's economic policies to Clinton's, and among independents, Reaganomics was the clear winner. "It was the downscale voters who turned against the Democrats and who produced the new Republican congressional majorities," Greenberg wrote. The competing explanations — ideology versus economics — diverged but were not contradictory. Just one in four voters said their economic conditions had improved, but many voters pointed the finger at government as the cause of their problems.

Finally, Clinton dragged down many Democrats, particularly in the South and West, where Republicans registered some of the greatest gains. The more a Democratic House member from one of these anti-Clinton districts had supported the President's programs, the more likely he or she was to lose in 1994. Democratic candidates who for years had learned to run apart from the national party were subsumed by the disaffection toward Clinton and the Democratic Congress. "All politics was not local in 1994," said Gary Jacobson of the University of California at San Diego. "Republicans succeeded in framing the local choice in national terms, making taxes, social discipline, big government and the Clinton presidency the dominant issues."

THE first returns arrived soon after the polls closed on election night, and for the second time in six months, the news from Kentucky was unexpectedly promising. Republicans already had notched their first surprising win when Mark Souder knocked off Democrat Jill Long in the Indiana district once represented by Dan Quayle. Now Kentucky showed not only that Ron Lewis would win in a landslide, but more surprisingly that the Republicans would pick up the neighboring First District, where most counties still had Democratic registrations of 80 percent or better. The Republicans instantly recognized the meaning of that victory: The First District was far down on the charts of likely pickups; if the First had fallen, there was no doubt about the strength of the wave that was coming that night.

The Senate officially tipped Republican at 9:26 P.M. when network analysts declared Jon Kyl the winner in Arizona, but by then the celebrations in Washington were in full swing. The Associated Press waited until nearly 3 A.M. to officially turn control of the House over to the Republicans. At that hour, Gingrich was already meeting with advisers in a Marietta, Georgia, hotel room to begin to set priorities for the transition to power. At Democratic headquarters, the high command huddled in David Wilhelm's office, where reports of bad news kept pouring in throughout the afternoon. About 8 P.M., political director Don Sweitzer took a call from one of his field coordinators, who was in New York. "He's not going to make it," she told him, choking back tears. Sweitzer dejectedly walked back into Wilhelm's office, by now strewn with bags of potato chips, empty pizza boxes, and half-eaten cartons of Chinese food. "Cuomo's not going to make it," he reported to the others, and then, emotionally drained himself, sat down and stared out the window in disbelief at the size of the Republican victory.

In the predawn darkness on the morning after the election, Gingrich sat on a chair outside his hotel, fielding questions from morning television and radio programs in Atlanta and around the country. On the biggest morning of his life, Gingrich seemed unwilling to allow himself to celebrate on camera; instead he answered the anchors' questions like a human machine gun spewing forth talking points from the Republican National Committee. "I think the American people at every level last night sent a signal for less government and lower taxes and a change of direction," he told Bryant Gumbel on the *Today* show. A knot of reporters huddled on the brick patio a few feet away, as technicians scrambled to replace one audio plug with another as Gingrich hopscotched his way through the morning interviews. When the last interview ended and the camera crews began to break down their equipment and the print reporters began to straggle away, a technician came over to remove the microphone from Gingrich's lapel. Now the Speaker-to-be seemed content to steal a second for himself, as if, finally, he was pausing to gulp in the significance of all that had happened. Suddenly, he reared back, and then he slapped his hands on his knees. "Incredible," he said, looking beyond the rapidly dispersing crowd to some far distant horizon. "Absolutely incredible!"

★★★

2

The Clinton Impasse

O N THE SUNDAY BEFORE the Republican landslide, Bill Clinton sat in the backseat of the presidential limousine and watched the city of San Francisco recede into the fog. His presidency seemed equally enshrouded in gloom. Clinton was in the midst of his final campaign swing of 1994, hoping to stave off disaster in the election just ahead. But the polls and his own instincts — and the pointed absence of Democratic candidates from some of the platforms on which he spoke — all told him there would be no reprieve. The chill in the air that morning was more than the damp West Coast air.

Clinton appeared braced for the cold slap of repudiation that he knew was imminent. Waving occasionally to pedestrians who stopped to watch the presidential motorcade pass, Clinton sipped coffee that he poured himself from a ceramic pitcher in a shopping bag left on the seat across from him. The limousine could have used some new up-holstery; the radio, tuned to a soft music station, crackled with static. Light rain dripped from the heavy gray sky. As he waved and sipped and talked, Clinton was alternately reflective and defiant. He looked tired, but not despondent. He seemed both embittered that Republicans were poised to reap the benefits of stalemating his agenda in Congress and painfully aware that his own mistakes, and the mistakes of his party, had handed them the tools to do so.

Those conflicting impulses came through most clearly when Clinton said that only two things had surprised him about his time in Washington. One sounded like a campaign speech point: "the intense partisanship of the congressional Republican leadership, and the fact that they got away with it, that they haven't been punished for it in public perception." The other sounded more heartfelt, almost plaintive. Leaning back, Clinton said he had been surprised by "the difficulty of staying in some harmony with the voters; how easy [it was] for a relatively insignificant issue like gays in the military . . . to get you all out of position with people when ninety-five percent of what you're doing is exactly what they hired you do to do." Clinton straightened up in his seat. "It's because symbols count. They always count. And you're so far away from folks, and it's so easy in this environment when they are just being bombarded with stuff for them to feel like they are out of touch with you."

Over the next half hour, as the motorcade rolled toward the airport, Clinton talked about many things. But his loss of connection with voters — a fissure that the Republican gains in the congressional election just two days later would starkly illuminate — always remained close to the surface. Even when the motorcade had stopped on the runway and aides were motioning for him to leave the limousine, he returned to it once again. "When I first came here," he said, "I was so interested in trying to put through the specifics of my plan that I gave a lot more thought to that, than how we keep the people in the process all the way." But he knew he had failed to make that connection; and at that moment, the leader of the free world seemed very much a man alone.

CLINTON had arrived in Washington in January 1993 lifted on hopes as buoyant as clouds. As the nation's first baby boomer President, Clinton appeared poised to inject a needed dose of energy and idealism into a capital mired in partisan conflict and petty scandal. His spare and eloquent inaugural address evoked comparisons with the speech delivered three decades earlier by his idol, John F. Kennedy.

But the promise of that moment faded almost as soon as he stepped away from the podium. Two days after his inaugural, Clinton was forced to withdraw his nomination of Zoe Baird, a Connecticut corporate attorney, as attorney general after talk radio fanned flames of outrage over the revelation she had hired two illegal aliens to care for her infant son. By the end of his first week, Clinton was embroiled in the dispute that still stuck in his mind on that Sunday morning drive in San Francisco almost two years later: whether openly homosexual soldiers would be allowed to serve in the military, as he had promised during the campaign.

Those misfortunes, following on the heels of Clinton's triumphant inaugural day, set a pattern that has never wavered. Throughout his presidency, Clinton has teetered constantly between success and despair, unable to consolidate a stable base of support for himself and his policies. One moment Clinton was winning a critical legislative victory — passing a $500 billion plan to reduce the deficit in 1993, or squeezing out a narrow vote in the House the next year to ban nineteen types of assault weapons. The next he was suffering a stinging reversal, when a new allegation emerged charging him with misconduct during his years as the governor of Arkansas, or when one of his prized initiatives ran aground in Congress.

After beginning with such promise, Clinton's first two years in office demonstrated the intractability of the problems confronting the Democratic Party. For the quarter century before Clinton's victory, Republicans had dominated presidential elections so thoroughly that some analysts argued the GOP had constructed a virtual "lock" on the electoral college. Breaking that lock and building a stable majority of public support for a new era of government activism was Clinton's goal from the moment he emerged on the national stage. He built his campaign's centrist "New Democrat" agenda — which balanced calls for government activism with promises of government reform — on the candid admission that white middle-class voters at the heart of the party's political coalition from the New Deal through the Great Society had lost faith in traditional liberal answers.

That New Democrat agenda allowed Clinton to capture the White House. But in office Clinton and the Democratic Congress undermined its promise with an unsteady and often chaotic performance that left many voters convinced the Democrats had defaulted on their pledges to reform Washington and attack the problems of middle-class families. The mutual failures of Clinton and the congressional Democrats inspired a backlash so strong that the 1994 election brought the Republicans their largest electoral gains in forty years. After surveying voters in the days following the explosion, even

Stanley B. Greenberg, Clinton's pollster, acknowledged, "Voters this year revolted against Democratic-dominated national politics that seemed corrupt, divisive and slow to address the needs of ordinary citizens."

Clinton's own missteps explained many of his failures, but his difficulties had deeper roots in a decade-long disagreement among Democrats over the reason for the party's decline — and how much of its liberal tradition had to be surrendered to survive. Clinton's victory in 1992 represented not only a personal success but a triumph for an alliance of Sunbelt and centrist Democrats known as the Democratic Leadership Council, who had called for the party to fundamentally rethink liberal approaches on all fronts: economic, social, and foreign policy. Clinton's subsequent reversals in office revealed not only his own flaws, but the weaknesses in that analysis — as well as the crippling resistance within the party to its strengths. To many on Capitol Hill, the surge toward the GOP in 1994 showed that Clinton was overmatched by the job. But it was just as reasonable to conclude from his experience that even an extremely talented politician could not overcome the internal ideological and racial divisions that hobbled the Democrats. To understand why, it is important first to understand the forces that undermined the Democratic hold on the public's imagination over the past generation, and how they shaped the political vision that Clinton carried with him to the Oval Office.

THE SEARCH FOR A DEMOCRATIC MAJORITY

Democrats ruled the political world in which Bill Clinton grew to adulthood, not only in Arkansas but in the nation. From Franklin Roosevelt's election in 1932 through 1968, Democrats held the White House for all but eight years, and for all but four years in that period they controlled both houses of Congress. Liberal ideas so dominated political debate that the critic Lionel Trilling once famously declared, "In the United States at this time liberalism is not only the dominant, but even the sole intellectual tradition."

This was Roosevelt's legacy. In the crucible of the Depression, Roosevelt endowed his party with a lasting vision and the means to implement it. Roosevelt identified the Democrats as the party of upward mobility and economic security for the middle class, and he forged a diverse political coalition of northern ethnics, blacks, union members, and southern whites that dominated national elections for the next generation.

Roosevelt's resilient New Deal coalition survived economic upheaval and world war, and even the death of its founder, but it could not survive the social turmoil of the 1960s. After 1968, Republicans controlled the White House for twenty of the next twenty-four years. The three-way presidential campaign of 1968 was the hinge between the two eras. Richard Nixon's victory that year was hardly decisive: He won the White House for the Republicans with just 43.4 percent of the vote. But under the pressure of the Vietnam War, racial tension, and social disorder, the Democratic coalition sundered; Hubert Humphrey, the Democratic nominee, won only 42.7 percent — down almost nineteen percentage points from Lyndon Johnson's landslide in 1964. Alabama Governor George Wallace, a Democrat running an economically populist, racially divisive independent campaign that declared "there isn't a dime's worth of difference" between the two parties, captured the remainder, peeling away millions of southern whites and northern Catholics who had grown up considering themselves Roosevelt Democrats.

Wallace's success foreshadowed the death of the Roosevelt majority in national politics. The New Deal coalition was torn apart by crosscutting pressures of race, culture, and class. From one side, Lyndon Johnson's Great Society and War on Poverty repositioned the Democrats less as the advocate for the great middle class than as the tribune for the poor. From the other, questions of race and social tolerance pressed at the cultural fault lines in the Democratic majority. Roosevelt's coalition had always contained incompatible views on race, but for decades the party had successfully bound together blacks and racially conservative whites through an appeal to their common economic interests. By 1968, though, those appeals to economic solidarity were attenuated by a widening prosperity that lifted more and more workers into a middle class that worried less about layoffs than taxes. With its economic bonds already weakened, the coalition could not survive the backlash among many white voters in the South against desegregation in the mid-1960s, or the anxiety in the North generated by race riots in dozens of cities, student protests, and rising fear about urban crime.

Humphrey's defeat in 1968 offered the first clear signal that Roosevelt's formula of economic solidarity could be trumped with an appeal based on shared cultural interests. And on that battlefield, it was the Republicans who successfully portrayed themselves as the voice of the common man — what Nixon called "the silent majority" — while Democrats were identified with the avant-garde forces of cultural elitism that millions of Americans saw as threats to moral order. That cultural and racial contrast — carefully nurtured by a generation of Republican political strategists and later reinforced by Ronald Reagan with an economic appeal based on opposition to both taxes and new government spending — became a central pillar of the reliable Republican presidential majority that emerged from the Democratic wreckage in 1968.

In 1968, the Wallace voters took only a first step, leaving the Democratic Party most had grown up with; but four years later, Nixon carried them the next step into the Republican camp and reshaped the landscape of presidential politics. Nixon courted the Wallace voters with an array of potent cultural symbols, from a proposed "moratorium" on school busing to denunciation of the "bums" protesting the Vietnam War on college campuses. In 1972, the Democrats cooperated by nominating for President South Dakota Senator George McGovern, a passionate opponent of the Vietnam War whose liberalism embodied almost everything alienating the Wallace voters from their former party. In an internal White House memo, Nixon said he intended to frame the election as a choice between "square America and radical America" and he succeeded beyond even his expectation, winning forty-nine states and nearly 61 percent of the popular vote against McGovern, including 80 percent of 1968 Wallace supporters. Joining the generally downscale Wallace vote from North and South to an upscale and suburban GOP base, Nixon's victory in 1972 marked a historic turning point. Nixon established a new conservative coalition — what he called "a new American majority" — as the dominant force in presidential politics.

The Watergate scandal that forced Nixon's resignation temporarily obscured the change. Gerald Ford, Nixon's successor, was weakened by his decision to pardon Nixon and by his own tendency toward malapropism, and in the 1976 election, former Georgia Governor Jimmy Carter, a born-again Christian running a centrist campaign and promising to return honesty and trust to government, brought back just enough moderate and southern votes to squeeze past Ford into the White House with 50.1 percent of the vote.

But Carter could not consolidate his breakthrough. Carter was buffeted by double-digit inflation and interest rates and humiliated by the seizure of American hostages in Iran. But he was also caught in the same conundrum that would ensnare Bill Clinton more than a decade later. The campaigns of 1968 and 1972 had demonstrated that the Democratic liberal base vote of minorities, union members, feminists, and the poor was no longer sufficient to win national elections. But that base remained the dominant voice inside the party — and its various constituencies resisted Carter's efforts to reach out to centrist voters on issues like welfare reform and reducing federal spending. Carter seemed trapped in a zero-sum game: Each step he took to increase his support in the center alienated party activists on the Left. Conversely, his gestures toward the Left — particularly on relations with the Soviet Union — alienated "neoconservative" Democrats like Senator Henry Jackson of Washington. In the 1980 primary, Carter beat back a liberal challenge from Senator Edward M. Kennedy, but in the fall, the President was an easy target for Ronald Reagan, the Republican nominee, who won a landslide victory and in the process mobilized ideological conservatives against an administration they believed had tilted too far to the left.

With Reagan's resounding victory, Democrats could no longer deny that *something* was wrong. Carter's defeat set off a decade-long debate within the Democratic Party over how to recover the White House — a process that ultimately produced Clinton and the New Democrat agenda that he rode to the presidency in 1992.

THE STRUGGLE OF THE 1980s

During the 1980s, advocates of three broad theories clashed over how to recapture the initiative from the Republicans and rebuild a Democratic majority. Each struck a different balance in the fundamental challenge confronting Democratic strategists: how to expand the party's appeal without alienating its base support. The first argued that Democrats did not really need to expand their support, but instead should pump life back into the New Deal coalition with a message of economic "fairness" and registration drives to bring millions of low-income and minority voters to the polls. The other two schools argued that the party had to reach out to centrist voters, but they differed on how to do it. Through 1988, the most prominent of these alternatives was the neoliberal movement identified with suburban reformers like Gary Hart, Michael Dukakis, and Paul Tsongas. But after the 1984 election, another reform camp developed around the Democratic Leadership Council, an alliance of centrist and conservative Democrats that drew its membership primarily from the Sunbelt.

In succession, each of these camps anointed the party's presidential nominee in the campaigns from 1984 through 1992. First was the party's New Deal wing, which powered former Vice President Walter Mondale's capture of the 1984 Democratic presidential nomination. Mondale almost prided himself on offering nothing new. "He dares to be cautious," his media adviser proclaimed. Mondale built his campaign message from a stack of liberal verities on both economic and social issues — compassion for the poor, protectionism in trade, lower defense budgets — that actually owed less to Roosevelt's muscular internationalism and middle-class sensibility than to the liberal social movements of the 1960s. Mondale's very absence of innovation made him the choice for a party elite who believed that Carter's failure was rooted in his deviation from traditional liberal approaches. Liberal interest groups like the AFL-CIO rallied around Mondale's campaign under the cry of nominating a "real Democrat."

But as the campaign unfolded, Mondale saw all of these institutional advantages turned against him by Gary Hart, a solitary and cerebral two-term Democratic senator from Colorado, who carried the flag of neoliberalism into national politics for the first time. Though less than nine years younger than Mondale, Hart seemed entirely from a different generation; he was stylish, darkly ironic, and committed to a different brand of politics. Mondale was "a collection of special interests," Hart declared, and a "spokesman from the past" — the embodiment of an interest-group politics that had lost both its practical relevance and political appeal. Hart presented himself as the voice of "new ideas" within a party that desperately needed to reexamine first principles. "Nostalgia," Hart insisted, "is not a program." "Where's the beef?" Mondale replied, as he sought to undermine Hart's credibility with the party faithful.

Hart was ahead of his time, offering a message of change to a party still steering with its eyes on the rearview mirror. But he was a flawed messenger, dogged by an often chilly public persona and persistent allegations of marital infidelity. Mondale's support from the party establishment — and the doubts about Hart among voters uneasy about revelations that he had changed his name and misstated his age — proved just enough to allow the former vice president to narrowly claim the nomination at the Democratic convention in San Francisco. But the general election bore out all of Hart's predictions about Mondale's vulnerability. With Republicans effectively painting Mondale as a return to a brand of liberalism discredited during the 1960s — Reagan's U.N. Ambassador Jeane Kirkpatrick, a neoconservative Democrat from the party's Henry Jackson wing, tagged Mondale the leader of the "San Francisco Democrats," whose instinct was to "blame America first" — the result was never in doubt. Reagan replayed Nixon's 1972 landslide, winning forty-nine states and 59 percent of the vote.

The 1984 campaign ended the dominance of the New Deal wing in Democratic presidential politics. Though Jesse Jackson continued to push the argument into the 1990s, Mondale's landslide defeat exposed as a dead end the vision of regaining the White House by mobilizing an army of the disaffected with a message of unreconstructed liberalism. The New Deal philosophy remains extremely influential within the party — indeed, it constitutes the dominant perspective among Democrats in the House of Representatives — but no one representing its viewpoint has come close to winning the party presidential nomination since Mondale.

The Mondale debacle opened the door not only to the neoliberals, but to the new Democratic Leadership Council, which forged a competing reform tradition. The group was born in the fears of Sunbelt Democrats that the party's continuing image of economic and cultural liberalism could lead to its extinction across the South and West. In January 1985, Al From, then an aide to Representative Gillis Long, a leading House moderate, drafted a memo urging that centrists build an ongoing organization to challenge the party's direction. Entitled "Saving the Democratic Party," From's memo starkly described the Democrats' deteriorating position: "[T]he leadership of the Democratic Party," From wrote, "has been unable to adapt the party's traditional concern for working people, the poor, and minorities — its compassion and sense of social justice — into a coherent agenda for governing a rapidly changing nation."

From called on Democratic elected officials to create what he called a "governing council" that would draft a "blueprint — for changing the party." The new group, From wrote, should work to disenthrall the party from organized labor, feminists, and other constituency groups — what he called "the new bosses." Subservient to those interests, From insisted, the Democratic Party "has projected an image to the nation of exactly what [it] is — a disorganized band with no sense of purpose that couldn't govern effectively even if elected."

From's bracing words amounted to a declaration of war on the forces within the party that had nominated Mondale, and his militance struck a chord with the moderate elected officials to whom he privately circulated his manifesto. With then–Virginia Governor Charles S. Robb heavily lobbying his colleagues, the DLC was born early in 1985. Within a few weeks, it counted seventy-five members, primarily governors and members of Congress, most of them from the Sunbelt, and almost all of them white; liberal critics instantly dubbed the group "the white male caucus."

The DLC and neoliberal camps united in rejecting the traditional liberal agenda. But they departed on exactly what should replace it. The neoliberals called for a new centrist economics based on growth (rather than redistribution), free trade, and fiscal restraint, but strongly reaffirmed the party's post-McGovern traditions on social and foreign policy. The DLC shared the commitment to centrist economics and free trade, but took a much harder line against liberal traditions on cultural and foreign policy issues than Hart and the other neoliberals. This approach reflected not only differences in political philosophy but divergent political strategies. The neoliberal appeal targeted mostly college-educated suburbanites; the DLC also hoped to reach those voters, but with its social agenda also courted working-class voters who had abandoned the Democratic party over issues connected by race, strength, and social permissiveness.

On foreign policy, arms control, defense, and relations with the Soviet Union, the DLC consistently assumed positions to the right of the neoliberals. "I remember," says Democratic political consultant Paul Begala, "people saying, 'we've got to find a Democratic missile system.'" DLC Democrats generally supported aid to the contras in

Nicaragua, while Hart opposed it; conversely, most DLC Democrats opposed the nuclear freeze that Hart and other neoliberals endorsed. The DLC displayed much less enthusiasm than the neoliberals for reducing defense spending; and while Hart was prescient in seeing the possibilities that Mikhail Gorbachev presented for renegotiating the relationship with the Soviet Union, DLC Democrats were so focused on demonstrating their toughness that even as late as 1986 Robb absurdly insisted that "Soviet aggression, real and potential, remains the most pressing danger to America."

On domestic social policy, the divide was even wider. The DLC denounced racial hiring quotas; put less priority than the neoliberals on environmental protection and women's rights as defining issues; and supported the death penalty (which neoliberals like Hart, Dukakis, and Tsongas opposed). Robb, who became chairman in 1986, declared in a head-turning speech to a conference on the Great Society that "while racial discrimination has by no means vanished from our society, it's time to shift the primary focus from racism — the traditional enemy without — to self-defeating patterns of behavior — the new enemy within." No Democrat in years had so candidly discussed the contribution of the inner-city poor to their own despair. In contrast, Hart and most neoliberals remained as reluctant as Mondale — "squeamish," as one of Hart's speechwriters put it — to discuss the rising rate of illegitimacy, violence, and social chaos engulfing the inner-city underclass.

The battle for the 1988 Democratic presidential nomination offered the first confrontation between the neoliberal and DLC messages. After his strong showing in 1984, Hart began the contest as the putative front-runner. But almost before the race began, he was forced to drop out after revelations that he had taken an excursion with a model named Donna Rice on a pleasure boat almost too deliciously named *Monkey Business*. With Hart's departure the race came down to Jesse Jackson (who ran on New Deal fundamentalism), Senator Al Gore (who ran a defense-tilted, Southern-oriented DLC campaign), Representative Richard A. Gephardt of Missouri (who had served as the first DLC chairman but moved toward the Mondale wing with a campaign based on protectionism), and Massachusetts Governor Michael S. Dukakis, who offered a particularly technocratic formulation of neoliberalism.

Dukakis's victory in the primaries marked the ascendance of the neoliberal approach over its two competitors. Dukakis was as centrist a candidate on economics as the Democrats had produced. Diminutive and self-contained, he was fierce only in his frugality: a movie introducing him at the convention raised to the level of cultural symbol his refusal to trade in his ancient snowblower for a new model. Dukakis proposed no new taxes (indeed his forces defeated a platform amendment from Jackson at the 1988 convention urging new taxes on the rich), emphasized his record balancing the budget in Massachusetts, and associated himself with high-technology entrepreneurs, investment, public-private partnerships — in short, the entire hive of neoliberal buzzwords. For his mission if he won the White House, Dukakis offered nothing more exotic than "good jobs at good wages."

On that message Dukakis surged to a large lead over the Republican nominee, Vice President George Bush, in the summer of 1988. But he could not hold the advantage. Throughout the summer and fall, Bush and his aggressive campaign manager, Lee Atwater, systematically erased the gap by stripping away the "neo" to brand Dukakis as a liberal. Their tools were a seemingly bottomless supply of issues that reopened the cultural divides of the 1960s: Dukakis's opposition to the death penalty, his support for gun control, his membership in the American Civil Liberties Union, his veto of a Massachusetts law requiring that students say the pledge of allegiance. Bush slammed Dukakis as a foreign-policy neophyte who would strip America's defenses, calling him a man who knew of the world only what he had learned "in Harvard Yard's boutique." Most damagingly, Bush assailed Dukakis over a Massachusetts prison furlough program that offered even convicted murderers weekend passes — a policy that allowed a black convicted murderer named Willie Horton to rape a woman and torture her husband in Maryland while out on a weekend pass.

On each of these controversies, Dukakis could mount reasonable arguments in his defense, but the cumulative portrait Bush painted was not inaccurate: On cultural issues, Dukakis embraced a mind-set that represented the center of opinion in Manhattan and Malibu but few places in between. In their ruthless and relentless attack on Dukakis's "values," Bush and Atwater exposed the fatal political vulnerability of neoliberalism: its adherence to traditional liberalism on social and foreign-policy issues. In 1988, Democrats tried to win back the white middle class by portraying Bush as an economic elitist blind to the daily concerns of average families: a man who was "born on third base and thought he hit a triple," as Ann Richards, then the Texas state treasurer, jibed. But Bush — a senator's son who could hardly have been a more perfect fit for that collar — countered by portraying Dukakis as a cultural elitist contemptuous of mainstream social values. As with Nixon and Humphrey two decades before, culture trumped economics. Though Bush's own weaknesses as a campaigner were manifest, and his vote significantly eroded from the Republican high point of 1984, the cultural offensive allowed the vice president to re-assemble most of the Republican coalition that elected Nixon and Reagan, and win the election going away. Like New Deal fundamentalism, neoliberalism had proven itself a dead end in national politics.

THE EMERGENCE OF THE NEW DEMOCRATS

The Dukakis disaster provoked another round of soul searching within the Democratic Party. For good reason. With Dukakis's defeat, Democrats had now lost five of the past six presidential elections. Over that period, they had won an average of just 43 percent of the vote — and collected even more meager percentages among whites and men. Looking at the electoral college, the Democratic situation was even more dire. Over those six elections, Republicans won an average of 417 electoral votes — more than one and a half times the 270 they needed for victory. Not even Democrats in the first six elections after Roosevelt's initial victory amassed such a consistently overwhelming advantage.

For Democrats, the 1988 loss was particularly disheartening because Bush appeared so vulnerable, a figure ridiculed on the nightly talk shows and a man declared a "wimp" on the cover of *Newsweek* magazine. But awkward and distracted as he was, Bush still carried a majority of white men at *every* income level, and white women earning more than $12,500 a year. The fact that Democrats could not win a majority of white working-class voters even against a Republican who was chauffeured to school during the Depression and asked a waitress for another "splash" of coffee during the campaign under-scored the collapse of the party's historic identity as the voice of average Americans.

The shock of Dukakis's defeat opened Democrats to the more radical critique of the party embodied in the DLC vision. In particular, the inability of Dukakis's economic moderation to protect him from Bush's ideological assault on such issues as crime and defense forced onto the table the debate over social and foreign policy that both the neoliberals and New Deal Democrats had resisted.

In a seminal 1989 paper for the DLC entitled "The Politics of Evasion," William A. Galston and Elaine Kamarck, two analysts at the DLC's Progressive Policy Institute, insisted the party would not regain the White House until it convinced Americans not only that it could manage the economy — the argument Dukakis stressed — but that it would also uphold the national interest in foreign affairs and defend mainstream social values on issues like crime. For the party, they wrote, there was no shortcut back to the White House, adding, "The next nominee must be fully credible as commander-in-chief of our armed forces and as the prime steward of our foreign policy; he must squarely reflect the moral sentiments of average Americans; and he must offer a progressive economic message, based on the values of upward mobility and individual effort, that can unite the interests of those already in the middle class with those struggling to get there."

The analysis by Galston and Kamarck tracked with the work of Stanley B. Greenberg, an owlish Yale University political scientist who had abandoned the cloistered life to plunge into Democratic politics as a pollster. Greenberg had achieved instant notoriety in 1985 when he conducted a historic series of focus groups with disaffected white working-class Democrats in Macomb County, a blue-collar suburb north of Detroit. Greenberg found them roiling with resentments at their ancestral party, much of it over race. He reported that for many of these former Democrats the party's pleas for economic "fairness" — the most cherished message of the liberal New Deal wing — conjured images of "racial minorities" or "some blacks . . . kicking up a storm." The result was so explosive that the Michigan Democratic Party, which commissioned the study, initially suppressed it. But the paper became an eagerly sought form of Democratic samizdat and sent Greenberg on his way as one of the most creative analysts of his party's faltering appeal.

Greenberg, who became the pollster for Clinton's 1992 presidential campaign, shared with Galston and Kamarck the central belief that

Democrats could not regain the White House except by reestablishing their credibility with white middle-class voters through broad-based economics and affirmation of mainstream social values. "The key to Democratic success," Greenberg wrote in the fall of 1991, "is becoming a middle-class centered, bottom-up coalition. . . . Democrats need to rediscover broad-based social policy that sends a larger message: Democrats are for 'everybody,' not just the 'have-nots.'"

These critiques of traditional liberalism from Greenberg and Galston and Kamarck became central strands in Bill Clinton's 1992 campaign. Clinton devoured these analyses of the Democrats' difficulties as if they were so many French fries; their conclusions broadly echoed themes he had employed during his long career in Arkansas, a state that held both government and liberal social ideas on a short leash. But it was not until Clinton accepted From's request, in March 1990, to become chairman of the DLC, that he synthesized this argument in his own terms.

In a series of speeches during his chairmanship, Clinton sharpened his focus on the middle-class swing voters who had rejected the party over the previous six presidential elections. The high point came in an address that effectively launched his national campaign, a May 1991 speech to a DLC convention in Cleveland. Before a large crowd of activists and reporters, Clinton candidly described the Democratic dilemma in terms lifted almost directly from the Galston/Kamarck manifesto, saying that "too many of the people that used to vote for us, the very burdened middle class we are talking about, have not trusted us in national elections to defend our national interests abroad, to put their values into our social policy at home, or to take their tax money and spend it with discipline."

As he filled in his policy agenda during his presidential campaign, Clinton remained focused on those disaffected ex-Democratic voters. He targeted his economic message directly at the economic strain and fears of the future afflicting the middle class, particularly the three-fourths of the workforce without four-year college degrees. Clinton proposed to reignite the growth in living standards by creating — and equipping less-skilled workers for — high-wage jobs through massive public investment in education, training, advanced technological research, and infrastructure, coupled with an aggressive effort to open markets for high-value American products abroad. (Though Clinton also promised to reduce the federal deficit, as a candidate he clearly subordinated that goal to these calls for new "investment" spending.) Following thinkers like the prominent black sociologist William Julius Wilson, as well as Greenberg's political analysis, Clinton emphasized "universal programs" like national health insurance and a broad-based tax cut that offered tangible benefits to both the middle class and the needy, while saying little about traditional liberal programs, like affirmative action, that targeted benefits solely to the poor and minorities. And though he hadn't shown much enthusiasm for confronting the clubby oligarchy that ruled Arkansas, as a presidential candidate he sought to identify with disgust over Washington's insular culture by promising "to put Congress in order" with political reform.

While none of this differed much from the recipe that neoliberals like Hart or Dukakis had offered, Clinton parted ways with them on issues related to values. One of these was foreign policy, which Republicans since Nixon had used to hammer Democrats as weak and unwilling to stand up for American interests abroad. Clinton broke from the neoliberal foreign policy by promising a more muscular assertion of American interests abroad. Reversing the partisan pattern of the previous quarter century, Clinton criticized Bush for being too soft on Bosnia, on the Chinese crackdown on pro-democracy demonstrators at Tiananmen Square, and on Saddam Hussein before the invasion of Kuwait. Some countervailing notes crept in: Clinton urged significantly greater reliance on the United Nations and proposed far deeper cuts in defense spending — money he needed to pay for his investment package. But overall, the signals he sent were sufficiently stout to win Clinton symbolically valuable endorsements from a long list of the neoconservative policy intellectuals — led by Paul Nitze, the venerable arms control negotiator — who had left their party after the rise of George McGovern.

The strongest break from liberal (and neoliberal) orthodoxy — and Clinton's enduring contribution to the Democratic message — came in his demand for reciprocal responsibility in social policy. Clinton brought to the national level the DLC message that government should do more to expand opportunity, but at the same time demand personal responsibility from those it helps. Welfare reform offered the most powerful example: Clinton proposed that government spend more on education, training, and child care to equip welfare recipients to advance, but also insisted that after two years on the rolls they be required to work as a condition of further aid. "We need to go beyond the competing ideas of the old political establishment," Clinton declared in one of his most appealing formulations, "beyond every man for himself on the one hand, and the right to something for nothing on the other." He reinforced the message of individual responsibility by supporting stern punishment for criminals, including the death penalty.

This agenda reflected both a policy and political analysis. Personal responsibility as a principle of social policy appealed to Clinton because his experience in Arkansas had convinced him that traditional entitlement programs amounted to spending "more and more money to fix broken lives that should have been kept whole." And his economic plan was undergirded by the academic work of his longtime friend (and later Labor Secretary) Robert B. Reich, who maintained that in a global economy, the only dependable route to prosperity was to make the nation more attractive for investment by improving its infrastructure, its laboratories, and especially the skills of its workers.

But Clinton's agenda also reflected the middle-class political focus championed by Greenberg and the DLC. Clinton conceded public disillusionment about liberalism and instead promised something distinct: a "third way" that rejected the "false choices" of ideologically polarized liberalism and conservatism. Above all, his agenda aimed to redefine government activism in a way that made it acceptable to the middle-class white voters who had turned against government and the Democrats over the past quarter century. Throughout his race for the White House, Clinton's overriding goal was to convince hard-working middle-class voters, particularly the non–college educated who had suffered the most in the economic upheavals since the early 1970s, that he would be their champion, and reform government to work for them. Clinton and his advisers, said Greenberg, operated on the belief "that the Democratic party had become a party of postgraduates and liberal elites combined with minority populations, and that had precluded it . . . from reaching broad middle-class voters. [We believed] that one had to change that equation, that instead of focusing on those two ends, one had to center your message on middle-class America and that was just a fundamentally different equation about how to think about the Democratic Party."

This message was endlessly nuanced and sometimes overly complex. But it amounted to more than simply moving to the right or abandoning the party's core constituencies. Instead, Clinton sought to continue government services to the needy, but in a manner that white middle-class voters could support. Faced with racial divisions, stagnant incomes, cultural regression, and a crisis of confidence in government that together had destroyed the New Deal coalition, Clinton proposed renegotiating the liberal ideal of the social contract, but not breaking it.

This approach placed Clinton on an ideological and racial tightrope. Initially the party's most liberal elements viewed him with suspicion. Industrial labor unions, particularly the United Auto Workers, bristled against his support for free trade, symbolized by his sympathy for the North American Free Trade Agreement with Mexico and Canada. Jesse Jackson, black leaders sympathetic to him, and many white liberals saw Clinton's focus on "the forgotten middle class" and calls for personal responsibility as thinly coded appeals to white resentments. Characteristically, Clinton contained these problems by expanding his appeal, rather than sharpening the lines of conflict and breaking decisively with his liberal critics. Late in the summer of 1991, he sought to make the theme of personal responsibility more acceptable to liberals by applying it not only to the poor but also to the wealthy. "It's important to remember," he said during the speech that launched his candidacy in October 1991, "that the most irresponsible people of all in the 1980s were those at the top . . . who sold out savings and loans with bad deals and spent billions on wasteful takeovers and mergers."

The escalating economic populism ringing through those remarks constituted a significant break for Clinton with both his neoliberal and DLC predecessors, few of whom felt comfortable stomping in those vineyards. Combined with his celebration of middle-class cultural values, Clinton's class-tinged economic message created a double-barreled populism that allowed him to bid for blue-collar Democratic voters who might have considered Hart or Dukakis good-government effetes.

The dissonance between the views of the Democratic Left and the centrist elements of Clinton's agenda, like welfare reform and his support for the death penalty, was never resolved. But after losing five of the six previous presidential elections, even many liberals were willing to grit their teeth in the hope of victory. Clinton's blend attracted support from enough liberal institutions (including the teachers' and public employees' unions) and elected officials (including many African-American members of Congress) to suppress the ideological and racial conflict through the primaries and the general election.

Clinton had anticipated a primary clash with the party's liberal wing in the formidable form of New York Governor Mario M. Cuomo, or Iowa Senator Tom Harkin, a much lesser light. Instead, with Cuomo choosing not to run and Harkin's campaign never leaving the runway, Clinton's most serious opponents were former Senator Paul E. Tsongas, who offered a blend of fiscal conservatism and social and foreign-policy liberalism that expanded on the neoliberal lineage of Hart and Dukakis; and former California Governor Edmund G. (Jerry) Brown Jr., who ran an iconoclastic populist campaign that prefigured Ross Perot. Tsongas and Brown actually proved less of a threat to Clinton than allegations that emerged early in 1992 accusing him of marital infidelity and dodging the draft during Vietnam. Each left deep wounds, but Clinton demonstrated his most appealing political characteristic — extraordinary tenacity — in battling his way past them to the nomination. In July, Clinton claimed his prize with a powerful, if lengthy, speech at the Democratic National Convention in New York, where he effectively portrayed himself as both the defender and the product of "the forgotten middle-class" — a small-town boy whose climb honored middle-class values of faith, work, and self-reliance.

In the fall, that imagery, combined with Clinton's New Democrat message, frustrated Bush's efforts to replay the cultural assault that demolished Dukakis in 1988. With his hard-line positions on welfare and crime, Clinton sealed the trap doors on values and forced Bush to fight the campaign on economic performance and opportunity. On those grounds Bush could not compete. Like a spendthrift trust-funder, Bush by 1992 had squandered nearly all of the potent political coalition bequeathed to him by Reagan. But he suffered most from anemic economic performance: Over his four years in office, the economy grew just 5.7 percent, by far the weakest performance under any President in a generation. Even under Carter, the economy had grown twice as fast.

Bush's seeming indifference to the economy's lackluster perfor-
mance repelled independents, blue-collar Democrats, and the other
voters loosely attached to the Republican presidential coalition. Their
economic disenchantment outweighed any sympathy they might have
felt for Bush's efforts to find a moderate center on other domestic is-
sues, particularly the federal budget. Instead, those deviations from
Reaganism succeeded only in depressing and dividing his political
base. "Read my lips, no new taxes," Bush had declared at the GOP
convention in 1988; when he moved his lips to a tax increase as part of
a 1990 budget deal with the Democrats he hopelessly split his own
coalition. "Read my lips," one Michigan woman told us two months
before the election, "you will not see me voting for Bush again." Ulti-
mately, Bush burned his candle at both ends, demoralizing his base
support and alienating the independent swing voters who had broken
his way in 1988.

Yet Clinton still could not capture the center of the electorate.
With his pox-on-both-their-houses populism, the iconoclastic billion-
aire Ross Perot swept into his independent campaign most of the cen-
trist voters Clinton's New Democrat message had targeted. Clinton
won the White House not by expanding his coalition, but by holding
together the Democratic base while the Republican coalition dissolved
under the pressure of Bush's failure and Perot's insurgency. In the
most closely watched swing counties around the country — and with
most of the key demographic groups who had abandoned Democrats
over the past quarter century — Clinton ran within a few percentage
points of Dukakis's 1988 showing, while Perot and Bush divided the
1988 Republican vote.

Merely holding Dukakis's two-way vote in a three-way race did
represent a form of progress for Clinton and his party. And in a race
without Perot, polls indicated, Clinton still would have won. But in
fact those voters did not support Clinton, preferring instead to cast
their ballots for a third-party candidate who had proven himself er-
ratic, unpredictable, and arguably paranoid. With almost perfect sym-
metry, Clinton's 43 percent victory in the three-way 1992 campaign
portended the end of the political era opened by Nixon's 43 percent
three-way victory in 1968. In that election, Nixon won by consolidat-
ing his party's core vote while Wallace irrevocably split the reigning
Democratic coalition. Over the next four years Nixon built a new

coalition by cementing the Wallace voters — who had taken a first step away from the Democratic Party of their roots — into a Republican presidential majority.

In 1992, Perot reversed Wallace, fracturing the reigning Republican coalition. Clinton thus faced the same kind of challenge that confronted Nixon after 1968: to lead the Perot voters who had abandoned the GOP the next step into his own coalition — just as Nixon had done with the Wallace supporters a quarter century earlier. Greenberg's verdict that 1992 constituted a "shattering" election captured its destructive velocity. Now it fell to Bill Clinton to pick up the pieces and assemble a Democratic political majority that could shape the direction of national life into the new century.

THE ROAD FROM HOPE TO DESPAIR

"Defined in terms of what we set out to do, we have accomplished a number of our goals," Clinton told us on that Sunday morning before the 1994 election as he made his way to the San Francisco airport. Measured simply by the volume of legislation passed, there was much in his first two years to justify the claim. At his prodding, Congress had approved a substantial deficit-reduction plan, the North American Free Trade Agreement, creating a giant free-trade zone between Mexico, the United States, and Canada, new gun-control laws, a law mandating that businesses provide their workers with unpaid family and medical leave, a huge expansion of the earned-income tax credit, which benefits the working poor, a crime bill that provided billions of dollars in new spending on police, prisons, and crime prevention, a scaled-down version of his national service plan that allowed young people to earn college scholarships by performing community service, and a substantial program to funnel money and tax breaks into blighted urban "empowerment zones." The breadth and diversity of the list reflected the voracity of his ambition.

Yet these achievements were only one part of the ledger. The pressures of the presidency crystallized all the tensions inherent in Clinton's campaign: between his agenda and traditional Democratic approaches; between conflicting priorities within his agenda; and between his personal and political identities. Rather than consolidating a new era of Democratic control, his election set in motion forces that brought Republicans back to power more rapidly than almost anyone in the GOP had dared to hope.

The most important of Clinton's legislative accomplishments — particularly his deficit-reduction and anticrime plans — came only after protracted struggles that revealed weakness in both the President and his party and frequently forced Clinton out of the political center that he controlled during the campaign. Over time, his legislative successes were eclipsed by legislative failures — particularly his inability to pass his massive plan to reform the health care system. And his political momentum was sapped by other controversies, particularly doubts about his command of foreign policy, a lengthy dispute in 1993 over his effort to allow openly homosexual soldiers to serve in the military, and a procession of ethical allegations that weakened not only Clinton but several of his cabinet officers.

Much of the contemporary commentary about Clinton's troubles focused on disorganization and inexperience in the White House, disagreement between Clinton's political and policy advisers, and the absence of a commanding presidential image. To varying degrees, all these arguments had merit. But far more telling were two overarching personal and political problems that entangled his presidency. One was his inability to resolve doubts about his character and competence. The grandeur of office brought Clinton no shelter from the personal accusations that had battered him during the campaign. Ethical allegations followed Clinton throughout his presidency like the cloud over Mr. Btfsplk in "Li'l Abner." The accusations ranged from drizzle to downpour — from a sexual harassment suit filed against Clinton by a former Arkansas state worker named Paula Corbin Jones to questions about whether his wife had improperly benefited from inside information in commodity trades conducted fifteen years earlier to investigations into his participation in an Arkansas land development known as Whitewater and the suicide of associate White House counsel Vincent Foster. In each instance Clinton denied wrongdoing, but the controversies sapped the time of top aides, forced the White House into a bunker mentality for long stretches of time, and undermined his personal authority.

Like a leak in a roof, these concerns seeped into the foundation of his presidency, creating damage far from the original point of contact. The questions about Clinton's ethics merged with the uncertainties many voters held about his strength of leadership, particularly on foreign affairs, where, in contrast to his firmness as a candidate, he often appeared hesitant and tentative. The perception that Clinton could not make firm decisions and lacked strong principles in domestic or foreign policy — from his tortured process of finding a Supreme Court justice to his repeated shifts of direction on Bosnia through much of his presidency — was as damaging as the ethical allegations against him. Ultimately these two streams of criticism combined into a single underlying current of unease about Clinton's character. To a loud and persistent core of critics, Clinton's maneuvers on policy demonstrated character flaws: evidence he did not have the courage of his convictions — or even any convictions at all.

The greatest difficulties of Clinton's presidency, however, were less personal than generic. They sprang from the continuing dilemma of the Democratic Party itself. The internal contradictions that Democrats submerged in their eagerness to win the White House during 1992 exploded as soon as the election was over — and in the process began the chain reaction that propelled the GOP back into power.

THESE pressures immediately surfaced during the two-month transition after Clinton's election, as the President-elect set out to staff his government. The first signal any President sends about his intentions comes through his appointments to the White House and the cabinet. For Clinton the choices were especially critical. During the campaign he had pledged to steer his party in new directions, but there were many in Washington — and, indeed, many voters around the country — who doubted that his promise of a "third way" was anything more than a campaign ploy to dodge the liberal label. In a memo during the transition, Bill Galston and Elaine Kamarck, the DLC analysts whose work had influenced Clinton's campaign themes, urged Clinton to send a firm message of his sincerity to Republicans and Democrats alike through his personnel appointments: The President, they wrote, should use the appointment process "to continue his break with the past and to avoid being captured by the very forces he has undertaken to reform."

In particular, the two authors urged Clinton to create what Galston later called "a government of national reconciliation" by offering top jobs to independents and centrist Republicans. Both believed that appointing Republicans and independents would give Clinton a strong base from which to seek support from the moderate voters he needed to enlarge his plurality electoral victory into a lasting majority political coalition. It was sound advice. Throughout this century, Presidents of both parties had recognized the opportunity to broaden their political coalition and divide their opponents by bringing into government members of the opposition party. Franklin Roosevelt included three Republicans in his first cabinet. John F. Kennedy bolstered his credentials with business by naming C. Douglas Dillon, Eisenhower's undersecretary of State, as his Treasury secretary. Ronald Reagan pressured the fractures in the Democratic coalition by appointing prominent neoconservatives like Jeane Kirkpatrick and Paul Nitze to senior foreign-policy positions.

As a candidate, Clinton appeared aware of those possibilities and more than once declared his intent to reach across party lines in constructing his government. But that impulse vanished almost as soon as he no longer needed Republican and independent votes. Other priorities quickly intruded. During the campaign, Clinton promised a government that "looked like America," and in the transition he was barraged with demands from Democratic interest groups to name women and minorities to top jobs. Clinton also wanted to find places for his endless network of old friends; and despite the unhappy experience of Carter's attempt to import his "Georgia Mafia" to Washington, Clinton wanted to find spots for Arkansas cronies like Webb Hubbell, a law partner of Hillary Clinton, whom he stashed into a top position at the Justice Department. Amid all of these conflicting pressures, the process of filling the cabinet quickly turned into a public spectacle of quotas and indecision that did not end until Christmas Eve 1992.

Clinton held his personnel decisions close to his vest, and as he deliberated, the names of the contenders rose and fell on obscure gusts of rumor. In this maelstrom of ambition and intrigue, the idea of appointing Republicans and independents "just died," said Dee Dee Myers, Clinton's first White House press secretary. "It died of internal opposition. There was this circling of the wagons, which said, 'Oh, God, we can only have people that will be loyal. . . .' There wasn't anybody at the table arguing that what we really need is to have a Republican."

All of Clinton's cabinet appointments went to Democrats. Later in his presidency, Clinton brought in to senior positions David Gergen, who had worked for four Republican presidents, and John White, who had written Ross Perot's budget plan in 1992, and he reportedly sounded out former Republican Senator Warren Rudman to run the Pentagon. But these were near-token exceptions that could not change the partisan stamp of his initial choices.

Even centrist Democrats didn't fare that well in the scramble. The neoconservative foreign-policy intellectuals who had endorsed Clinton were shunted into secondary positions or frozen out altogether. In one meeting well into his presidency, Clinton blustered: "Where are all my neocons?" With a few exceptions, the DLC Democrats were not shut out, but neither did they secure the senior positions that Clinton's campaign might have predicted. DLC alumni like Galston and Kamarck, Bruce Reed (who had served as Clinton's campaign policy director), and Jeremy Rosner moved into White House jobs sufficiently senior to affect a broad range of specific policies but not powerful enough to influence the administration's overall direction.

When all the boxes were filled, Clinton had appointed a government that looked not too different from the one Michael Dukakis might have chosen. This was an early fork in the road, whose impact echoed throughout Clinton's presidency. Rather than using the appointment process to expand his coalition and point his presidency toward a clear break with the past, Clinton applied it almost entirely to consolidate his support with the existing Democratic base — and to reward longtime friends and allies. The practical impact of these staffing decisions was to lock Clinton into a partisan posture from the outset and to guarantee internal resistance to policy positions that confronted the Democratic base. Their symbolic impact was to embolden the traditional Democratic powers on Capitol Hill and in the interest groups to believe that Clinton might not be as committed to transforming the party as it seemed during the campaign. The few DLC officials inside the administration consoled each other with a bitter joke: I always knew that signing on early to the campaign would help you get a job, they would say. I just didn't know it was the Dukakis campaign.

*   *   *

THE narrowing tendencies of Clinton's key personnel decisions were emphatically reinforced by the second major strategic choice of the transition, his decision to create an intimate partnership in which the Democratic congressional leadership gained a virtual veto over his agenda. Clinton and his advisers came to Washington haunted by the mistakes of Jimmy Carter. Democrats in Washington held as an article of faith that Carter's failure to establish close relations with the Democratic congressional leadership had doomed his presidency. Clinton's advisers insisted they would not replicate that mistake. "There was a terrific fear in the first year that he would become like Carter," said Paul Begala, one of Clinton's key political advisers.

From the start, Clinton moved to minimize the possibility of conflict with the Democratic leadership. In the White House, operatives with experience on Capitol Hill assumed key positions. George Stephanopoulos, Clinton's all-purpose senior adviser, and David Dreyer, the deputy director of communications, were both alumni of Gephardt's office; Howard Paster, the first White House legislative affairs director, was a veteran Democratic lobbyist bound by instinct and experience to the party's congressional wing; former California Representative Leon E. Panetta, first as budget director and later as White House chief of staff, reinforced the voice of Congress in the White House. Later, former House Democratic Whip Tony Coelho was brought into the circle, particularly in planning for the 1994 campaign. At almost every turn, these advisers urged cooperation, not confrontation, with Congress as the way to steer clear of Carter's difficulties.

But Clinton's experience only demonstrated that those who remember the past can also be condemned to repeat it. By the end of 1994, Clinton found himself in a position uncannily similar to Carter's. He was in open combat with Congress and simultaneously under fire from the Left and Right of his party. His dilemma, ironically, was a direct result of his decision during the transition to bind his fate to the Democratic leadership.

CLINTON, CONGRESS, AND THE
DEATH OF REFORM

The three men who journeyed to Little Rock for dinner with Bill Clinton the second Sunday after his election knew very much about Washington and very little about him. One was George Mitchell of Maine, the Senate majority leader. During the Bush administration, the cool and cerebral Mitchell had been the single most powerful Democrat in Washington, a keen and agile adversary for the President. Over his long career, Mitchell had served as both the Democratic state party chairman in Maine and a federal judge, and his personality reflected both of those experiences. He was a fierce partisan, and an ardent liberal, but an extraordinarily precise and punctilious political operator. In public, Mitchell chose each word as carefully as if he had just been read his Miranda rights. He would prove a staunch ally of the new President — to the point where Clinton later offered him a seat on the Supreme Court.

Joining Mitchell in Little Rock was the Speaker of the House, Thomas S. Foley. Tall and loping, and improbably buffed by a late-in-life conversion to weight lifting and diet, Foley had first been elected to Congress from his district in eastern Washington state in November 1964 — just a few weeks after Bill Clinton began his freshman year at Georgetown. As he climbed the slippery pole of House influence over the next three decades, Foley was known less for any particular policy preferences than for fairness, integrity, and caution. His message was his mildness, which was enough for Democrats searching for leadership after the impulsive and overbearing Jim Wright had been forced to resign over ethical allegations in 1989. Foley projected little vision other than maintaining harmony among his members, and thus his position as their leader.

In the House leadership, vision was the province of the third man who flew to Little Rock that Sunday night, House Majority Leader Richard A. Gephardt; an ally of organized labor and other Democratic interest groups, Gephardt had effectively assumed leadership of the New Deal faction once headed by Mondale. Foley and Mitchell were each more than a decade older than Clinton, but Gephardt was a contemporary, just five years the new President's senior. A tow-headed former Eagle Scout, Gephardt was as ambitious and tenacious as any politician in Washington. His loss to Dukakis in the 1988 presidential race barely dented his ambition. Though he had sat out the 1992 presidential race (after briefly considering the prospect), there was no question that Gephardt saw himself someday occupying the position Bill Clinton now held.

For Clinton and his visitors, the dinner in Little Rock was very much a first date. Clinton had hundreds, even thousands, of friends salted throughout the Democratic Party, but very few of them sat on Capitol Hill. During his campaign for the nomination, Clinton's support among congressional Democrats had been notable only for its absence. Especially after he was wounded by the allegations about womanizing and the draft, they tended to view him as a likely loser in November who could drag many of them down to defeat as well, and even after it was clear he would be the nominee, Democrats on Capitol Hill continued to flail in feverish but ineffectual intrigues aimed at finding a new candidate to stop him. Widening the distance was anger among congressional Democrats, particularly in the House, over Clinton's criticism of Congress during the campaign. Clinton invariably disparaged the salary increase Congress had voted itself in 1989 as a "midnight pay raise" and picked at the House post office and banking scandals — both of which had seen legislators accused of misusing public institutions for their own gains.

For many Capitol Hill Democrats, Clinton's criticisms were fingernails on the chalkboard. Representative David R. Obey of Wisconsin, among the most liberal and caustic legislators in the House, insisted that Clinton had told him in 1989 that he supported the pay raise; after Clinton ran an ad in the New Hampshire primary criticizing the pay hike, Obey called him a "goddamned liar." Even after Clinton's victory, at a Democratic retreat, Representative Robert G. Torricelli of New Jersey, a stylish baby boomer known for dating Bianca Jagger, had raged at Paul Begala when Begala said that political reform would be one of Clinton's top priorities. "That's inside stuff," Torricelli howled. "Nobody cares about that stuff."

So there was much personal and political ground for Clinton and his guests to cover as they gathered at the governor's mansion in Little Rock on Sunday, November 15. Together with Vice President–elect Al Gore and Hillary Clinton, the three legislators and the new President talked cordially for several hours, and the next morning, all the participants in the dinner (except Hillary Clinton) filed out to meet with reporters at the Arkansas State House. One by one, as if reading off cue cards, they announced the end of the gridlock between the White House and Congress that had marked Bush's last years. "Our dinner last night marks a new era of cooperation and action in our nation's capital," the new President said. "Gridlock is over and cooperation and teamwork have begun," Gephardt said.

But the very first question from a reporter pointed toward a different interpretation of the previous evening's events. During the campaign, as part of his pledge to reform Washington, Clinton had called for a 25 percent reduction in the staff of both Congress and the White House, and for the President to be given the authority to veto individual line items in appropriations bills. Most congressional Democrats viewed the line-item veto as a threat to their own control over spending and dismissed the talk of staff cuts as demagoguery. Now that he was talking about ending the "Cold War" with Congress, the reporter asked, was Clinton still committed to pushing those ideas?

Clinton shuffled his feet. Congressional staff increases were not so much the problem, he said, after insisting the opposite for the better part of a year; the problem was that the White House staff "exploded in the last four years." Rather than demand that Congress cut its staff, Clinton said, "I'm going to get out there and set an example" by cutting the White House staff. As for the line-item veto, Clinton said that Speaker Foley — an ardent opponent of the idea — had proposed an elaborate alternative mechanism that provided less direct authority for the President. That idea, Clinton said, "is at least a good place for us to begin discussion."

In fact, the dinner in Little Rock effectively ended discussion of the congressional staff cut and line-item veto. While neither had been at the center of Clinton's campaign, both constituted valuable symbols of his intent to change the culture in Washington. Now in deference to his congressional visitors, Clinton had abandoned both of them. The effect of their demise was to derail the entire project of political reform. That became clear shortly after Clinton took office, when Mitchell pushed for quick action on campaign finance reform, an issue he had pushed aggressively under Bush. But Foley, representing a House Democratic membership that viewed any change in the rules as a threat to their electoral advantages, insisted on delay.

Clinton once again bent to Foley's demand. With only intermittent public squeaks of protest from the President, the House Democrats bottled up campaign finance legislation until so late in the 1994 session that its defeat in the face of Republican objections became inevitable; however cynical the Republican obstruction that finally killed the proposal, it amounted to throwing the last shovel of dirt into a grave that Democrats had dug themselves. Likewise, congressional Democrats delayed action on legislation to limit lobbyist gifts to legislators until so late in the session that they virtually invited the Republican filibuster that killed it. The bill for the dinner in Little Rock thus finally arrived: Clinton completed the first half of his presidency with almost nothing to show for his promise of cleaning up the Capitol.

Clinton's backsliding on political reform set the tone for much that followed during his first two years in the White House. His concessions encouraged the congressional Democratic leaders to substitute their vision for his own. Looking back, senior Clinton administration officials from all ideological perspectives now consider that Sunday evening session with Mitchell, Foley, and Gephardt the first step on Clinton's road to despair. Mandy Grunwald, one of Clinton's campaign political advisers, would later bitterly describe the session as the administration's "original sin."

As a candidate, Clinton repeatedly declared himself the opponent not just of Republican policies, but of "brain-dead politics in both parties." Many of his most popular campaign promises — welfare reform, downsizing and "reinventing" the federal government, pursuing a hard line against crime — threatened positions held by congressional Democrats tied to the party's liberal constituency groups. Almost immediately, the pressure to avoid confrontation with the Democratic Congress forced Clinton to dilute or discard many of those ideas. Clinton may have believed he could persuade the congressional Democrats to follow his lead, said Galston, but he "underestimated their capacity to become not his loyal followers but in some respects his jailers."

Those in the White House urging Clinton to accommodate Congress mounted many reasonable arguments. Clinton needed support from the congressional leadership to pass the core elements in his agenda, particularly his economic and health care reform plans. Stephanopoulos, Paster, and their allies argued repeatedly that to keep

Democrats in line behind these central goals he could not antagonize them on lesser issues. But this focus on the inside game of legislative maneuver failed to recognize the extent to which congressional politics was now itself driven by public opinion — and the degree to which public opinion now punished anything that appeared to perpetuate Washington business as usual. Clinton, the putative candidate of change, entombed himself in the past — playing backroom, back-scratching politics in the era of Ross Perot, C-SPAN, and near-universal public distrust of Congress. His endless deals with Democratic legislators put Clinton on a path toward fusing his political identity with that of Congress — the least popular institution in American government. "We took Secretariat," said Begala, with a trainer's enthusiasm about his horse, "and hooked him to a fucking plow."

Begala's formulation understated Clinton's complicity in the transformation. It was not an accident that Clinton deferred to Congress or looked inward toward the Democratic base in making his key personnel appointments. Both decisions reflected his own hesitation about pursuing the revolution within the party that he had promised in 1992. That endemic ambivalence was an old pattern for Clinton. Throughout his career, Clinton had often embraced bold ideas — but just as often backed away from political conflict. Exactly why was perhaps the central riddle of his political character. Many Clinton-watchers believed his tendency to avoid conflict was rooted in his youth; having grown up as the son of an alcoholic, abusive stepfather in a house jagged with conflict, Clinton instinctively looked to mediate rather than confront. Other observers, less inclined to psychoanalysis, said Clinton bobbed and weaved simply because he lacked spine. The most charitable interpretation was that Clinton genuinely believed in what he called the third way — his ability to find compromises that bridged seemingly unbridgeable alternatives.

Like blind men describing the elephant, those around Clinton variously pointed to each of these explanations. But whatever the cause, the result was the same: to tilt Clinton consistently back toward the more traditional liberal priorities of the congressional Democrats and away from the agenda that had won him the White House.

DEMOCRATIC congressional leaders hardly set out to undermine Clinton's presidency, and today vehemently insist they did nothing of the sort. On many issues they worked themselves to exhaustion on his behalf. But their interests were not identical with his, which both sides refused to acknowledge until too late. The House Democrats, who were bound most tightly to the party interest groups that defended the New Deal liberal vision, typically exerted the greatest resistance to new approaches. In shaping the party agenda, Gephardt and Foley understandably saw their responsibility as maximizing consensus among those House Democrats — the electorate that decided whether they would keep their leadership positions. But policies that satisfied the House Democrats often failed Clinton's larger goal of reaching out to voters beyond the Democratic base. Once Clinton linked himself to the congressional leadership, he found himself searching for the center of the Democratic caucus, which was measurably to the left of the center of the country.

This recalibration of Clinton's compass led him into dead ends on both of the values-related issues that had been critical to his campaign success: crime and welfare.

During the campaign, Clinton's repeated declarations that he intended to "end welfare as we know it" by requiring recipients to work after two years on the rolls proved a powerful shield against Bush's efforts to paint him a traditional liberal; but his promises created great expectations for action in office. In an internal transition memo to Clinton, Al From and Bruce Reed, who headed his domestic policy transition team, urged the new President to move forward immediately on welfare reform, warning: "Your promise to take on permanent welfare could be your albatross if you don't make it happen." But once Clinton took office, welfare reform instantly took a backseat.

At first, administration officials said Clinton had decided to put off his plan because the cost of moving welfare recipients to work interfered with his goal of reducing the deficit. But over time it became clear that the pressure to shelve welfare derived more from reluctance within the administration to confront liberals who opposed Clinton's promise of requiring welfare recipients to work after two years on the rolls. In private meetings with the President, Foley and Gephardt, who feared the issue would divide the Democratic caucus along racial lines, constantly counseled delay, often using the overload of other legislation as an excuse. "In the first two years," said Clinton pollster Stan Greenberg, "it was strongly advised from Congress that he could not bring forward the welfare bill." As on crime, the congressional leaders and their White House allies argued that advancing welfare reform could alienate the liberal votes the administration needed to pass its health care package. "Welfare was always seen as something that was likely to divide the party, to make things more difficult for the party," said David T. Ellwood, who co-chaired the Clinton administration's welfare reform task force as an assistant secretary of Health and Human Services. "It was always the issue that [people said] would screw up health care because some folks on the Hill would say, 'I'm not going to be with you on health care because . . . this just pushes me over the edge.'"

Nothing could dislodge the House intransigence. As Clinton's massive health care reform bill slipped into its terminal stages in the summer of 1994, Greenberg, with the White House's approval, met with Foley and Gephardt to urge them to shift their attention toward welfare. But they summarily rejected the proposal, insisting the risks were too great: Welfare would "blow up" the Democratic caucus, they argued, and with the Democrats divided, Republicans would pass their own bill on the floor. Again the administration backed down. Those who worked on the plan within the administration believed Clinton was personally committed to reform; but that commitment was not deep enough to lead him to confront the forces in Congress and his own administration urging that the issue be shelved. Ironically, in refusing to act during Clinton's first two years, the House liberals and the White House turned over control of the issue to the Republicans — who used the opportunity to wrench the debate sharply to the right in 1995.

Democratic disarray over crime also allowed the Republicans to seize control, this time well before the 1994 election. Initially, the administration appeared well on track to redeeming Clinton's promise of a new federal offensive against crime. In November 1993 the Senate approved, with broad bipartisan support, a crime bill that contained all the key elements Clinton supported: billions of dollars for prisons and police, a ban on nineteen types of semi-automatic assault weapons, expansion of the federal death penalty, and a moderate sum of money for programs that proposed to prevent crime by combating violence against women and providing alternatives for young people in poor neighborhoods. At that point, some administration officials urged the

House, which had passed a smaller package of anticrime bills earlier, to move immediately to resolve the differences in a House-Senate conference. But under pressure both from liberals who considered the Senate bill punitive and Judiciary Committee leaders defending their legislative territory, Foley and Gephardt insisted that the House be allowed to work through the bill again. Once again, with barely a shrug of resistance, the administration acceded.

House Democrats then spent months tilting the bill to the left. Onto the foundation of the Senate's crime prevention program, House liberals lathered billions of dollars in new social spending — all under the name of "crime prevention." Some of this supported narrowly targeted projects with broad support among community leaders — like "midnight basketball" leagues and all-day after-school programs for children in troubled neighborhoods. But the House liberals also stuffed into the bill a stack of loosely defined grant programs that rained money on cities, from $1.3 billion in "ounce of prevention" grants to $2 billion in Local Partnership Act grants only tangentially related to fighting crime.

This exceeded even the usual Washington inclination to throw money at a problem. The profusion of programs established under the name of crime prevention amounted to creating an urban slush fund aimed at buying off House liberals who believed the bill bent too far to the right. Yet Clinton was so fearful that liberals would abandon the legislation that he raised no public protest as the price tag on the legislation soared.

House liberals also insisted on another alteration that would create even greater problems for the bill. House opponents of the death penalty, led by the Congressional Black Caucus, inserted into the legislation a provision that would allow convicts on death row to challenge their sentences with statistics showing discrimination in the application of the death penalty. The battle over this Racial Justice Act became a revealing microcosm of Clinton's difficulties in moving the party in new directions — and the uncertainty of his commitment to doing so.

The statistical arguments on racial discrimination in the application of the death penalty were complex and even contradictory. But in a basic sense, by allowing sentences for murderers to be determined by broad notions of social equity rather than judgments about their individual crimes, the provision violated Clinton's insistence on personal responsibility. Still Clinton proceeded cautiously. Administration officials knew from the outset that the racial justice provision had no chance of ever passing the Senate. Some senior administration officials, like Ron Klain, the Justice Department chief of staff directing the administration effort on the legislation, privately even considered the provision a poison pill inserted by House liberals with the intent of killing the overall bill.

Clinton and his advisers, however, did not want to take the risk of directly confronting the House liberals by urging them to remove it. For weeks, administration officials slogged through inconclusive negotiations with House Democrats trying to find a way to levitate the provision from the bill without taking the blame for its removal. Throughout, Clinton's own inclinations remained obscure. Clinton never took a public position on the measure. Asked about the racial justice bill in April, he gave the sort of answer that encouraged the adjective "Clintonesque": He did not endorse the specific provision in the bill, but he added, "We think that you can absolutely have a racial justice provision that will do some good." Even in private, Clinton sent different signals at different times. Some White House advisers working on the crime bill said he clearly opposed the measure. Others in the White House felt he was at least ambivalent if not leaning slightly toward support. As he did on other occasions, Clinton left the impression that he agreed with everyone he spoke to about the issue.

The talks incredibly dragged on into the summer, preventing final action on the overall crime bill. At times, Clinton's advisers said they could not demand the provision's removal because the Congressional Black Caucus would vote against the overall bill. At other points, White House officials suggested that alienating the Black Caucus over the Racial Justice Act could cost their votes on health care. Mostly it appeared Clinton and his advisers were afraid of a racially tinged confrontation with the Left. The administration continued to hope that the House liberals would conclude the situation was hopeless in the Senate and agree to voluntarily remove the provision themselves — sparing Clinton from the blame of doing so. But they might as well have hoped for the sun to rise in the West. Finally in mid-July, Leon Panetta, recently designated the new White House chief of staff precisely to end such indecision, informed the Black Caucus the

administration would negotiate no more. The House-Senate confer-
ence committee completing work on the crime bill then removed the
racial justice measure.

But by then the damage was done. The long delay allowed conser-
vative opponents led by the National Rifle Association (which opposed
the assault weapon ban) to mobilize a powerful lobbying campaign
that targeted the spending programs House liberals had inflated the
previous spring. In the last act, defections from a core of black Dem-
ocrats angry over the Racial Justice Act, and four dozen white Demo-
crats opposed to gun control, allowed Republicans to kill the bill on
the House floor in August 1994. After a humiliating renegotiation
with the GOP, Clinton ultimately salvaged a scaled-down bill that cut
billions of dollars from the social spending that the House liberals had
added in the spring. But the victory was Pyrrhic. The crime bill's ini-
tial failure struck a devastating blow to the Democratic hopes in No-
vember. "When you get to the failure of the crime bill," said one
senior congressional Democratic strategist, "that was the beginning of
the end."*

The crime bill demonstrated the high cost of Clinton's desire to
avoid conflict with Congress. He began with a strong combination of
ideas that offered the opportunity for a new consensus. But Clinton
proved more clever than wise: He wanted to dodge the racial justice
dispute without ruffling either side; he wanted a tough centrist bill but
one that would not generate any alarms on the Left. In seeking to
dance around conflict within his own party, he allowed Republicans to
regain control of the issue — and cause him and the Democrats far
more pain than if they had honestly confronted their internal differ-
ences in the spring.

MISJUDGING THE TIDE

Clinton's concessions to congressional Democrats on political reform,
crime, and welfare reform were intended above all to win support for
his central domestic initiatives: his economic plan in 1993 and his pro-
posal to reform the health care system in 1994. But the Democratic

---

*For a detailed account of the NRA campaign against the crime bill and the negotia-
tions that led to its resurrection, see chapter 4.

leaders could not uphold their half of the bargain: efficiently producing the votes for Clinton's core proposals. His deficit-reduction plan did win congressional approval, but only on razor-thin margins after a disordered legislative struggle that left a lasting image of chaos. The health care plan fared even more poorly, dying without reaching the floor for a vote in either the House or the Senate.

In both cases, innumerable tactical mistakes in the legislative scrum contributed to Clinton's disappointments. But both initiatives suffered from a more fundamental flaw: Like the final crime bill, each was tilted too far toward finding the center of opinion within the Democratic Party rather than the center of the country as a whole. With both his budget and health care plans, Clinton underestimated the degree of public antipathy toward government, and sought new taxes and federal powers more sweeping than public opinion would support.

As Bush had learned before Clinton, the gaping federal budget deficit was a problem without attractive solutions. Clinton could no more shrink the deficit without straining his political coalition than Bush could. As a candidate, Clinton had dodged that reality. Instead he promised both to cut the deficit in half (the priority of more affluent voters and the Wall Street wing of the party) and to finance new investment aimed at economically anxious voters, without raising taxes on the middle class or cutting programs that would affect Democratic constituencies. Inevitably, he found those promises incompatible.

The persistent hostility toward government that polls had registered throughout Clinton's presidency left him with no real choice but to seek large reductions in the deficit; but as he finalized his economic plan during his first weeks in office, something else had to give. Clinton chose to minimize the backlash from congressional Democrats and core Democratic constituencies by limiting his proposals to reduce spending in existing programs. At one point early in 1993, Leon Panetta, then Clinton's budget director, promised that the President's plan would cut spending by two dollars for every dollar it raised taxes. But as the administration worked through the plan, virtually each proposed cut threatened some entrenched Democratic interest in Congress. "The discussion was, 'The chairman won't like this, the subcommittee chairman won't like that,'" said Begala. In the end, Clinton and his advisers could agree on cuts that only slightly exceeded their proposed new taxes.

Clinton's insistence on slashing the deficit (by nearly $500 billion over five years) placed him in tune with public opinion. But his unwillingness to seek deeper spending cuts for fear of offending congressional Democrats distorted the plan in ways that diminished its public appeal. To meet his deficit-reduction targets without massive reductions in existing programs, Clinton was forced to abandon the middle-class tax cut he promised during the campaign, and to scale back (though not eliminate) his new public investments. These were the two elements of his campaign economic agenda most attractive to working-class voters whose support he needed to consolidate. He might still have survived those transgressions but he deviated from his campaign promises in one final, fatal respect: After promising not to raise taxes on the middle class, he proposed a broad-based energy tax that did just that.

Clinton launched the plan with an energetic nationally televised speech to a joint session of Congress in February 1993 that repeatedly brought Democrats to their feet in applause. But against the head wind of public skepticism about new taxes and spending, the proposal steadily lost altitude. The depth of those emotions became apparent during a visit we took to Edison, New Jersey, in the midst of the debate. A racially mixed, middle-class community of ninety thousand, Edison had narrowly voted for Clinton in the 1992 election, but just nine months later, it was almost impossible to find a voice of support for his economic plan. In conversations on Little League ball fields, at a church bazaar, and at a summer night's carnival, men and women found it difficult to understand why Clinton was pursuing new spending — even on so-called investments — while simultaneously trying to reduce the deficit. But mostly they found it unacceptable that he was asking for new taxes before demanding the harshest possible reductions in federal programs they almost universally considered ineffective. "Nobody minds paying if you get something for it," said the owner of a small auto-repair business. "But we're not getting anything." "In the final analysis," said another man, "I am going to be paying for a lot of programs that are just crap."

These attitudes, echoed in communities around the country, converged with violent force over Clinton's economic plan in the summer of 1993. The Senate rejected his broad-based energy tax and replaced it with a smaller gasoline tax similar to those that Clinton had criticized during the campaign. The Senate also added more spending cuts. But even so, as Republicans and conservative groups kept up their drumbeat against the taxes in the package, moderate Democrats in both chambers recoiled. On the final House vote in August, even the Democratic congressman from Little Rock, Ray Thornton, cast his ballot against Clinton. Near desperation, Clinton twisted arms, cajoled, and pleaded for votes. Just enough, and no more, came to him: Clinton squeezed his economic plan through by two votes in the House and on Vice President Al Gore's tie-breaking vote in the Senate.

But the price of the victory was enormous. Clinton's success at convincing reluctant congressional Democrats to make deficit reduction their top economic priority was still an impressive political feat. But in seeking to appease the Democratic Congress on the *means* of reducing the deficit, by raising taxes too much and cutting spending too little, Clinton lost the country, and then nearly lost the Congress as well. Like Clinton's initial cabinet appointments and his decisions to defer political and welfare reform, the debate over his economic plan worked against his larger goal of broadening his political coalition. Instead, the lines in the country were hardening — with a majority against him.

THE rise and fall of Clinton's health care reform plan — and the reasons for its demise — followed the arc of his budget proposal. The President launched the health care plan with a ringing national address in September 1993. So commanding was Clinton that none of the legislators who assembled for his remarks in the House chamber realized that he ad-libbed the first five minutes of the speech because aides had placed the wrong address in the TelePrompTer. The plan he introduced that night was the most ambitious government proposal since the Great Society and perhaps even since Harry Truman tried, and failed, to reform the health care system forty-five years earlier. Clinton proposed to guarantee universal health insurance for all Americans by requiring employers to purchase insurance for their employees; to limit health care costs by capping insurance premiums; to restructure the health insurance market by requiring most Americans to buy their insurance through vast new purchasing cooperatives called alliances.

Overnight polls showed a surge of public support for the proposal. Hillary Clinton, who had midwifed its development along with an old Clinton friend, a business consultant named Ira Magaziner, blitzed Capitol Hill to rave reviews. In the first weeks after its unveiling, the plan seemed propelled by an unstoppable tailwind; even Haley Barbour and Bob Dole suggested Republicans might negotiate a compromise.

But as on the budget Clinton could not maintain the momentum. So long as the public was focused on the problem of cost and access to health care, Clinton controlled the debate. But as critics focused on the role of the government in solving those problems, support for Clinton's plan again eroded. Initially, only a handful of conservatives, like Texas Senator Phil Gramm and party strategist Bill Kristol, camped out in positions of outright opposition to the health care plan. But as the Health Insurance Association of America, the trade association for health insurance companies, the National Federation of Independent Business, and other industry groups launched huge advertising and lobbying campaigns that portrayed the plan as a government takeover of the health care industry, more Republicans lined up in opposition, invariably denouncing bureaucrats and big government themselves. "The President's idea," Bob Dole declared in his response to Clinton's State of the Union address early in 1994, "is to put a mountain of bureaucrats between you and your doctor."

From the outset many in and around the administration had feared the plan would be vulnerable on just that front. While the task force led by Hillary Clinton and Ira Magaziner completed the plan, Treasury Secretary Lloyd Bentsen, White House economic coordinator Robert Rubin, and other administration economic advisers warned Clinton against seeking a revolution in the health care industry out of balance with his own political strength or the public tolerance for new government programs. Eventually, Clinton himself seemed to recognize the problem. When Clinton was conducting his final rehearsal for his second State of the Union address an adviser urged him to describe the health care initiative with the word "approach" rather than "plan" because listeners found the word plan "a little bit" frightening. "Okay," the President said wryly, "Our 1,367-page approach."

Hillary Clinton was not the doctrinaire liberal that her critics sometimes painted her, but she did have more confidence than Clinton's centrist advisers in the capacity of government programs to change the world for the better — and more faith that the public could be convinced to accept a vast new government enterprise. To insiders, that was apparent from the outset. During the administration's first weeks, the Clintons brought in a group of outside health care experts to discuss a communications strategy for their developing plan. Most of the advice was predictable, urging that Clinton use kitchen-table talk, not the dead language of policy. When it came time for Jeremy Rosner to speak he suggested to the President that the discussion was focusing on the wrong form of communication. Rosner, who studied health care for the DLC (and later became a speechwriter for Clinton's National Security Council), told Clinton that what he did on health care would communicate an enormous amount about him — particularly whether he meant to govern as the New Democrat he promised. "If the plan is a big government plan, and a centralized plan, that will communicate something else," Rosner told him. Clinton nodded in agreement, but Rosner could also see Hillary Clinton glaring across the table at him.

Another factor pushed the administration to inflate its plan. Throughout, Magaziner and Hillary Clinton were focused on consolidating congressional support on the Left, particularly among House liberals who preferred a complete government takeover of the health care industry, an option known as the "single-payer" approach. As on the budget, the White House sought to build its legislative coalition on health care from the Left in: by first attracting as much support from liberals as possible, and only then reaching out to moderates. Inside the White House, officials talked about their mammoth proposal as an onion — whose layers could be peeled away to win over more support in the center. But they believed that as their opening bid, the plan had to be as sweeping as possible, to generate enthusiastic support on the Left.

That turned out to be a fatal miscalculation. Many on the Left, who preferred the single-payer approach, remained unenthusiastic about Clinton's blueprint. And the size and scope of the plan provided critics with their opening to attack it. The relentless assault on the plan as an extension of big government that would endanger the quality of health care steadily drove Americans away from it: In early 1994, opposition to the plan rose above support in the polls, and the lines never crossed again.

In the face of this withering counterattack, the White House could never settle on a clear legislative strategy. In contrast to the budget, many in the administration knew from the outset that Clinton could not pass health care reform solely with Democratic votes. Hillary Clinton tenaciously courted Rhode Island Republican Senator John Chafee, who was seen as the bridge to the GOP moderates. But the White House never clearly determined what price it was willing to pay for Republican support — or abandoned the vain hope that it could pass the bill from the "Left in" solely with Democratic votes and avoid significant compromise at all. Hillary Clinton was especially resistant to concession, particularly before the two sides had tested their strength in actual legislative votes. One ranking White House official who worked on the health care task force said later: "Once she makes her decision she becomes the most self-righteous person on earth. If you ask any senator, even those who agreed with us, they would say that even though she was a great driving force, and smart as hell, she did not know how to compromise."

Delay proved fatal. As it stalled in five separate congressional committees, health care reform was ripped apart by the two largest forces of 1994: deepening disarray among Democrats, and rising militance on the Right. As public anxiety about the proposal increased with each passing month, Republican conservatives felt more emboldened to increase their attacks. That underlying current of polarization in Congress tugged Chafee and the Republican moderates, as well as the centrist Democrats, more to the right and diminished their enthusiasm for reaching any accommodation with Clinton. Each downward twist in the spiral encouraged the next until the plan finally collapsed without reaching a vote on the floor of either the House or Senate. Like the battle over the budget, the collapse of Clinton's health care initiative demonstrated how easy it was to mobilize opposition against the expansion of government — and how deeply Clinton had endangered his presidency by underestimating that sentiment.

THE DEMOCRATS IN DISARRAY

For all of Clinton's miscalculations, the chaos that surrounded his budget and health care initiatives spoke just as profoundly about the inability of congressional Democrats to unite behind a common goal. At times, the doomed, dysfunctional relationship of Clinton and the congressional Democrats seemed to cry out for spectral intervention from Sam Rayburn and Lyndon Johnson. At other points, it appeared nothing less than a psychologist would do.

When Clinton took office, over two-thirds of House Democrats and half of Senate Democrats had never served under a President of their own party. Under Clinton, they adamantly refused to be harnessed to an agenda driven by the White House. The congressional Democrats preached community and acted like libertarians. "It wasn't in their psyche [to cooperate]," said Stephanopoulos. "Their work habits retained something of an adversarial stance toward the White House."

More than habit explained their attitude. Few congressional Democrats felt Clinton had contributed to their election; few (especially in the House) fully supported the New Democrat agenda on which he was elected; and fewer still felt any personal loyalty to him. Most important, few believed their own political success was tied to Clinton's. Bred on Tip O'Neill's commandment that all politics is local, most congressional Democrats acted as though they could entirely separate their own fate from Clinton's. In so doing, they fundamentally misinterpreted their situation. Through the succession of Republican presidential landslides during the 1980s, most congressional Democrats had routinely attracted far more votes in their districts than the party's hapless presidential nominees. That convinced many of them they could thrive even if Clinton did not. What they failed to understand was that with Democrats holding both Congress and the White House, they would now all be held jointly accountable for success or failure in Washington. They could run away from Clinton as fast as they wished; but they could not run away from the record that the President and Congress compiled.

Congressional Democrats had legitimate grievances about White House reversals that left them politically exposed. Clinton's decision during the budget fight in 1993 to abandon the broad-based energy tax in the Senate — after the House had gone out on a limb to support it — cut the mold for an unpredictable pattern of concession that left many congressional Democrats muttering that the President's word was a rapidly depreciating asset. "I think," the acerbic liberal Representative David Obey said much later, "some of us learned some time ago that if you don't like the President's position on a particular issue, you simply need to wait a few weeks."

But the larger problem was the lack of loyalty in the opposite direction. Many congressional Democrats worked faithfully on Clinton's behalf. But many others said and did whatever they believed served their interests regardless of its impact on his presidency. Senate Armed Services Committee Chairman Sam Nunn, a precise and solitary Georgia Democrat, led the opposition to the new President over his campaign promise to allow homosexuals to serve openly in the military — inflaming a dispute that damaged Clinton with culturally conservative voters, especially in the South, more than any other.* At one point, Senator Daniel Patrick Moynihan, the chairman of the Finance Committee — which was expected to play the lead role in passing the health care reform package — seconded on national television the Republican claim that there was no health care crisis. Nebraska Senator Robert Kerrey, one of Clinton's rivals for the 1992 nomination, provided the winning vote for the budget plan only after delivering an angry speech on the Senate floor in which he dismissed the package as timid and unworthy of support. The struggle to pass the plan had taken all of Clinton's energy and nearly brought his presidency to its knees, and yet Kerrey lectured him: "The price of this plan is too low."

On it went for Clinton. Like Carter he found himself simultaneously under fire from both the Left and Right of his party. One month

---

* Clinton ultimately was forced to abandon his campaign promise to allow gays to serve openly and accept Nunn's "don't ask, don't tell" compromise, which prohibited the military from asking recruits about their sexual orientation but still allowed them to remove from active duty known homosexuals. Nunn insisted his compromise saved Clinton from Republican efforts to write into law the existing policy barring known gays from service. But White House officials felt Nunn's long campaign against Clinton's proposal — highlighted by a field trip to the Norfolk naval base, where Nunn led a troupe of television cameras through the barracks and bathrooms of eight ships to highlight the cramped quarters sailors lived in — was intended to assert his dominance over defense policy even under a Democratic administration. For all the pain Nunn imposed in forcing Clinton to abandon his promise, said one embittered White House official, "It could have been Strom Thurmond as chairman of the committee."

conservative Western Democrats opposed the administration's plans to reduce subsidies to ranchers who grazed their cattle on public lands. The next month House liberals resisted Clinton's plan for national educational standards as unfair to minorities and the poor. The demands multiplied as congressional Democrats realized that each of Clinton's major initiatives typically teetered on the edge of defeat — making every vote crucial. As if dealing with terrorists, the White House found its willingness to make concessions only encouraged ever greater demands. "We showed we would bargain with anyone to get those last few votes," said David Wilhelm, the Democratic National Committee chairman during Clinton's first two years. "And those who were loyal did not get any huge benefits from being loyal. . . . The benefits in this process went to those who held out." It reached the point where Mel Reynolds, a Chicago Democratic Representative (who was later forced to resign from Congress after he was convicted of having sexual relations with a minor), once demanded that in return for a vote, the President come to his house and have his picture taken with his family.

Eventually, the Democratic refusal to hang together cornered the party in a conundrum familiar to students of game theory. In the prisoner's dilemma, two prisoners can escape their jailers only if they cooperate; but if each takes actions to maximize his individual prospects of escaping, they increase the odds that both will be caught. So it was for Democrats throughout Clinton's tumultuous first two years. Conservatives thought they were strengthening their position at home by opposing the budget plan, health care reform, Clinton's effort to open the military to homosexuals, and the ban on assault weapons. Liberals thought they were protecting their flank by fighting welfare reform and rewriting the crime bill. Democrats of all ideologies believed they were safeguarding their electoral advantages by blocking campaign finance and lobbying reform.

But in protecting their individual interests, the Democrats produced a record of division and confusion that undermined public support for the party as a whole. In looking to fortify their personal defenses, the congressional Democrats summoned the deluge that submerged all of them. Provided with unified control of government for the first time in twelve years, the Democrats reverted to the fratricidal chaos of the Carter era — and reminded millions of Americans why they were so reluctant to grant the party power in the first place. "In 1992, people suspended their distrust of the Democratic Party and said, 'Govern,' " said Wilhelm. "That was the challenge we had: We were always going to be judged on whether or not we took advantage of this suspension of disbelief. The fact that we didn't, and we didn't repeatedly, was the opposite of what people had hoped for in 1992, and that more than any other factor explains the 1994 midterm results."

In 1993 and the first months of 1994, the Democrats controlled these centrifugal impulses long enough to pass a steady flow of legislation. In the White House, those successes justified the course of cooperation with Congress, notwithstanding anxiety about all the compromises it demanded. But as Clinton's legislative agenda stalled and his political position eroded through 1994, gloom spread through Clinton's circles over what had become (in Greenberg's phrase) "an impossible embrace" with the Democratic congressional leadership. Clinton himself understood the escalating cost of the course he had chosen. As his presidency slipped under the waves in the dispiriting summer of 1994 Clinton turned to an aide in the Oval Office and ruefully declared, "I've lashed myself to Congress like Ahab to Moby Dick."

CLINTON's options dwindled as time went on. The alternative to reliance on the Democratic leadership was a posture of independent challenge to Congress that sought to attract bipartisan alliances behind his initiatives. Advocates of this approach, who clustered mostly around the DLC, saw it as the key to Clinton's liberation and revival. By attempting to pass his major initiatives solely with Democratic votes, they argued, Clinton left himself so little margin for error that he could not afford to offend any significant block of liberals. Only if he could lock in support from a core of moderates in *both* parties, the argument went, could Clinton establish his independence from the congressional Democratic leadership and regain control of his agenda.

Clinton was not indifferent to these arguments. But once he established a sharply partisan direction at his administration's outset, he found it increasingly difficult to shift his course toward bipartisanship.

It were as if he were traveling on a road that had forked: With each step the distance between the two paths widened.

Building a bipartisan alliance with Republicans would never have been easy for Clinton. With the emergence of Newt Gingrich as spiritual leader in the House, and the pressure on Dole from an increasingly conservative caucus in the Senate, there was never any possibility of broad bipartisan agreement. The real question was more precise: Could Clinton consistently split off a nucleus of Republican moderates — eight to ten in the Senate, two dozen to forty in the House, depending on the issue — and consolidate them into his governing coalition the way Ronald Reagan did on his key economic votes with the southern Democratic Boll Weevils?

Just before Clinton took office, one of Gingrich's top lieutenants said privately that he feared just that. One conservative Republican senator said there was "a fear all along that we would lose that group of our members." Likewise, at a breakfast after the 1994 election, Haley Barbour told David Wilhelm of the DNC that his greatest fear over the past two years had been that Clinton would divide the GOP by striking a deal with the Senate Republican moderates on health care. In the Senate, Bob Dole shared that fear. But Clinton never split the Republican legislative coalition. Though the President regularly praised the virtues of bipartisanship, the White House from the start appeared ambivalent at best about seeking Republican support. "I don't think they worked the Hill very hard," Dole said. "As compared to any administration I've been around, we never really had much contact. And if I didn't as the leader [have contact], I'm sure others didn't have." Representative Steve Gunderson, a Republican moderate from Wisconsin, maintains that Clinton simply ignored potential Republican allies: "With the exception of national service, they really did nothing [to attract Republican moderates.] It was really one of the great mistakes they made. I remember, [Democratic Representatives Dave] McCurdy and [Charlie] Stenholm said, 'I'm going to love Bill Clinton; he's one of us.' And after the election, we put together a list of forty some moderates in the last Congress. The White House never once had us down. . . . It was clearly a direct signal."

Gunderson's judgment is too sweeping. Clinton attracted a respectable number of Republican votes for several of his second-tier domestic initiatives, particularly those related to education, like his national service plan. But with the exception of the fight to pass NAFTA, at no point was attracting Republican support a central element of Clinton's legislative strategy. Generally it was more an afterthought; Clinton would accept Republican votes, but he would not seek them if the cost included alienating the Left. "I believe that a fundamental decision was made very early in the transition that the President-elect was going to try to function as the leader of his party," said Galston. "And that if he could get others to join, fine. But the first consideration would be getting the overwhelming majority of his own party behind his initiatives."

In that sectarian instinct, Clinton inevitably was reinforced by the Democratic congressional leadership, especially in the House. The Senate demanded at least some bipartisanship, if only because it took sixty votes to overcome a filibuster and neither party usually controlled that many. But in the House, which had been racked by partisan warfare since Reagan's election, Democrats instinctively recoiled from any talk of détente with Republicans. On the other side, Republicans were embittered over House rules and procedures that they believed advantaged the Democrats. "There was a pretty clear signal from the House and Senate Democrats [that] we're in charge now, and we're going to make you irrelevant," said Dick Armey. "Clinton would never have been able to reach through the foreground noise of what our guys were seeing."

Surmounting those divisions — and the pressure from congressional Republican leaders on their members to reject compromise with Clinton — demanded more than presidential socializing. It would have required Clinton to recalibrate his policy agenda toward the sentiments of the moderates in both parties. In practice, such an approach would have compelled Clinton to increase his emphasis on deficit reduction, reinventing government, and welfare reform, while scaling back his ambitions to redesign the health care system and slowing his efforts to launch new investment programs. This price Clinton proved unwilling to pay.

A bipartisan legislative strategy offered Clinton no guarantee of success. So polarized was the political debate he inherited that even a strategy consciously aimed at the center might not have assured a consistent legislative majority. Congressional alumni in the White House staunchly believed this road was a dead end, that any effort to enlist Republicans would cost more Democratic votes than Clinton would gain — and provoke a revolt from the Left in the process.

But it is difficult to see how this path could have produced worse results than the strictly partisan approach Clinton chose. The cost of Clinton's failure to lock in support from moderate Republicans early in his administration rose exponentially through 1994. As the Republican leadership escalated its attacks on his proposals, Clinton had no Republican support he could call on to isolate his opponents as obstructionists (or, for that matter, to help break the Dole-led Senate filibusters that became routine).

Instead, after the crippling divisions of the Bush years, the GOP coalesced in opposition to the administration's agenda, and in the process reopened many of the ideological divides between the parties that Clinton had suppressed in the 1992 campaign. Through the legislative battles of 1993 and 1994, the Republicans in effect ran against Clinton the ideologically polarizing campaign that it directed against Dukakis in 1988 — but had been unable to make stick against Clinton as a candidate. "In 1992, Bill Clinton ran as a new kind of Democrat," said Haley Barbour, with his signature tone of syrupy disdain. "Now we know a new kind of Democrat is someone who campaigns as a moderate but governs as a liberal." Everywhere, as election day neared, Republican candidates swelled that chorus.

LIKE any good partisan, Barbour overstated his case. But the maelstrom of Clinton's first two years muddied each of his attempts to improve on the New Deal and neoliberal messages that had failed in the 1980s. As a candidate, Clinton had identified with middle-class Americans in three distinct respects: as an economic populist, a cultural populist, and an outsider committed to reforming a political system they considered stacked against them. But his own failures as President and the mistakes of the Democratic Congress blurred each of those identities and narrowed his appeal to voters beyond the traditional Democratic base.

Once he left the campaign trail, Clinton's identity as a cultural populist vanished almost entirely. The fight over gays in the military created the most damage, but it was only one cut among many: The symbolism of his quotalike insistence on diversity in appointments, the failure to move on welfare reform, news coverage of his socializing with Hollywood celebrities, even the prominent role granted to his wife — reinforced in rural parts of the country by his pursuit of gun control — all left their mark. In his acceptance speech at the Democratic convention in 1992, Clinton had portrayed himself as a small-town boy who learned more from his grandfather who "ran a little country store in our little town of Hope" than from all his professors in college. But by embracing so many positions identified with the cultural elite, he looked very much like a man whose values were shaped at Georgetown, Yale, and Oxford, not by serving Slim Jims and chewing tobacco.

Clinton's credibility as an outsider committed to reforming government collapsed almost as completely. The failure to pursue political reform, the inclusion of new taxes in his budget plan, the attempt to impose a health care plan viewed in the end as a threatening expansion of big government, and his pattern of concession to congressional Democrats, all stamped him as part of the entrenched Washington culture he had condemned as a candidate.

Clinton's identity as an economic populist also suffered. As President, he retained his campaign's rhetorical focus on the need to improve living standards for middle-class workers, particularly less-skilled workers threatened by trade or new technology. But, apart from lower interest rates, he could offer working-class Americans little more than empathy. Family incomes and wages for most workers remained flat or falling despite the economic recovery of his first two years. And the elements of his economic agenda most popular among more affluent and better-educated voters, such as deficit reduction and the expansion of free trade, enjoyed much greater legislative success than the components of his plan intended to directly benefit downscale workers — increased spending on job training and education, and the guarantee of health care that could not be taken away.

Clinton's promises of new government initiatives for the struggling middle class crashed against the wall of public doubt about government. The persistence of those attitudes, even among the intended targets of his largesse, confronted Clinton with the defining paradox of his presidency. His election unmistakably signaled a desire for more aggressive attention to domestic problems and a rejection of Bush's disengaged economic management. But polling evidence from the outset strongly suggested that most Americans remained dubious that new government programs were the route to renewal. The challenge Clinton faced was carving out the political space to reinvigorate government by convincing a skeptical public he was first reforming it. But Clinton tried to move forward with new government programs before he had cleared the road.

The hostility to government did not guarantee Clinton's failure. There was another path available to Clinton, one that tried to assuage the underlying resentment toward government rather than confronting it head on with new taxes and a massive health care plan. Had he moderated his health care goals, limited his tax increase to the wealthy, and deferred his investment agenda until after he had first pursued an aggressive program of government reform and reductions in existing spending — had he demonstrated to Americans he was serious about cleaning up Washington — Clinton might have begun to rebuild public confidence in government and slowly cultivate support for new federal initiatives. But that required a patience and a willingness to confront the demands for new programs within his own party and his own administration that Clinton did not display.

As it turned out, Clinton went into the midterm election with something close to the worst of both worlds. Among Republicans and more affluent independents he acquired a reputation as a traditional Democrat too quick to expand government and too slow to cut spending programs favored by powerful party constituencies. But he delivered to his base and economically anxious working-class voters only small amounts of new investment spending, and no progress on ensuring their health care. To the first group of voters, Clinton came to look like Walter Mondale, an unreconstructed big-government liberal; to the second, he came to resemble Michael Dukakis or Paul Tsongas, a neoliberal advancing elite concerns on both the economic and cultural fronts.

From either direction, the 1994 election testified to political failure. Among independents, Democratic support in the 1994 election dropped thirteen points compared to the previous three congressional elections. And, compared to the same period, the Democratic vote collapsed among voters without college degrees — the people Clinton always had in mind when he cast himself as the defender of men and women who worked hard and played by the rules. After two years of

Democratic control in Washington, the voters the President coveted for his own coalition — the silent legions of "the forgotten middle class" — turned away from Clinton as sharply as they had rejected George Bush only two years before.

The midterm results dashed Clinton's hopes of assembling a new majority coalition that would rejoin white swing voters to the liberal and minority Democratic base. Indeed, the backlash against Clinton's first two years accelerated many of the demographic and political trends he hoped to reverse, particularly the movement of men and white voters into the GOP, and the Republican consolidation of the South. For all the questions about his character, Clinton had understood as keenly as any Democrat how his party would have to change to renew itself. His 1992 agenda offered a more promising blueprint for revival than Mondale, Hart, or Dukakis had produced. Yet even he could not implement the design. Under Clinton, the Democratic dilemma remained unresolved.

THE afternoon following the midterm election, Clinton filed into the East Room at the White House to meet with reporters. He looked drawn and a bit dazed. The weight of his repudiation seemed to press physically on his shoulders. Ordinarily Clinton thrived at press conferences. This day he stumbled and rambled. He tried gallows humor, contrition, conciliation, and defiance. He groped for a meaning that amounted to anything other than rejection. "I think [the voters] were saying two things to me," he said at one point. "Or maybe three . . . maybe three hundred." A moment later, he suggested the voters were somehow agreeing with his agenda, only complaining that it had not been implemented fast enough. Clinton filled the room with great billowing clouds of words. But he could find no silver lining to pluck from the wreckage; the election results had been written in black and white. When he left the podium the conclusion was as inescapable as when he stepped behind it: As a positive force, with the capacity to shape the nation's agenda for the next two years, Clinton's presidency was over.

★★★

II

The Republican Transformation

★★★

3

_____

The Long March

T HE MORNING OF JANUARY 4, 1995, crackled
with all the anticipation of Inauguration Day, but it was the
Republican-controlled 104th Congress, not a new President,
taking the oath of office in Washington. There was an ecu-
menical prayer service at St. Peter's Catholic Church on Capitol Hill
early in the day and an appearance by the Mighty Morphin Power
Rangers for the kids in the afternoon. The television networks had
moved their broadcasts to Washington for the day, but it was the most
rambunctious allies of the new GOP majority, the radio talk show
hosts, who commanded the best seats. They were allowed to broadcast
from inside the Capitol itself, long considered the heart of enemy ter-
ritory. "God Bless America! Normal people are back in charge," ex-
ulted Cincinnati talk show host Bill Cunningham.

In the House chamber, exuberant chaos reigned. The galleries were
packed, and children romped on the thick blue-and-red carpet on the
House floor. Old-timers like Bob Michel, newly retired as the Repub-
lican leader after thirty-eight years in the House, prowled the floor
with the enthusiasm of a raw recruit, and a number of senators, nor-
mally disdainful of the lower body, had come over to watch the cere-
monies. But it was the seventy-three-member Republican freshman
class that best symbolized the transformation under way. Conserva-
tive, impatient, anti-Washington, and determined to exercise their

113

power like a cattle prod on the party, the freshman class was the collective personification of the architect of the new Republican majority, House Speaker Newt Gingrich.

The balloting for Speaker began about 12:40 P.M., and it took the clerk about forty minutes to call the roll. The voting held no suspense. Long before this day, Gingrich had been anointed the next Republican leader; when Michel announced his retirement in October 1993, no other Republican chose to challenge him. It was a measure of the power he had amassed after sixteen years in the House that he could win the most powerful position in Congress by acclamation within his own party. When the balloting was over and Gingrich officially declared the winner, the Republicans suddenly let loose with a war chant that echoed through the chamber in a most undignified way: "Newt! Newt! Newt! Newt!" The doors at the back broke open and an exultant Gingrich strode down the center aisle to a fresh round of cheers. Several children who had remained on the floor with their parents rushed to shake his hand and one member pumped her fist in the air in a gesture of triumph. As Gingrich mounted the Speaker's rostrum, another enormous wave of applause spilled across the chamber, and then someone yelled out, "It's a whole Newt world!"

Indeed it was, for the ceremony marked more than the installation of a new Speaker or the transition from Democratic to Republican rule in the House. It symbolized the triumph of an entire generation of Republicans — Newt Gingrich's generation. The rise of the Gingrich wing was neither a quiet coup nor a simple passing of power. The turn came only after a long and sometimes bloody battle for power within the party. Bob Dole, standing in the back of the House chamber as an observer, represented the party's senior leader and its leading candidate for President, but he also symbolized the old order whose dominance had passed. Gingrich's ascension, and the boisterous class of Republican freshmen who led the cheering, dramatically underscored the degree to which the locus of power had shifted. Despite Dole's seniority and stature, the Gingrich generation now drove the Republican agenda.

Gingrich's election as Speaker marked the coming of age of the baby boomers within the GOP, just as Clinton's inauguration two years earlier symbolized their arrival among the Democrats. Immediate similarities in the backgrounds of the President and the new

Speaker caught the public's attention, from their devoted and loving mothers and their difficult relationships with their adoptive fathers down to their long quests for power and their ownership of 1967 Ford Mustangs. But there was an important difference between Clinton and Gingrich, the two men who dominated the politics of Washington in 1995. Clinton won his presidency without taking control of his party. Gingrich reshaped his party, then he took it over. "There are two ways to rise," Gingrich once said. "One is to figure out the current system and figure out how you fit into it. The other is to figure out the system that ought to be, and as you change the current system into the system that ought to be, at some point it becomes more practical for you to be a leader than for somebody who grew out of the old order." Not by accident did the House chamber ring out with "Newt! Newt! Newt! Newt!"

As the ceremony began, Democratic leader Richard Gephardt was the first to speak, promising cooperation with the new Republican majority but continued fealty to his own party's principles. Let the great debate begin, he said. But for the Democrats, his concluding words pierced through the chamber with a gloomy sense of finality. "With partnership but with purpose, I pass this great gavel of our government," he said. "With resignation but with resolve, I hereby end forty years of Democratic rule of this House." There was a brief pause as the audience seemed to take a deep breath over Gephardt's last word — and then the applause broke out again as Gingrich accepted the gavel. Forty years of Democratic rule were now gone: The Berlin Wall of American politics stood in a heap of rubble.

Hours earlier, Gingrich had excoriated the Democratic minority during a morning press conference for raising questions about his ethical conduct. But the spirit of the bipartisan prayer service now infused his rhetoric as Speaker. He spoke from notes scrawled on pages from a three-ring binder, and on the lectern at his side was a copy of *The Portable Lincoln*, recommended reading from one of his colleagues. He quoted from de Tocqueville's description of the House — "Often there is not a distinguished man among them" — and then read from the Contract With America "to remind all of us what we're about to go through and why," a warning that for the next three months he would drive the members at a punishing pace to complete work on all ten items pledged to the American people. Gingrich paid tribute to predecessors from both parties, describing Franklin Roosevelt as "the greatest President of the twentieth century," and he reminded the Republicans that it was the liberal wing of the Democratic Party that had courageously led the nation out of segregation. And then he called on Democrats to put aside their prejudices toward Ronald Reagan, saying there was much they could learn from him and from other Republicans struggling to rein in the federal government and reform the policies of the Great Society.

The speech was Gingrichesque — long, didactic, and entirely unlike what might have been expected for the occasion. But it was also remarkable for its tone of conciliation. He had found an uplifting way to talk about what in reality was the opening round of a gut-wrenching debate of the most fundamental sort, about the role of government after a half century of New Deal liberalism; about society's obligations to its most vulnerable; about the deterioration of the American cities; about who would gain or lose power and which interests would now have their way in Washington. Gingrich's balming words camouflaged a coming battle of monumental proportions.

The address was even more startling when set against the history of the Gingrich wing's rise in the party, a record of partisanship, confrontation, and ruthlessness that frightened the fainthearted and made Gingrich one of the nation's most polarizing politicians. Often through sheer force of personality and conviction, Gingrich had brought along others in his party who desperately sought an end to their minority status in the House. Gingrich's ascent had stretched over a decade and involved a series of partisan and intraparty battles defined by his own strategic impulses and remarkable self-assurance. One battle was designed to discredit liberalism and the Democratic Party, the other to embed Gingrich's updated version of Reagan conservatism — fusing Reagan's optimism with the antigovernment anger of the '90s — as the only acceptable orthodoxy within the Republican Party.

In the battle with the Democrats, which drew most of the attention from the press, Gingrich used issues ranging from anticommunism to school prayer to crime to fracture the crumbling New Deal coalition. At the same time he incessantly portrayed the House as an institution corrupted by decades of entrenched power as part of his strategy to undermine public support for Democratic rule.

The battle within the Republican Party was equally fierce. At one level it was a clash over how to get things done. Gingrich's generation favored activism and conflict, the old guard preferred comity with the Democrats, which too often translated into passivity. Gingrich wanted to shake the minority mind-set out of his party and force it to think like a future governing majority. His intellectual energy and motivational talents gradually brought many converts to his side. He was always the teacher, the professor, the theoretician, the idea man behind the movement, and for every ten or twenty loony ideas, there was always one that worked. "We'd finish up one of our meetings at nine-thirty at night and I'd be ready to go home," recalled Connie Mack, a close ally of Gingrich's and now a Republican senator from Florida. "At ten o'clock, Newt was back in his office preparing a memo for the meeting the next morning."

The internal battle within the Republican Party, however, was about more than political style. It centered equally on core values of Republican doctrine, pitting those trying to preserve and extend Reaganism against those who favored moderation and pragmatism. At the heart of this battle were the issues of deficits and taxes. For more than a decade, Republicans fought repeated battles that set the Gingrich wing (or what began as the Jack Kemp wing) of young, antitax conservatives against the Dole generation of traditional Republicans, who worried more about the size of the deficit than the size of government. Gingrich's wing viewed Dole as an accommodationist willing to sell out the party's conservative principles; Dole saw Gingrich and his allies as irresponsible adolescents outside the mainstream of their own party.

But now, on this day, as Gingrich took the oath as Speaker, Dole walked forward from the back of the chamber to congratulate his longtime adversary. Their dislike of one another was legendary. For more than a decade they had sparred from opposite sides of the Capitol and from opposing camps within the party. During the first two years of Clinton's presidency, each had played a pivotal role in helping to revive the Republican Party. Now they were ready to begin a new relationship and to reconcile their differences over taxes and deficits. But this time, it was on terms established by Gingrich and his impatient band of followers.

THE 1980s: CONFRONTING THE DEMOCRATS

Gingrich considers himself a disciple of Ronald Reagan, but he turned to Richard Nixon for the advice that began his ascent in the House. It was the fall of 1982. The country was in the grip of a severe recession, and the Republicans had just suffered a serious defeat in the midterm elections, losing twenty-six seats in the House. Reagan had asked the country to "stay the course," but the voters weren't buying. Reagan's working majority in the House was gone and worse, in Gingrich's mind, there was no new agenda coming from the White House. Led by Dole, Congress had already begun to roll back the Reagan tax cuts of 1981, and now the Democrats would have enough votes to block further efforts to cut spending. Gingrich feared the Reagan revolution had crested.

Gingrich had little in common with Nixon and in fact had been a Rockefeller supporter in 1968, his first involvement in national politics. But he respected the exiled former President as one of the party's shrewdest political analysts, and so he went to New York to ask him how to revitalize the Republican minority in the House. For several hours, the brooding old man and the impulsive young Georgian swapped ideas. No single person could transform an institution the size of the House, Nixon counseled. Nixon had been elected to Congress in the GOP landslide of 1946 and twice within a decade had seen the Republicans lose their House majority after just two years in power. House Republicans, he said, had never displayed enough teamwork, aggressiveness, or interest in ideas to make them an effective counterforce in a Democratic-controlled body, and he urged Gingrich to start assembling a team of committed activists who could develop an agenda of issues around which the party could rally.

Thus was born the Conservative Opportunity Society (COS), the first important vehicle Gingrich rode to power. Gingrich returned to Washington and began recruiting a small team of young conservatives. One of the first people he approached was Vin Weber of Minnesota, who was elected to Congress with Reagan in 1980 and did not want to spend his political career in the House minority. "He said to me, 'What are you planning to do next year — and maybe the next ten years?'" Weber recalled. Gingrich soon had drawn in half a dozen or so others who he believed had the right combination of conservative philosophy and activist energy: Bob Walker of Pennsylvania; Dan Lungren of California; Judd Gregg of New Hampshire; Dan Coats of Indiana; Duncan Hunter of California. Connie Mack, elected in 1982, joined soon after he arrived the following year.

The group began regular meetings to talk about the future of the party and what small steps they could take toward changing it. They gathered in the mornings before the House began its sessions or over dinner at the end of the day. They organized weekend retreats, and Walker would drive back from Pennsylvania on Saturday morning to spend the day listening to speakers, like the futurist Alvin Toffler or author John Naisbitt. They drafted a manifesto of principles written in the flavor of Colonial American revolutionaries, declaring themselves to be the political descendants of the Founding Fathers. They spent hours talking about ideas and issues and the use of language in political combat; even their name, the Conservative Opportunity Society, was carefully selected as the antithesis of what they were seeking to topple, the hated "liberal welfare state."

In those days, the aspiring revolutionaries had three goals: discredit the Democrats, develop a positive agenda for the Republican Party, and eventually dominate the party itself. They joked among themselves that only two things stood in their way: the Democrats and the Republicans. They looked for wedge issues (such as crime or welfare reform) that would force Democrats to choose between their core constituencies and the middle class, and for magnet issues (such as tax cuts) that could attract more people to the conservative cause. In December 1983, Judd Gregg wrote a memo to Weber outlining the issues COS should emphasize the next year, and it now reads like a rough draft of the 1994 Contract With America: balanced budget, line-item veto, crime, drugs, welfare reform, school prayer, even reforming the rules of the House. Gingrich believed that after half a century of New Deal liberalism, the issues were moving their way; eventually the voters would follow. "It's like Kondratieff's long-wave theory of economics," he said. "It's a long-wave theory of politics."

Issues were fine, but publicity was essential too, and to attract attention, COS began to throw spitballs at the Democrats. When COS was formed, live television coverage of the House was still in its infancy. But the group quickly realized that C-SPAN provided an extraordinary tool to reach a new audience. Bob Walker recognized the opportunity first. As the party's "official objector," he spent hours on the House floor protecting the minority's interests, and after nasty exchanges with the Democrats, he would return to his office and find a pile of phone messages waiting for him from around the country. Whenever Gingrich traveled for speeches, people would ask him, "Do you know this fellow Bob Walker?"

Gingrich and Co. decided to take advantage of the new medium and the House rules to propagate their conservative ideas and harass the Democratic majority. They would meet just before the House opened in the morning, pick a topic for the day, and stream across Independence Avenue to the Capitol for one-minute speeches attacking the Democrats. Toward the end of the day, they would gather along the back rail on the House floor, agree on the topic for the evening debate, and then, after regular business had been concluded, soak up an hour or two of time set aside for "special orders," carrying on the equivalent of a college bull session before an empty chamber. Gingrich was the intellectual leader and helped engender the discipline to carry out their projects, but in many other respects, they were all interchangeable, and Weber, Walker, and Mack played equally significant roles in shaping the organization's strategy. The members were sufficiently thorough in their planning that, on the opening day of the new session in 1984, Walker asked the House to set aside four hours at the end of every day for COS and listed every speaker for the entire session by name. The Democrats killed the motion, but Walker's request was a sign of things to come. "It's going to be like Chinese water torture," Gingrich said at the time.

Tip O'Neill, the garrulous old Boston pol who, as House Speaker, personified the Democratic majority, put Gingrich and Co. on the map in the spring of 1984. One night, Gingrich and several others from COS commandeered the floor during special orders to flay the Democrats over opposing aid to the Nicaraguan contras. Gingrich accused them of appeasement, saying they had a "pessimistic, defeatist, and skeptical view toward the American role in the world." He accused several Democrats by name of being "blind to communism" and challenged them to respond. None could, of course, because regular business was over and the chamber was deserted. A few days later, an angry O'Neill roared back. "You deliberately stood in the well before an empty House and challenged these people and you challenged their

Americanism," the Speaker said, shaking with rage. "It's the lowest thing I've ever seen in my life in thirty-two years in Congress." Trent Lott, the Republican whip, jumped from his seat to protest; O'Neill was reprimanded for his remarks and his words were excised from the Congressional Record, the first time since 1798 that a Speaker had suffered such an indignity. O'Neill next ordered the C-SPAN cameras to pan the chamber during special orders to show viewers that no one in Washington paid any attention to these youngsters. But the COS cadre didn't care whether anyone was in the chamber or not, nor did they think television viewers would stop listening just because no other House members were. Someone, they believed, was always watching. As Weber put it, "We never thought it was an empty chamber."

The Democrats hated COS. O'Neill referred to Gingrich, Walker, and Weber as "The Three Stooges." Most senior Republicans spoke of them in only slightly more charitable terms, regarding the group as a right-wing fringe of troublemakers. Bob Michel told reporters he had given COS some "fatherly advice" about how to conduct themselves, and other Republicans warned incoming freshman members to steer clear of COS if they hoped to advance their careers in the House. Even some of the original recruits grew squeamish about COS tactics. "Newt's belief that to ultimately succeed you almost had to destroy the system so that you could rebuild it . . . was kind of scary stuff," said Dan Coats, who drifted away and later moved to the Senate. A few members of the Republican leadership offered aid and comfort, however, among them Jack Kemp, Trent Lott, and Dick Cheney. Kemp, as the leading advocate of tax cuts and an "opportunity society," was the godfather of the group and regarded by many inside and outside the organization as its spiritual leader. But the Buffalo congressman was uneasy with the COS tactics and never joined the group. Lott, a member of the House leadership and an aggressive partisan himself, quietly supported COS in his activities and was seen by the younger members as their chief protector. Cheney, who served as Gerald Ford's White House chief of staff, offered the Young Turks insights into the mindset of White House officials or the way Congress was seen from the other end of Pennsylvania Avenue. From time to time, Kemp, Lott, or Cheney would pop into COS meetings, take temperatures, offer words of encouragement, and then leave them on their own.

*　　*　　*

GINGRICH and the other COS members tried to persuade their Republican colleagues that cooperating with the Democrats was a dead end, that the Democrats would always trample on the rights of the minority. Most Republicans rejected Gingrich's analysis, but in 1985, a bitter dispute over a contested election in Indiana's Eighth Congressional District brought new converts to his cause. On election night 1984, Democratic incumbent Frank McCloskey led Republican Richard McIntyre by seventy-two votes. But election officials discovered a counting error in one county, and a new tally gave McIntyre a thirty-four-vote margin. The Indiana secretary of state certified him as the winner — then recertified the result by an even larger margin after another recount. But there were several thousand disputed ballots, and when the new Congress convened in January, the Democratic majority refused to seat McIntyre. Instead, they established a task force to investigate, chaired by Leon Panetta, who was then a California congressman. Republicans were outraged at what they regarded as a flagrant abuse of power.

The battle raged for months, polarizing the House and triggering an intensive debate among Republicans about their status in the minority. Gingrich saw the fight as an opportunity to rally Republicans to his larger cause. Together with his allies, he pushed the caucus to confront the Democrats and disrupt the House if necessary. Like so many student radicals from the 1960s, some frustrated Republicans suggested setting off smoke bombs in the House chamber or chaining themselves to O'Neill's chair. Others proposed using physical force to block McCloskey from taking his seat.

At the end of April, the task force of two Democrats and one Republican voted along party lines to declare McCloskey the winner, and on May 1, 1985, the full House approved a resolution allowing him to take his seat. Every Republican (and ten Democrats) opposed the resolution, and moments after the vote, the entire Republican caucus staged a walkout, marching from the chamber down the steps of the Capitol in a symbolic protest for the cameras. Most Democrats just laughed, and Michel almost immediately returned to the chamber as if nothing had happened. But for many other Republicans, who believed the Democrats had stolen the election, the fight had been a radicalizing experience that made them more receptive to Gingrich's message. "It was essential to Newt and his success to drive home the point that . . . something corrupting had happened to Democratic rule and that it was not just not in our interest, but really wrong, to be in bed with Democrats," Weber said. "I don't think Republicans ever looked upon the Democrats the same."

Gingrich also seized on moral or ethical problems of his colleagues, particularly but not exclusively when the cases involved a Democrat. In his first term, he moved to expel Democratic Representative Charles Diggs, who had been convicted of converting payroll funds to personal use. Later he pushed to censure, rather than merely reprimand, Democrat Gerry Studds and Republican Dan Crane after they admitted to sexual involvement with congressional pages. He unsuccessfully urged the House to take tougher action against Democratic Representative Fernand St Germain, after the ethics committee proposed a slap on the wrist over his failure to file proper financial disclosure forms and his acceptance of rides on an airplane owned by a savings and loan institution. The committee also had investigated a generous loan St Germain received from a bank to purchase a pancake house and complaints that a member of his staff had intervened with regulators in behalf of a savings and loan friendly to the chairman. But when Gingrich tried to force the full House to air the charges, only one Democrat voted for his resolution and it was soundly defeated.

Gingrich's biggest target, however, was Jim Wright of Texas, the man who succeeded O'Neill as Speaker. Gingrich stalked Wright with an intensity and ferocity that frightened his closest friends in Congress. At the time, author John Barry was working on a book about Wright, *The Ambition and The Power*, and he spent many hours with Gingrich throughout the bitter fight. The power Wright was amassing as Speaker clearly alarmed Gingrich, who feared that the Republican leaders had no effective strategy for countering him. With only a few shards of evidence at first, Gingrich moved to build an ethics case against Wright. He sent a staff member to Texas to investigate Wright's past; he used Wright's relationship to savings and loan executives to raise questions about his personal integrity; and when the *Washington Post* reported in September 1987 that Wright had a sweetheart deal on a privately published book (royalties of 55 percent compared to the normal 10–15 percent in most contracts), he intensified his offensive. Gingrich prepared a thick file of clippings raising questions about Wright's business dealings, and made them available to anyone who would listen. He talked to reporters and editorial writers around the country. He made floor speeches and held press conferences wherever he traveled to build public support for an investigation.

His friends feared he was committing political suicide. They worried that by attempting to personalize the case against Democratic corruption around Wright, Gingrich invited a counterattack from the Democrats that would destroy him and their movement. They doubted Gingrich's case could survive rebuttal, and even if it could, they didn't think it was possible to dislodge a sitting Speaker. Gingrich was adamant. "Look, all of us have failings," he told his allies, "and if nobody can come forward and identify genuine corruption for fear that they will be vilified for the average failings that all of us are guilty of, then the place is doomed." Whatever skeletons rattled in his own past, Gingrich told his colleagues, paled in comparison to what he believed Wright had done. That was at least a debatable proposition in the minds of some people. Gingrich had divorced his first wife, his former high school teacher, who was seven years his senior, under unflattering circumstances. She once said he had come to the hospital while she was recovering from cancer surgery, pulled out a tablet, and began to discuss the details of the divorce. Gingrich long claimed it did not happen in the way described, but never offered his own account. There were also repeated reports of marital infidelity during the breakup of the first marriage. Asked about those stories, Gingrich told the *Washington Post*'s Dale Russakoff, "I've led a human life."

House leaders had grave reservations about the path of Gingrich's drive against Wright. In March 1988, Bob Michel asked two Republicans with prosecutorial experience, Bob Livingston of Louisiana and James Sensenbrenner of Wisconsin, to review Gingrich's material. They concluded he did not have a case strong enough to take to the Ethics Committee, and so Gingrich returned once again to the media. "We worked on the assumption that if enough newspapers said there should be an investigation, Common Cause would have to say so. Then members would say it. It would happen," he told Barry. Gingrich was correct. A few months later, Common Cause called on the Ethics Committee to open a formal inquiry and shortly thereafter, Gingrich filed his own complaint against Wright.

The investigation had a poisonous effect on the House, to the discomfort of Gingrich's Republican elders. Wright, as tough and as partisan as Gingrich, snarled "as a fire hydrant to a dog," when he was asked one day what he thought of his accuser. Long after the fight was over, he wrote: "At heart, Gingrich is a nihilist. Throughout his career, he has been intent on destroying and demoralizing the existing order. . . . He is a bit like those who burned the Reichstag in Germany so they could blame it on the 'Communists.' Torpedoing Congress and blaming the Democrats has been Newt's route to power."

By the spring of 1989, the House had become an ethics swamp and an institution mired in partisanship. In April, the House Ethics Committee issued a five-count indictment of Wright, charging him with sixty-nine specific violations of House rules, from the book deal to improper financial relationships with friends to the acceptance of "gifts" beyond the limits of the House. Shortly after the Ethics Committee report, newspapers disclosed that House Democratic Whip Tony Coelho of California, one of his party's most skillful, partisan operators, had been involved in a questionable junk bond deal. By late May, Democrats were in turmoil, and pressure mounted on Wright to resign to spare the House further embarrassment. Coelho added to that pressure by suddenly announcing on Memorial Day weekend that he would quit the House. On May 31, Wright finally succumbed to the inevitable, announcing his resignation after an emotional, hour-long speech on the floor of the House. Wright defended his actions and then called for an end to the "mindless cannibalism" that he said had consumed the institution. At that, Democrats rose to give their fallen leader a standing ovation. Gingrich sat emotionless, then stood up with his colleagues, his hands alternatively clasped behind his back or thrust in his pockets — but never joining the applause. "Let me give you back this job you gave me as a propitiation for all of this season of bad will that has grown up among us," Wright said as he bid farewell to the House. "Let me give it back to you. . . . I do not want to be a party to tearing this institution up. I love it."

The embittered Democrats threatened revenge against Gingrich. "There's an evil wind blowing in the halls of Congress today that's reminiscent of the Spanish Inquisition," said Representative Jack Brooks of Texas. "We've replaced comity and compassion with hatred and malice." But Republicans had little sympathy for Wright, and in Gingrich they now recognized a steeliness of will that elevated him above the others in COS. Gingrich's relentless and often singular pursuit of Wright convinced many of his colleagues that he was more than an intellectual gadfly, more than a disruptive ideologue. Some of them actually began to see him as a leader, someone who could carry them out of their long period of exile. When House Republicans caucused on the morning after Wright's resignation, Gingrich received a standing ovation.

THE 1980s: BATTLING THE REPUBLICANS

If Gingrich and his COS allies spent much of their time attacking the Democrats, they also battled the pragmatists in their own party over Reagan's legacy. Many of these battles came over taxes and deficits, with Bob Dole their principal antagonist. As chairman of the Senate Finance Committee, Dole had reluctantly supported the 1981 Reagan tax cuts, but he made no secret that he thought George Bush had it about right when he referred to the Reagan-Kemp theory as voodoo economics. "I never really understood all that supply-side business," Dole said in the summer of 1982. In fact, he ridiculed the supply-siders whenever he could. "The good news is a busload of supply-siders went over the cliff," he often joked. "The bad news is there were three empty seats."

When it came to fiscal policy, Dole was a traditionalist who believed the government had a moral obligation to live within its means, except in times of an economic or military emergency. To Kemp, that was old thinking: Deficits didn't matter, tax cuts did. Tax cuts were the holy grail, the elixir for unlocking the economy's potential. Cut them deep enough and they would produce not only prosperity but plenty of new revenues for the government from the expanding economy.

The first real fight came in 1982. Reagan had signed his 1981 tax cuts during the August congressional recess, but by the time everyone returned to Washington a month later, the economy had softened and the deficit projections skyrocketed. By early 1982, Dole felt Congress had to recapture some of the revenue lost through the Reagan tax cuts and he began drafting a bill that would do so without raising income tax rates. He looked for ways to broaden the tax base and close existing loopholes, and when he finally proposed it, "everyone went crazy," said Robert Lighthizer, who was the staff director of the Senate Finance Committee at the time.

The bill raised taxes by $98 billion over three years, with about half the increase aimed at business and the rest at individuals. Its supporters defended the measure as sound economics. "This bill is specifically designed to improve the economy by closing the deficit gap and to bring interest rates down," Representative Barber Conable of New York, the ranking Republican on the House Ways and Means Committee, told his colleagues. Kemp denounced the bill. "Whether we call this reform or compliance or a tax increase, we are taking $100 billion out of the economy, out of the pockets of the American people, out of the nation's businesses." On the Senate floor, Dole pleaded for support. "Call it a tax increase, call it a tax reform bill, call it anything you want, but vote for it because it is good policy," he said. Responding to critics who opposed raising taxes in the midst of a recession, Dole said, "I do not know what choice we had."

Dole passed the bill with Republican votes in the Senate, but in the House, where it was approved 226–107, Dole needed help from the Democrats. Only 103 Republicans voted in favor, while 89 opposed the Dole plan, among them Gingrich. "More taxes are not the way to help this economy," he told his constituents. "Instead we need to get people back to work and make America more productive, not give the government more of each taxpayer's hard-earned dollars." Dole's leadership in passing the bill made him Washington's and Wall Street's darling. There was talk of a "new Dole," not the dark, vicious partisan of the 1976 vice presidential campaign — who labeled World War I, World War II, Korea, and Vietnam "Democrat wars" — but a leader who had finally forced Reagan to put governing ahead of ideology.

Dole considered the bill good economics and good politics. "The perception out there was that we were being unfair," he said at the time. "That we were hitting people in the bottom who were helpless and vulnerable, that we were just helping the people at the top. Then the deficits wouldn't go down. In fact they were soaring. . . . We could see as a party we weren't expanding. The President was okay but the Republican Party was not strong." Dole insisted he had no reason to feel defensive — though the impact of his protest suggested he was. "You know, I'm not going to be defensive about my political philosophy. I think I'm as conservative as some of these House Republicans who think we've lost our minds, particularly me." But to Gingrich, Dole was anything but a statesman; he was, in one of Gingrich's most memorable lines, nothing less than "the tax collector for the welfare state."

In 1984 the tax issue was joined again, this time at the Republican national convention in Dallas. Democratic nominee Walter Mondale, in his acceptance speech the month before, had said that, if elected President, he would propose a tax increase to reduce the deficit, and he warned that Reagan would have to do the same. Kemp, Gingrich, Weber, Representative Tom Loeffler of Texas, and Trent Lott, who was chairman of the platform committee, were determined to make Reagan be Reagan by nailing down a platform plank opposing any new taxes. A few days before the platform committee convened, Gingrich called for enactment of a "Dole-proof plank" on taxes, adding that Republicans "should soundly reject the idea that we need to raise taxes next year." Where Reagan actually stood was a mystery, but his top White House advisers, Chief of Staff James A. Baker III and Deputy Chief of Staff Richard Darman, two master inside operators, wanted to leave the President plenty of wiggle room in his second term. Both were instinctively wary of the conservative hard-liners. Meanwhile, a group of moderate Republicans, clearly taking the minority position within their party, proposed a plank that said that, in addition to spending cuts, "tax increases may also be necessary" to balance the budget.

Dole argued that the party must take a credible position on taxes, code for leaving open the door for an increase. "We can't escape the fact that we have to do something about the deficit," he said. "If we say no tax hike and the President says no defense cuts, Walter Mondale will have a field day asking, 'Mr. President, how do you cut the deficit?'" Gingrich accused Dole of offering "an automatic, old-time, Republican answer" to the tax question. "He is saying the Democrats raise taxes a lot and we raise taxes a little."

Drew Lewis, the White House point man on the platform, tilted toward Dole and the soft-liners. Lewis urged the platform committee not to lock in the President, and he developed compromise language he thought would be acceptable. But the conservatives balked when he presented them with the compromise the next morning. They considered the language too squishy; their solution was a change in punctuation, a comma after the word "taxes" in the key sentence, which fundamentally altered the meaning and put the party firmly on record against any new taxes. The committee adopted their proposal and the plank now read, "We therefore oppose any attempts to increase taxes, which would harm the recovery and reverse the trend toward restoring control of the economy to individual Americans." Kemp, Gingrich, and the others declared victory, while a humiliated Lewis tried to put the best face on the fact that the President of the United States had just been rolled. A month later, Dole was still fuming. Calling Gingrich and the others who had staged the Dallas rebellion a bunch of "young hypocrites," he said, "They think they can peddle the idea that they've taken over the party. Well, they aren't the Republican Party and they aren't going to be."

The two sides clashed again the following year, principally over efforts by Dole to reduce the deficit. Dole produced one of the most hawkish deficit-reduction plans of the decade, which reduced the deficit $56 billion in fiscal 1986 and $300 billion over three years by freezing Social Security Cost-of-Living Adjustments (COLAs), limiting the increase in defense spending to the rate of inflation, and eliminating thirteen domestic programs. Dole's plan also held the line against new taxes. After a fifteen-hour debate, California Senator Pete Wilson, still recovering from an appendectomy, was rolled into the Senate chamber on a gurney in the middle of the night to make the vote 49–49, and with Vice President Bush breaking the tie, Dole passed his budget.

Two months later, however, the deal was in ruins and Republicans were at war with one another over the collapse. Pressured by both Tip O'Neill and House Republicans, Reagan lost his nerve. At a White House cocktail party that came to be known as the Oak Tree Agreement, Reagan agreed to give up the freeze on Social Security COLAs and O'Neill agreed to accept the Senate's figure for defense spending, which was higher than many Democrats wanted. That agreement also reflected behind-the-scenes pressure from Kemp and his allies, who had maneuvered to kill the Senate plan and head off any compromise that might include new taxes. Kemp also opposed the freeze on Social Security COLAs as a violation of the implicit agreement between the government and the elderly. "I didn't feel like I was torpedoing the budget, I thought I was torpedoing a very, very bad deal," Kemp said. Kemp arranged secret negotiating meetings between White House Chief of Staff Don Regan and key House Republicans that deliberately excluded Dole, and sixty-seven House Republicans sent a letter to the Senate Budget Committee chairman urging him to abandon the COLAs freeze.

The struggles of 1985 highlighted the evolving divisions within the Republican Party over both taxes and deficits. Dole and Senate Budget Committee Chairman Pete Domenici of New Mexico headed the school of deficit hawks, who argued that deficits mattered most and that reducing them should be the party's highest priority. That had been Republican doctrine for generations. Kemp, of course, believed just the opposite. Worrying about the deficit, he feared, turned the Republicans into a party of Scrooges; to Kemp, that was hardly the way to build a majority. But another view was also beginning to evolve, symbolized by people like Weber and Gingrich. They obviously shared Kemp's view on taxes, particularly his resistance to higher taxes, but they also believed the deficit represented a threat to the country's future and would have to be confronted. "A lot of us privately argued with Jack about deficits," Weber said. "I can remember an argument in the Speaker's lobby that I sort of refereed between Kemp and Gingrich over the Balanced Budget Amendment, and it got so heated that they literally got up and just walked away from each other. There was a lot of tension within the group."

The 1985 fight did little to settle the long-running debate. In its aftermath, Congress decided to use a blunt instrument to bludgeon the deficit into submission, enacting the Gramm-Rudman-Hollings Act. But the debate continued to rage within the party, symbolized by the opposing postures of Dole and Bush in their 1988 presidential campaigns. Dole refused to sign an antitax pledge during the New Hampshire primary; Bush said, "read my lips, no new taxes." That set the stage for the most disruptive fight of Bush's presidency.

1989–1990: BREAKING WITH BUSH

Bush's tenure in the White House proved to be a terrible disappointment to the Gingrich generation in the House, but at the same time marked their period of passage to political independence. However they may feel about Bush personally, the members of the Gingrich generation remember his presidency with all the enthusiasm of a bad blind date. Some are circumspect about their feelings, but one who does little to hide his disdain is House Majority Leader Dick Armey of Texas, a blunt-spoken conservative who dismissively referred to the "Bush-Clinton era" in his 1995 book, *The Freedom Revolution.* "When Ronald Reagan left for California on January 20, 1989, George Bush was left with more assets than any president in history," Armey wrote. "A thriving economy. A world awakening to new freedoms. Socialist ideas in disgrace. All his generation's labors and sacrifices were coming to fruition. . . . At home fresh blood in Congress was ready to carry out freedom's mandate. . . . Seeing liberalism in its death throes, voters turned to George Bush and said, 'Finish it off!' Instead, they got a reversal of the Reagan revolution."

Like many conservatives, Armey romanticizes the Reagan era. Other right-leaning analysts, like author David Frum, note Reagan's loss of nerve in confronting the welfare state after 1982. But Armey's conclusion reflects the intensity of frustration that Bush inspired among the activist conservatives. Tom DeLay, the Republican whip in the House, described his experience as one continuous battle against the moderates in his own party. "I spent the entire four years fighting Republicans, not Democrats," he said.

The first step toward independence came early in Bush's presidency and was, ironically, triggered by Bush himself when he named Dick Cheney secretary of defense after the Senate rejected his first choice, John Tower. Cheney's nomination unexpectedly opened a rung on the House leadership ladder, and Gingrich quickly decided to enter the competition, even though few people outside his circle of friends saw Gingrich as a natural choice for the job. Throughout his career, he had played the role of intellectual incendiary, idea man, visionary, partisan slasher. But to the outside world, he lacked the smooth edges Washington expected of its leaders.

Gingrich heard about Cheney's nomination from a newspaper reporter shortly after the announcement was made, and within hours he and his supporters were making calls about the race. Gingrich needed little encouragement; he had already surveyed the potential field, sensed a vacuum, and characteristically believed he was uniquely qualified to fill it. Weber opposed the idea, fearing that Gingrich risked a defeat that could set back their cause immeasurably. But when Gingrich made clear he wanted to run, Weber agreed to manage the campaign. Analyzing the race, Gingrich and Weber saw three potential opponents: Jerry Lewis of California, then the chairman of the Republican Conference; Henry Hyde of Illinois, a popular conservative best known as one the House's staunchest opponents of abortion; and Edward Madigan, another Illinois legislator, who was chief deputy whip and stylistically a carbon copy of Bob Michel. Recognizing his own reputation as a conservative ideologue, Gingrich wanted to avoid a fight over political philosophies. Instead he sought to frame the race as a debate over the means by which Republicans could gain more power. Hoping to appeal to oppressed moderates as well as his conservative corps of supporters, he cast the conflict as a choice between accepting the status quo or taking action to change it.

Hyde decided not to run. Lewis bowed out too, fearing he would divide the anti-Gingrich vote. Edward Rollins, a top party strategist then running the National Republican Congressional Committee (NRCC) and a California friend, had called Lewis the day Cheney was nominated for the Pentagon and urged him to run, arguing that only he could prevent Gingrich from getting the job. Rollins and Gingrich, both strong personalities, had clashed at the NRCC, and Rollins believed Lewis would make a better whip. But Lewis first wanted to talk to Michel, and when Michel assured him that Madigan could win the race, he stepped back. "I asked the leader [to] see to it that Madigan had the votes, and he said he would," Lewis recalled. But Lewis capitulated too fast. Led by Bob Walker, a delegation of about two dozen conservatives urged Michel to stop playing an active role in the whip race. They had no objections, they told him, to his open support for Madigan, but insisted it was wrong for him to lobby others to vote for Madigan. Ever the gracious leader, Michel agreed to their request — and paid a high price.

Among the first people Gingrich called for help that weekend were two moderates, Steve Gunderson of Wisconsin and Nancy Johnson of Connecticut. Both were members of an organization formed in the middle 1980s as a rival of COS called the 92 Group, whose philosophical leanings were far closer to Bush's than Reagan's. The 92 Group members generally disagreed with the tactics of turmoil favored by Gingrich and COS, but Gingrich quietly began courting them in the mid-1980s, and the two sides concluded that, if the party ever hoped to reach majority status, they had to find a way to work together. Their fear was that the more factions like COS and the 92 Group gained power, the greater the chances that Republicans would splinter exactly as the Democrats had. Gingrich, Weber, and several others from COS began to hold regular talks with the 92 Group leaders to look for issues they could work on together, and the more time they spent together, the less one-dimensional Gingrich seemed to the moderates. For one thing, Gingrich radiated energy at a time when the Republican leadership in the House appeared lifeless and resigned to permanent minority status. "Newt was first and foremost the intellectual leader behind activism," Gunderson said. But more than that, Gingrich convinced them that their differences on a few issues need not be debilitating. He understood how to deal with those differences "without eroding what united us," Johnson said. When he called Johnson and Gunderson for help, both enthusiastically agreed. Other moderates were shocked, but Johnson told them Gingrich had "the vision to build a majority party and the strength and charisma to do it."

The outcome of the whip's race stunned everyone. Gingrich emerged with a two-vote victory. His success testified to the frustration of many House Republicans and the risks they would take to try to change it. Gingrich had managed to reach far beyond his narrow base to moderates and more senior Republicans, politicians like Bill Frenzel of Minnesota, who shared none of Gingrich's faith in aggressive tactics, but believed Republicans needed "someone who was both imaginative and had a breadth of vision" to break the Democrats' grip on power in the House.

The result appalled the Democrats; they knew Gingrich only as an inflammatory partisan. Others in the Washington political community found it difficult to understand why, in the Bush era of kinder and gentler politics, the House Republicans would entrust their futures to such a controversial figure. The outcome was equally unnerving to the Bush White House, where most officials assumed Madigan would win. Moreover, they didn't trust Gingrich, nor did they believe Gingrich could fulfill the job's principal requirement of counting votes for their legislative proposals. (Gingrich agreed, saying in one interview, "I don't count." So he hired Weber aide Dan Meyer to do the job and delegated much of the day-to-day work to his friend Bob Walker.)

The whip election, however, offered powerful evidence of the degree to which Gingrich already had transformed the House. "I came here [in 1978] and the party would never elect Newt Gingrich to be whip, and for ten years I changed the party," Gingrich said. "I didn't run for leadership. I just changed the party. In 1989 I went from being back-bencher to the second-ranking Republican."

To his critics — in both parties and outside the political system — Gingrich represented much that was wrong with American politics. As one congressional Democrat once said, Gingrich tried to take over the House not at the ballot box "but with hand grenades." Few people understood the nuances of power and policy better than Gingrich, but in combat he fought mostly with blunt instruments. Many politicians often hid their resentment at probing questions or political criticism, but Gingrich was as predictable as Old Faithful in his eruptions. He exploded in anger at his opponents and his bombastic rhetoric was salted with the kinds of words — "grotesque," "stupid," "immoral," "corrupt," "sick," "despicable" — that other politicians used sparingly, if at all. He saw the world in black and white, almost exclusively through an ideological lens. If he was attacked or criticized, it was because the accuser was a vicious liberal or a tool of the welfare state. He once described Clinton as "the enemy of normal people," and his own human frailties rarely seemed to temper his criticism of others. His certitude shocked those who did not know him well, and though he regularly regretted the times he flew off the handle by recklessly criticizing an opponent with only partial facts in hand, he did not appear overly concerned about suppressing the instinct.

His life, Gingrich once said, was "a classic psychodrama," and he often seemed lifted from the pages of a particularly baroque novel. He was at once ruthless and vulnerable, harsh and compassionate, ebullient and petulant. He surrounded people with energy and ideas, and yet even some of those closest to him believed he yearned for true friendship in his life. He married at nineteen to a woman seven years his senior who had been his high school teacher, but early in his congressional career they were divorced. At times, his second wife, Marianne, publicly described the strains of being married to someone out to change the world. Around the time he was elected whip, she described the marriage as "off and on for some time." Gingrich, as if handicapping a political contest, gave it a 53–47 percent chance of survival.

That was one side of this complex character. The other side, the side Republicans who elected him as whip bet on, involved organizational and political talents that few of his peers matched, talents he displayed throughout 1995 in holding his slender majority together. Gingrich had studied the works of great leaders and emulated their methods, from the "vision, strategies, tactics, projects" model patterned after General George C. Marshall and General Motors president Alfred P. Sloan to the "listen, learn, help, lead" approach that he said guided his efforts to reform the country. He operated to his own drummer, which is what encouraged his House colleagues and frightened the Democrats and some of Bush's advisers in the White House.

THE White House, of course, was right to worry, for Gingrich's election as whip set the stage for what would become the defining political battle of Bush's presidency: the 1990 budget fight, when the Gingrich conservatives declared their independence from the White House and sought to dictate the terms of Republican governance for the 1990s. In their eyes, the Bush presidency threatened to reverse the gains Republicans had made under Reagan. They were particularly hostile to Bush's top economic advisers, Treasury Secretary Nick Brady and Budget Director Richard Darman, both of whom symbolized Wall Street's influence in the party and, like Dole throughout the 1980s, an accommodation with big government. On issues ranging from the environment to government regulation to the economy, the conservatives believed Bush was steadily moving the party away from Reagan conservatism toward a more moderate middle ground and they were determined to block him. "The only way we could take over Congress and be a party of prominence was to have a very clear distinction between the Democrats and the Republicans," Tom DeLay said. "The Bush administration muddied that distinction. The Bush administration wanted to work with Congress, rather than beat Congress. And so it was contrary to what we were doing. We were trying to build a party and take over the Congress. The Bush administration was trying to run the country and be reelected."

In the spring of 1990, with his own reelection clearly in mind, Bush opened negotiations with the Democrats over the deficit. His advisers convinced him that if he could make progress in reducing the deficit that summer, the financial markets would respond favorably and the economy would revive in time for the 1992 campaign. The talks began in May, but after six weeks the two sides had made no progress. Hoping to jump-start the process, Bush invited the Democratic and Republican congressional leaders to the White House for breakfast on June 26, where the Democrats insisted on a statement from Bush reaffirming his willingness to consider new taxes as part of an overall package. Darman drafted the language, and the Democrats asked for a moment to review it privately. It read: "It is clear that both the size of the deficit problem and the need for a package that can be enacted require all of the following: entitlement and mandatory program reform; tax revenue increases; growth incentives; discretionary-spending reductions; orderly reductions in defense expenditures; and budget process reform." The Democrats returned with a final demand. It had to be more personal. They wanted Bush to add two words to the first sentence, making it read, "It is clear *to me* . . ." Bush accepted the change, to his later chagrin.

Hoping to avoid an eruption within the party, White House officials quietly tacked the statement on the bulletin board in the White House pressroom. But when Republicans heard the news, they were apoplectic. Gingrich, in Washington, could not believe it, nor a continent away in California could Vice President Dan Quayle. Both thought the White House had disastrously miscalculated. White House Chief of Staff John Sununu called Gingrich to reassure him that the statement did not mean what people were suggesting, that in the end Bush could easily walk away from a deal that included new taxes. But everyone else knew it meant exactly what it said. Bush's no-tax pledge, the single strongest statement of his 1988 campaign, was now dead.

"Sununu explicitly misled me," Gingrich said. "I believe because he was misled. He went through this very embarrassing twenty-four hours where he said it didn't really mean what it meant and then they came back and said yes, it did mean what it meant." By that afternoon, Bob Walker had rounded up ninety signatures on a letter from House Republicans warning Bush they would vote against any package that "increases tax rates for the American people." A similar letter with two dozen signatures came from the Senate. For the conservatives, the ultimate indignity came when Walter Mondale praised Bush in the *New York Times*. "He had the courage to change his mind, to acknowledge the truth about our nation's troubled finances, to 'think anew,' as he admitted," Mondale wrote. "The president should also be given credit for resisting the tremendous pressure from many of his Republican colleagues to sacrifice our nation's fiscal responsibility to a shortsighted campaign slogan."

As a member of the Republican leadership, Gingrich was nominally part of the negotiating team, but he came to believe he should have walked out of the talks the minute Bush broke his pledge. "I think I should have seen the President and said this summit is over and if you proceed down this line you will split your party," he said. "But there were a lot of things going on. One, I was a brand new whip, I was trying to work with [Bob] Michel, I was trying to learn to work with a Republican administration." Gingrich admits that from that point on, he and the White House essentially misled one another about the endgame in the talks. At the time Bush began the negotiations, Gingrich hinted that he and other House Republicans could accept a package with taxes other than income taxes as long as the Democrats agreed to cut capital gains taxes in return. (One of the taxes he was then willing to accept was a broad-based energy tax of the kind Clinton proposed, and the Republicans attacked, in 1993.) But from the moment Bush reneged on his pledge, Gingrich's resistance to any new taxes stiffened. The hard-liners in the House believed they had to draw an inflexible line against new taxes to reestablish the GOP as the antitax party in America.

The warning signals from House Republicans grew louder throughout the summer. In July, the Republican Conference overwhelmingly approved an Armey-sponsored resolution that said they would oppose a summit deal that included new taxes. Later that summer, Gingrich gave a belligerent speech at the Heritage Foundation in what he said was a deliberate effort to warn the White House to avoid the trap of a deal that included new taxes or that did not include a capital gains tax cut. On Labor Day weekend, en route to visit U.S. troops in the Persian Gulf, Gingrich had a long discussion with White House congressional liaison Nick Calio in which he argued that he owed his loyalty to the House and his own principles, not to the White House.

Whatever he was suggesting in private conversations with Darman and Sununu, who still believed he would support a final deal, Gingrich seemed firm in his discussions with other House Republicans. "Outside the room there was not vacillation on his part," Weber said. "He kept in very close touch with all his supporters to make sure he didn't get far afield from what we were doing."

The White House ignored the danger signs. Like everyone else in Washington, administration officials had a low opinion of the House Republicans. They also believed that in the end Gingrich would have to support the deal, and if he did, so too would many of his followers. "What they were using on him was, you're now a member of the leadership, you signed up to be a member of the leadership, your President needs you right now," Walker said. In late September, Gingrich sent a memo to Sununu and Darman that seemed to hint at compromise. "With a good agreement and full partnership in the decision process on the other items, the Republican leadership and membership will work hard," he concluded. Darman took it as an implicit pledge to accept what the negotiators worked out. "He never led other people to believe he might bolt," Darman later complained.

After Labor Day, the negotiators moved their operations to Andrews Air Force Base, where day after day they argued to stalemate. Gingrich displayed his disdain for the talks by reading books and magazines or catching up on his mail at the table. About ten days before the negotiators' self-imposed deadline of October 1, when huge, automatic spending cuts mandated under Gramm-Rudman-Hollings would take effect, most of the negotiators were dismissed and the fate of the summit was placed in the hands of what became known as the Big Eight: Sununu, Darman, and Brady from the administration; and from the Congress, Dole, Michel, Senate Majority Leader George Mitchell, House Speaker Tom Foley, and House Majority Leader Dick Gephardt. Gingrich was not welcome.

Neither Dole nor Michel was wedded to the capital gains tax cut that many House Republicans saw as an essential part of any package. At one point, Dole urged the Republicans to drop the capital gains tax cut, proposing that it be packaged separately with Democratic proposals for new spending. Darman and Sununu, however, resisted. At another point, Dole indicated a willingness to accept higher individual rates on the wealthy in exchange for a capital gains cut. "I think we have to have balance," he said. "We have to have progressivity." Michel thought the Democratic price for a capital gains cut was simply too high to accept. Nervous House Republicans began sporting bright yellow "Junk the Summit" buttons and accused Democrats of sabotaging the process. Their continued protests rankled Dole, who thought he was watching a rerun of his earlier conflicts with the Gingrich wing. "There are new generations coming along all of the time, and maybe after they have been here awhile they will change their views," he said acidly.

On Saturday, September 29, the Big Eight concluded the negotiations, with plans to unveil the package formally at a Rose Garden ceremony the next day. Sununu called Gingrich that night to brief him on the outlines of the deal, but Gingrich was not impressed. The proposal included almost $134 billion in new taxes over five years, but contained neither the capital gains tax cut favored by the Republicans nor the income tax rate increases sought by the Democrats. Gingrich said House Republicans would not buy it. Sununu suggested Gingrich come to the White House the next day an hour before the other negotiators. "There's no point to that," Gingrich said.

The next day the negotiators met with Bush at the White House, and one by one were asked their opinion of the agreement. Gingrich spoke near the end. "I can't support this," he said. "I don't think it will pass." He turned to Bush and said, "I think you may destroy your presidency and I think it'd be an enormous mistake." But after five months of talks, neither Bush nor the Democratic leaders were prepared to turn back. Bush and the negotiators began filing out to the Rose Garden to meet the press; Gingrich walked the other way, out of the White House compound and back up to Capitol Hill to lead the resistance. As it turned out, he was also taking the first decisive step toward building a new Republican Party. "I am still to this day astonished," he said. "There are certain things — if you do them, you destroy the party base. These guys sat down there [at the White House] and thought that this twenty-year-long movement, or thirty-year-long movement, was just sort of a chimera. It's an astonishing moment."

Gingrich understood his troops. They were in open rebellion by the end of the day. One called the summit agreement "the fiscal equivalent of Yalta," while another claimed it was "a road map to recession" and a "cave-in to the Democratic liberal big spenders." Gingrich,

Walker, and Weber opened discussions on how to organize the opposition. Dole and Michel urged Republicans to support their President. Even Phil Gramm, who participated in the summit talks, stuck by the President for the first week, even going so far as to lobby House Republicans to support Bush and the agreement. The House opened debate on the package on October 4 and throughout the day a bitter argument ensued. Early the next morning, the House rejected the package, a stunning defeat for Bush engineered by the rebels in his own party. With Gingrich leading the opposition, 105 Republicans voted against the budget deal, while only 71 voted for it. A majority of Democrats, led by liberals like Wisconsin's David Obey, joined them in opposition. It took the exhausted negotiators the rest of the month to agree on a new package, but in the eyes of the Gingrich wing, the second one looked worse than the original. Bush still did not get his capital gains tax cut, while Democrats succeeded in raising the top tax rate from 28 percent to 31 percent. The final agreement passed with the help of the Democrats, while Republicans, looking toward their reelection prospects a month down the road, ran away from the deal and the White House. Bush had won the battle but lost his party.

THE 1990s: EXPANDING THE CIRCLE

Gingrich and his allies shared a clear, strategic goal in their bitter fight with Bush over the budget in 1990: to reassert as dramatically as possible the conservative principles they believed explained Reagan's electoral success. "The number one thing we had to prove in the fall of '90 was that, if you explicitly decided to govern from the center, we could make it so unbelievably expensive you couldn't sustain it," he said.

The modern conservative era in national elections began with Nixon in 1968, but he was hardly a model for conservative governance. Though he campaigned using conservative, hot-button issues like crime and school busing, he governed by accommodating and even expanding the liberal vision of the state. Nixon created the Environmental Protection Agency and the Occupational Health and Safety Administration, signed the Clean Air Act, imposed wage and price controls, and even proposed national health insurance.

Most current-day conservatives look to Reagan's first election as the time when conservative governance came to Washington. Reagan had led the conservative wing of the party throughout the 1970s, nearly defeating Ford for the GOP nomination in 1976 and, after an early stumble, winning the nomination and the presidency in 1980. Reagan campaigned on a pledge to "get government off your backs" and argued that government was not the answer to many of the country's problems but part of the problem itself. He wanted to cut taxes, cut spending, clip back the regulatory hedge, rebuild America's arsenal, and return power to the states, and in his first year he took a series of bold steps in that direction. But almost as quickly as he started, he stopped. The recession of 1982 blunted his moves to cut taxes and spending, and his revolution quickly lost its momentum. His fiscal legacy was a period of economic prosperity and a mountain of debt.

Bush marked a turn away from Reagan and what he and his senior advisers — and much of the electorate — saw as the excesses of eight years of conservative policies, which he captured rhetorically by calling for a "kinder and gentler" style of conservatism (coming, ironically, after a slashing, negative campaign in 1988). The Bush style meant enactment of the Clean Air Act, the Americans with Disabilities Act, and the civil rights reforms of 1991 that reversed a series of Supreme Court rulings trimming affirmative action. It also meant a domestic agenda that was practically nonexistent after Bush's first two years in office, a point Sununu indelicately made when he said he could see no reason Congress should stay around and work because the administration had nothing to offer them in terms of legislative initiatives.

There were pockets of conservative innovation scattered through Bush's government — in the vice president's office, where Quayle and his chief of staff, Bill Kristol, pushed such ideas as regulatory and legal reform and waged war against the "cultural elite" in the name of "family values"; at the Department of Housing and Urban Development, where Kemp, a self-described "bleeding-heart conservative," preached the virtues of conveying capitalism to the poor; in the White House domestic policy office, where a young aide named James Pinkerton propounded a grand, if ephemeral, "new paradigm" of conservative social reform built around themes of bureaucratic decentralization and personal empowerment — and embodied in ideas such as school choice or tenant homeownership — that Kemp also favored. But these outposts were as isolated as dissident cells in a dictatorship. Their ideas never gripped the President and without presidential interest, they floated as aimlessly as balloons in a summer breeze.

The fog on domestic issues that enveloped the Bush administration was only partly explained by the President's disinterest. To some extent, Bush's reluctance to advance an aggressive conservative assault on government reflected his reading of public opinion. In the late 1980s, polls did show a temporary increase in the percentage of Americans looking for Washington to take action against problems they perceived to have been neglected during the previous eight years.

On most issues, though, Bush's instinct was neither moderate nor conservative but timid. At the core of Bush's passivity was an unspoken belief common to Republicans of his generation — that domestic policy belonged to the Democrats. On issues like health care, welfare, and the inner city, Bush-era Republicans believed their role was more to deflect Democratic initiatives than advance their own. Vin Weber saw this thinking raised to its paralyzing essence whenever he argued with Sununu over the administration's direction. There was no percentage for Bush in pushing a conservative domestic agenda, Sununu would tell him; the Democrats would take whatever he proposed and only bloat it with new spending. That calculation had an element of realism: Democrats did after all control both houses of Congress, and Bush felt deeply burned by the result of the budget summit. But implicitly, Weber believed, Bush's approach assumed that conservatives could not win the argument with Democrats on how to confront domestic problems. "If you go back to Bush," says Weber, "we not only didn't have much to say, we had a consistent strategy of not saying anything."

The Gingrich wing viewed this strategy as defeatist. They believed in activist conservatism and while they wanted to restore Reaganism as the heart of the Republican Party's governing agenda, they actually were preparing to take conservatism to places the Gipper had only dreamed about. To advance his vision, Gingrich turned his attention in the last half of the Bush administration from legislation to politics and elections. He was burrowing deep beneath the surface of the party, methodically recruiting allies for an eventual takeover. For more than a decade, Gingrich had pursued a clear-eyed strategy for taking over the party. "You would capture seventy or eighty percent of the incoming freshman class every two years and at some point you would have transformed the whole structure," he said.

GINGRICH used an ever-expanding empire of organizations to spread his ideas and doctrine, recruiting and inculcating younger conservatives around the country. At the time he became Speaker, many Americans didn't know enough about him to have a firm opinion about whether they liked him, but long before that, he had emerged as a cult figure to a growing corps of young Republican candidates.

Gingrich embodied his own "third-wave, information age" mantra, turning himself into a multimedia Whirling Dervish of books, writings, lectures, tapes, and television, spewing out ideas — some brilliant, some just plain wacky — with energy and audacity that exhausted those around him. "I have an enormous personal ambition," he said modestly in 1985. "I want to shift the entire planet. And I'm doing it." He believed in the power of ideas, particularly his own, and he looked to spread them through every medium possible. Gingrich became his own political conglomerate; he was the Harold Geneen of the House. There was a think tank called the American Opportunity Foundation, and a book, *Window of Opportunity*, timed for release just before the 1984 Republican national convention. There was a political action committee called GOPAC. There was the National Republican Congressional Committee. Later came a lecture series beamed by satellite to sites around the country and a weekly television program on the conservative National Empowerment Television network, both underwritten by the Progress and Freedom Foundation, an organization that also bore the Gingrich stamp. Even his unprecedented notoriety as Speaker didn't satisfy his restless ambition. In June 1995 he descended on New Hampshire with a horde of reporters in tow to ensure that the presidential candidates were listening to his ideas. Along the way, he snared Clinton into staging a joint appearance at a senior citizen center on a muggy Sunday afternoon. And of course there was his controversial book *To Renew America*, which in the summer of 1995 became a number one bestseller; the publicity generated by his nationwide promotional tour gave him yet another outlet for propagating his views.

Always it was the same gospel of smaller government, entrepreneurship, opportunity, futurism, technology, and a critique of the welfare state, dispensed to any audience, any reporter, any television camera that would give him a forum. But if the purpose was to spread his ideas, it was also to promote himself. For as he put it one day shortly before the 1994 elections, "I think I am a transformational figure." His critics saw him as something else, as a walking conflict of interest, who took money from wealthy contributors, some of them with business before the Congress, and used it to advance his climb to power. Though he had pilloried Jim Wright and other Democrats in the 1980s over conflicts of interest, Gingrich failed to understand how his own business affairs looked to others. He was furious when Democrats objected to the $4.5 million advance he accepted from Rupert Murdoch's publishing company, raging at his critics during an intemperate speech to the Republican National Committee in January 1995. "I am a genuine revolutionary," he said. "They are genuine reactionaries. We are going to change their world, they will do anything to stop us. They will use any tool: There is no grotesquerie, no distortion, no dishonesty too great for them to come after us." But even many Republicans thought the book deal compromised Gingrich at a time when the party needed him to concentrate on running the House, and they were relieved when he decided to take only royalties from the book's sales. He refused for years to make public the names of GOPAC's contributors, then as he severed his ties to the group, cavalierly told his colleagues there that *they* should do it.

Gingrich built his power from the inside out. Although extraordinarily skilled at attracting attention to himself, it was his ability to inspire and motivate other Republican office seekers that ultimately returned the biggest dividends, both for the party and for himself. Gingrich never seemed to run short of ideas, although he needed savvy people around him to sift the good from the bad. One day the staff at the National Republican Congressional Committee relabeled the drawers on the file cabinets to read "Newt's Ideas," "Newt's Ideas," "Newt's Ideas." Only one carried the label "Newt's Good Ideas." He often called one senior Reagan White House official at 6:30 in the morning, believing that if he got him early enough, he could influence his thinking for the whole day. He would drop in to see White House press secretary Marlin Fitzwater, always with new proposals for communicating the President's message strategy, most of them too complicated to be of use.

By far the most important of the organizations in the Gingrich network was GOPAC, which fell into his lap when Pete DuPont, the former Delaware governor, ran for President in 1988. DuPont had founded GOPAC to help develop a Republican farm team in the state legislatures. But fearing that the organization would become entangled in his own presidential campaign, DuPont searched for an energetic young conservative to replace him. "We were looking for someone who wanted to build the party at the grass roots," DuPont said. "Newt seemed head and shoulders above everybody."

Gingrich transformed GOPAC from a political bank that dispensed money to candidates into an educational and recruitment machine designed to give candidates the wherewithal to run and win on their own. He believed that while campaign contributions were important, candidates needed much more to be successful; they needed ideas and advice and the ability to withstand the combat of a vigorous campaign. Mostly they needed a sense of the larger picture and where they could fit into it. "GOPAC tried to give people confidence to get into the arena and stay," Joe Gaylord said. Gingrich wanted to help candidates win elections, but even more he wanted to transform their thinking about what it meant to be a Republican. Jeffrey Eisenach, the executive director of GOPAC in the early 1990s, said, "It was his understanding that political parties are cultures and that cultures are self-reinforcing and that a political party that had been a minority for as long as the Republican Party had been a minority party had learned all the habits of being a minority and that the set of habits that one needed to have in order to become a majority was very different from the set of habits one needed to have to be a comfortable minority."

Instead of cash, Gingrich sent audiotapes and videotapes. They would arrive unsolicited nearly every month in the mailboxes of candidates around the country, tapes on tactics and strategy and ideas and issues, lectures from Gingrich or his political advisers, interviews with other successful Republicans. It was like subscribing to a motivational course, with Gingrich a cross between Norman Vincent Peale and a Marine drill sergeant. As he put it in one lecture, "A healthy society starts out saying, 'Life is hard.'" GOPAC offered candidates everything from broad policy prescriptions for ending the welfare state or rethinking America's role in a post–Cold War world to literary

stilettos for attacking Democrats. One famous 1990 memo was enti-
tled "Language, a Key Mechanism of Control," outlining sixty words
that would negatively define the opposition. Word one: "decay."

John Boehner, now the third-ranking Republican in the House,
was in the Ohio legislature when the first tape unexpectedly arrived in
his mail. He popped it into the tape player in his car and was quickly
addicted to the Gingrich vision for America. The tapes were like polit-
ical methadone. "If it weren't for the tapes every month, I probably
wouldn't have run for Congress," Boehner said. Roger Wicker, elected
to the House from Mississippi in 1994 and later chosen as the leader of
the freshman class, was another GOPAC devotee, claiming he has lis-
tened to every tape produced in the last seven or eight years. "A great
deal of the political philosophy I brought to Washington was shaped
by Newt Gingrich," he said.

Gingrich also shifted the focus of the organization toward winning
control of the House. In a 1986 letter to Republican fund-raiser Ted
Welch of Tennessee, Gingrich said GOPAC's program now is "to
build party strength and groom promising future congressional candi-
dates in congressional districts where there may not be a possibility of
winning a seat right away, but where voting demographics show there
is a Republican voting strength and that with the right candidate and
sufficient party strength, a win can be ours." The letter surfaced in
1995 in a lawsuit against GOPAC charging that the organization had
violated federal campaign finance laws. By the early 1990s, GOPAC
was working intimately with the NRCC to help recruit candidates for
Congress, according to Spencer Abraham, who was the NRCC execu-
tive director and won election to the Senate in 1994. "GOPAC did a
lot to help recruit candidates in 1992," Abraham said. "GOPAC made
that their top priority."

IN the late 1980s and early 1990s, newly arriving Republican House
members became ready enlistees in Gingrich's army, fresh troops will-
ing to hurl themselves against the Democratic barricades with as much
enthusiasm as Gingrich himself once displayed. With Gingrich now in
the party leadership, COS lost its rationale, but other members, with
Gingrich's explicit blessing, picked up his mantle. Tom DeLay, who
had guessed wrong by supporting Ed Madigan in the whip's race,
feared exile under the Gingrich regime. He took over the Republican

Study Committee and quickly developed links to outside conservative organizations. Younger members helped lead the Republican attack against Democratic handling of the scandal over the House bank, which for years had routinely allowed members to bounce checks with no penalties. Likewise they banged the drums over the House post office scandal, in which members were allowed to convert their allowances for stamps to cash and which ultimately brought about the 1994 indictment of Ways and Means Committee chairman Dan Rostenkowski of Chicago. When the bank scandal broke, Democratic leaders quickly shut down the institution, but attempted to contain the damage by releasing only the names of the most egregious offenders in the mountain of overdrafts that had piled up over the years. Boehner and Jim Nussle, two freshman Republicans who had come to Washington promising to reform the House, led a boisterous counterattack against the Democratic leadership, even though it meant disclosing the names of scores of Republicans. Nussle, in what became the most memorable visual image of the protest, appeared on the House floor with a paper bag over his head, claiming he was embarrassed to be recognized as a member of the House. With five other freshmen from the Class of 1990 (Rick Santorum of Pennsylvania, Scott Klug of Wisconsin, Charles Taylor of North Carolina, and Frank Riggs and John Doolittle of California) who also had run on reform platforms, they formed the Gang of Seven and demanded that the leadership release the names of all 325 sitting and former House members who had overdrawn their accounts. It didn't matter if they drove the reputation of Congress even lower in the public's esteem; that too was part of the Gingrich plan.*

Gingrich's domination of the House became clear after the 1992 elections. Bush's defeat emancipated the younger rebels, and for many of them there was a sense of relief, even exuberance, on the night he was defeated. "Oh, man, yeah, it was fabulous," said Tom DeLay, who feared a second Bush term meant "another four years of misery." DeLay believed the Republicans had a greater chance of becoming a majority with Clinton in the White House. "You know, you're kind of torn," he said one day in the summer of 1995, sitting in the spacious

---

*After the 1994 election, Nussle became director of the transition and Boehner was elected Conference chairman. Santorum was elected to the Senate.

offices of the Majority whip in the Capitol. "You want to keep the White House but at the same time you knew that if we had another four years of this, we'd never take over the Congress."

Despite Bush's defeat, House Republicans gained ten seats, and the freshman class numbered forty-seven because of the record number of retirements. Nearly all the freshman Republicans had benefited directly from GOPAC materials; they shared Gingrich's ideological vision for the party and Ross Perot's fervor for reform. When Republicans met to elect their leaders, the Gingrich generation swept every significant position except the top job, which Michel held. But even the leader's days were numbered, as Gingrich made clear by hinting that if Michel did not retire at the end of 1994, he would challenge him. Michel capitulated and gradually ceded power to Gingrich.

The most significant change in the leadership elections that year came when the Republicans removed Jerry Lewis of California as chairman of the Republican Conference and installed Dick Armey of Texas in his place. Lewis was out of the Michel school of Republicans, a conservative conformist with a seat on the Appropriations Committee who preferred dealing with Democrats to confronting them over ideological differences. Even today, as majority leader, Armey has trouble hiding his disdain for the thinking that Lewis represented. "Jerry's typical of Appropriations guys," he said. "They'll sit down and work out a compromise." No one would say that about Dick Armey, whom Weber once described as a "one-man think tank in cowboy boots" and others described as a man who made Gingrich look diplomatic. Gingrich openly supported Armey in the race, and his four-vote victory over Lewis was aided by at least thirty votes among the freshman class.

Lewis harbored the notion that he yet might succeed Michel as GOP leader, and he blamed Gingrich for his unceremonious ouster. He knew Gingrich's game. As he put it, "Not many people go around carrying war generals' books under their arms. There's little question that Newt felt if there was a competitor on the leadership ladder who might be in the way, it was probably me. I was moved out of the way."

Armey's victory reflected the changing Republican attitude toward 1992. Within months of Clinton's victory, an internal consensus hardened into political theology: Bush had given away the White House through passivity, misguided moderation, and inattention to the conservative base; notwithstanding qualms about the culture war rhetoric of the Houston convention, the dominant view became that Bush lost not because he had been too ideological, but rather because he was not ideological enough. Democratic strategists like Stanley Greenberg saw in the 1992 result a clear repudiation of Reagan and particularly Reagan economics, but by mid-1993, most Republicans had reached the opposite conclusion. They believed that Bush was defeated because he had deviated from Reaganism, particularly in raising taxes, and that revival lay in reclaiming the inheritance that Bush had squandered. Nobody felt that more strongly than the House Republicans, as their leadership elections demonstrated. As Gingrich had said, governing from the center held no appeal to them. When he won the conference chairmanship, Armey sent a note to Dick Darman, with whom he had feuded bitterly during the Bush years. The note read, "Thanks, Dick, I couldn't have done it without you."

Armey was, if anything, more conservative than Gingrich. Pure ideology ran through his veins. He seemed to relish offending his opponents, no matter which party they were in, and he was often either clumsy or deliberately blunt in some of his attacks. He infuriated Democrats during the crime bill debate by saying of Clinton, "*Your* President is just not that important to us." During health care hearings, he said to Hillary Rodham Clinton, "The reports on your charm are overstated and the reports on your wit are understated." In what he called an embarrassing slip of the tongue, he referred to Democrat Barney Frank, an openly gay member of the House, as "Barney Fag."

Large and rumpled, Armey was an ex-economics professor who grew up in North Dakota and migrated to Texas, became a Ronald Reagan disciple, and won election to the House in 1984 in a district plunked between Dallas and Fort Worth. He developed the idea of the Base Closing Commission, a creative device designed to remove some of the politics from the process of shrinking the defense structure after the Cold War, and he used his position on the Joint Economic Committee to critique and attack Democratic economic initiatives. In 1995 he published *The Freedom Revolution*, which was overshadowed by Gingrich's heavily promoted book, but which offered a conservative blueprint toward a radically smaller federal government that made Gingrich seem the voice of moderation. "Just 10 years ago, even during the Reagan years, many of the proposals here would have been dismissed as wildly impractical," he wrote. "We are turning to self-government, to a world in which free people may confidently navigate the roads for themselves. . . . At the end of a century defined by government expansion, we are yearning again for individual freedom and for modest, competent government."

FREED from the Bush White House, the Gingrich generation pressed to accelerate the revolution. Gingrich had instilled in them the belief in teamwork, unity, and a vision of their own future. They added the antigovernment fervor that was growing at the grass roots. During a Republican retreat in Princeton, New Jersey, in early 1993, the young activists erupted in anger over the desultory discussion. At the time, the GOP's future still appeared shaky; the new members said it was time to talk candidly about their problems, and they couldn't do that while lobbyists and other outsiders sat at the table with them. What was to have been a half-hour meeting turned into a ninety-minute gripe session. "We said, 'This is ridiculous,'" Nussle said. "We said, 'Why are we here? Who are we? What is the Republican Party? What do we stand for? Our message of "We're not them" isn't working.'"

Even Gingrich was worried. In the summer of 1993, he said in an interview, "The Republican Party faces three or four enormous challenges. One is that Perot could run [in 1996] in such a way that even if Clinton's doing badly he survives. And second is that Republicans can stumble into a victory they don't understand and spend four years pulling the White House away and further crippling the party. And the third is that they could end up as the anti-Clinton party in a way which doesn't allow them any coherent ability to govern on anything."

The eruption by the backbenchers in Princeton laid the groundwork for another retreat in early 1994 in Salisbury, Maryland, this time without lobbyists present, where the House Republicans began to focus more systematically on a message for the coming campaign. After a year in which Republicans had won a Senate seat in Texas, the governorships of New Jersey and Virginia, and the city halls in New York and Los Angeles, there were sharp exchanges about the mood of the electorate. Frank Luntz offered a gloomy portrait of public attitudes toward the Republicans (not that perceptions of the Democrats were much better) and when challenged by DeLay about the victories in 1993, fired back, "We won because we were not the incumbent. It was an anti-incumbent vote, not a pro-Republican vote."

The Republicans were by then desperate to escape from the minority. Tom Tauke, who had formed the 92 Group in the mid-1980s but was now a corporate executive, helped chair the Salisbury meetings and likened them to the kind of sessions that have occurred in many American companies as they reorient themselves to a changing global economy. "They really did want to say, 'If we get into the majority, what is it that we will do? How will we be different from the Democrats?'" Tauke said. "That was a much different kind of discussion from anything that I engaged in when I was a member of Congress."

But the classes of 1990 and 1992 paled in their anti-Washington fervor when compared to the rambunctious Class of 1994. Even before they were elected, this new crop of Republicans lifted Gingrich's vision to the forefront of the party. Once in Washington, they provided him with the troops to help push through the Contract With America; later they displayed their independence by challenging Gingrich and other Republican leaders to live up to the rhetoric of the campaign about changing Washington. Not since the Democratic Watergate babies of the Class of 1974 had a new group of House members arrived in Washington to as much fanfare. They were described as the most conservative class in modern times, the most anti-Washington class in memory. The *New York Times* described them as "73 Mr. Smiths," a not entirely flattering portrayal. Many arrived not with a commitment to careers in Washington, but with an impatience to reform the capital, and they were given an unusual amount of power by Gingrich and Armey: key spots on committees like Ways and Means and Appropriations and, in two cases, subcommittee chairmanships.

They had won their elections with the help of the anti-Washington coalition, with the votes of term limits activists, gun owners, religious conservatives, Perot supporters. Many came directly from those movements: Steve Stockman of Texas with gun owners; Linda Smith of Washington with antitax activists and religious conservatives; Helen Chenoweth of Idaho with the opponents of Clinton's western policies and more radical elements on their fringe; Bob Inglis of South Carolina with term limits activists; David McIntosh of Indiana with antiregulatory advocates. But mostly they were creatures of the architect of the revolution himself: Newt Gingrich. If the Conservative Opportunity Society represented the truest of the Reagan true believers in the House in the early 1980s, then the new class of Republicans in the House represented the purest strain of the Gingrich philosophy. They took Gingrich at his word to reform Washington. They held up the House to cut more deeply into budgets for the National Endowment for the Arts, for example. They balked at compromise with the Senate or the White House. Linda Smith became a thorn in the side of Republican leaders over their leisurely pace to consider campaign finance reform. Democrats said they were proof the GOP was in the hands of extremists. As freshman Representative Mark Foley of Florida told the *New York Times*, "Newt's looking at us in his own likeness." It was the likeness of Gingrich in his younger years.

1995: TO BALANCE THE BUDGET

Nowhere were the changes in the party more clear than in the effort to move the GOP's long debate over taxes and deficits to another level. Gingrich's election as Speaker and the antigovernment fervor of the freshman brigade in the House provided the impetus for what would become the Republican's boldest and riskiest policy initiative of the new Congress, the proposal to balance the budget by the year 2002 and cut taxes at the same time, a formula that would require the Republicans to tackle the same issue that brought about Clinton's downfall — health care — by attempting to restructure Medicare and Medicaid and slash projected spending to meet their deficit targets.

The budget initiative once again opened up Republicans to attacks that they were extremists, that they were selling out to big business and the rich, that they were willing to hurt the elderly and the poor in order to provide the rich with tax cuts they didn't need. But to those Republicans who pushed the hardest for the budget plan, an irrefutable logic bound the overall effort: Balancing the budget served the ideological end of reducing the size of government, and reducing the size of government served the political end of further identifying the Republicans as the anti-Washington party.

In the broadest sense, the decision to cut taxes and balance the budget represented an accommodation between the Gingrich-Kemp tax-cutting wing of the party and the Dole-led deficit hawks. Each side seemed to be a winner. But Dole moved farther to accommodate Gingrich than Gingrich moved toward Dole. In the new alignment of power within the party, it was the House Republicans who proved more determined to cut taxes and more anxious to balance the budget as quickly as possible. It was Gingrich and the House who made the Balanced Budget Amendment to the Constitution the first item in the Contract With America; it was Gingrich personally — to the surprise and dismay of many of his House colleagues — who declared that, no matter what happened to the constitutional amendment in the Senate, the House would produce a seven-year plan to balance the budget; and it was Gingrich and the House who insisted, over the resistance of many Republicans in the Senate, that the plan include massive tax cuts. That, of course, is not the way Dole sees it. "I have the view that they're [the House] finally catching up," he said. "I hear all these young guys talking and I say, 'Well we've been there so long we're glad the cavalry got here. We've been holding out for years.'"

The Republican budget proposal, adopted in June 1995, underscored the shifts within the party and the changing politics of deficits and taxes. When Dole and Senate Budget Committee Chairman Pete Domenici of New Mexico tried to coax through their budget resolution in 1985, the constituency behind their effort included the political elite, Wall Street, some economists, and what the Kemp Republicans derided as the "green eyeshade wing" of the GOP. Kemp correctly perceived that the politics of deficit reduction was mostly the politics of pain, and that the Democrats had remained in power not by dispensing pain but by providing pleasure through spending programs financed by a progressive tax system. But by 1995, the terms of debate had changed. Gingrich and Co. rarely talked about balancing the budget in terms of the economy; they rarely talked about jobs at all. Instead, balancing the budget was described in moral terms — and as an instrument for reducing the power of the federal government.

The Perot campaign of 1992 had helped to create a new constituency for deficit reduction. With his infomercials and his easy-to-read charts, Perot almost single-handedly put the deficit near the top of the political agenda, and while the voters remained conflicted over their true priorities (polls showed strong majorities wanted to reduce the deficit, but equally strong majorities wanted to protect favored spending programs like Medicare and Social Security), the growing awareness of the size of the problem made it easier for politicians to tackle.

Grassroots anger with the federal government gave many Republicans a new rationale to balance the budget. Deficit reduction became not only an end in itself, but also a means to redistribute power outside Washington. As Dick Armey put it, "Balancing the budget in my mind is the attention-getting device that enables me to reduce the size of government. Because the national concern over the deficit is larger than life. . . . So I take what I can get and focus it on the job I want. If you're anxious about the deficit, then let me use your anxiety to cut the size of the government."

This conclusion reshaped the debate over spending cuts between the party's populist and traditional fiscal wings. In the 1980s, Kemp and his sympathizers argued that spending cuts alone reflected an accountant's mentality, a static and ultimately self-defeating strategy that kept the party mired in the traditions of the midwestern Republicans of the 1950s and prevented them from gaining the upper hand in the debate with the Democrats. These conservatives viewed tax cuts as the key to expanding the GOP's appeal. But by the 1990s, many young conservatives saw spending cuts as equally popular, because of the pain the cuts would inflict on Washington. For their own reasons, both the fiscal and the populist conservatives found common cause in a program of unprecedented spending reductions.

For all practical purposes, the 1990 budget fight with Bush had settled the issue of whether the new Republican Party would support tax increases in the foreseeable future. But events outside the Beltway reinforced those sentiments. A new generation of activist, Republican governors — Michigan's John Engler, Wisconsin's Tommy Thompson, Massachusetts's William Weld, Ohio's George Voinovich — had closed budget deficits in the 1990s by cutting spending rather than raising taxes, then won landslide reelections in 1994. Their political health contrasted with the travails of California Governor Pete Wilson, who had raised taxes by $7 billion in 1991 as part of a package designed to close a huge budget gap brought on by the national recession and defense cuts that decimated the state's aerospace industry. Like Bob Dole in the 1980s, Wilson won praise for his political courage, but the decision nearly cost him his job. His party did not miss the lesson.

If Wilson personified the path to avoid, New Jersey's Christine Todd Whitman, who was elected in 1993 on a Kemp-Reagan platform to cut taxes by 30 percent over three years, became the model to emulate. Her victory over unpopular Democrat Jim Florio stemmed mostly from his decision to raise taxes by $2.8 billion at the beginning of his term, triggering an antitax revolt that cost Democrats control of the state legislature in 1991 and that drove his own approval ratings down to 20 percent. But when Whitman scored a come-from-behind victory over Florio, a revisionist theory took hold: The tax cuts did it. Her success in office quickly bred imitators, and in 1994 a number of Republican challengers, including George Pataki in New York, adopted her model as their own.

The new message made its strongest impression on Bob Dole, the man who had ridiculed supply-siders throughout the 1980s and who had often equated the need to raise taxes with the obligations of governing responsibly. Preparing for another presidential campaign, Dole scrambled to catch up with the shifting sentiment within his own party. The first step was to repair the damage from his 1988 campaign, when he had refused to sign an antitax pledge during the New Hampshire primary, where Bush attacked him as "Senator Straddle" for his past record of raising taxes. "Stop lying about my record," Dole snarled at Bush on the night he saw his presidential aspirations die in New Hampshire. Dole decided to shuck off that part of his political resume, and on April 7, 1995 — which just happened to be the day House Republicans were celebrating the completion of work on the Contract With America — Dole summoned Grover G. Norquist of Americans for Tax Reform to his office in the Capitol. With photographers there to record the scene, Dole signed his name on the same antitax pledge he had spurned seven years earlier.

Dole faced pressure not simply to resist new taxes but to cut existing taxes and he was buffeted from four directions: from Phil Gramm looking to sharpen distinctions for the '96 campaign; from the need to appeal to the conservative, Republican primary electorate; from Gingrich and the hard-charging House; and just as important, from the younger conservatives in his own Senate caucus. Gingrich and the

House drove Dole and the Senate to balance the budget, and nowhere was the difference between the two bodies more clear than in the personalities of two men who had the responsibility for developing the budget blueprint, Pete Domenici and John Kasich. Domenici was, with Dole, perhaps the leading deficit hawk in the Congress, but he had layers of scar tissue from his battles of the 1980s and he was reluctant to begin another round unless everyone was prepared to finish the job. More than anyone, Domenici knew how difficult it would be for Republicans to balance the budget, particularly without a constitutional amendment, and he feared that his younger colleagues would flinch in the face of the Democratic counterattack on Medicare and cuts in education and other domestic programs. The last thing he wanted was to start down the balanced budget path one more time, only to fall short.

Kasich, the son of a postman from the blue-collar community of McKees Rocks, Pennsylvania, was another story entirely. Young, rebellious, exuberant, Kasich would not listen to those who insisted the budget could not be balanced. He had joined the Republican Party in the 1970s, he said, for one simple reason. "I don't like to be hassled, I don't like to be told what to do. I don't like bureaucracy and I hate rules," he said. "And I saw the Democratic Party as favoring all that: rules, bureaucracy, and standing in line." He claimed to be one of the few young Republicans "with hair over my collar and riding a motorcycle," but like other young conservatives, he worshiped Ronald Reagan. After the 1992 elections, he bid successfully for the ranking Republican slot on the Budget Committee and soon became the House's most relentless deficit cutter and the author of several alternative Republican budgets. If Domenici was always dour and pessimistic about the long road ahead, Kasich appeared to be the optimistic executioner, impatient with everyone who doubted it could be done and insistent that Republicans not play favorites as they wielded their razors.

Gingrich believed there was almost mystical power in the number zero, that by hanging a "0" on the budget scoreboard, the party could gain the political high ground in what would be a crippling debate with the Democrats over spending priorities. The Senate had less enthusiasm for the strategy. They had stared into this abyss before and knew that a balanced budget would mean enormous reductions in projected spending for Medicare and Medicaid, plus terminations of other domestic programs. "The Senate was never interested in going to zero," one top House Republican said. "They fought us every step of the way and they constantly argued it couldn't be done and then at the end of the day, of course, they stand on a mountain top, pound their chest and say didn't we have a great idea." The RNC's Don Fierce, who was keeping a close eye on the evolving budget strategy in behalf of Haley Barbour, recalled one meeting in Gingrich's office shortly after the Senate had defeated the Balanced Budget Amendment. "Newt looked around the room and he said, 'This is where Stockman and Darman blinked. I will not blink. I'm going forward. I hope we all go forward.'" Dole, however, scoffed at the idea that he and the Senate had taken a backseat to the House on balancing the budget. "Some of these House guys have short memories," he said. "We've been trying to do this for years."

House Republicans believed they owed their new constituency a tax cut, particularly the pro-family groups who had lost a fight to include school prayer in the Contract and received as a consolation prize the inclusion of their proposed $500 per child tax credit. Despite resistance in the Senate to any tax cuts, the House formula eventually won the day, but only after substantial negotiations. The House originally called for $350 billion in tax cuts; the Senate included none unless the spending cuts were in place to eliminate the deficit, in which case the Senate said $170 billion. Eventually they compromised at $245 billion. The final compromise budget blueprint called for nearly $1 billion in deficit reduction, including reducing projected spending on Medicare by $270 billion and on Medicaid by $180 billion.

The Medicare fight alone put the party's future in peril, and by late 1995 it was clearly damaging the GOP's standing with the American people. One poll in the heat of the debate showed only about a quarter of the people approved of the changes Republicans were making in the program, an anemic level of support substantially *below* the nadir of public backing for Clinton's health care plan. Gingrich himself became as much a lightning rod for attacks from the Democrats as Clinton had been for Republicans in 1993 and 1994. The Democrats maintained control of the governorship in Kentucky and fended off Republican dreams of capturing both houses of the Virginia legislature in the 1995 elections in part by personalizing the Republican revolution around Gingrich, and Republican strategists talked openly about their fears that in 1996, Democratic political ads would morph their candidates into Gingrich in the same way Republicans had morphed Democrats into Clinton in 1994.

Coupled with the huge tax cuts, an assault on Medicaid and other safety net programs for the poor, the Medicare restructuring and the budget blueprint represented an enormous political gamble. But more than any other single document, the budget resolution reflected the bulging coalition of the new Republican Party: Perot and his followers had shaped the climate for an all-out attack on the deficit; religious conservatives had shaped the tax cuts; the supply-siders and tax cutters from the 1980s emerged triumphant in the long war over using tax increases to help balance the budget; and the antigovernment movement made it possible to think about shrinking the size of government beyond anything the party had tried before. The resolution of this debate within the party framed the political dialogue with Clinton and the Democrats over the future of the country, but equally important, it demonstrated how tightly Gingrich and his generation controlled the party's agenda.

Throughout 1995, Gingrich often marveled privately at the power he had amassed as Speaker. In part he knew it reflected the built-in powers of the Speaker bestowed by the Founding Fathers. Compared to Bob Dole in the Senate, he told friends, the Speaker had enormous power. But Gingrich expanded his reach beyond anything the Founding Fathers had imagined, marrying the authority of the institution with a persistent strategy to speak to a larger audience through the power of television and a message that transcended the gritty legislative details of Capitol Hill. Even before the elections of 1994, Gingrich had talked about 1995 as a year in which he and his followers would stamp their vision on the party, effectively forcing the Republican presidential candidates to run on a platform established in the House. In so doing, Gingrich created a political figure the country had not seen in generations: a congressional leader as powerful — and as polarizing — as a President.

★★★

4

Leave Us Alone

WHAT BOTHERS JOHN COLLINS is not so much the new gun-control laws — he expected as much from Bill Clinton and the Democrats in Congress — as the video cameras on the highways in his hometown of Las Vegas. The progression worries him, the small steps, the imperceptible advances. Remember, at first, they were supposed to keep an eye on traffic? Now the cameras are being used to give out traffic tickets. What's next? Monitoring where people drive? Cataloguing license plates? "Little by little," he said ominously, letting the thought trail off in a haze of cigarette smoke.

Tanned and leathery, Collins delivered this warning while standing outside a ballroom in a downtown Phoenix hotel one sizzling afternoon in May 1995. Inside, leaders of the National Rifle Association (NRA), at once perhaps the most powerful and embattled lobby in the country, were handing out awards at a gala luncheon. Collins was one of some twenty thousand gun enthusiasts who had gathered for the NRA's annual convention. A few blocks away, in the Phoenix Convention Center, dozens of manufacturers had set up booths, displaying the latest in shotguns and handguns and telescopic sights. There were hunting bows, crafted as carefully as sculptures, and camouflage outfits and leather jackets with the names of gun manufacturers emblazoned across the back like baseball teams.

Browsing through the stacks of merchandise (down to infant-sized NRA T-shirts that read "Protecting your right to keep and bear arms, for now and for the future") was one of the two principal activities at the convention. The other was talking politics. Stephen Donnell, an NRA board member who has been with the organization for fifty years, waited until Collins had finished his disquisition on highway cameras before offering his own opinion on the state of the nation. "The real issue isn't gun control," he said. "The question is whether we are going to be subjects of the government or whether we are going to be citizens and the government is going to be subject to us." Donnell suggested digging up old newsreels of Hitler and Mussolini to gain an understanding of where Clinton was trying to take the country. What was the connection? "The similarity," John Collins jumped in, "is in the direction they are going."

Not far from Collins and Donnell, David Dutton, a slim, bearded psychologist from the small town of Coarsegold, California, was sitting on a bench, wearing a T-shirt with pictures of Bill and Hillary Clinton above the inscription "Dual Airbags." Friendly but passionate, Dutton picked up where Collins and Donnell left off. "The federal government has become a hydra-headed monster," Dutton said. "Almost any federal agency they want to cut, I would be in favor of. It's grown out of hand. It's a malignant cancer." People used to be free in America, he said almost wistfully. "Now if you pump leaded gas in your car, it's a federal offense."

Not everyone who gathered at the NRA convention was so angry at government. But most were. Like Collins, they had grievances that extended well beyond guns and gun control. Indeed, few of them said they had suffered any personal inconvenience from either the ban on semi-automatic assault weapons or the waiting period for handgun purchases Congress had approved over the previous two years. To most of them, gun control had ascended from the practical to the symbolic. Gun control was just the means to the end of enlarging government and giving Washington more power to control the lives of its citizens. Washington was taking away guns to clear the path for taking away other rights: This was the article of faith. One man from Colorado raged at being required to give his fingerprints to obtain a driver's license. Another complained about federal environmental regulations that favored turtles over farmers and snails over ranchers.

Another said government welfare programs were undermining traditional moral values. Speed limits, restraints on the use of public lands, all the infringements on liberty that society demands to uphold order seemed to them an intolerable web of rules and regulations too thick to evade or even comprehend.

What made these sentiments all the more remarkable was their source. The NRA convention had a small-town, blue-collar flavor, and the men who pored over shotguns and swapped hunting stories seemed like the sort who might have broken up antiwar demonstrations with their fists twenty-five years ago. Now they sounded like the Weathermen themselves, branding the government as corrupt, voracious, malevolent. "We're going into a situation where there is a police state mentality," one man said. Another man added: "I'm not saying there is any definite, immediate conspiracy to turn America into a tyranny. But as a matter of principle, people should be afraid of their government."

At their most extreme, these beliefs bordered on the antigovernment paranoia expressed by the two men accused of blowing up a federal office building in Oklahoma City just a month before the NRA meeting. Yet they usually stopped short. Everyone in Phoenix condemned the violence, and if there was any sympathy for the bombers it was kept well hidden. Still, the intensity of the alienation from government was palpable. When these men talked about Washington, many of them conjured up images of revolution — peaceful or political, but revolution nonetheless. In the same way they once might have spoken of Moscow as a threat to their freedom, now they pointed at their own capital. "I consider the federal government to be the greatest threat to our liberty today," Dutton said. "We've defeated communism. We've defeated Nazism. The last threat is inside the Beltway."

THESE angry white men are one legion in a grassroots movement that has rewritten the political equation of the 1990s, and in the process helped to transform the Republican Party. With social movements on the left like labor unions and civil rights organizations diminished in power, an army of conservative grassroots groups has mobilized middle-class discontent with government into a militant political force, reaching for an idealized past with the tools of the onrushing future: fax machines, computer bulletin boards, and the shrill buzz of talk radio. They have forged alliances with the Gingrich generation of conservatives and strengthened their hand as the dominant voice within the GOP family. Like a boulder in a highway, the conservative populist movement has become an enormous, often impassable obstacle in the path of President Clinton. No single factor in the Republican revival after Bush's defeat has been more important than the party's success at reconnecting with and invigorating the profusion of anti-Washington and antigovernment movements sprouting in every state.

These movements exist in concentric circles of alienation from government. At the farthest edge are extremist tax protesters, survivalists, and elements of the militia movement so alienated from society that they can imagine taking up arms against it. But most of the energy has been contained within the boundaries of mainstream politics. Probably not in this century have so many distinct groups, with such a broad range of grievances, simultaneously targeted the government in Washington as their enemy. The conservative, or antigovernment, populist coalition operates on at least half a dozen fronts: gun owners led by the 3.5-million-member NRA; Christian conservatives organized primarily through televangelist Marion G. (Pat) Robertson's Christian Coalition, which now counts 1.7 million members in seventeen hundred local chapters; the movement to impose term limits on members of Congress; the network of more than eight hundred state and local antitax organizations; small-business owners spearheaded by the six-hundred-thousand-member National Federation of Independent Business (NFIB), which has surpassed more conciliatory big business organizations as a legislative force in Washington; the Perot movement; and the "wise use" and property rights movements that have amalgamated ranchers, farmers, off-road enthusiasts, loggers, and miners — as well as multinational mining and timber companies — into a coalition demanding the rollback of environmental regulations, increased access to public lands, and government compensation for environmental rules that prevent landowners from developing their property.

Even this list doesn't encompass the entire range of populist right-of-center uprisings through the early 1990s, from the movements that opposed the North American Free Trade Agreement (NAFTA) and the world trade treaty known as GATT to the anti-immigration and anti–affirmative action movements that began in California and have spread elsewhere over time. "There is a synergy," said conservative political consultant Craig Shirley. "It is feeding on itself. It is keeping itself in motion."

These movements sort largely into two camps. In one are the Christian Coalition and other groups drawn to politics primarily by fears of cultural decline and the breakdown of the family. In the other are the secular organizations — like the National Federation of Independent Business, the followers of Ross Perot, the term limits and property rights movements, and the NRA — motivated mostly by opposition to the expansion of government spending and regulation. There are significant differences between and even within these camps, but the conservative populist coalition is more demographically and ideologically coherent than many on the left assume. To a striking degree, Americans in these groups express common attitudes and exhibit similar lifestyles. Gun ownership is considerably more common among groups within the antigovernment coalition than among the population as a whole. Nearly half of small-business owners consider themselves born-again Christians. Gun owners, Christian conservatives, and small-business owners are all heavy listeners to talk radio. In many states, small-business owners, antitax advocates, and Perot activists provided the foundation of support for the term limits movement. The 1995 term limits ballot initiative in Mississippi, for example, was directed by Mike Crook, a field organizer for the Christian Coalition who was also a member of the NRA. "The links are all there," Crook says. "They are all interrelated. All of these grassroots organizations . . . amount to taking back our country for the people."

THE ROAR OF THE CROWD

Knitting together these groups is not only shared experience but also the uninhibited, anti-establishment voice of talk radio. Henry Luce once said a successful magazine created a community that previously had been unaware of its common bonds. Talk radio encourages a community of the disaffected. It offers solidarity and reinforcement for those alienated from government, and provides its audience with an endless stream of outrages to harden their discontent. It has become a mass-market version of what the *Wall Street Journal* editorial page provides the conservative elite, a bulletin board that transmits ideas, but, more important, reassures like-minded people they are not alone. Talk radio shows give a voice to voter outrage more intimate and unvarnished than ever would have appeared in the mainstream press, and in so doing strengthens and validates those feelings for a wider audience. "Conservatives felt very isolated," said Paul Weyrich, a veteran conservative strategist. "What talk radio has done . . . is taught them there are lots of people who feel like they do." By encouraging conservatives in the conviction that they represented the majority of opinion, talk radio emboldened them in their crusade against liberalism and consolidated the dominance of conservative populism as the voice of the post-Bush Republican Party.

Call-in talk radio had been around at least since the 1950s, but it grew explosively in the 1980s, with the number of stations devoted to talk radio more than doubling between 1988 and 1995 to about twelve hundred. Many factors propelled the turn toward talk. The superiority of FM sound quality forced AM stations to seek alternatives to music programming; advances in satellite technology allowed easier and less costly distribution of nationally syndicated talk programs; and the Reagan administration's repeal of the Fairness Doctrine in 1987 erased managers' fears that they might have to provide equal time to views opposing those of the combative talk show hosts. Talk radio's success also reflected declining faith in the mainstream media. In the basic divide that increasingly defined American politics in the 1990s, talk radio was firmly situated with the army of the discontented storming the castle, while the major newspapers and television networks were widely perceived as speaking for the elite barricaded within. Talk radio was both more personal than the mainstream press and more interactive. The hosts, most of whom affected a blue-collar, guy-down-the-block style, were far more approachable than the Olympian newscasters in network television; and the two-way dialogue between the hosts and their audiences gave many listeners the sense that the shows reflected their experience, rather than the opinions of the distant political elite. "The whole communication works because voters believe it to be of themselves rather than of the establishment," says Democratic pollster Celinda Lake. "Something that appears on talk radio has twice the credibility almost of the evening news."

Politics wasn't the only, or even the dominant, focus for most radio talk shows. But as distrust of Washington grew through the 1960s and 1970s, talk radio emerged as a magnet for feelings of discontent that were often filtered or overlooked in the mainstream press. Talk radio's characteristic tone was a dumbfounded outrage, the amazement of those on the outside at the imbecility of those on the inside. Its voice was the voice of the angry baseball fan bellowing from the bleachers, or the cabby firing off opinions from the front seat as he weaved through the traffic. Bound by neither the standards of factual accuracy nor objectivity to which the mainstream press aspired (even if it didn't always reach), talk radio exploded into the political world like a cluster bomb.

For years, talk show hosts tapped a wellspring of anti-establishment sentiment on local issues. The targets varied, but the message was always the same: The big boys — the local government, the phone companies, the liberal national media — were ganging up on the little people. In Boston, host Jerry Williams, a classic New Deal Democrat suspicious of all entrenched authority, led a successful fight in 1986 to repeal a state mandatory seat-belt law. In Miami, Michael Siegel, another centrist Democrat, led a campaign against phone rate increases.

Talk radio first mobilized as a force in national politics at the end of 1988, when Williams, Siegel, and several dozen of their colleagues joined to oppose the congressional pay raise. Hoping to minimize public attention, the congressional leadership had constructed a complex parliamentary system by which legislators would receive a 51 percent pay raise without ever having to take a vote, a plan designed to buffer them from an unpopular act that proponents insisted was necessary to make service in Congress attractive to able people. But the maneuver had the opposite effect, generating anger over both the pay raise itself and the duplicity of the process. Talk radio became the nervous system for the opposition that erupted in the winter of 1988–1989.

Leading that charge was consumer advocate Ralph Nader, who for years had solicited talk radio hosts to promote his causes. He bombarded them with material opposing what he invariably termed the congressional "pay grab," and in a matter of weeks, Nader appeared on two hundred programs, colorfully denouncing Congress and always giving out phone numbers for listeners to register their disapproval with their representatives. Nader's most important recruit was

Jerry Williams, who then enlisted hosts around the country to the cause. In fact, many were already being driven to it by their callers. One was Michael Siegel, who had launched a new show in Seattle in November 1988. Soon after he arrived, a caller angry about the pay raise suggested that voters hold another Boston Tea Party on December 16 — the 215th anniversary of the original. That gave Siegel the idea of urging listeners to send tea bags to Congress as a symbol of opposition to the pay hike. Working with the liberal Nader and the conservative National Taxpayers Union, he encouraged his talk radio host colleagues to join the crusade. Eventually, some seventy-five thousand tea bags flooded into Washington. Amid this fragrant tide of opposition, Congress angrily abandoned their raise — though they voted themselves a smaller increase later in the session.

The talk radio crusade against the pay hike had its roots on the Left with Nader, but it turned heads mostly on the Right. More than anyone else in Washington, a handful of House Republicans recognized the political implications of the talk show uprising against the pay raise. Beyond the ideological attractions, there was a natural emotional affinity between the House Republicans and talk show hosts, for they shared a personal sense of exclusion. The mainstream press mostly treated talk show hosts with scorn, but scorn would have been a big step up for the House Republicans, who had spent more than three decades in the minority and were regularly ignored even by George Bush's White House. The average House Republican had as good a chance of being abducted by aliens as appearing on one of the Sunday morning television interview shows like *Meet the Press* or *Face the Nation*. Talk radio offered a microphone to legislators who otherwise stood mute in the national press.

The classic example was California Representative Robert K. Dornan, a bombastic conservative who attacked Democrats so passionately that he sometimes seemed disappointed words were the only weapons permitted on the House floor. He described one Democratic opponent for his congressional seat as a "sick, pompous little ass." Another time he grabbed the collar of Democratic Representative Tom Downey and called him a "draft-dodging wimp." After a while, Dornan's apoplectic assaults on Democrats drew only shrugs or groans from most reporters. But beginning in the late 1980s, those same excesses made Dornan a prized guest on talk radio shows. Paul Morrell,

Dornan's press aide, found himself fielding as many as ten or fifteen requests a week for Dornan, from stations far outside of his Orange County congressional district. That demand for Dornan, combined with the furor talk radio whipped up over the pay raise, convinced Morrell that the talk shows constituted an underutilized resource for conservatives. "It just hit me about the power of talk radio," Morrell said. "Even if the hosts didn't identify themselves as conservatives or Republicans, there was an underlying commonsense attitude [about them] that would appeal to Republicans. And I figured there ought to be a way to tap into that."

Working with Ed Gillespie, another GOP aide, Morrell asked all press secretaries for House Republicans to compile a list of sympathetic talk radio hosts in their districts. Eventually Morrell collected several hundred names, and sold the House Republican Study Committee on a program to systematically cultivate them. Under a program that became known as Talk Right, the Republican Committee regularly sent the hosts issue briefs listing GOP talking points on current issues and offering half a dozen House Republican legislators as guests. For a few minutes each day, and for longer periods at night, Republican legislators began turning up on the air in Milwaukee or Chicago or Salt Lake City, summoning listeners to point their frustration at bureaucrats, corrupt politicians, and big-spending liberals in Washington. "I talked to the nation sitting at my desk," recalled House Majority Whip Tom DeLay, who assumed control of the Study Committee as the Talk Right effort began. In the first months, no one could point to any votes that were turned by talk radio, no districts where Republicans were suddenly more competitive. But the Republicans were bulldozing a new path for distributing the antigovernment, anti-Congress message, clearing an opening that would widen into a highway under President Clinton.

ON LOAN FROM GOD

The most important development in the political mobilization of talk radio was one that nobody cultivated and few could have anticipated: the unlikely ascent of Rush Hudson Limbaugh III. Limbaugh was born in the small town of Cape Girardeau, Missouri, in a family known for lawyers and Republicans. His father was the most prominent attorney in town and a staunchly conservative former Republican county chairman; his mother was active in Republican politics, too, and his grandfather, also a lawyer, had served Eisenhower as ambassador to India. Overweight and physically awkward, Limbaugh passed through adolescence almost untouched by the 1960s; he was a large round peg who could never find quite the right hole. By his account, school "never interested" him. Instead, he was drawn to the radio, and, like many entertainers, seemed to come to life only onstage. Under pressure from his father, who expected another lawyer, Limbaugh tried college, but he didn't fit there either. After only one year he dropped out and went off to make his name behind the microphone.

For the next decade, Limbaugh experienced unbroken downward mobility: Each year he earned less money than the year before. He flunked out of radio in Pittsburgh, and then flunked out again in Kansas City. In something close to despair, he took a job selling group tickets for the Kansas City Royals baseball team. For five years he treaded water, until he found a low-level news-reading job at another Kansas City station. A broadcast consultant, amused by Limbaugh's impertinent patter, recommended him as a daytime talk host to a Sacramento station that had recently fired shock jock Morton Downey Jr. In 1984, Limbaugh moved west and turned his life around. From the start his format was unique: no guests, just Limbaugh and his manic blend of satire and commentary. This time, his mixture clicked, and came to the attention of a national program syndicator. In the summer of 1988, Limbaugh moved to New York and launched the nationally syndicated program that would make him a household name less than a decade after he hustled Kiwanis clubs to come out and root for the Royals.

From a modest beginning (only fifty-eight stations signed on at first), Limbaugh's audience grew exponentially to heights unmatched in contemporary radio: eight million a week, eleven million a week, ultimately twenty million a week listening on 660 stations. On the national stage, his talents blossomed. Limbaugh proved to be a gifted entertainer with a quick sense of humor, a voice built for the boom box, and a Reaganesque tendency never to let an inconvenient fact interrupt a good anecdote. His show bounded from humor to invective, from monologue to skits, from egomaniacal vanity to deflating self-parody, all to the rhythm of an insistent rock-and-roll beat. Outside his studio, Limbaugh still sometimes seemed the awkward teen. Appearing one Sunday morning with the gray eminences on ABC's *This Week with David Brinkley*, he was oddly tentative and passive. But in his own domain, "with talent on loan from God," and a predominantly male audience that received his every word as if it were borne to them on tablets, he was a graceful high-wire act, a stream-of-consciousness provocateur who leapt from note to note with cool assurance. On any given show he might denounce the mainstream media, lacerate the latest bit of liberal lunacy, or recast Vice President Al Gore, a frequent nemesis, as the star of a new movie: *Forrest Gore*, the adventures of "a man with a room temperature IQ."

Behind the humor was a staunchly conservative message that blended elements of Ronald Reagan, Jack Kemp, and William Bennett, the former education secretary and virtue czar who became an intellectual mentor to Limbaugh. "If you combine Kemp's optimism about America with Bill Bennett's deep concern about the collapse of families and our culture, I think you've got Rush Limbaugh," said Adam Meyerson, the editor of the Heritage Foundation's *Policy Review*. Limbaugh instinctively spoke the language of conservative populism. He was effortlessly middlebrow in his tastes: On the air he talked about football and Tom Clancy novels and complained about "pointy-headed academic think tank types." Like all conservative populists, Limbaugh presented himself as the voice of the people in between — the Americans who carry the load and feel they are blamed by the people on top for the suffering of the people on the bottom. In his second book, he told his fans,

> You are the ones trying to hold society together in the face of a full-frontal assault on your values. You are the ones who obey the law, pay the taxes, raise your children to be moral and productive citizens. . . . And you are doing it all with the help of God and your family, never once whining about the lack of federal funding or burning down your neighborhood because the government is "neglecting" you.
>
> And what has been your reward? You are called selfish and greedy. . . . And the worst of it is, you are the ones who have to pick up the pieces and pay more taxes for yet another program when the liberal social experiments fail once again.

Those arguments merely followed the grooves that conservative populists from Richard Nixon to George Wallace to Ronald Reagan had laid down for decades. Limbaugh's unique contribution was to infuse these appeals to middle America with the irreverent spirit of baby boomer humor and rock and roll. Like conservative satirist P. J. O'Rourke, but on a far larger platform, Limbaugh applied the subversive cultural impudence of the '60s against the very liberal establishment the '60s had spawned. Limbaugh sometimes barreled past propriety (he was forced to drop an early routine ridiculing AIDS patients after a gay rights group disrupted one of his television appearances), but more often he found colorful, confrontational language ("femi-nazis" for feminists; "tree-hugging wackos" for environmentalists) that infuriated his critics and exhilarated his fans by voicing and validating emotions usually left unspoken. For three hours every day, Limbaugh presided over a shotgun wedding between the *National Lampoon* and the *National Review*.

The result was to open vast new audiences for the conservative populist message. "The truth," says John Fund of the *Wall Street Journal*, who collaborated with Limbaugh on his first book, "is that he took ideas that had been current in the conservative movement for decades, popularized them, made them entertaining, and brought an entire non-policy audience the benefits of that work. . . . Because of his entertainment gifts, he was able to attract a much larger audience than anybody who had gone before him."

As his audience grew, Limbaugh functioned like a trawling ship for the Right, bringing home nets full of new recruits. The circulation of the *American Spectator*, a take-no-prisoners monthly conservative journal, increased tenfold largely because of its advertising on Limbaugh's show. The Heritage Foundation once offered free copies of a book by Bennett on Limbaugh's show — and within days received seventy-five thousand phone calls. At the libertarian Cato Institute, the phones would ring into hysteria any time Limbaugh mentioned one of its reports on the air. "Our receptionist would just go nuts," said Anna McCollister, the group's former communications director. "She would practically tell you what time he went on the air because the phones would start ringing immediately."

Limbaugh operated as a megaphone, too, enormously amplifying the message that conservatives in Washington typically felt was diluted or ignored in the mainstream press. He played an especially crucial role in opening a new front in the systematic drive by Gingrich and his allies to stigmatize the Democratic Congress as enfeebled and corrupt. As a satirist — to say nothing of a political propagandist — Limbaugh couldn't have asked for better material than the Democrats served him up into the early 1990s with the congressional banking and post office scandals. One routine he played during the banking scandal ended with the tag line: "Capitol Hill Bank, member FLEECE, a special privilege lender." With Limbaugh and other talk show hosts augmenting the complaints of younger House Republicans, the reluctant Democratic leadership was forced to make public the list of members who had bounced checks at the House bank — a milestone in the decade-long Gingrich effort to discredit the House.

Limbaugh's emergence in the early 1990s was only one sign of talk radio's potential to turbocharge the conservative populist movement. Another indication came in New Jersey, where a Trenton radio station that combined oldies music and nervy talk led a revolt against New Jersey Democratic Governor James J. Florio's massive tax hike. Following prevailing wisdom in the Democratic Party, Florio almost immediately after taking office in 1990 sought to cement his hold on middle-class voters by funding educational improvement and property tax relief with increases in income and sales taxes targeted mainly at the affluent. His office produced elaborate calculations demonstrating that middle-class taxpayers would come out ahead and sold the package as an effort to ensure that the rich paid their fair share. But in another signal of distrust with government, middle-class voters turned vehemently against him.

At the center of the storm was WKXW-FM in Trenton, where hosts more accustomed to raffling off concert tickets promoted an anti-tax petition drive that collected over four hundred thousand signatures and inspired a raucous demonstration at the state capitol. One morning disk jockey urged his listeners to open "not a period of mourning, but a period of mooning" at the statehouse. It wasn't so-phisticated debate, but no one missed the point. "They had what they called a New Jersey hour of rage," said political consultant Paul Begala, who worked for Florio. "One guy called in and did a primal scream for thirty seconds. . . . A woman called in and said, 'When I think of Jim Florio, I think of a colostomy bag.'" In this swirling cacophony, Democrats lost control of both chambers of the state House in 1991, and two years later, Florio himself lost his job to Republican Christine Todd Whitman, who had hosted a show on WKXW after losing a 1990 Senate bid and who promised sweeping cuts in state taxes during her 1993 gubernatorial campaign.

The Bush White House and many other establishment Republicans failed to recognize this new vehicle. "Talk radio was not much of a factor at all in our thinking," recalled Bush's press secretary Marlin Fitzwater. "I don't ever remember having a discussion of talk radio as an entity. I don't recall any effort to reach out to them as a group." Even Limbaugh largely escaped their notice. Limbaugh emerged as a true national phenomenon early in Bush's presidency, with a following so fervent they labeled themselves "dittoheads" to honor their practice of endorsing their hero's effusions with a simple "ditto." But the White House paid Limbaugh no attention until he urged listeners to register their disappointment with Bush by voting for Pat Buchanan (a talk radio host himself) in the 1992 New Hampshire primary. Later that spring Bush invited Limbaugh to stay overnight at the White House and both Bush and Quayle subsequently appeared on his show (becoming the first studio guests on the program).

Limbaugh's enthusiasm for Bush always appeared measured, but his distaste for Clinton knew virtually no bounds. Mary Matalin, the Bush reelection campaign's sharp-tongued political director, stayed in close touch with Limbaugh throughout the fall campaign, often tipping him off privately to coming attacks against the Democratic nominee. But even Matalin didn't see talk radio as a means to reach a specific constituency of voters disaffected with government. And most people around Bush saw talk show hosts as a minor evolutionary advance from carnival barkers: at once peripheral and beneath the dignity of the presidency. "There was no sense of it as a tool," Fitzwater remembers somewhat ruefully. "We didn't recognize what was happening." The full political mobilization of talk radio and the populist, conservative network it served would await a different generation of Republicans — and another President.

FROM BRYAN TO REAGAN

Behind all of these swirling, swelling movements on the Right is the fear of a world spinning out of control. Populism has always combined reform with nostalgia. Since the days of Andrew Jackson, populists have sought to purify society by restoring seemingly abandoned ideals. With those conflicting impulses — moving forward by reaching back — populist movements uneasily join evangelical hopes of remaking society with an exaggerated sense of defensiveness. Now, as much as in the nineteenth century, the populist impulse is foremost about restoration: of values, of a way of life, and of the prominence of Americans who feel their status endangered by change. Populist movements flourish in broken soil, at times when large numbers of Americans feel themselves uprooted by developments that they cannot understand or control. As the economy restructures under the pressures of globalization and advancing technology, and society's cultural framework strains under the breakdown of the two-parent family, this is again one of those times. "People feel they don't have control over their own lives," said Republican pollster Frank Luntz. "That they can no longer shape their future."

For the populists of William Jennings Bryan in the 1890s, mostly farmers but also small businessmen and some urban workers, the forces cracking the foundations of their lives arose from the transformation of America into a modern industrial economy: the great railroads, the new trusts like Standard Oil and Carnegie Steel, the shadowy Wall Street financiers like J. P. Morgan. Reversing the Jeffersonian suspicion of centralized power that defined the Democratic Party through the nineteenth century, Bryan and his fellow populists saw a muscular federal government as a counterweight to this unaccountable economic power. They envisioned government as the tool through which the "plain people" (as the populists called them) could regain control over a society suddenly dominated by private powers beyond their reach. That ideal of government as a means of empowering individuals against the excesses of private economic power has echoed through liberal populism from Franklin Roosevelt to Ralph Nader. It reverberated in Bill Clinton's 1992 promises to mobilize government against "savings and loans crooks" and "corporate executives [who] raised their own salaries when . . . their workers were losing their jobs."

Economic grievance defined the voice of populism for most of American history, but beginning after World War II, conservatives built a competing populist tradition focused around cultural grievance. Here the enemy was not business and the wealthy, but government and an intellectual "new class" hostile to the hometown values of the "plain people." While liberal populists portrayed government as a means for ordinary people to assert their economic interests, conservative populists portrayed it as a weapon for a cosmopolitan elite to advance an insidious cultural agenda.

In the years after World War II, anticommunist conservatives like Richard Nixon and Joe McCarthy marshaled this imagery to present themselves as the voice of a silent majority straining to reclaim and protect America from treacherous elitists: Ivy League diplomats whose loyalty, grasp of true American principles, religious faith, and even sexuality were questionable. In the 1960s, George Wallace and Spiro Agnew updated the arguments to condemn the media, "permissive" liberals who coddled violent criminals, and intellectuals — the professor who "knows how to run the Vietnam War but can't park his bicycle straight," as Wallace put it.

In the 1980s, Ronald Reagan brought these cultural and economic grievances together, targeting "welfare queens" and bureaucrats scheming to expand their power in the "puzzle palaces on the Potomac," all at the cost of higher taxes on the hard-working middle class. Later in the 1980s, a succession of populist voices, beginning with term limit advocates and talk radio hosts, reinforced by Ross Perot's 1992 campaign, focused their fire not only on government in the abstract, but on politicians themselves. "You don't have to look very far to see the main source of [our] problem," wrote one term limits group in 1994 mailings against members of Congress who opposed the idea. "Career politicians at every level who have built little empires at our expense. Corruption . . . pork barrel spending to buy votes at the next election . . . taxpayer funded perks and privileges that would make a Third World autocrat blush."

This assault on the political system itself provided the final brick in the modern conservative populist argument. Today, the successors to Nixon and Wallace and Reagan fuse economic and cultural grievance to create a dichotomy between a virtuous public and a corrupt political class. In conservative populist imagery, government has been turned on its head by an insular liberal elite and now penalizes the productive to reward the unproductive. Hard-working small-business owners struggling to create jobs are buried under social engineering schemes from "politicians and bureaucrats" who see them only "as the means to solve problem after problem facing our society," writes NFIB president Jack Faris. Government coddles criminals while stripping law-abiding Americans of the capacity for self-defense with self-defeating gun-control laws: "They are going to walk [us] up that blind alley until they take away the right of honest people in this country to own a gun and at the end of that blind alley is going to be a criminal with a gun," says Wayne R. LaPierre, the executive vice president of the NRA. Government oppresses struggling working families with taxes to pay for the immorality and indolence of the welfare-dependent underclass: "The destructive vise of government policy tightens on those families that stay together, work and save," writes Ralph Reed, executive director of the Christian Coalition. "Like a twisted Robin Hood, the government takes from intact families and gives to those who bring children into the world without taking responsibility for providing for them."

These arguments combine legitimate dispute with scapegoating into a mixture more explosive than either would be alone. In the past three decades, the federal government has grown larger and more assertive about intruding on decisions — from the legality of abortion to the nature of classroom instruction — once determined almost entirely by local custom. But by indicting government for the unsettling changes in the economy and culture, the conservative populists blame complex problems common across the industrialized West — from rising rates of illegitimacy and crime to a decline in economic opportunity for average families — on the failures of a misguided domestic political class.

Yet it is that very simplification that gives their message such power. In its certainty, the conservative populist message contests hopelessness: If one government created these problems by reaching too far, these groups tell their uneasy followers, a different government can solve them by withdrawing its hands. These conservative activists and their congressional allies may be seeding disappointment by overestimating the impact of reducing government as much as liberals oversold the impact of enlarging government during the 1960s. But the conservative insurgency is likely to continue growing for some time before that reckoning arrives.

Indeed all signs point toward a widening conservative uprising against Washington. Though conservative populism was born largely with the Cold War, the conflict with the Soviets for years imposed a boundary on the Right's anger against the government. Even as distrust in Washington grew rapidly after the 1960s, for most on the Right government retained authority as a source of defense against the Soviets and internal subversion that might weaken those defenses. But with the end of the Cold War, that last line of defense for Washington crumbled. Suddenly there was no reason for the insurgents to hold their fire.

"In 1989, the whole world changed and it changed fairly rapidly," says Paul Jacob, the executive director of U.S. Term Limits, the largest group pushing that cause. "The Cold War was gone. At the same time the Cold War was gone, we saw the streets of Prague fill up and the government in Czechoslovakia go overnight. We saw the [Berlin] wall just tumble. . . . Then, with that inspiration, people were free to start looking at city hall and their state capitol and Washington. And all of a sudden they said, 'Geez, they're dictating to us. We don't really control our government.'"

The power of that sentiment was initially most visible in the rapid emergence of the term limits movement itself. From 1990 through 1994, term limits were approved in twenty-two states, including virtually every state that allows voters to pass law by referendum, by an average vote of nearly two to one. The movement's future was cast into doubt by a 1995 Supreme Court ruling that only a constitutional amendment can limit the terms for members of Congress, but its initiative campaigns furrowed the ground for the anti-politician arguments that became central both to Ross Perot's 1992 presidential campaign and the GOP drive against the Democratic Congress two years later. Leaders in the term limits movement effectively argued that in the world of unlimited tenure, the only people who sought political office were careerists who would not serve the public interest. It was a twist on the old Groucho Marx line: Anyone who wanted to join the club was the sort of person who shouldn't be let in. As Ed Crane, president of the libertarian think tank Cato Institute and a leading theorist of the term limits movement, wrote: "Ironically, the kind of person we should have in Congress is the person who would prefer to be in the productive, private sector. . . . By contrast, the kind of person who eagerly anticipates spending the rest of his life in politics is not likely to be 'representative' of his community." In the perfectly sealed catch-22 logic of term limit advocates, anyone who sought political office under the existing rules was unrepresentative.

THROUGH the early 1990s, the powerful response to those arguments in the term limit ballot campaigns demonstrated the growing alienation from Washington — and the solidifying strength of the conservative populist movement at the grassroots. But in Washington, divisions within the Right over the Bush administration muted the political impact of these changes. Though Ronald Reagan had disappointed some of the most ardent conservatives by failing to push seriously to restrict abortion, or limiting his attacks on the welfare state after 1982, he was still an inspiring figure that activists mobilized to support. With Bush, the populist Right was caught in no-man's land: He was not enough of an ally to inspire enthusiasm, nor enough of an enemy to rally against.

Though Bush, under the tutelage of his campaign manager, Lee Atwater, battered Michael S. Dukakis with conservative wedge issues in the 1988 general election, the conservative groups never considered him one of their own. Nor did Bush truly feel comfortable with them. Part of the problem was cultural: An administration of George Herbert Walker Bush, James A. Baker III, and Nicholas Brady, wealthy men who attended the finest schools, not surprisingly felt more comfortable with corporate executives than gun owners or small businessmen who selected their neckwear from J. C. Penney, not Hermès. But the larger problem was Bush's rejection of the unyielding antigovernment crusade that animated the conservative populist network. Lacking strong preferences on domestic policy, Bush vacillated between the polarizing tactics that marked his 1988 campaign and vestigial instincts toward moderation that alienated the conservative activists.

Gun control typified his drift. In the 1988 campaign, Bush had actively solicited the NRA's support and benefited from their $7 million independent expenditure on his behalf. During his presidency, he staunchly opposed the Brady bill to impose a waiting period on hand-gun purchases, as well as Democratic efforts to ban the sale of semi-automatic assault weapons (both of which became law under Clinton). But after a drug-abusing drifter with an AK-47 sprayed 105 rounds across a schoolyard in Stockton, California, in January 1989, killing five children in the process, Bush moved to preempt the more restrictive Democratic proposals by prohibiting merely the import of such assault weapons. That was hardly an extremist position: After the Stockton shooting, even Ronald Reagan criticized assault weapons. But Bush's stab at compromise infuriated the NRA, which opposed any concession. Once Bush implemented the import ban, the group never forgave him.

That pattern cut the mold. Bush's support for the Americans with Disabilities Act, and the Clean Air Act — legislation he considered essential for bolstering his credentials as a reasonable centrist — angered the NFIB, which considered them fountainheads of burdensome regulation. His acceptance of compromise civil rights legislation in 1991, after vetoing similar legislation one year earlier as a quota bill, pleased lobbyists for major corporations eager to tamp down the racially charged dispute but bitterly disappointed both social conservatives and small business. Regulations limiting development on environmentally sensitive wetlands angered the emerging property rights movement. Most important was Bush's decision to abandon his emphatic "read my lips, no new taxes" pledge from the 1988 campaign, which stamped him as a traitor not only to the small-business lobby and the antitax network, but to the conservative movement more broadly.

In the 1992 campaign the populist Right was dispirited and disorganized. Only Robertson's newly formed Christian Coalition stood loyally by Bush. The NRA sharply criticized Clinton but remained officially neutral. At the NFIB, there was no organizational push behind Bush. Clinton remained an object of suspicion among the members, but "they just didn't like George Bush," said John J. Motley, the NFIB's vice president at the time. The same was true among the emerging wise use groups in the West. This lack of enthusiasm was mirrored at Bush's reelection campaign, where the effort to mobilize the conservative coalitions extended little beyond checking the spelling on the names assembled for endorsement letters. Across the board, conservative groups experienced massive defection among their members to Perot; Bush's share of the vote from 1988 to 1992 dropped by twenty percentage points even among evangelical Christians. The conservative movement, like the GOP itself, looked dead on its feet.

THE CLINTON BACKLASH

The resurrection came with dizzying speed. For the conservative populist movement, Clinton's victory in 1992 was like a shot of adrenaline to the heart: painful but invigorating. With Clinton's election, the ambivalence of the Bush administration was replaced by the clarity of opposition. Clinton erased contradictions and submerged differences. The frustration pent up under Bush burst free in a frenzy of mobilization against the man that displaced him.

The reaction against Clinton added an ideological and ultimately partisan focus to what had been a broadly populist uprising against Congress and the government in Washington. Though conservatives seized on them first, both talk radio and the term limits movement appealed to more than just conservative voters. Up through Clinton's election, liberal reformers like Nader thought they could channel and benefit from the anti-establishment currents in these developments.

But Clinton polarized the electorate in a way that hastened the rightward drift of the populist current. Just like Jimmy Carter's, Clinton's struggle to find a centrist formula for governing had the paradoxical result of activating the Right without inspiring the Left. He produced a reaction without an initial action. The Left sulked over the centrist elements of Clinton's agenda — his support of the death penalty and the North American Free Trade Agreement, his failure to endorse a single-payer government-run health care system. But the antigovernment coalition was systematically enraged by Clinton's left-leaning initiatives — support for abortion rights and allowing gays to serve in the military; health care reform and higher taxes on the affluent; environmental reform of public lands policies in the West; gun control. "By the end of the two years," said Don Fierce, the director of strategic planning at the Republican National Committee, "he had activated each and every group." Together these groups joined in an uprising as powerful as any Washington had seen in years — powerful enough to help bring the Clinton administration to its knees.

Early in the administration a young conservative activist named Grover Norquist moved to channel and collect this backlash energy. If Rush Limbaugh symbolized the public face of the conservative populist movement, the little-known Norquist embodied its internal workings. Norquist was a bearded Harvard Business School graduate in his mid-thirties with the requisitely impudent baby boomer touches in his office near DuPont Circle. On his wall is a photo of Janis Joplin, and the screensaver on his computer flashes a succession of conservative heroes — from Limbaugh and William F. Buckley to Reagan and Margaret Thatcher. Norquist was an extravagant supporter of anticommunist insurgencies in the 1980s, and photos of him posing with various large-caliber weapons in Afghanistan, Albania, and Angola hang on his walls like bears' heads in a hunting lodge. He was known for hosting exuberant parties at a Capitol Hill town house crowded with political memorabilia. But his manner was a bit guarded and oddly formal: He often answered the phone by saying, "Grover G. Norquist."

Norquist's organization, Americans for Tax Reform, was somewhat less grand. Operating on a relatively small budget, it functioned as a clearinghouse linking local antitax activists and promoting antitax ballot initiatives in the states. It was best known for promoting a document Norquist described simply as "the pledge," in which politicians took an oath to oppose tax increases. With its theological simplicity, the pledge captured the essence of Norquist's political philosophy: He believed the Republican Party existed to reduce taxes and retrench government, and anyone who veered from those principles was at least a subject of suspicion and more commonly an obstacle to be crushed. Like Newt Gingrich, Norquist tended to view political disputes in quasi-Marxian terms, as the collision of historic forces proceeding like planets along unalterable courses. His posture toward Clinton's health care proposal typified his instinct for apocalyptic analysis: "Government-run health care was the whole onslaught," he said one blustery afternoon as evenly as if he were describing the weather. "Government-run health care meant that America would cease to be America. It would be a social democracy. Social democracies don't have free-market parties. They do not have antigovernment parties. They don't have Republican parties."

Listening to such soliloquies, there were those in Republican circles who considered Norquist a bit much, but his fans included Gingrich and Armey and the people around them. They saw in Norquist the rare operative with the capacity both to conceive the big picture and execute the intricate tactical maneuvers that advanced it. In truth, there were few people anywhere in the country who understood the nature of the changing conservative coalition as deeply as Norquist.

Norquist's passion was matching people and causes; even at Harvard Business School, while most of his classmates were producing treatises on how to structure a stock portfolio, he wrote a paper on how to properly structure the Republican coalition. He was especially ardent about aligning the two principal poles of the antigovernment movement: the economic and social conservatives, who had often been at odds during the Reagan and Bush years. Early in the Clinton administration, Norquist saw the opportunity to impart a structure to his vision. Groups of conservatives were gathering constantly in ad hoc meetings to oppose various elements of Clinton's agenda. Norquist organized a regular Wednesday morning meeting to bring together the most active grassroots organizations in the antigovernment coalition. His initial impulse was to unite the Right against Clinton's health care plan. But quickly, the group widened the offensive to encompass just about anything Clinton hoped to achieve — "everything that would slow them down and hurt them," Norquist recalls. "Everything that would make it less likely that they could take over the health industry." Meeting in Norquist's small office, sharing strategies, dreaming of better days, they fashioned themselves a council of war.

Paul Weyrich, the veteran conservative strategist, also hosted a weekly meeting of conservatives on Wednesday. But Norquist's quickly became seen as closer to the cutting edge. The cast of characters Norquist drew sometimes approached the eccentric: One occasional participant said the meetings made him feel as though he were stepping into the intergalactic bar in *Star Wars*. But Norquist attracted all the core elements of the antigovernment coalition: property rights groups, the NRA, antispending and antitax groups, the Christian Coalition, U.S. Term Limits. Party guru Bill Kristol or his associates sometimes dropped by, while Don Fierce of the RNC and Ed

Gillespie from the House Republican leadership attended regularly. "Everybody who thinks they are important wants to be there," said one regular attendee.

The presence of the RNC and House leadership aides at the Norquist meetings was particularly revealing. Under Clinton, the Republican Party's ties to the antigovernment coalition revitalized. Bitterness from the Bush administration lingered; at his first few Norquist meetings, RNC strategist Fierce felt he was there primarily to be yelled at. As traditional midwestern conservatives, Republican congressional leaders Bob Dole and Bob Michel (the prototypical "pre-Reagan Republicans" in Norquist's dismissive argot) weren't much more attuned to this grassroots network than Bush. Even Gingrich, though philosophically in sync, didn't fully understand its potential political impact, some thought.

But Clinton forced the GOP and the antigovernment coalition to bury their grudges. With Democrats holding both chambers of Congress and the White House, Republicans controlled no institutional platform from which to contest Clinton. They were compelled to find new means of carrying the battle, and mobilizing the conservative grassroots became one of the most important. Day after day, the groups and the Republicans found their interests converging. When House Democrats took their first recess in 1993 after approving Clinton's tax and budget plan, the National Republican Congressional Committee strafed legislators in twenty-four vulnerable districts with radio ads and faxes to talk radio show hosts attacking the vote; at the same time, Norquist's group and other tax opponents mobilized local antitax activists to pack the legislators' town meetings. ("You had the groups on the ground, us up here with air support, and the Democratic incumbent in the middle," said Dan Leonard, the communications director at the congressional committee.) When the U.S. Chamber of Commerce moved toward accommodation with Clinton at the outset of his term — refusing to oppose his tax increases and issuing a statement that offered support for requiring employers to purchase health insurance for their employees — groups in the antigovernment coalition joined with House Republicans in a bare-knuckled lobbying campaign that forced the chamber by early 1994 to fire the architect of the conciliatory strategy, William T. Archey.

That insurrection symbolized the shift in power within conservative ranks away from large companies toward small business. Even as late as the 1980s, many Democrats hoped to build alliances with the nation's twelve million small businesses as a counterweight to the power of big business in Washington. But small business proved a far more aggressive opponent of Clinton's initiatives than big business. "I'm not necessarily sure that you could even categorize the big-business community's attitude today that the government is the enemy," said John Motley, the NFIB's vice president for government affairs until leaving the organization halfway through 1995. "But certainly within the medium- and small-business sectors that is the attitude."

The gap between large and small business became particularly evident in the legislative debate over health care. Not only the chamber but most big-business organizations hesitated before taking a stand against Clinton's plan. But small business, opposed to the mandate that employers purchase insurance for their workers, became the backbone of the massive conservative organizing effort that bled away support on Capitol Hill for the administration's blueprint through 1994.

The health care fight knit together the conservative movement and the GOP in a complex feedback loop. While Republicans cast around for a response to Clinton's plan after its well-received introduction in fall 1993, groups in the antigovernment coalition, and sympathizers like Bill Kristol, pushed the party toward unconditional opposition. When Republicans finally moved to that position in 1994, they turned to conservative groups like the Christian Coalition and NFIB to organize the grassroots pressure they needed to support their resistance. They responded with faxes, phone calls, town meetings, and mailings that put enormous pressure on Democrats in competitive seats, particularly from the South and West. These lobbying efforts not only helped to derail Clinton's top domestic priority, but also reinforced the alliance between the groups in the conservative network and the most conservative elements within the GOP. Especially for small-business owners, the health care fight marked a turning point in what appears a long-term realignment into alliance with Republicans. "Our stand on the health care debate . . . has really cemented that relationship," said Motley.

The same calculations that allied the GOP and the groups in the conservative populist network also compelled the Republicans to deepen their efforts to co-opt talk radio. "It became an audience that we simply had to talk to every day," said Chuck Greener, who arrived as Republican National Committee communications director early in 1993. On one level, talk radio had for Republicans the appeal of a life vest to a drowning man. With Democrats controlling both ends of Pennsylvania Avenue, the Republicans held no levers of power, and power was the only reliable lure for the mainstream Washington press. Without power, the Republicans understood they were the chirp of dissent at the bottom of newspaper stories on the new majority's plans. "One thing that didn't take too long to figure out was if we didn't use new technology we were never going to get heard," Greener said. Talk radio assured Republicans a back channel of communication to the public.

But the talk circuit also offered Republicans something more. Greener and other Republican strategists understood that in an era when voters were skeptical of all politicians, talk show hosts could often make the case against Clinton and the Democratic Congress more persuasively than GOP politicians could themselves. To the extent talk show hosts echoed Republican arguments about health care or taxes or Clinton's ethics, Greener believed, they invested the indictment with more credibility than it would have coming from a purely partisan source. "They can often make the case to a broader universe than we can and more effectively," Greener said.

Technology enabled the Republicans to cement their new relationship with the talk show hosts. The key was the fax, which allowed the party to communicate with hundreds of shows — instantly. That speed revolutionized political argument. Republicans couldn't match Clinton's access to the network news, but even without such a national platform, the "blast fax" to hundreds of talk show hosts, other media outlets, and sympathetic grassroots groups allowed them to shower their response to his initiatives across the country as soon as he announced them — and sometimes before.

Congressional Democrats, left complacent by their seemingly impervious majority, were far behind. But the Clinton White House tried to exploit the new technologies. During the campaign, Clinton had been much more nimble than Bush about using the alternative means of communication; besieged by Jerry Brown and the Manhattan

tabloids during the New York primary in 1992, he refurbished his bat-
tered image with a folksy good-ol'-boy turn on the morning show of
Don Imus. "Don't be cruel, to a heart that's true," Clinton croaked in
a cracked voice when Imus asked him if he had any last words for New
Yorkers.

In office, the White House set up its own site on the Internet and
established an office under the direction of communications aide Jeff
Eller to book administration officials on talk radio. The morning after
Clinton announced his health care plan in September 1993, the White
House invited dozens of talk show hosts to broadcast from card tables
set up on the North Lawn. (Limbaugh declined the invitation.) Yet all
the attention the White House lavished on talk radio produced dimin-
ishing returns. Even the most aggressive marketing could not over-
come the rising hostility toward Clinton among many right-leaning
hosts and the reserve army of the discontented who tuned them in.
"I'm not sure Republicans are any better at it," said Eller after he left
the White House to join a political consulting firm in Texas. "They
just have a more receptive ear to the policies they want to put forth."

For Republicans, the most important ears — and lungs — on talk
radio belonged to Limbaugh. The Republicans barraged hundreds of
talk show hosts with faxes and phone calls, pitching guests, offering
new ideas on how to skewer Clinton and the Democrats. But on Lim-
baugh they lavished special attention. In the same way that an earlier
generation of Democratic leaders might have opened lines to the edi-
torial page editors of the *New York Times* and the *Washington Post*, Re-
publican leaders courted Limbaugh and sought his benediction for
their efforts. "He is an independent power," said Ed Gillespie, the aide
to Armey. "You have to know where he is and let him know where
you are."

Gingrich, Dick Armey, and RNC chairman Haley Barbour all
communicated directly with Limbaugh. On issues like health care and
the crime bill, they often provided Limbaugh with advance notice of
the party's strategy, hoping that he would begin to build an audience
for the arguments they intended to raise against Clinton. "The idea
was to start a public education campaign that you would then roll out
to a broader audience," said one GOP operative involved in the ef-
forts. Another Republican familiar with the courting of Limbaugh
said, "We'll call him and talk to him and let him know what our

strategy is. . . . Rush has a very keen strategic sense in terms of what's good timing and what matters. If you say to him, 'Look, we want to do this, but we can't do it tomorrow, we want to do it back after the August recess, or whatever,' he'll listen to you and listen to your side of that story on that front."

Limbaugh was actually cautious about maintaining his independence from the GOP. His support for conservative causes was indivisible. But he was always conscious of avoiding the appearance that he was merely the voice of the RNC. Unlike many other leading talk show hosts he almost never urged his listeners to call legislators that Republicans were hoping to pressure on an upcoming vote. (A rare exception to his no-phone-numbers rule came when he pointed his audience at Congress over the bank scandal in 1992.) He would listen to Republican entreaties to steer his commentary this way or that, but never offer them guarantees. "He thinks he is bigger than any party," said his collaborator John Fund. "He never does anyone else's handiwork. Because he got so big so fast, he is a creature of no one."

Yet for all his insistence on procedural independence, Limbaugh's substantive interests and the interests of the Republican leadership almost always converged. Limbaugh's distaste for Bill and Hillary Clinton was epic: He pursued the Clintons as tenaciously as Texas Ranger Frank Hamer pursued Bonnie and Clyde, and with as much conviction that he was on the trail of absolute evil. Limbaugh pounded Clinton's health care bill, highlighting each new conservative critique of the plan that appeared. He was one of the first conservatives to take up arms against the crime bill in 1994. And he worked tirelessly to keep the ethical charges against Clinton in the public eye; when Limbaugh reported on an account in a shadowy financial newsletter claiming — incorrectly — that associate White House counsel Vincent Foster's body had been moved before his death, the stock market tumbled. So relentlessly did Limbaugh cudgel Clinton that the conservative magazine *National Review* late in 1993 anointed him over Dole and Gingrich as "The Leader of the Opposition."

Limbaugh's increased prominence brought increased notoriety. More than once President Clinton lashed out against Limbaugh by name. In a testy interview from Air Force One with a St. Louis radio station, Clinton complained that Limbaugh would follow him on the air for three hours, without anyone challenging his facts or being offered an opportunity for rebuttal. "There's no truth detector," the President complained. "You won't get on afterwards and say what was true and what wasn't." Clinton had a case. Limbaugh let his ideological enthusiasms exceed the facts so often that the liberal advocacy group Fairness and Accuracy in Reporting was able to collect an entire book's worth of his inaccuracies. Limbaugh — who squealed under criticism to a degree surprising for someone who served up so much of it — fired back that the report was an attempt by the national media to silence him because "liberals are terrified of me." Several of the alleged mistakes, in fact, were more ideological quibbles than factual disputes. But on points large and small — from his assertion that more American Indians were alive today than when Columbus discovered the New World to his mistaken insistence that illegal immigrants were eligible for "everything you want" in social welfare benefits — the group found Limbaugh tangled in inconvenient facts. Limbaugh's detailed rebuttal refuted some of the claims, but failed to dent several of the group's accusations of inaccuracy, and even Fund acknowledged the report was "not a complete fabrication."

Limbaugh increasingly polarized opinion. As in the case of the other key institutions in the conservative populist network, his power derived more from the intensity than the breadth of his support. One national survey found that significantly more Americans held a negative than positive impression of him. But to his fans — more men than women, many of them college educated and younger — he could do no wrong. And each day for three hours, Limbaugh stirred that huge and receptive audience toward outrage at that man in the White House — and encouraged them to count the days to an election that would give them their chance to strip the President of his power.

OTHER groups in the coalition joined the Republicans in courting talk radio and creating new communications links between conservatives. The Heritage Foundation, the leading conservative think tank, even built a studio in its office just off Capitol Hill to entice talk hosts to broadcast from Washington. But the groups pushed out beyond the party institutions to stretch the possibilities of the new media. The Heritage Foundation and the *National Review* joined forces to launch an Internet Web site known as Town Hall that gathered in one place reports, articles, and other ideological ammunition from more than a dozen leading conservative organizations. The NRA and Christian Coalition likewise launched programs to communicate with their members and other sympathizers through internal computer bulletin boards and by posting information on the Internet. Characteristically, the NRA operation was particularly aggressive. Anyone interested in the cause (even those who did not belong to the organization) could sign up for regular e-mail alerts that sometimes came at the pace of four or five a day; switching on their computers, gun aficionados would receive notices to call the governor of Oregon to support an NRA bill, or the locations for congressional town meetings where they could make the case against the assault weapon ban — along with the helpful instruction to "please dress appropriately — suits and/or ties make a better impression than sports or outdoor wear."

In January 1994, the RNC launched its hour-long weekly television show, *Rising Tide*. Weyrich, the veteran conservative organizer, went the RNC one better, opening his own television network known as National Empowerment Television. Operating from his Capitol Hill office, with a bare-bones staff, the network offered to limited distribution at first a succession of aspiring Limbaughs and George Wills — from the "Mitchells in the Morning," a self-caffeinated young husband-and-wife team of right-thinking economists, to the "Youngbloods," a strictly conservative twenty-something version of the McLaughlin Group. Gingrich hosted a program on technology. The NRA and the Cato Institute sponsored their own shows. As surely as if some "environmental wacko" had designed the operation, everything was recycled. Every morning, Weyrich's office collected highlights from the previous day's shows and faxed them to a list of over one thousand talk show hosts. The NRA posted transcripts of its shows — often devoted to gun owners claiming abuse by federal law enforcement officials — on the Internet.

Liberals could point to nothing comparable. Bob Chlopak, a veteran liberal organizer who had directed a coalition supporting Clinton's health care plan, appeared on a show at NET one night and came away muttering the way an Iraqi general might have if given a tour of the American force in Desert Storm. "A huge part of the conservative revolution is they have mastered modern communications," he said later. "You have Christian radio, and all the talk on the mainstream stations. And we have nothing like that. The ability to communicate quickly, to inject emotion into people's living rooms, is a very powerful weapon."

In comparison to talk radio, however, this Niagara of conservative chatter reached only limited audiences, almost all of whom supported the cause to begin with. The computer networks spoke to a potentially larger constituency, but their impact was measured mostly in anticipation. Even Herb Berkowitz, the Heritage Foundation's top public relations official, felt that "the jury . . . is still out on the Internet and the 'information superhighway.'" Moreover, the new computer technologies exposed their sponsors to risks difficult to control — as the NRA learned when it was forced to shut down a public computer bulletin board it maintained following the revelation that someone posted on it a recipe for constructing a bomb.

Talk radio reached almost half the country — at least sometimes — with about one in six Americans a regular listener. Even there polls showed the audience was predominantly conservative to begin with. That led some to denigrate talk radio as only preaching to the converted. But that was precisely its strength. The affinity between host and audience made talk radio a mobilizing tool of great power. It stoked anger, sharpened resentments, personalized policy disputes, and clarified issues in a manner that reduced the middle ground. The widening reach of talk radio emboldened Republicans and the conservative populist groups to greater militance against Clinton by bolstering their confidence that they could reach their constituency even when the networks and major newspapers sided with the President. And, as talk radio's impact on its audience became more apparent, it created a powerful echo effect, as the mainstream press felt compelled to devote more coverage to the issues that burned up the phone lines. The conservatives knew they could not ignore traditional forums like the Sunday morning talk shows or the network news, but they feared opposition from these institutions less. They didn't need kind words from Tim Russert or Peter Jennings. They had their own channel. They had Rush.

THE NEW CONSERVATIVE NETWORK

In fact, by the middle of the Clinton administration, the conservative populist movement had developed what might be termed an alternative mobilization network — a powerful system of inculcating and activating support that functioned largely under the radar of its Democratic opponents and the national media.

Through Clinton's first year, this system took its fledgling steps. Talk radio rebellions, some encouraged with faxes from Republican operatives, fanned brush fires over Clinton's missteps on gays in the military, the administration's budget package, and its reforms in western land policies. Limbaugh, Perot, the *Wall Street Journal* editorial page, and several dozen other talk show hosts helped Republicans push through a change in House rules that made it easier for the minority to bring directly to a floor vote legislation that Democratic committee chairmen had bottled up. Even more powerful evidence of the new network's potential came early in 1994 when advocates of home-schooling, many of them religious conservatives, barraged Congress with faxes and phone calls protesting a Democratic education bill that they believed would require parents teaching their children at home to obtain federal certification. Democrats insisted the bill would do no such thing; the home-schoolers didn't believe them. Fueled by talk radio, religious broadcasters, messages posted on computer bulletin boards, and fax trees that spread their roots at blistering speed, the uprising against the bill hit Congress with such unanticipated ferocity that Democrats were forced to scramble in retreat. Within days the House voted 424–1 to exempt home schools from the certification requirements.

These were preliminary skirmishes for the battle over the crime bill that consumed Washington the next summer. More than anything before it, the struggle over the crime bill showed the strength of the antigovernment coalition and the power of its alternative communication network to move public opinion. It revealed to the White House, to the RNC, and to congressional Republicans how powerful a force was converging in the populist Right.

At the center of this insurgent army was a middle-aged grandmother named Tanya K. Metaksa. Metaksa had only recently been appointed as the NRA's chief lobbyist, or more formally, executive director of the NRA's Institute for Legislative Affairs. That was the second-ranking position in the NRA hierarchy. The top job was held by Wayne LaPierre, the organization's executive vice president, who frequently pleaded the group's case on television. LaPierre moved into control in 1991, the representative of a hard-line faction that felt Warren Cassidy, his predecessor, had been too conciliatory with gun-control advocates. Under LaPierre the organization lavished money on direct mail to enlarge its membership and restore its faded reputation as an enforcer on Capitol Hill. LaPierre spent so heavily that he drew internal criticism for depleting the organization's financial reserves: Leaked internal documents showed the organization ran cumulative operating deficits of $69 million between 1991 and 1993. But the aggressive mail program did boost the group's membership from a low point of about 2.3 million back to 3.5 million halfway through the Clinton administration, which was like adding another million or so bullets to the political arsenal the NRA pointed at unfriendly legislators. In early 1994, the organization brought in Metaksa to manage the armory.

LaPierre had a slightly distracted air, as though focusing on something in the distance. Metaksa is the opposite: short, squat, and intense. She has steel-gray hair and a steely manner somehow hardened rather than softened by a quick, rueful laugh. She looks like she would be equally comfortable as a schoolteacher or a prison guard.

Metaksa had actually taught school — high school history in Connecticut — in her roundabout route to the NRA. The stepdaughter of conservative columnist John Chamberlain, she found her calling in hardball politics only after exhausting a succession of more genteel alternatives. As a young Smith graduate in the late 1950s, she worked as a photographer in New York, snapping babies and memorializing medical procedures; then she married, and followed her husband to Colorado and Connecticut, where she worked in a variety of jobs and raised three children in a small town near Hartford. Her husband liked target shooting, and Metaksa picked up the avocation: "We would get a baby-sitter once a week," she said, "and instead of bowling we went shooting." After Congress passed a crime bill in 1968 that banned the mail-order sale of guns and ammunition, she took her first step into politics, organizing Connecticut hunters in 1970 against Thomas Dodd, a Democratic senator seeking reelection. Metaksa liked politics, had a good feel for the rough and tumble, and a few years later accepted an offer from the NRA to run its campaign against a Massachusetts ballot initiative to ban handguns. The campaign crushed the initiative by a margin of more than two to one, a showing that left the desired impression in the NRA headquarters. After the campaign she moved her family to Washington and began work as an NRA lobbyist.

The NRA is not an easy place to work; like a banana republic, it combines palace intrigues, contending factions, lots of guns, and periodic coups. Before too long, Metaksa was caught on the wrong side of an uprising; she left the organization in 1980, and though she insists she jumped, Cassidy, her boss at the time, says she was pushed out for being too confrontational. Metaksa landed at the 1980 Reagan campaign, organizing support from gun owners, then worked for New York Senator Al D'Amato, before launching yet another career by forming a computer consulting company. But she retained her ties to the NRA and inched back toward power by joining the organization's board in 1991. As the organization moved steadily to the right through the early 1990s, her pugnacity no longer appeared a handicap. The dominant forces on the board, led by Neal Knox, a former gun magazine editor and NRA lobbyist who once suggested that the assassinations of John and Robert Kennedy and Martin Luther King were part of a conspiracy to disarm gun owners, were looking for a lobbyist who would wage house-to-house combat against Clinton. In Metaksa they found an eager recruit.

It is the lot of the NRA lobbyist to challenge the conventional definition of "unreasonable." Gun-control advocates wave at them the grisly evidence of mass shootings in a Sacramento schoolyard or a Long Island railroad commuter train and the NRA response is unwavering: all the more reason to punish criminals and not deny ordinary citizens the means to defend themselves. In the NRA's hands, the arguments of the antigovernment coalition ascend to a dizzying, if purist, pinnacle — the point at which the government becomes literally the enemy. "The right to keep and bear arms," LaPierre writes in his 1994 book, *Guns, Crime and Freedom*, "[is] the ultimate safeguard against despotism and genocide." In the NRA, it is an article of faith that it can happen here.

The NRA's crystalline intransigence made it a singular group in a city built on the deal. The NRA's refusal to compromise deepened its sense of encirclement and embattlement, which hardened its conviction not to compromise. It has borne the scorn of editorial pages, denunciations from the White House, high-profile resignations from longtime supporters like former President George Bush and Democratic Representative John D. Dingell, internal grumbling from its conservationist and sportsman wings, and a rift with many police organizations (once among its closest allies) over its refusal to support even the banning of armor-piercing "cop-killer" bullets, much less semi-automatic assault weapons. But on its core concerns, the NRA has never shifted direction, never softened, never conceded. It could not be reasoned with, or bought off, or intimidated. It was the Terminator of lobbying organizations.

That was the case with the crime bill. The NRA lost when the Senate approved a ban on nineteen types of semi-automatic assault weapons by two votes in November 1993. It lost again when the House banned assault weapons by two votes in May 1994. As the crime bill moved into a House-Senate conference that summer, even some of the NRA's principal supporters despaired of removing a provision that already had cleared both chambers and was supported by roughly two-thirds of the public. House Judiciary Committee Chairman Jack Brooks of Texas, a crusty longtime NRA ally who had led the fight against the assault weapon ban, privately urged the organization to accept some limits on the semi-automatic weapons. The NRA instead set out to stop the crime bill.

At first it appeared they would have about as much chance as of stopping a bullet. Crime topped the polls as the voters' highest priority. The House had approved the assault weapon ban as a stand-alone measure, but the Senate had embedded it into the overall crime bill, and the conference followed that precedent. That meant the assault ban was now linked to a bill that contained nearly $9 billion in funding for prisons, another $9 billion to redeem Clinton's campaign promise of funding one hundred thousand new police officers, and nearly $8 billion in social programs aimed at "crime prevention," with billions more sloshing around to reimburse states for incarcerating illegal aliens or to launch programs to deter violence against women, some $33 billion in all.

Legislators from all points on the ideological spectrum could find something objectionable in the huge package, but the administration assumed that, in the end, a majority would find too much in it too attractive to walk away. Metaksa, her own job threatened by the administration's successes on gun control, had no choice but to believe otherwise. The administration gave her the opening she needed by wasting weeks in negotiations with House liberals over the provision in the legislation allowing prisoners on death row to challenge their sentences as racially biased. With the administration focused on mollifying the Left, Metaksa seized the opportunity to agitate the right. To pressure the seventy-seven Democrats who had opposed the assault weapon ban in May, she mobilized gun owners in their districts with the stealth tools of the conservative network: direct mail, faxes, and notices on the Internet. She also accelerated the distribution of campaign contributions to NRA supporters. Then on the weekend of July 4, she hired Craig Shirley, a conservative public relations specialist, to organize a media campaign against the bill.

Shirley's plan of action showed how dramatically the new means of communication had enlarged the political options for conservatives. He did not spend a moment worrying about convincing the *Washington Post* or the television networks. From the start his focus was making the case against the bill on talk radio, where he knew he could find an audience both sympathetic to his message and eager to take up arms against any initiative dear to Clinton. Once, twice, sometimes three times a day through the month of July, Shirley "blast-faxed" talking points against the bill to 735 right-of-center talk radio stations. "It was anecdotal bite-sized information," he said, "all designed to get people mad." From some twenty different organizations in the antigovernment coalition, Shirley recruited spokesmen and dispatched them onto the airwaves to batter the bill. Typical was Steve Moore at the Cato Institute. For two weeks in the damp depths of the Washington summer, Moore barely left his desk; hour after hour he sat behind his speakerphone, seeding doubts about the bill on programs in San Diego and Baton Rouge and Richmond. Shirley lined up drive time in Hazeltown, Pennsylvania, and Christian radio in Louisiana. Moore delivered his pitch. He felt like a guerrilla, operating behind enemy lines.

Like most of Shirley's recruits, Moore pounded away at the billions of dollars in social spending that House Democrats had added to the bill to cement support from liberal and minority members. That theme — which Limbaugh had been among the first to emphasize — became the centerpiece of the NRA campaign against the bill. The focus was revealing in two respects. In deciding to tar the legislation as a "pork bill," Metaksa showed a keen sense for the package's Achilles' heel at a time when many Americans viewed government spending itself as a crime. But the decision to fight the bill on fiscal grounds also implicitly acknowledged that the NRA could not win the argument on the central issue of its concern, the assault weapon ban. In that sense, the NRA's public campaign against the crime bill testified simultaneously to its strength and its weakness.

Yet it was only the NRA's strength that was most immediately apparent. On Thursday, August 11, by a vote of 225–210, the House voted down Clinton's crime bill by rejecting the procedural rule to bring it to the floor. As usual almost all Republicans voted against the rule; they typically voted against such procedural measures en bloc to protest the manner in which the majority Democrats manipulated the House rules to their advantage. The shock was that fifty-eight Democrats joined with them. Ten were members of the Black Caucus opposed to the death penalty. The other forty-eight were white Democrats — all but one of whom had originally voted against the assault weapon ban. Those Democrats, most of them representing rural districts, had been forced to choose between the President and the NRA — and the NRA campaign had convinced them they had more to fear from gun owners than from the President.

Coming late on a hot, rainy afternoon, the vote was the rare moment of genuine astonishment in Washington. Initially no one knew how to react. The vote marked the arrival of the conservative coalition's new methods of political mobilization. Republicans basked in the credit for the most traumatic moment of Clinton's presidency (direct mail contributions to the RNC soared in the days after the vote), but the party had less to do with the result than the NRA and the network of conservative activists and talk radio hosts it assembled. The crime bill was the Right's Tet; the moment the guerrilla army came out of the jungle. This was not an obscure contest over internal House rules or home-schooling. The bill was a top presidential priority that had drawn praise from most newspapers and the mainstream media; until the very last days before the vote, the conservative fax and talk radio campaign against it had been almost invisible in Washington.

In the hours immediately after the defeat, President Clinton sought to rally the public against the NRA and the Republicans. His goal was to force the House to reconsider the same bill and pass it. Over the weekend, he marshaled the traditional tools of presidential persuasion, denouncing his opponents in speeches and appearances, all widely covered in the national press. But the public uprising never occurred. With NRA television ads (featuring Charlton Heston as the spokesman) and an all-points offensive on talk radio, the conservative coalition fought the White House to a standstill. In their hearts, those who voted against the bill were almost certainly motivated more by opposition to the assault ban or simple partisanship than concern about wasteful spending. But the fortress that the NRA had built around that opposition — the argument that the bill was stuffed with misguided liberal "pork" — did not crack. Primarily through the powerful imprint of talk radio, the conservative campaign stamped the pork label on the bill so firmly that both the moderate Republicans and pro-gun Democrats, the principal targets of Clinton's efforts, felt safe in defying him. "Millions of Americans knew the pork argument before anybody sat down and wrote it in the *Washington Post* or the *New York Times*," marveled Ron Klain, the chief administration strategist on the bill. Within days the White House glumly concluded that the Hill could not be moved.

By the Monday following the vote, Clinton was forced to shift gears and open negotiations to revise the bill. Many conservative Republicans and the NRA were hoping to kill the legislation entirely. But Gingrich — in a decision that Metaksa and others would bitterly second-guess for months — concluded he could not hold the moderate Republicans to a posture of total opposition and allowed them to negotiate a deal with the administration. Around-the-clock bargaining reduced some social spending and toughened other sections of the bill but retained the assault weapon ban, which many of the moderate Republicans supported. The revised package passed the House ten days after the initial vote, and after another harrowing passage, cleared the Senate later in August. At the RNC headquarters, angry conservatives offered their own verdict on the result. The flood of contributions temporarily fell to a trickle: better to fight and lose than compromise and win, Barbour and his aides concluded.

The crime bill's narrow escape suggested limits to the conservative network's power to shape public opinion: The moderate suburban Republicans still felt uncomfortable going home without a bill. But that was just one small step from total victory. Crime was to be one of the crowning achievements of Clinton and the Democratic Congress. But in the fall, Republicans used the bill as a sword far more than Democrats raised it as a shield. On the day the House finally approved the crime bill, Craig Shirley called Tanya Metaksa at the NRA. "I feel like it's the Alamo," Shirley said. "We lost the battle but we did enough damage that we're going to win the war."

INDEED, as Congress finally left Washington to contest the fall election, an enormous gulf in enthusiasm and energy separated the two coalitions. The Left stumbled toward the election as dazed as the survivors of an earthquake, while the Right pulsed with the sense of opportunity. Everywhere Republican candidates spoke the language of conservative populism, promising to defend the productive elements of society against a parasitic political class and an indolent, violent underclass. Limbaugh summoned his legions to the battlements: "We're going to go in," he declared. "We're going to conquer. And we ain't getting out." The House Republicans consulted closely with the groups in drafting their Contract and designed its specifics largely to reflect their priorities. Hearing their own agenda echoed, the antigovernment coalition poured money and volunteers into Republican campaigns. "They had the only foot soldiers out there," said Celinda Lake, the Democratic pollster.

In some races, Democrats turned the focus back on their critics in the conservative populist movement, particularly the NRA; in Nebraska, Senator Bob Kerrey, a Medal of Honor winner, responded to an NRA attack ad with a powerful commercial that linked his opposition to assault weapons with his service in Vietnam. But across the South and Mountain West, and in many rural districts of the Midwest, Democrats felt as though they were running into a gale. The campaigns from the populist antigovernment groups and the insistent blare of talk radio provided a powerful echo for the direct Republican efforts, reinforcing the GOP themes, energizing their core voters, and exerting a powerful crossover appeal for conservative Democrats. "I hauled the union members to the polls," lamented Democratic Oklahoma Representative Dave McCurdy, who lost a race for the Senate, "and they voted with the NRA."

So it went, for Democrats across the country. It was too easy for Clinton to claim, as he did after the election, that the NRA had cost the Democrats control of the House; that exaggerated the group's role

198 / *Storming the Gates*

and minimized his own (not to mention the failure of the congressional Democrats themselves). Likewise, the Republican freshmen overstated their debt to Limbaugh when they honored him at a dinner as their "majority maker." Much larger forces of alienation against Clinton and government propelled the GOP sweep. But the groups in the antigovernment coalition, and their sympathizers in the talk radio studios, had delivered critical contributions to the Republican cause. Exit polls and other post-election surveys showed that the key elements of the coalition all broke decisively toward the GOP: Nearly eight in ten fundamentalist Christians, 69 percent of gun owners, two-thirds of Ross Perot supporters, nearly two-thirds of regular talk radio listeners, and almost 60 percent of small-business owners, small-business employees, and term limit supporters, all voted Republican in the congressional election. Gun owners alone provided one-third of the total votes Republican congressional candidates received in the midterm election.

After the disarray of 1992, the groups that comprise the conservative populist coalition could not have demonstrated their vitality in any more emphatic terms. In the wreckage of the Democratic Congress stood the evidence of their own revival.

THE power and drive of these groups make them the most turbulent force in American politics. Republicans have always disparaged the Democratic Party as merely a collection of interests — an amalgam of feminists, public sector unions, minorities, and gays — who view the party as a vehicle to advance their own ambitions and agendas but extend it no overriding loyalty. Now, the Republicans are evolving into the same position, where the driving energy in the party is actually *outside* the party — and sometimes outside the political mainstream — in the property rights and antitax activists, small-business owners, term limit advocates, gun owners, Perot-style independents, and conservative Christians who comprise the antigovernment coalition.

In the short run, this alliance has undeniably bolstered the GOP. After the congressional sweep in 1994, the new Republican leadership in the House integrated the conservative network into a smoothly functioning machine lobbying for the Contract With America. Norquist's dream of bringing together social and economic conservatives was taken to a new level every Thursday in a Capitol meeting room, where Representative John Boehner, the chairman of the House Republican Conference, presided over a weekly strategy session with representatives of almost two dozen interest groups, many of whom had never worked together before. Those attending included officials from trade associations and traditional business interests long allied with the GOP; but the core groups were two pillars of the populist antigovernment coalition: the National Federation of Independent Business and the Christian Coalition. The Christian Coalition alone invested $1 million in lobbying for the Contract, and the small-business owners activated their extensive grassroots network behind key elements, such as regulatory reform, and the tax plan; at one point, the NFIB was generating 265,000 pieces of mail per week behind the Contract bill to limit private lawsuits. In return for their support, the groups were systematically included in tactical and substantive legislative deliberations to an almost unprecedented degree. Likewise, Gingrich provided talk radio unprecedented access, soliciting hosts to broadcast directly from the Capitol, including his own chambers, throughout the drive to pass the Contract. These unprecedented efforts helped the Republican leadership pass all the elements in the Contract through the House, with the exception only of the constitutional amendment to impose term limits on Congress.

Yet this embrace imposes obligations on both sides. The groups' increasing influence means that the Republicans, like Democrats on such issues as civil rights, are maneuvering within narrowing boundaries of permissible dissent. It may be just as difficult now for Republicans to nominate a candidate who supports abortion rights or gun control as it is for Democrats to select a nominee who would abandon affirmative action or champion right-to-work laws. Bob Dole's posture in the period leading into his presidential announcement in 1995 signified the change. As the clear front-runner for the party nomination, Dole was in a position to define the party. But in the weeks before his presidential announcement, he behaved more like Walter Mondale in 1984, pledging fealty to the demands of one constituency group after another. At one point, he wrote the NRA promising to lead the fight to repeal the ban on assault weapons Congress had approved the previous year. (Both Dole and Gingrich have promised the NRA that Congress will pass no gun-control legislation so long as Republicans control the gavels.) Then he embraced a property rights bill far more expansive than earlier versions he supported. Finally, he summoned Norquist to his office and signed the no-new-taxes pledge Norquist's group promotes — the same pledge that Dole had refused to sign during the campaign in 1988.

Already the groups in the antigovernment coalition play a significant role in shaping the GOP's internal balance of power. As the groups' voices grow louder inside the party, moderate and even more traditionally conservative voices are further drowned out. The groups' ties are strongest to the most devoutly antigovernment House Republicans and House alumni in the Senate. As the House raced to complete passage of the Contract With America, the groups at times effectively functioned as agents of the House leadership, turning the screws on Republicans wavering over aspects of Gingrich's blueprint. When a coalition of deficit hawks and moderates launched a mini-rebellion against the cost of the Contract's tax cut, Norquist's group sent a clear shot across their bow by flooding faxes and direct mail into the district of one of the revolt's leaders, Fred Upton of Michigan; another conservative group fired off a burst of radio ads. "Fred," said one House leadership aide, "hit the panic button in a heartbeat." With Gingrich and Armey providing enormous pressure from the other end, the rebels saw themselves trapped in a pincer movement. The revolt collapsed and the bill passed comfortably. Norquist later let it be known that he refused even to accept Upton's calls — until Gingrich, in the name of party harmony, asked him to do so. That spoke volumes about the shifting locus of power within the party.

THE vibrancy of the Right poses complex challenges to the Republicans. Over the long run, meeting the expectations of the groups in the antigovernment alliance could threaten the GOP as much as disappointing them. By their nature advocacy groups are insatiable; however much policy moves in their direction, they seek to take it another step. While the groups in the conservative coalition have proven enormously successful at orchestrating a backlash against Clinton's excesses, all at times have inspired backlashes against their own. Independent voters are as skeptical of many of the conservative groups' priorities — like banning abortion and loosening gun control — as they are of liberal agendas like affirmative action.

The catastrophic bombing of a federal office building in Oklahoma City in April 1995 underscored the risk of giving any group too much sway over the party's agenda. After the bombing, some liberal commentators quickly suggested that the relentless conservative attempt to portray government as the enemy had contributed to a climate conducive to the attack. Most analysts rightly rejected that broad-brush association. But more specific areas of convergence raised uncomfortable questions for Republican politicians about their allies.

Particularly troubling were the vituperative attacks from mainstream gun-owner groups and other conservative voices on gun-control laws and the federal agents who enforce them. The NRA, of course, does not advocate violence. But NRA condemnation of the Bureau of Alcohol, Tobacco and Firearms, the agency charged with enforcing federal gun laws, veered dangerously close to the rhetoric of the militantly anti–gun control antitax citizens' militias linked to the Oklahoma City attack. In one fund-raising letter, Wayne LaPierre of the NRA warned of "jackbooted government thugs [who] . . . take away our constitutional rights, break in our doors, seize our guns, destroy our property, and even injure or kill us." That language led former President Bush to resign from the group, and created many uncomfortable moments for Republicans (led by Bob Dole) who had annealed themselves to the NRA. (Ultimately the NRA was forced to apologize for its language.) And with public attention riveted on shadowy militia corps marching through the woods with assault weapons, congressional Republicans were forced to place on hold their plans to repeal the assault weapon ban or loosen other gun laws. These contortions provided Democrats an opening to effectively charge the GOP with carrying the water for an extremist special interest, the same weapon conservatives had wielded with great effectiveness against Democrats for the previous twenty years.

The rapidly shifting ground suggested a larger moral. The resurgence of the conservative populist movement has fueled the Republican political revival and created a political structure both to channel and amplify the widespread discontent about government. But the movement is a fundamentally centrifugal, destabilizing political force that threatens the GOP position over the long term even as it bolsters it in the near term. The Republicans face an ongoing challenge to convince these protest movements that they are the most effective vehicle to advance their ambitions. If that convergence of interest shatters, there is no larger glue to hold these movements to the Republican coalition — or perhaps to the two-party system at all. "The two-party system is in a deteriorating position because of declining trust," says Don Fierce of the RNC. "If we don't live up to what we say we'll do, what will these groups do? They go to a third party."

5

Dixie Rising

I N 1994, THE REPUBLICAN PARTY captured the
South, and the South captured the Republican Party. Both sides of
this transformation will change American politics into the foresee-
able future. In a geographical shift of seismic proportions, the
1994 elections affirmed the South, the largest prize of all the political
regions in the country, as the new Republican heartland. Republicans
made significant — in some cases startling — advances throughout
the region, significantly raising the strength of the Dixie accent in a
party that had its origins in opposition to southern slave owners.
While the differences that separate southern and northern Republi-
cans may be far smaller than those that historically divided southern
and northern Democrats, Republicans who sprouted from southern
soil remain culturally and philosophically distinct from those in the
North. Added to the GOP's long-standing western base, the expansion
of Republican power in the South deepens all the conservative tenden-
cies of the party, from opposition to new taxes and support for higher
defense spending to a more central role for social issues such as abor-
tion and school prayer. "Southern Republicans tend to be more con-
servative, they tend to be more philosophically committed, and they
tend to be more confrontational," said Texas Senator Phil Gramm,
whose career is the walking embodiment of all three.

Few stories in modern American politics are as rich or as enduring as the partisan transformation of the South. Over the past half century, politicians, political scientists, historians, journalists, and others have chronicled the breakup of the southern Democratic Party and the steady erosion of the one-party South. The current state of this evolution to two-party politics makes it easy to forget how far and how fast the Republicans actually have traveled. One measure of the distance between then and now is the judgment on the party delivered by the late V. O. Key Jr., whose pioneering work, *Southern Politics in State and Nation*, remains an essential companion in understanding the political geography of the country's most distinctive region. In 1949, Key wrote of the Republican Party, "It scarcely deserves the name of party. It wavers somewhat between an esoteric cult on the order of a lodge and a conspiracy for plunder in accord with the accepted customs of our politics. Its exact position on the cult-conspiracy scale varies from place to place and from time to time. Only in North Carolina, Virginia and Tennessee do the Republicans approximate the reality of a political party." A few years later, on the eve of the 1952 election that would prove to be a breakthrough for the Republicans, political scientist Alex Heard wrote, "To many citizens of the South, a Republican is a curiosity." Such a curiosity that in east Texas they tell the story of a sheriff who years ago tossed out two votes for a Republican presidential candidate on the presumption that someone had voted twice.

No one would claim that today, for the Republican Party in America wears a distinctly southern face, particularly in the Congress. This is no longer the party that, for a generation, was led in Congress by politicians from the Midwest or Northeast, men like Joseph Martin of Massachusetts, the last Republican Speaker before Newt Gingrich; Everett Dirksen of Illinois, the Senate Republican leader in the 1960s; or a succession of House Republican leaders: Charles Halleck of Indiana; Gerald Ford of Michigan; and Bob Michel of Illinois. Today, the three top-ranking Republicans in the House are all southerners: Speaker Newt Gingrich of Georgia, Majority Leader Dick Armey, and GOP Whip Tom DeLay, both of Texas. So are the chairmen of two of the most powerful committees in the chamber: Texan Bill Archer of the Ways and Means Committee, and Louisianan Bob Livingston of the Appropriations Committee. Bob Dole may be the majority leader of the Senate, but beneath him in the next tiers of leadership stands a virtual army of southern conservatives: Trent Lott and Thad Cochran of Mississippi, Don Nickles of Oklahoma, Connie Mack of Florida, and of course Gramm, who surrendered his leadership position to run for President.

After a century as the smallest of minorities, the Republican Party now stands as a vibrant force throughout the South — in some states the dominant force — with little on the horizon likely to reverse trends that have been increasing the party's strength for a generation. Twenty-six years ago, political analyst Kevin Phillips, then a young veteran of Richard Nixon's 1968 campaign, predicted Republicans would seize control of the South in his book *The Emerging Republican Majority*. Phillips cited a host of evidence, from the growing disaffection of white southerners to the national Democratic Party and the increasing hold on the Democratic Party's southern apparatus by African-Americans to the growing suburban middle class and the influx of migrants from the North, all of which drove southern politics to a new balance of power in the postwar era. To read Phillips today is a little like watching the movie *Back to the Future*. Democrats understood their own predicament, but appeared powerless to stop the forces that overwhelmed them from almost every direction. In 1968, a young college professor and executive director of the Democratic Party in South Carolina wrote an essay that, like Phillips's work, examined the political trends in his region and concluded that, unless something dramatic and unexpected occurred to halt them, the roles of the two political parties would be reversed by the end of the century. The Democrats, he predicted, faced a future as the lesser party in the South, a strained coalition consisting largely of white liberals and African-Americans, while the Republican Party would consolidate the white middle and upper class into the new majority. The author of that monograph was Don Fowler, who in early 1995, after southern Democrats had suffered one of their worst defeats ever, was chosen as chairman of the Democratic National Committee and presented with the task of attempting to dam up what has been a mighty river of change in his native region.

The elections of 1994 represented not just another step forward for the Republicans, but the kind of quantum change that has the power to remake the politics of a region — and by implication the entire nation — for a generation. For the first time in this century, southern Republicans emerged from an election in control of a majority of the governorships, a majority of the seats in the U.S. Senate, and, most significant of all, a majority of the seats in the U.S. House. Republicans also gained 119 southern state legislative seats and captured control of three state legislative chambers, the Florida Senate, North Carolina House, and the South Carolina House. For the first time since Reconstruction, Republicans elected the Speakers of two southern legislatures.

Results in some states were nothing short of extraordinary. In Tennessee, Republicans won the governorship, both Senate seats, and two more seats in the House. In North Carolina, they added twenty-six seats in the state House and thirteen in the state Senate. In Texas and South Carolina, they won a majority of statewide constitutional offices. In just four years, the Georgia congressional delegation went from nine Democrats and one Republican to seven Republicans and four Democrats. When Democrat Nathan Deal switched to the GOP in the spring of 1995, that left the split at eight to three in favor of the GOP, with all eight Republicans white and all three Democrats African-Americans. Republicans won not only high-profile contests for governor or Senate but penetrated far down the ballot to win local offices like sheriff or justice of the peace. As the University of South Carolina's Blease Graham said, "When the Republicans start electing sheriffs, watch out. That's as grassroots as it gets."

Given the inexorable trends in presidential elections over the past four decades, the changes may not seem startling, but few people anticipated that the Republican force would hit the South with such a pounding fury in November 1994. Despite the defection problems in presidential elections, Democratic candidates in the South long assumed that they could insulate themselves from what southern voters regarded as the most unappealing aspects of the national party. The 1994 elections robbed them of that illusion, perhaps for good, in large part because white southern voters rebelled against one of their own in the White House. Several factors combined to produce the earthquake, from the "rising tide lifts all boats" nature of national voting patterns, to the impact of redistricting on boundaries that long had favored Democrats, to the evolutionary nature of the changes that had been under way in the region. But Clinton's presidency became a solidifying force for Republican voters in the South that southern Democratic candidates could not overcome, and southern Republican leaders like Gingrich and party chairman Haley Barbour, intuitively recognizing the possibility for a historical transformation in their region, made the South a special focus in their election strategy.

Congressional Quarterly's Rhodes Cook, in one of a number of perceptive post-election articles about 1994, pointed out that, in the postwar period, southern Democratic congressional candidates have fared worst when southern Democrats held the presidency. Although Lyndon Johnson won a landslide in 1964, his civil rights policies, while morally necessary for the future of the country, fractured his own political party, and Republicans more than doubled their strength in the House during his tenure in the White House. Jimmy Carter's presidency not only reinforced the ideological differences between southern Democrats and the national party, but embarrassed his native South by Carter's failures of leadership, symbolized by the long Iranian hostage crisis. During Carter's presidency Republicans further added to their strength in the House and Senate and among southern governors. But if Carter embarrassed southern voters, Clinton's presidency produced outright rebellion. Clinton had earned praise as one of the brightest, most agile governors in his region; but as President his policies, from his advocacy of ending discrimination against homosexuals in the military to his economic and health care programs that stressed big-government activism, often seemed like a stick in the eye to his native South. Having been burned once by Carter, white southerners refused to be taken in again, and their bile spilled over on other southern Democrats in Congress. If the best of a generation of southern Democrats had surrendered so quickly to the liberals in his party, how could any of the others be trusted in Washington? "In my opinion, Bill Clinton's 1992 campaign was the last hurrah for the Democratic Party in the South," insisted South Carolina Representative Lindsey Graham, who in 1994 became the first Republican ever elected to Congress from his up-country district.

Even assuming some reversals from the landslide of 1994, Republicans are in a position to expand their standing at nearly every level in the region in future elections. Although Democratic enclaves exist in many parts of the rural South (and of course in the minority communities), two-party politics is now the norm throughout the South, with the Republicans holding the advantage in many places; in some GOP districts, in fact, Democrats are not even competitive anymore. For the first time in the postwar period, the midterm elections of 1994 re-sembled a presidential election in the South, with white voters flock-ing to congressional and legislative candidates in numbers comparable to their vote for Republican presidential candidates over the past three decades. Today Republicans hold 80 percent of the southern congres-sional districts where Bush received at least 60 percent of the vote. If the Solid South ever re-creates itself in the future, it likely will be as a largely Republican stronghold.

The presidential contours of the 1994 vote show up clearly in the exit polls, which paint the picture in vivid tones: 63 percent of south-ern white voters supported Republican candidates, a level consistent with their support for Republican presidential candidates over the past two decades (with the exception of Bush in 1992). Analysts enshrined 1994 as the Year of the White Male, but in the South they might have written just as easily about the White Female. According to exit polls, 68 percent of southern white men cast votes for Republican House candidates — but so did 59 percent of southern white women. From any angle, the results looked the same: White southerners of all cate-gories had abandoned the Democrats. Republicans won substantial majorities among white voters in every income category other than those earning less than $15,000 a year. They also won majorities of white voters by every category of educational achievement, from those with college degrees to those who never graduated from high school. In 1994, Democratic appeals to class warfare failed, and their historic links to downscale, southern populists shattered in the face of a Re-publican campaign built on traditional values that resonate deeply throughout the South. In the South, culture counts for as much as or more politically than class.

As important as the 1994 elections were in transforming the politi-cal balance in the South, they were equally significant in affecting the balance of power with the Republican Party. Those changes will shape the style, culture, and priorities of the GOP into the next century. The elections solidified Sun Belt preeminence within a party long accus-tomed to dominance by the Northeast and Midwest. Compared to the last time Republicans held the House, the geographic conversion ap-pears stunning. The South and West now control more than 55 per-cent of Republican seats in the House, where forty years ago, the Northeast and Midwest held roughly 75 percent. In 1955, Republicans held just 10 of 120 southern congressional districts; at the end of 1995 they controlled 78 of 137, and during that same period, their strength in the Senate went from none of the 26 seats to 16 today.*

White southerners, whose long memories of the Civil War made them among the most loyal of Democratic constituencies, now identify with the Republican Party in roughly the same percentages as northern Protestants, upon whose shoulders the GOP was founded. In practical terms, these white southerners, drawn over the years to the GOP's brand of economic and cultural conservatism, now represent the most loyal of all conservative constituencies — and are more likely to shape the future than their northern brethren.

LONG TIME COMING

Like the rise of the Gingrich generation within the Republican Party, the geographic transformation of American politics did not occur suddenly, nor was it the result of transitory currents or a few dominant personalities. Powerful forces changed the South and the political allegiances of the people there, and it has taken a generation for them to fully flower.

The most significant, of course, is race and the civil rights movement of the 1950s and 1960s, which empowered African-Americans in the South, drove white voters out of the old Democratic Party, and established a new Republican Party as their refuge. In 1994, southern Republicans received 94 percent of their votes from whites and just 2 percent from African-Americans. The Voting Rights Act of 1965 enfranchised millions of black voters in the decade after its passage by Congress, and allowed blacks who had long been excluded from the political process not only to vote but to play increasingly powerful roles within the Democratic Party. But those changes also had the effect of driving many white voters out of the Democratic Party toward the Republicans. Ironically, the Republicans then used that same legislation as the legal centerpiece of a redistricting strategy after the 1990 census that was designed to maximize the number of legislative and congressional districts with black or Hispanic majorities and, as a

---

*Figures are based on *Congressional Quarterly*'s definition of the South, which is the eleven states of the Old Confederacy plus Oklahoma and Kentucky.

consequence, diminish Democratic chances of winning the adjacent, increasingly white districts. Thus, the civil rights revolution constructed the pilings of the modern Republican Party in the South and the movement's legal legacy topped off the GOP's new southern mansion with their victories in 1994. It would be a gross oversimplification to say that the racial politics of the 1960s primarily produced the results of the 1994 elections. But Republicans struggling to move beyond race deny reality when they attempt to wipe away their party's use of racial prejudice and paranoia to erode the strength of the Democratic Party and cement their relationship with a generation of white voters.

Nearly as powerful as race in transforming southern politics was the region's economic conversion throughout the post–World War II era. Long the nation's most impoverished region, the South over this period rose closer to national standards. The decline of the agrarian South and the rise of a modern economy grounded in manufacturing, defense, tourism, services, and technology has been, by anyone's measure, one of the great success stories of the late twentieth century — but in creating a more diversified society, the South's economic transformation made it difficult for Democrats to speak for the interests of all, as they once claimed to do. And the absence of labor unions robbed the Democrats in the South of a key organizing tool available in the white ethnic wards of the North.

Between 1961 and 1991, median family income in the South (adjusted for inflation) increased from $20,228 to $31,940, while the percentage of southerners holding college degrees rose from 6.9 percent to 12.3 percent. From 1980 to 1993, personal income grew slightly faster in the South than in any other region of the country, with several states among the nation's leaders. Southern governors of both parties were among the most active economic salesmen in the nation, and virtually every southern state can point to major new industrial investment that has helped to boost wages and job opportunities. Traditionally the southern elite favored low-skill industries staffed by poorly educated workers, but by the 1980s, southern governors recognized they could never achieve prosperity unless they could guarantee new industry an educated workforce; farsighted politicians in both parties, like Bill Clinton, Jim Hunt, Lamar Alexander, and Richard

Riley, became the country's leaders in promoting higher educational standards.

The third great current of change was population growth, fueled by the influx of northern migrants drawn by the South's expanding economic opportunities, warm weather, cheaper living standards, and more relaxed lifestyle. (Immigration from abroad reinforced the population growth, particularly in Texas and Florida.) Over a forty-year span, the population of the South grew by 81 percent, faster than the nation as a whole, and in states like Florida (366 percent) and Texas (120 percent), exploded at a breathtaking pace. Not every state, of course, shared equally in this growth. North Carolina and Georgia gained significantly; Mississippi and Alabama, long impoverished, did not. The Outer South, or Peripheral South, gained far more than the states of the Deep South, but as a whole, the region was transformed by the flood of new arrivals.

In concert with the economic changes, in-migration from the North and the swell of refugees from the farms to the cities and the imposition of court-ordered busing gave rise to a suburban South where one had never existed. Around cities like Dallas and Houston, Atlanta, Birmingham, Orlando, Raleigh, Richmond, Charlotte, and Greenville, suburbs sprouted relentlessly. Between 1980 and 1990, the South could boast of thirteen of the twenty-five fastest-growing congressional districts in the country (seven of the other twelve were in California alone), while only four of the twenty-five slowest-growing were southern based (and three of them were majority-black districts). A wave of blue-collar migration hit during the early 1980s, when hard times humbled the Rust Belt, but for the most part the migration brought middle-class, middle-income families to the corporations establishing operations in the South. Almost every new housing development rising in the suburban and exurban counties of the South represented another potential Republican enclave and a further nail in the Democrats' coffin.

These great forces transformed southern life in fundamental ways, but they did not dislodge the region's most salient political characteristic, its abiding conservatism. "Conservatism occupies an exalted position in the South," wrote brothers Earl Black and Merle Black, two political scientists who study southern politics. "Although the region has sometimes been portrayed as ripe for the construction of successful biracial coalitions of have-littles and have-nots, the growth of the urban middle class and the popularity of middle-class beliefs among southern white workers have worked against explicit class politics and in favor of conservative politics generally."

Southern conservatism remains a unique blend of patriotism, religion, faith in free markets, and distrust of outsiders. Through the enduring prism of the Civil War, the South long saw itself besieged by the moneyed interests and hostile values of the North, creating a sense of beleaguerment that made the region more protective of its own culture and cohesive in its conservatism. The arrival of millions of northern immigrants somewhat diluted this sense of embattlement, but it has not made the South significantly less conservative. No region is more resolute in its support for a strong defense, and no region has so benefited from defense spending. The network of military bases and installations across the South testifies to the tenacity of southern power brokers, from Richard Russell to Sam Nunn. But despite its dependence on federal largesse, the South long has viewed government suspiciously, and its legislatures have been far more protective of the economic elites and major industries than of using government to redistribute wealth to the impoverished masses. Southern states have historically provided the least generous benefits to welfare recipients, for example, while providing the most attractive incentives to local industries or to lure corporations to their states, although, to be fair, the mostly impoverished southern states had fewer resources to redistribute. Like the culture of the military, religion is woven more deeply into the daily life of the South than it is in any other region. The conservative values of the pulpit spill regularly into the public arena, and on a wide variety of social and cultural issues, the South is the country's most conservative section.

GIVEN the power of these demographic and sociological forces, it was inevitable that the political infrastructure of the South would come unhinged after World War II. The first intimation came in the 1948 presidential race. That year, Strom Thurmond, then the governor of South Carolina, bolted from the Democratic Party over its civil rights platform plank and Harry Truman's civil rights policies. Running for President on the Dixiecrat ticket, Thurmond carried not only his home state, but also Alabama, Mississippi, and Louisiana. Thurmond's racially based crusade, built on resistance to the prospect of desegregation, represented the first challenge to Democratic preeminence of southern politics.

The first true Republican breakthrough, however, came in 1952 with Eisenhower's campaign for President. Until Eisenhower, Republican presidential candidates, conceding the obvious, rarely campaigned in the South. Why spend time in states like Mississippi, Georgia, or South Carolina, all of which gave Franklin Roosevelt at least 90 percent of the vote in 1932? But Eisenhower's standing as a war hero offered him an entree to southern voters that transcended party politics. He campaigned in every southern state except Mississippi, carried half the white vote, and won Virginia, Tennessee, Florida, Texas, and Oklahoma. Four years later, although he lost ground in some of the Deep South states because of the 1954 Supreme Court decision on school desegregation, Eisenhower added Louisiana and Kentucky to his column, and for the first time, the Democrats failed to win a majority of the southern electoral vote.

Eisenhower, however, did not simply replicate Thurmond's 1948 campaign. Eisenhower appealed most to the rising middle class in the South, and he scored best in the growing Outer South states with smaller concentration of African-Americans; Thurmond won those where African-American percentages were greatest. The difference between 1948 and 1952 reflected patterns that existed throughout the postwar period: racially polarized voting occurred in those areas with the most black citizens and where whites felt most threatened by the impending civil rights movement. The pattern of the general's vote reflected support for his conservative values far more than the racial paranoia that had begun to infect the region. Strategically, however, his most important contribution was to help the Republicans neutralize the South as a bastion of Democratic strength in presidential elections, an electoral reversal that became decisive in later years.

Once Eisenhower left office, the conversion of the South stalled temporarily. In 1960, John F. Kennedy recaptured Texas (thanks to the presence of Lyndon Johnson on the ticket) and Louisiana, while holding the other southern states (except Mississippi, which voted for an unpledged slate of electors). Nationally, Richard Nixon received about a third of the black vote, according to a post-election Gallup poll.

Beneath the surface, however, the fissures of racial polarization in the South grew deeper, creating an enormous opportunity for the Republicans if they positioned themselves as more conservative on race than the national Democrats. Democratic machine politics of the South, as Theodore H. White pointed out in *The Making of the President 1960*, already was driving many southerners toward the Republican Party. But the more significant force powering a potential Republican conversion was the growing link between the national Democratic Party and its support for the emancipation of southern blacks.

The policies of the Kennedy and Johnson administrations, particularly the passage of the 1964 Civil Rights Act and the Voting Rights Act of 1965, imprinted a partisan label on racial politics. As late as 1962, polls showed the public found little difference in the two parties on issues of race, but by 1964, 60 percent said Democrats were more likely to favor "fair treatment in jobs for blacks," compared to only 7 percent who cited the Republicans. "By 1964 the Democratic Party was on its way to becoming the home of racial liberalism and the Republican Party was on its way to becoming the home of racial conservatism," wrote Thomas Byrne Edsall and Mary Edsall in their book *Chain Reaction*.

Johnson's leadership on civil rights helped propel him to a landslide reelection victory in 1964, but it also drove southern whites in the Deep South to Barry Goldwater and the Republicans. Johnson won 61 percent of the vote that year, but Goldwater, in an alliance signaling the coming power of the South and West within the Republican Party, captured every one of the Deep South states, virtually replicating Thurmond's performance in 1948. Goldwater made little headway in the Outer South, where his extreme conservative views alarmed the southern middle class as much as they did voters elsewhere, and his southern electoral count was less than Nixon's four years earlier. But the significance of Goldwater's candidacy came in underscoring the irrevocable split between the national Democratic Party and its segregationist wing in the South; his doomed candidacy provided the outlines of what would become a Republican electoral advantage in presidential politics for a generation to come. Racial conservatism represented the vehicle for Republicans to expand their beachhead in the South.

In 1968, the South fractured as never before, due to the independent candidacy of Alabama governor George Wallace. With the allegiance of downscale, white populists resistant to the civil rights movement, Wallace won all the Deep South states except South Carolina, where Strom Thurmond's support saved the state for Nixon. Nixon won most of the Outer South and Hubert Humphrey carried Texas for the Democrats. "The presidential election of 1968 marked a historic first occasion — the Negrophobe Deep South and the modern Outer South simultaneously abandoned the Democratic Party," Kevin Phillips wrote. The Deep South continued its rebellion over racial issues, while voters in the Outer South revolted against Johnson's Great Society and what they saw as its abandonment of the principles of Roosevelt's New Deal liberalism. To many southerners, Johnson was less interested in helping the broad middle class than he was in helping the poor. Phillips correctly predicted that the Deep South would inevitably follow the Outer South into the Republican orbit, and in the aftermath of the 1968 election, Nixon immediately embarked on his "southern strategy," effectively driving a racial wedge deeper into the Democratic Party by exploiting issues like school busing and law and order.

With the racial identities of the two parties now firmly fixed in the minds of southern voters, Nixon also moved to profit from growing the ideological chasm between the national Democratic Party and its southern wing. Nixon's southern strategy inaugurated a period in which Republicans emphasized cultural and social issues to cement their ties with white southerners. But nothing Nixon did was more effective in enlarging the divisions than the Democrats' decision in 1972 to nominate George McGovern for President. McGovern's left-liberal voting record and vehement opposition to the Vietnam War drove the entire South into the hands of a Republican presidential nominee for the first time in the twentieth century. Nixon's election marked another strategic breakthrough for the Republicans, akin to Eisenhower's in 1952, for in consolidating the southern electoral vote, the GOP needed to win barely more than a third of the northern electoral vote to secure the White House. Nixon became the model for the Republican landslides of the 1980s, and, had it not been for the Watergate scandal, might have hastened the realignment of the region below the presidential level.

In 1976, Jimmy Carter, the first Deep South politician to head a national party ticket since the Civil War, arrested the Republican surge.

But the Democratic comeback was short-lived. In 1980, Reagan proved to be the ideal candidate to bind the antigovernment conservatism of the West with the patriotic, populist conservatism of the South. His campaigns in 1980 and especially 1984 represented historic landmarks in expanding the GOP's appeal in the South. Reagan's allure was grounded not only in his advocacy of a strong national defense and a muscular foreign policy, but in his invocation of religion and the use of cultural issues ranging from gun control to abortion. That blend attracted downscale southern whites who historically had responded to the populist, economic policies of the Democrats that had propped up farm prices, railed against Wall Street, fought the utility companies, and jawboned to keep interest rates low. To most southerners, Walter Mondale, the Democratic nominee in 1984, was further evidence that the national Democratic Party had abandoned them.

Shrewd Republicans understood the key to their southern success hinged on dividing the electorate by cultural, not economic, allegiance. As Lee Atwater, the South Carolina political operative who held a top role in Reagan's 1984 campaign, managed Bush's 1988 campaign, and died of a brain tumor shortly after becoming chairman of the Republican National Committee, wrote in a 1983 strategy memo,

> It is critical to our future success in the South that we understand the reasons for our inroads into the populist vote. Populists have always been liberal on economics. So long as the crucial issues were generally confined to economics — as during the New Deal — the liberal candidate could expect to get most of the populist vote. But populists are conservatives on most social issues, including abortion, gun control and ERA [Equal Rights Amendment]. Also, populists usually lean conservative on foreign policy and national security issues. . . . Thus when Republicans are successful in getting certain social issues to the forefront, the populist vote is ours.

It was in the cultivation of those populist voters, Atwater said, "that our hope for a Republican South rests." Atwater ran a textbook version of this strategy in George Bush's 1988 campaign, and again the Democrats cooperated by nominating another northern liberal, this time the technocractic governor of Massachusetts, Michael Dukakis.

The week of the Republican convention in New Orleans, when Dukakis still held a lead in the polls, Fred Meyer, then the GOP chairman in Texas, confidently outlined the strategy for winning the South. "We're going to raise a number of issues," he said matter-of-factly in the sunlit atrium of his hotel. "Gun control, defense, crime and drugs, the death penalty, and taxes. Gun control and taxes are the top two." Using that blueprint, Bush again swept the entire South.

Chastened by their string of humiliating defeats, the Democrats in 1992 countered with an all-southern ticket of Clinton and Albert Gore of Tennessee. The two exuberant baby boomers campaigned throughout the South and carried their home states of Arkansas and Tennessee as well as Georgia, Louisiana, and Kentucky. Democrats crowed that they had finally picked the Republican lock on the door of the electoral college, but the voting patterns told a different story. Clinton's success owed much to the candidacy of Ross Perot. While the South proved to be his weakest region nationally, Perot siphoned off enough votes from George Bush to give the Democrats several states they otherwise might have lost. Compared to Dukakis, Clinton had held his own, but compared to fellow native son Jimmy Carter more than a decade earlier, he looked far weaker. Even in victory, Clinton's performance provided another telling sign of the continuing deterioration of the Democratic Party in the region.

LONE STARS AND PALMETTOS

Republican leaders like Reagan and Nixon were successful in accentuating the differences between the two political parties nationally, but it was left to a generation of southern politicians and political activists to transfer their success in national elections down to the grass roots. Progress has come in fits and starts, with 1994 the most stunning example of success to date, and the results of 1995, when the GOP failed to win control of the Virginia legislature or the governorship of Kentucky, a reminder that Democrats will continue to battle for position. But unless there is a dramatic reversal of Democratic Party fortunes in the region, Republicans appear likely to build on the advances throughout the decade.

Through the wide lens of presidential politics, the conversion of the South is a story of race, geography, and ideology. Those factors intermingled as well in transforming local politics across the region, but in unique and idiosyncratic combinations from state to state. No two states followed the same path, for as historians long have said, there is not one South but several. To describe the larger story, we have chosen two states that exemplify different regions and distinctive histories in the political evolution of the South. One state is South Carolina, born of the slave trade but today a state economically and politically transformed, perhaps the leading Republican state in the entire region. The other is Texas — big, brawling, bragging Texas — where the South meets the West, and the future lies with the GOP.

The two states are in many respects opposites. Texas is the prototypical Sun Belt megastate, with a population of more than seventeen million people and a cultural amalgam of the South, the West, and of Mexico. Almost 10 percent of its population is foreign born, and Hispanics (26 percent of the population), not African-Americans (12 percent), are its largest minority. Despite its continuing romance with the myth of the American cowboy, Texas is today one of the most urbanized states in the nation, with 91 percent of its residents living in and around cities. Rapidly growing and rapidly changing, Texas has maintained its fierce pride and independence as a kind of nation-state, and its politics, like its people, have a bigger-than-life quality. But the evolution of Texas from a Democratic bastion to a state where Republicans now hold a narrow advantage is best understood as an example of the power of conservative ideas, images, and ideology — and of the struggle between the two parties to claim that mantle for themselves.

South Carolina, on the other hand, draws its lineage from the old cotton and plantation South, where low-country planters built enormous fortunes on the backs of imported slaves. The end of slavery and the beginnings of the breakup of the agrarian economy brought the textile industry to the state, factories that depended on low-wage, nonunionized workers — and protectionist trade policies — for their survival. Historically South Carolina remained an impoverished state and one with among the highest percentages of blacks in its population. Today blacks account for 30 percent of the population, and 45 percent of South Carolinians still reside in rural areas. And while its per capita income remains in the lower tier nationally, the economic progress over the past two decades is indisputable, thanks to the governance of both Democrats and Republicans. It is a political success story, however, only for the Republicans. Its rapid evolution toward the Republicans was powered initially by the bitter racial divisions that affected the entire tier of Deep South states. But the consolidation of Republican power over the past few years owes more to the GOP's success in assembling a coalition of suburban conservatives and rural populists and to the determination of two-term governor Carroll Campbell to build a party from the ground up.

CARROLL Campbell always looked like he stepped straight out of the boardrooms of corporate America. Impeccably groomed with a youthful, athletic appearance, his chiseled face and conservative clothes spoke of the business world, not the back rooms of southern politics. Had he been in business rather than politics during the 1980s, he no doubt would have found his way into mergers and acquisitions, for during that period he engineered one of the most dramatic — and hostile — political takeovers in the country. During his eight years as governor, from 1987 to 1995, South Carolina turned decisively toward the Republican Party, with Campbell driving the transformation.

On the night of March 3, 1995, Republican activists in South Carolina gathered at the state fairgrounds a mile from the capitol in Columbia for an annual fund-raising event known as the Silver Elephant Dinner. The affair originated some years ago when the Republican Party was more a social club than political machine, and in a good year a few hundred optimistic people might show up to socialize and assure one another there were brighter days ahead. But on this damp and chilly evening, the banquet hall was jammed with two thousand jubilant Republicans who represented a far more diverse, if still overwhelmingly white, portion of the population. The dignitaries that night included almost every significant South Carolina Republican for the past three decades, beginning with the antiquarian Strom Thurmond and ending with David Beasley, the newly elected governor, and David Wilkins, who in December 1994 became the first Republican Speaker of a southern legislature since Reconstruction. Five prospective presidential candidates also mingled with the crowd, drawn by a meaningless straw poll of the sort that fills up the early calendar of a presidential campaign. But the most acclaimed politician of all was Carroll Campbell, then out of office only a few months. Many in the crowd sported buttons touting their favorite candidate for

President in 1996 — but they all wanted Campbell for vice president, for Campbell had changed the face of Republicans in the Palmetto state.

Thirty years earlier, the party had a far more dubious image, certainly outside the state. In South Carolina, the modern Republican Party was born on September 16, 1964, when Strom Thurmond quit the Democratic Party and became a Republican and announced his intention to campaign for Barry Goldwater. Thurmond blamed the Democrats for deserting the people of South Carolina, but he meant they had abandoned the southern segregationists opposed to the burgeoning civil rights revolution. His long battle with the national Democrats had culminated that summer with his opposition to the Civil Rights Act of 1964, and his defection marked the opening of a wave of white flight out of the Democratic Party and into the waiting arms of the Republicans. The small, southern Republican Party in those days was lily white, and as if to advertise its no-blacks-need-apply mentality, South Carolina Republicans in 1966 held their state convention beneath a huge Confederate flag.

Thurmond's defection represented a turning point in southern politics and provided an enormous boost to the Republicans in his state. No other southern Republican Party had been able to claim a politician of such stature. "He was an established institution with major influence in the whole state," Don Fowler said. Thurmond's status made it more socially acceptable for other whites to break historic bonds and vote Republican. Four years later, he proved to be Richard Nixon's most prominent and effective southern supporter, first protecting Nixon's southern flank against an incursion by the Reagan forces at the Republican national convention, and later by holding South Carolina in Nixon's column against Wallace's racially charged, populist campaign.

Thurmond's overt racial politics ended during the Nixon administration, as the Voting Rights Act enfranchised enough black voters to make them a force to be reckoned with, and as attitudes changed the terms of acceptable public debate. By then, few southerners wanted to turn back the clock to segregation, and even Thurmond began to court black voters, providing them with services through his Senate office and hiring African-Americans for his staff. But despite Thurmond's popularity and Nixon's southern landslide in 1972, the Republican surge in South Carolina stalled. Below the presidential level, lower-income South Carolinians remained true to their Democratic heritage. By a fluke, Republican James Edwards won the governorship in 1974, after the Democratic nominee was ruled ineligible because he did not meet the state's residency requirement. But in the face of an overwhelming Democratic majority in the legislature, Edwards proved to be little more than a well-liked caretaker, and in 1978, the governorship reverted to the Democrats, when Richard Riley, a reform-minded state senator, was elected.

That same year, Campbell won election to Congress in what became the first wave of the Reagan revolution, joining a freshman class that included Newt Gingrich. Campbell charted his own course, but he was as partisan and conservative as Gingrich and Co. Opposed to new taxes and most new spending, he strongly supported more money for the Pentagon, a crucial employer in the South Carolina economy. Campbell exemplified the suburban southern conservative who would come to dominate the congressional Republicans a decade later.

For two decades, Campbell had ascended through the Republican ranks, starting as a poll watcher for Nixon in 1960, running campaigns around his hometown of Greenville (a Republican stronghold), and later winning election to the state House and state Senate. Shortly after entering the legislature in 1970, he joined forces with Lee Atwater, then a college student, and they became an inseparable team. Atwater was the more explosive and excitable, Campbell the more polished and contained; but they were brothers beneath the skin — competitive, conservative, partisan, and enthusiastic practitioners of the negative politics that earned Atwater his national reputation. Later another young Republican, Warren Tompkins, a high school friend of Atwater's, joined the team, and together the triumvirate of Campbell-Atwater-Tompkins set their sights on converting South Carolina into a Republican state.

Dick Riley served successfully for two terms as governor, establishing himself as a leader in the South in reforming and improving education and in attracting economic investment to his state. But among his political priorities was changing the state's constitution to permit governors to serve a second term, an effort designed to enhance the power of the Democratic majority in the state. In 1986, his lieutenant governor, Mike Daniel, sought to extend the Democrats' reign, but in

Campbell he found an opponent beyond his strength. Campbell shared Riley's (and Daniel's) commitment to education and economic development, but he displayed Atwater's acumen for enlarging the fissures within the Democratic coalition. In one campaign debate, Campbell declared that he believed the state should continue to fly the Confederate flag over the state capitol, and, in challenging Daniel to state his position, in essence dared his opponent to choose between the white populists or the African-Americans, whose uneasy alliance had kept Democrats in power. Daniel instantly understood the danger not only to his own candidacy but to Democratic hegemony throughout the South. "If we don't win this race," he said in what amounted to a warning to every Democrat in the region, "every officeholder in the state will have Republican opposition." That fall, Republicans lost control of the U.S. Senate in part because a surge of black voters helped to elect Democrats in four southern states, and in South Carolina, Democrat Senator Ernest Hollings was reelected with 63 percent of the vote. But in the governor's race, Campbell won a twenty-three-hundred-vote victory, 51–49 percent, a dramatic breakthrough for the Republicans that signaled a coming crack-up among the Democrats.

Daniel's prophecy about the impact of a Campbell victory proved correct. Campbell governed as a pro-business conservative and played politics as a hard-charging partisan whose involvement in presidential politics gave him a sophistication that few others in the state shared. He became a national leader among governors on education, co-chairing with Clinton a National Governors' Association committee on education reform and standards, and later chairing the NGA itself. Armed with promises of educational reforms in his state, he ceaselessly recruited new business to South Carolina. He pared the state budget and sought to reform Medicaid, food stamps, and welfare. He displayed a new style of Republican leadership, light years beyond the Old South, an activist conservative with a modern, appealing style. Campbell reached out to black voters and appointed blacks and women to state jobs. But all the while he stressed patriotic and pro-family values designed constantly to enlarge his conservative, white base. Campbell became the face of responsible, conservative governance, the first time many South Carolinians had seen that package under the banner of the Republicans. At one point, Bill Clinton, who had worked extensively with Campbell at the governors' association, described the South Carolina governor as the conservative he admired most. "He governed well," Lindsey Graham said. "He was a fiscal conservative and a social conservative, but he didn't scare the hell out of people."

Politically, Campbell was at heart a precinct organizer, and he loved the minutiae of politics as much as he enjoyed manipulating the levers of power from the governor's office. He believed in taking risks and quickly eclipsed Thurmond as the state's most astute player in national politics. As a freshman member of the House, he backed Reagan's 1980 candidacy while Thurmond supported John Connally, the flamboyant Texan who spent more than $10 million to win just one delegate. In 1988, Campbell and Atwater conspired to move up the South Carolina primary a few days before the South's Super Tuesday, and his vigorous support of Bush formed the cornerstone of the southern "firewall" that clinched Bush's nomination. At home, he and Tompkins, with Atwater's advice, moved with similar dexterity. Given the economic and demographic trends in the South, there is little doubt that South Carolina would have continued to move toward the Republicans, but Campbell's aggressiveness and his determination put the state on a fast track. "If we had had a Carroll Campbell in Florida," said Tom Slade, Florida's Republican chairman, "we'd have owned this state."

When Campbell was inaugurated in January 1987, Republicans held just two of the six congressional districts, 29 of 124 seats in the state House and 10 of the 46 seats in the state Senate. One sign of the GOP's problems was that Campbell's election as governor had cost Republicans his old congressional seat. With Tompkins as his top adviser, Campbell laid out a step-by-step strategy designed to produce a Republican majority, or at least something approaching it. The first step was to obtain a veto-proof House to give him the power to demonstrate the difference between Republican and Democratic governance. To do that, he needed either to convert conservative Democratic legislators or find Republicans who could win in conservative districts those Democrats held. Tompkins already had a long list of targets, and he and Campbell made clear they would fight for those districts until the Democrats proved decisively that Republicans could not win them. "The theory was, these are districts that ought to be Republican, and we're going to run somebody in there every time or we're going to switch the incumbent," Tompkins said. "We're going to keep going after them year after year until they either join us or wear down and quit." Initially, Campbell had more success winning converts than elections. Whenever a Democrat announced his decision to join the party, the tireless Campbell showed up offering money and a pledge to support the convert against a subsequent primary challenge. Campbell and Tompkins exhibited the same vigor recruiting candidates, but they wanted aggressive politicians like themselves, not GOP place-holders. Campbell promised support on one condition. "You either run to win or we don't want you on the ballot," he told them.

The near collapse of the Democratic Party in South Carolina eased Campbell's task, a pattern repeated throughout the South in the past decade. The Democrats were a party in name only, a historical institution that had ceased to operate with anything approaching a unified purpose. Republicans succeeded in part because, in their infancy as a party, they learned to depend on one another, not on the family ties that prompted so many southerners to cast their ballots for Democrats. Faced with aggressive challenges from the Republicans, many Democrats in the South floundered, fought one another, or collapsed. "The South Carolina experience between 1986 and 1994 was the face of a political party not fulfilling its responsibilities to the public," Fowler, who was Democratic national committeeman at the time, said. "We just were not aggressive. We said, 'Oh, he'll pass and things will go back to normal.' There was not an effective response to what he was doing, and the field of effective politics was just almost abdicated to him and his people." The best evidence came in Campbell's 1990 reelection campaign, when the Democrats nominated an outspokenly liberal African-American state senator named Theo Mitchell, whose campaign reinforced the image of the Democrats as a party out of touch with the southern mainstream.

Campbell helped enhance the image of the Republican Party. During his first three years in office, Republican identification among white voters rose from 30 percent to 54 percent, while identification with the Democrats fell from 24 to 15 percent. Republican identification later declined after a scandal in the legislature, but Democrats reaped no benefit. During the fall of 1994, Republican pollster Whit

Ayres found that only 8 percent of white men in South Carolina iden-
tified themselves as Democrats. But even after his landslide reelection
in 1990, Campbell faced a heavily Democratic legislature. In the Sen-
ate, Republicans were outnumbered four to one, and in the House it
was still nearly two to one. But a legislative scandal in 1990 and 1991,
in which a total of sixteen legislators were convicted of taking money
in exchange for votes, unexpectedly worked to strengthen Campbell at
the expense of the entrenched, legislative Old Boy network that had
ruled the state for generations. In that face-off, Campbell represented
the modern model of governance, while the Democrats symbolized
the corrupt politics of the past. Though the sting operation caught
legislators from both parties, Campbell used the public reaction to
push through reforms that strengthened his own hand. Meanwhile,
the scandal left incumbent Democrats in the South Carolina legisla-
ture vulnerable to the same kind of charges that Gingrich and the Re-
publicans were making in Washington over the House bank and post
office scandals — that it was time to clean house. The scandal en-
hanced Campbell's image, and with it a Republican Party eager to
seize power.

Redistricting provided Campbell with the other weapon he needed
to remake the legislature. Like Republicans elsewhere, Campbell and
his forces allied themselves with black legislators, who were seeking to
construct the maximum number of majority-black districts. The Bush
Justice Department cooperated by brandishing the act like a club on
behalf of minorities. The political math was simple: the more major-
ity-black districts, the fewer the number of black voters in adjacent
districts. Given the flight of white voters into the Republican Party,
GOP leaders believed those districts, drained of black votes to create
the new affirmative-action seats, would topple into their column. "We
felt like we could beat any Democrat when the minority population of
a district was less than twenty-five percent," Tompkins said. Which
meant the Republicans were confident they could win almost two-
thirds of the white vote in such districts.

One reason for their confidence was the growing involvement of
the Christian Coalition in Republican politics in South Carolina and the
shift of white evangelical Christians away from their historic ties to the
Democratic Party. Bob Jones University, one of the leading Christian
colleges in the country, long had exerted political influence around its

home in Greenville, but it took Pat Robertson's 1988 presidential campaign to activate a religious conservative political movement. As the first white evangelical minister to run for President, Robertson tapped a network of support largely untouched by other politicians. For generations, white evangelicals had steered clear of politics, but Robertson's campaign not only aroused their interest but converted them into precinct political activists. Robertson had targeted South Carolina during his campaign, and despite his poor showing against George Bush in the primary there, the disappointed supporters he left behind quickly became the core of one of the most effective political organizations in the state.

Campbell, as Bush's strongest ally in the state, had bitterly fought the Robertson forces during the primary. But once Bush had secured the nomination, Campbell moved to heal the wounds and draw Robertson supporters into the party. The South Carolina chapter of the Christian Coalition now stands as one of the strongest in the country, and when it held its spring banquet shortly after the Silver Elephant Dinner in the spring of 1995, more than fifteen hundred people showed up, including many of the Republican leaders who had shared the stage in Columbia. Their success in seizing control of the party apparatus in some parts of the state and relentless focus on opposition to abortion created strains between the Christian Coalition and the regular wing of the party that persist today. Indeed, many traditional Republicans now feel disenfranchised from their own party. Yet the party leaders had no choice but to pay that price: Without the mobilization of the religious conservatives, they would remain a minority in the state. "Until the religious conservative movement broke its behavioral Democratic patterns and started voting in large part in Republican primaries and for Republican candidates, we weren't winning elections in the South," Tompkins said.

Armed with the new redistricting map and riding the currents that already were flowing in their direction, Republican leaders concluded they would eventually seize control of the legislature, but not as quickly as they did. "Most people thought it would be '96, not '94," said David Wilkins, the House Speaker. As it turned out, salvation arrived one election ahead of schedule. The Republican House caucus grew to fifty-two members after the 1992 election, a gain large enough for party leaders to advance their timetable to 1994. With Republicans posting gains across the region on election night 1994, South Carolina Republicans picked up nine more seats in the state House, and then, with Campbell and Wilkins applying the pressure, they quickly converted enough Democrats to assure them a majority. With Campbell tearfully watching from the balcony of the old state-house, Wilkins took the oath of office in early December in a preview of the historic transfer of power that soon unfolded in Washington.

Campbell's retirement as governor brought to power a new generation of Republican leaders in South Carolina, led by thirty-seven-year-old David Beasley, a former Democrat who in his own way typified the new southern Republican Party. Young, personable, and extremely conservative, Beasley underwent a political conversion in 1991, seven years after becoming a born-again Christian. Beasley's campaign for governor depended heavily on support from the Christian Coalition, and while his ties to the religious right scared off some of the suburban white vote, his strength among evangelical Christians helped him to win some rural areas of the state Campbell failed to capture during his first campaign for governor in 1986. Beasley represents the continuing evolution of the Republican Party in the South, and as with the party's challenge nationally, his ability to speak for the interests of both traditional Republicans and the religious conservatives will determine the course of South Carolina politics toward the end of the decade. However Beasley performs, though, the impact of Carroll Campbell's eight years in office is not likely to erode soon. "We're winning everywhere now," said John Morgan, a Republican demographer who helped the South Carolina Republicans in 1994. "The only thing we're not getting is the minority vote. South Carolina is like a lot of southern states. Once it goes, it goes for good."

AN old adage in presidential politics said Democrats could not win the White House without winning Texas. Bill Clinton disproved that maxim in 1992, but his national victory only served to confirm that, in presidential races, Texas had become one of the most Republican states in the nation. It took George W. Bush, the son of the man Clinton ousted from the White House, however, to demonstrate just how deep those Republican roots have sunk.

Appearances can be deceiving. Democrats hold more seats in the

Texas delegation in the U.S. House and still control the state legislature, though with shrinking margins, while below Bush sit a Democratic lieutenant governor, attorney general, comptroller, and land commissioner. By those measures, Texas lags behind a number of other southern states in its evolution toward the GOP. But much of that apparent strength is an artifact of tilted redistricting plans the Democratic state legislature has drawn to protect the party. In terms of raw votes, Republicans increasingly dominate the Lone Star State. In 1994, Republicans actually won 56 percent of the total vote for House candidates, but ended up with just eleven of the thirty House seats. (They added another in 1995 when Representative Greg Laughlin switched parties.) Over the past three decades, no state in the country showed more significant growth in Republican votes in House elections than Texas, according to a 1995 study by the Committee for the Study of the American Electorate.

The 1994 elections tilted the balance even more sharply toward the Republicans. Even as the state turned Republican in presidential elections, Democrats generally held the high ground in state and local elections. Republicans won a share of the big races, but in most contests, the presumption of advantage rested with the Democrats. The Republican earthquake of 1994 shattered that equilibrium. "I think 1994 switched that for a long time to come," said Matthew Dowd, a leading Democratic analyst in Austin. "The Democrats can still win elections here, but it's got to be the right money, the right person, the right time. It was headed in that direction, but it came to a head in 1994."

Few states can boast of the political heritage of Texas, where the raw and robust energy of the culture produced a succession of political figures whose exploits, personalities, and achievements etched themselves into the national consciousness generations ago, from Sam Rayburn to Lyndon Johnson to John Connally. Later another generation of Texas politicians, less overpowering perhaps but still imposing, succeeded them in the 1970s and 1980s, from John Tower to Barbara Jordan to Lloyd Bentsen to Jim Wright, and, even more recently, Ann Richards, Phil Gramm, James A. Baker III, and two men named Bush. But ideology, not personality, represented the grinding wheel of Texas politics. Unlike many Deep South states, racial animosities rarely drove Texas politics; instead, sharply contrasting views of government and business often formed the clash points of the political wars, although for many years they were fought out inside the Democratic Party, where three factions — the Tory conservatives, the regulars, and the liberals — wrestled for advantage. Conservatives saw government as an agent of the business interests, particularly the oil and gas industry. Liberals wanted government to play a more active role in checking the power of the big companies and in helping the poor.

Sometimes these Democratic intraparty feuds helped to elect Republicans, as happened in 1952, when conservative governor Allen Shivers broke with the Democratic Party over Adlai Stevenson's support for federal control of offshore oil leasing and led a band of Shivercrats, who deserted the national party and delivered Texas to Dwight Eisenhower. In 1961, liberals decided they couldn't vote for the arch-conservative Democrat running to fill the Senate seat vacated by Lyndon Johnson when he became vice president, and their opposition in a special election runoff elected a dapper and diminutive college professor named John Tower as the South's first Republican senator since Reconstruction.

But by the late 1970s, these philosophical splits increasingly played out in a partisan struggle of Republicans versus Democrats, with the Republicans closer to the philosophical heart of the state, but Democrats able to sustain themselves on tradition and guile. Over time, however, the Republicans proved more adept at capitalizing on the increasingly suburban character of the Lone Star State. Boots and blue jeans remained the uniform of any self-respecting Texan and barbecue the food of choice, but the personality of the state increasingly reflected a suburban and corporate mentality, not the cowboy culture. The new demographics of Texas played to Republican advantages, a fact Democrats resisted throughout the 1980s. Democrats often tried to will the voters back toward their ancestral roots as Yellow Dog Democrats (so named because they would vote a yellow dog before throwing a vote to a Republican), hoping that old habits would eventually bring about their restoration. Republicans preached the gospel of less government, lower taxes, and cultural values that squared more with Texans' sense of independence than LBJ's welfare state, and their proselytizing produced a steady and perceptible migration of conservative Texans out of the Democratic Party and eventually into the Republican Party. Equally important was the Republicans' success in capturing a younger generation of Texans. In small towns that had been bastions of conservative Democrats, younger people entering politics more often than not gravitated to the GOP.

The Republican Party looked upscale and corporate, grounded initially in old money and in a new management class that arrived in Texas in the 1970s and 1980s. The oil boom of the late '70s changed the shape of Texas and of its politics, bringing into the state a deluge of northern migrants who shared many of the same conservative values as native Texans but did not have the historical ties to the Democrats. Those were remarkable days, when Houston added almost a thousand people a week in a dizzying rush to profit from rising oil prices and the speculative land boom that accompanied it. *Dallas*, America's favorite prime-time soap opera, glamorized the mixture of oil, sex, cattle, and money that seemed to typify life in the Texas fast lane, while a Houston honky-tonk called Gilley's, where the crews from the nearby oil refineries tested their manhood on mechanical bulls and drank beer from long-neck bottles, was memorialized by John Travolta in the movie *Urban Cowboy*. Some of the Yankee migrants came out of the auto plants of Michigan and Ohio, where Japanese competition had battered the big three auto companies. But as many or more of the new arrivals worked for the corporations that fled New York and the Northeast, or for the defense plants running overtime shifts fueled by Reagan's arms buildup, or for the high-tech firms around Austin or Dallas that caught the front end of the microchip revolution and hurtled Texas from the space age into the information age. When the Boy Scouts of America abandoned their home in New Jersey for space in one of the sparkling office parks along the freeway between the sprawling Dallas–Fort Worth Airport and the glass towers of downtown Dallas, the symbolism of Texas as America's new political heartland seemed complete.

Numbers tell an intriguing tale of the political evolution in Texas over the past dozen years, as conservatives increasingly took up residence with the Republicans. Over the past fifteen years, conservatives have become only a slightly larger share of the Texas electorate, but they are now the dominant part of the Republican coalition, according to network exit polls. In 1982, a year of Democratic victories in Texas, slightly more than four in ten white voters called themselves conservatives. Among those "conservative" voters, 43 percent identified themselves as Republicans, while 23 percent said they were Democrats. In 1988, when Bush won the presidency, 48 percent of the white electorate called themselves conservatives, but by then 59 percent of them identified with the Republican Party, against only 13 percent who said they were Democrats. By the fall of 1994, conservatives still accounted for 48 percent of the white electorate, but 68 percent now said they were Republicans and only 7 percent said they were Democrats.

This shifting allegiance among conservative Texans permanently upset the partisan balance in the state. Many Texans, moderates and some conservatives, continue to straddle the two parties, splitting their tickets in major elections. But two polling firms that have tracked the habits and attitudes of Texas voters over the past fifteen years — the Republican Tarrance Group and Democratic Shipley and Associates — demonstrate convincingly the steady drift to the GOP. Between 1982 and 1994, the Tarrance Group conducted more than twenty-five thousand interviews with Texas voters, and their results show that the percentage of voters who said they usually vote for Republican candidates rose from 33 percent to 48 percent. Among white voters, the increase was from 37.5 percent to 55.5 percent. George Shipley's firm, measuring the change in a slightly different way, shows the percentage of regular Republican voters rising from 41 to 45 percent between 1988 and 1995, while the percentage of regular Democratic voters fell from 46 percent to 38 percent. "The motion since 1978 and maybe even earlier has been the same: Republicans going up, Democrats going down," said Karl Rove, a Texas political operative who is George W. Bush's chief strategist. "And there's got to be something that causes that to sort of freeze before you can start to change back."

The Republican rise in Texas came in three waves. The first began in 1978 with the election of Bill Clements, a curmudgeonly Dallas oil man, who became the state's first Republican governor since Reconstruction. Clements won by just seventeen thousand votes in the first gubernatorial election that presented voters with a choice between a nominally liberal Democrat and a conservative Republican. In their primary, Democrats had rebuffed the incumbent governor, conservative Dolph Briscoe, in favor of liberal attorney John Hill, whose victory cemented the growing minority-liberal alliance within the Democratic Party. Clements carried Dallas County and Harris

County by sixty-nine thousand votes and lost the rest of the state by fifty-two thousand votes. His victory demonstrated the Republicans were then little more than an enclave party, huddled in Dallas, Houston, and a few other cities like Midland in oil-rich west Texas, where George Bush made his fortune. But they were surrounded by what the swing bands in the old road houses used to call "miles and miles of Texas" still controlled by the Democrats. The classic example of this urban-rural division came in the 1970 Senate race, when Lloyd Bentsen lost the four biggest counties in the state and swamped George Bush in the rural areas.

Bill Clements lasted only one term, brought down in 1982 by his own prickly personality, a downturn in the economy, and the political machinery of Senator Lloyd Bentsen, who led a party sweep that mobilized an army of Democratic voters. Clements's pollster, Lance Tarrance, generally considered one of the best analysts of Texas at the time, was so far off the mark in his final numbers that he later joked that, in his first post-election meeting with the defeated governor, he felt like "Bonaparte's intelligence officer after Waterloo." But the GOP quickly recovered, and the mid-1980s produced a second wave of Republican growth, as the GOP expanded its reach into the rural areas, first through Phil Gramm's election to the Senate in 1984 and then in 1986, when Clements ousted Democrat Mark White, the man who defeated him four years earlier. Gramm, whose first campaign was a primary challenge to Bentsen in 1976, was elected to Congress in 1978 as a Democrat, then switched parties in 1983 after the Democrats removed him from the Budget Committee in retaliation for sponsoring Reagan's 1981 budget. He quit Congress, then regained his House seat in a special election. After Tower's retirement, he moved to the Senate.

Both Gramm and Reagan ran polarizing elections that year, and the Democrats played into their hands by nominating two liberals, Mondale for President and Lloyd Doggett, now an Austin congressman, for Senate — neither of whom had a chance of winning. Their nominations helped drive conservative and moderate Democrats into the Republican Party. Gramm ran an extraordinarily ideological campaign, highlighted by a radio attack centered on Doggett's acceptance of a campaign contribution raised at an all-male strip show. "You couldn't turn on a radio in Texas and not hear it," Gramm said. Republicans begged Gramm to take the ad off the air, claiming it was alienating potential voters. "They said, 'Stop this radio spot, take it off,'" Gramm said. Instead he ordered aides to double the buy, and in Gramm's description, Doggett "never got up after that." Although Doggett had not known about the source of the money, the contribution from the gay strip-joint fund-raiser symbolized the diverging cultural images of the two parties, with Democrats trapped on the wrong side of a growing divide. For Gramm and the Republicans, the issue proved to be their pipeline into the rural voters, who remained staunchly Democratic in registration. "I spent a tremendous amount of time in the winter, spring, and summer before the fall election working every small town in the state," Gramm said, and the radio ad on Doggett's campaign contribution played heavily in those same small towns. Reagan won 230 of the 254 counties in Texas, and Gramm captured 203, a tremendous breakthrough for the Republican Party.

Gramm represented the antithesis of the country-club Republican. Born poor in Georgia, he drove himself to succeed, first as an economics professor at Texas A&M University and later in politics. This was no to-the-manor-born Republican. Gramm was all elbows. He was an antigovernment, pro-market conservative with a brusque personality and the stamina of a young Lyndon Johnson. As Senator Hank Brown once said, "Phil Gramm's a little like getting a drink of water from a fire hose. He has a blowtorch intellect and an incredible energy level." He led the Democratic Boll Weevils in the House, who passed Reagan's economic plan, and later sponsored the Gramm-Rudman-Hollings deficit-reduction bill his first year in the Senate. His colleagues found him abrasive and too anxious to take credit for things they did, but his political instincts were surer than most of his opponents'. Unlike Clements, Gramm had little use for Democrats in Texas. "I took the view that they were never going to be with me and that I wanted to displace them. And I took them on, head-on, everywhere."

Like Gramm's election in 1984, Clements's return to office in 1986 demonstrated the GOP's widening reach in Texas. Clements carried 194 counties in 1986, compared to just 95 counties in his losing race in 1982. A post-election analysis by Republican strategist Karl Rove showed that the shift toward Clements came disproportionately from rural counties that had been historically resistant to Republican candidates below the level of President. "The movement away from the Democratic Party that began in earnest in 1978 made Clements's victory possible," Rove wrote. "Without a willingness by rural Texans to vote for a Republican candidate and without the growth of the Republican base in metro and suburban counties to augment the party's traditional urban county core, it would have been difficult for any Republican candidate to win. . . . If successful, Clements could alter the political landscape of Texas for decades to come."

But Clements displayed no interest in the kind of party-building that Carroll Campbell had thrived on in South Carolina. He left that job to others, principally Gramm and a hyperactive Dallas businessman named Fred Meyer, who first made headlines by convincing enough local officials in Dallas to switch parties to give the Republicans a majority of the courthouse there. "Bill Clements is really not a politician," Meyer said, who served as state chairman from 1986 to 1994. "I give him credit because he's the first one to win the governorship. But he didn't understand. He still doesn't." Gramm and Meyer worked tirelessly to recruit candidates and promote the party both in rural Texas and in the still-growing suburbs. Over a period of fifteen years, the number of Republican officeholders in the state increased tenfold. Like Republicans in other southern states, Texas Republicans benefited enormously from a Democratic Party riven by factionalism, slow to recognize the changes in the state, and increasingly identified with the national party's liberal image. Democratic leaders couldn't decide whether to denounce the Republicans as right-wing zealots or claim the Democrats' own agenda was only slightly less conservative than the GOP's. But in a state with 254 counties and a history of Democratic control of the courthouses, the conversion of Texas sometimes seemed painfully slow. Republicans often counted their advances on one hand — a Railroad Commission seat here, a state Supreme Court justice there — while Democrats maintained control of the legislature and the congressional delegation. Each time Republicans stood poised for a major breakthrough, the Democrats mustered enough strength to hurl them back yet another time.

The biggest Republican disappointment came in 1990, when Gramm won his reelection contest with 60 percent of the vote, but Democrat Ann Richards won the governor's race over Clayton Williams, a west Texas rancher and oil man, by 51–49 percent.

Richards had survived one of the meanest Democratic primaries in history, eclipsing former governor Mark White in the first round of the primary and then slaying liberal pit bull Jim Mattox in the runoff. Mattox threw everything he could at Richards, including accusations of past drug use (she is a recovering alcoholic), but his tactics backfired, permanently crippling his own career.

In Williams, Richards faced an untested politician who had roared out of the primary largely on the strength of a television commercial in which he promised to introduce youthful offenders to "the joys of bustin' rocks." Claytie Williams seemed to exemplify the traits Texans loved best: rugged independence, a deep suspicion of government, and unbridled faith in free markets. But on closer inspection he was a caricature of Texas past and an embarrassment to a state that had grown more sophisticated throughout the 1970s and 1980s. Williams offended women with crude sexual comments and turned off hardworking middle-class voters by admitting he had not paid federal income taxes in 1986. Despite her liberal credentials, Richards's personality bridged a cultural divide between Bubba and Bella Abzug. She held on to her Democratic base, attracted suburban Republican women, and sent Williams back to his west Texas ranch to ponder a political career that had crashed like a meteor. Among men, Richards lost by 58–41, but among women, who made up 53 percent of the electorate, she won 56–43.

Richards became an instant Democratic star and a potential nominee for a national ticket. Her 1988 keynote address at the Democratic convention first put her in the national spotlight. Given the job of pillorying Republican nominee George Bush, Richards delivered a devastating speech full of biting, sarcastic humor that culminated with the line: "Poor George, he just can't help it. He was born with a silver foot in his mouth." Richards's gritty but grandmotherly personality captivated Texans, and her big head of white hair and Texas twang softened the edges of her liberal, feminist political background. Richards offered few dramatic legislative initiatives. Instead she hoped to bring about a "new Texas" by appointing to power those who historically had been locked out: women, blacks, Hispanics, gays. One of her most publicized appointees was forced to quit after admitting she had lied about graduating from college, an embarrassment that cost Richards considerable capital. On one of the most pressing issues facing the state, equalizing school financing, she deferred to the legislature after her own plan went nowhere. When the legislature produced its own plan, she campaigned actively for it, but the voters turned it down by a two-to-one margin. But despite her middling legislative record and her even more mixed record of appointments, Richards became one of the most popular politicians in the state's history. Were it not for her friend Bill Clinton, Richards might still be governor today.

The 1992 election, ironically, dealt a savage blow to Democrats in Texas. Clinton's victory proved devastating for Texas Democrats. Despite his southern roots, Clinton's policies reinforced the Democratic Party's liberal cast, while the problems in his personal life and his oscillating style of leadership offended the values of Texans of both parties. It is difficult to find a major state where Clinton stands in lower esteem than Texas.

But Clinton's performance as President represented only part of the damage his presidency inflicted on Texas Democrats. Equally harmful was his decision to select Lloyd Bentsen, the one Democrat who had held the party together, as his treasury secretary. For more than a decade, Bentsen acted as the security blanket for Democrats of all ideologies. Personally, he was a pro-business Democrat who looked after the oil and gas industries from the Senate Finance Committee, and his standing among Texas voters gave cover to liberal Democratic office seekers who had his blessing. What he lacked in charisma he made up for with the stature that came from his powerful committee chairmanship (and his party's 1988 vice presidential nomination), keen political instincts, and a statewide political team led by able strategist Jack Martin that was one of the best in the country. His conservative-to-moderate philosophy appealed to the broad middle of the Texas electorate, and his personal prestige gave him the freedom to exercise his partisanship aggressively when events required. The Treasury nomination capped Bentsen's distinguished political career, but his departure from Texas left a vacuum that no other Democrat could fill. It is difficult to imagine a presidential personnel decision made with less regard for its political impact in one of the country's most important states.

Richards's failure to find a suitable successor to Bentsen compounded the Democrats' problem. For years, Texas Democrats never lacked for attractive young candidates to run for higher office, but when Richards began hunting for a replacement, she found an empty cupboard. One of the brightest young stars in Texas was Henry Cisneros, who had an impressive record while mayor of San Antonio. But he left the mayor's office tarnished by the fallout from an extramarital affair. Neither he nor Richards was game for naming him to the Senate or a brutal, statewide campaign. (Cisneros preferred a cabinet slot, and Clinton obliged, naming him secretary of Housing and Urban Development.) Richards dithered for weeks, finally naming Bob Kreuger, a bland former congressman and failed Senate candidate who was then on the Railroad Commission, to the vacant seat. Kreuger's appointment proved to be an utter disaster for the party. Trapped between his desire to be loyal to Clinton and the state's conservative, anti-Clinton majority, Kreuger forfeited any advantages he had as an incumbent and surrendered the seat in a humiliating special election in June 1993 won by Republican Kay Bailey Hutchison. Hutchison captured 239 of the 254 counties and 67 percent of the vote, reconsolidating the Republican regulars with most of the Perot voters who had defected in 1992.

Hutchison's triumph boosted the sagging spirits of the national Republican Party, and provided the first clear warning that Richards was vulnerable in 1994, despite her personal popularity. A month earlier, Texas voters had rejected a school finance plan advocated by the governor, and she lacked a clear agenda for a second term. Even so, with the Texas economy rebounding after successive shocks from the oil bust, a collapse in real estate development, and the national recession, Richards still should have been one of the most secure incumbents in the country — were it not for her ties to the unpopular Clinton and the conservative Republican trend that continued to take root.

Richards's battle against George W. Bush in 1994 epitomized the kind of contest that made Texas politics such a popular spectator sport, pitting what *Texas Monthly* called "the most popular Democrat in decades" against someone with the most famous Republican name in the state. Richards sought to capitalize on her personality, while Bush built a remarkably disciplined campaign around issues and ideology. He refrained from attacking Richards personally, doggedly sticking to a conservative message that emphasized four issues: welfare reform, lowering the age at which juveniles would be tried as adults, tort reform, and education reform. Richards attacked Bush's record as a businessman, questioned his qualifications to be governor, and lost her cool several times by referring to Bush as "shrub" and "jerk." They met once in debate, and while Bush appeared more nervous, it was Richards who sounded ill-prepared for the only question that counted, which came from Paul Burka of *Texas Monthly*, who asked her what she would do with a second term. Her unfocused answer summed up the core weakness of her campaign.

The morning after their debate, Bush began his stretch run in east Texas, long the heart and soul of the Democratic Party, and everywhere he went that day he delivered the same message: The election was not about personality or party, it was about philosophy — and he was the conservative. Waiting for his campaign bus in Marshall late in the afternoon, Dorothy Ruthven described a personal political evolution that illustrated the state's transformation: "My parents were Democrats and you just sort of grew up that way," she said. "My daughter and son are staunch Republicans." A lifelong Democrat herself, Ruthven had switched parties and planned to vote for Bush. Ruthven represented the target of Bush's strategy for winning the election, which combined maximizing the growing Republican suburban areas with an all-out effort in rural Democratic strongholds, particularly in east Texas. Karl Rove had divided the state into three categories: the big urban and suburban counties populated by what Rove liked to call loyal, "paint-me-red Republicans"; smaller metropolitan areas that showed increasing Republican tendencies; and once-Democratic rural counties that had become competitive since 1990. Throughout the spring, Bush quietly traveled to these rural counties, spending half a day or more in each of them, getting to know the people and the power structure. In the fall he returned on campaign whistle-stops.

On election day, the strategy paid huge dividends, as Bush dispatched Richards with surprising ease, 53–47 percent. The victory marked another major step in the evolution of Texas away from the Democrats. Bush's rural strategy helped deliver east Texas, where he received 53 percent of the vote (up eight points over Williams in 1990), while in the urban and suburban areas, he swamped Richards, even though she actually won more raw votes in both Dallas and Houston than she had in 1990. For example, her vote in Houston rose from 412,000 to 434,000, but the Republican vote leaped from 407,000 to 554,000. In Dallas–Fort Worth, Richards went from

535,000 to 580,000, while the GOP vote jumped from 528,000 to 701,000. Much of Bush's advantage came in the rapidly growing collar counties around the state's major cities. The ten fastest-growing of those counties gave Bush majorities ranging from 54 percent to 73 percent, one more indication why the future lies more with the Republicans in Texas as in much of the rest of the South.

Bush's victory was not simply the product of angry white men turning against a feminist idol. Bush won the male vote by the same margin (58–41) as Williams had. Among all women, he lost by only 50–49, improving significantly on the 43 percent that Williams had received in 1990. Among white women, however, he won 59 percent of the vote, convincingly demonstrating that pro-choice Republican women would support a quietly pro-life Republican man if he did not polarize the election around social issues, as he carefully avoided. After winning five of the eight major geographic areas of the state in 1990, Richards won only two in 1994: the area of central Texas between Austin and Dallas, and the traditional Democratic bastion of South Texas, which is the most heavily Hispanic area of the state. South Texas may represent the next Republican target, however, and there are signs that the Democrats' strength there has begun to erode. If the Republicans go part of the way in converting South Texas to a more competitive playing field, the Democrats will find it even more difficult to win statewide elections.

Bush's victory changed the balance of power in Texas. If he governs successfully, he could solidify the Republican advantage into the next century. As governor, Bush has been a kinder, gentler version of the Republicanism practiced by Phil Gramm. Working with a Democratic lieutenant governor and a Democratic House Speaker, Bush concluded his first legislative session in June 1995 having won nearly everything on his agenda; he even promised not to campaign in 1996 against Democratic legislators who helped pass his programs. "I've been around Texas long enough to know that when I look at the sheriff in the eyes in [some] rural county and I say, 'Pal, you've got to be with me only if you're a Republican,' there's no way he's going to be for me."

Bush may appear on the surface somewhat out of step with the style and tactics of other southern conservatives, for he has the same gentlemanly politeness of his father and has opposed Gramm's stance on welfare and Pete Wilson's position on immigration. But like his brother, Jeb, who ran unsuccessfully for governor of Florida in 1994, George W. Bush's conservatism carries a harder edge than anything his father practiced. "I think you're the product of your upbringing," Bush said one day in the summer of 1995, sitting in his capitol office adorned with Texas art. "I was raised in Midland, Texas. He was raised in Greenwich, Connecticut. Greenwich was a very lovely community, [but] I grew up with sons of roughnecks. I think I'm a little more populist . . . than he would be. . . . I think being raised in Midland, which was kind of a frontier at the time — unbelievably egalitarian world — I think it's a little different perspective." He is, in other words, much less a product of the old Republican Party of his father, and if not quite a Gingrich Republican, far more in tune with the new party.

THE REPUBLICAN FUTURE

With the same trends that transformed Texas and South Carolina coursing through the entire region, the South now stands as the Republicans' bastion. This represents perhaps the most strategically significant of all the shifts that have occurred in the political balance in this decade. The old Solid South provided enough extra congressional seats to protect the Democrats from losses in other regions and keep them in power for four decades. But in 1994, Republicans did for congressional races what Eisenhower did in 1952 to the presidential equation: They neutralized a long-held Democratic advantage and for the first time significantly turned the tide in their direction.

The demographic and political trends of today's South suggest, in the words of Merle Black, that the region could become a "surplus supplier" of congressional seats for the Republicans. What that means is that the South now may be able to offset potential losses in the North and West that could come in the settling from the 1994 earthquake, giving the Republicans a much greater opportunity to maintain control of both the Senate and House in coming years. At Republican Party headquarters in Washington, the GOP targeting maps for 1996 show a preponderance of districts in the South considered ripe for harvesting, while among Democratic strategists, the conundrum of the South remains the most challenging aspect of charting a course back to majority status in the House and Senate.

For election after election, southern Democrats scraped by on guile, independence, and the argument that voting Republican in congressional or legislative races meant throwing away a vote, given the partisan balance in both Congress and state legislature. By erasing the presumption of Democratic control, the 1994 elections removed that argument, and the once-dominant southern Democratic power barons have fallen by the wayside.

The growing number of Republican officeholders provides the party with something else it has never enjoyed in the South: an expanding farm team of experienced candidates and the appeal of a winning franchise to talented and aspiring young politicians. Lindsey Graham, the young South Carolinian who captured a House seat in 1994 held by Democrats since Reconstruction, said he hopes to do in his district what Carroll Campbell did statewide, which is to present an attractive model of Republican governance locally and thereby encourage younger South Carolinians to follow him into the party. Graham argues that talented Democrats can still win elections in his district, but not for long. "We're one generation away where you can't do that," he said. "If I succeed as a congressman to build a farm system of Republicans to win local offices like I'm trying to do, the next generation of young people who want to get into politics and run as Democrats will have to be extremely lucky to win." With roughly two in three white southern voters under age forty-five supporting Republican House candidates in 1994, Graham's expectations hardly seem farfetched.

The hardening of racial lines between the two parties represents the most troubling aspect of southern political trends. The Republicans may aspire to become the nation's majority party, but can a political institution that derives 94 percent of its vote in the South from whites ever pretend to offer credible representation to African-Americans? Most southern politicians, Republicans and Democrats, have long since abandoned overtly racial campaign appeals, but Republicans still struggle to escape their own history in the South. Younger Republicans, those who came of age with or in the aftermath of the civil rights movement, have tried to move beyond race-based campaigning. "The southern strategy, in my opinion, has been very destructive for the Republican Party," said Bob Inglis, a second-term House member from South Carolina. "You can't be a majority party if you write off 30 percent of the vote. You can't hold on. You've got to prove that conservative doesn't equal racist."

Colin Powell's decision to become an active member of the party represents an enormous boost for the GOP. But at a time when Republicans seek dramatic reforms in welfare programs that many blacks see as punitive, and when leading Republican officials press to eliminate affirmative action programs, the burden of proof on the party remains enormously high, as Powell himself has said. Who can forget the 1990 Senate race in North Carolina, in which Jesse Helms played the race card in the final month of the campaign to defeat Harvey Gantt, the black former mayor of Charlotte? Helms aired a television commercial that showed a pair of white hands holding a letter saying the recipient had been rejected for a job in favor of a minority applicant with fewer qualifications. Democrats mistake these purely racial appeals as the principal reason for their decline in the South. In reality, Republicans have gained much more in recent elections by identifying themselves with less government, fiscal conservatism, and lower taxes than by race-based arguments. But the current agenda in Washington, coupled with the desire by many prominent Republicans to end affirmative-action programs, hinders the GOP's ability to reach out to black voters. Some Republican strategists posit a future in which GOP candidates routinely receive 15–20 percent of the black vote in the South, built upon the emerging black middle class. Some candidates have achieved those numbers, but not many: The party as a whole remains suspect to the most significant minority in the region, and the current agenda nationally likely will prevent the GOP from reaching those targets.

The Supreme Court's 1995 decision on redistricting threatens further polarization in the South, at least in the short run. In *Miller v. Johnson*, the Court threw out Georgia's congressional boundaries on the basis that race was the "predominant factor" in dictating the shape of the districts. The immediate impact was to threaten the career of Cynthia McKinney, the black Democrat elected in 1992 who represents Georgia's Eleventh District. But it could have wider implications for black representation throughout the South. The map grew out of an alliance between black and Republican legislators common throughout the country after the 1990 census: Republicans agreed to maximize the number of majority-minority districts, knowing they could more easily win the surrounding majority-white districts. That is particularly true in the South, given trends in white voting practices, and as a result the Georgia decision could wreak more havoc within the Democratic Party than with the Republican Party. But many black voters interpreted the decision as another indication that the court as now constituted is hostile to their interests. Over the longer run, however, the shift back toward congressional and legislative districts that are more balanced racially should be a healthy development because it will force all candidates, white or black, once again to appeal to a biracial constituency. If both Republicans and Democrats, for their own reasons, feel the need to make genuine appeals to black voters, the political system in the South will be far healthier than it is today.

The wreckage of the Democrats, increasingly divided between its liberal-minority wing and its shrinking moderate wing, lies strewn across the region. The movement of conservative voters into the GOP ensures that the liberal wing of the Democratic Party increasingly will dominate primary elections in the South, making the party's nominees less electable in general elections. The safest Democratic seats (other than those held by longtime white incumbents) belong to some of the most liberal members of the Democratic caucus, many of them African-Americans in newly created majority-minority districts. Moderate-to-conservative Democrats have become an endangered species. Of forty-two white southern Democrats in the House in 1995, twenty-eight were elected before 1990, while forty-four of seventy-seven white southern Republicans arrived after the 1990 elections. The process of generational replacement augurs well for the Republicans, for increasingly, white voters see the GOP as the party that will protect their interests. The 1994 elections, rather than strengthening the hand of moderates within the party, nearly decimated the wing symbolized by the Democratic Leadership Council, the organization founded largely by southern Democrats after the 1984 election to push the party toward the center, and the party switches and retirements in 1995 — most notably Senator Sam Nunn of Georgia — underscored the sense of gloom now pervasive among Democrats in the South. "The only conservative Democrats who can survive in the South are those known as conservatives, not Democrats," Merle Black said. "In the minds of white voters, a conservative Democrat is an unreliable conservative." Unless Democrats find some new way to reverse these trends, the old-fashioned conservative Democrat could soon face extinction, as a young generation of white politicians looks to the Republicans to fulfill their ambitions. The one hope for Democrats may lie in their ability to attract populist voters fearful about the changes Republicans are making in Washington, a strategy that showed some potential in the 1995 elections.

While the Democrats are pulled left, southern Republicans have assembled a coalition that is more purely conservative than anywhere else in the country, with the possible exception of parts of the West. The southern GOP draws on a voter base that includes not only economic conservatives but far more religious and cultural conservatives than elsewhere as well. Exit polls from 1994 showed that a quarter of white southern voters identified themselves as Christian fundamentalists, compared to less than one in six nationally. The growing strength of this constituency, and its locus in a region that has become the party's new base of power, not only guarantees greater attention by the party to divisive issues like school prayer and abortion, but threatens to make secular conservatives and moderates think twice about their longer-term allegiance with the GOP. Comments by Republicans like Mississippi's Kirk Fordice that America is a "Christian nation" represent a minority view even among the most religious of the GOP leadership, but they still damage the party's national image.

The new southern Republican coalition doesn't just reinforce the party's conservative tendencies, it threatens to accelerate them. No region, with the possible exception of the West, better typifies the strength of the conservative, antigovernment coalition that helped drive the Republicans to power. Exit polls showed that a quarter of white southern voters owned guns, that one in five regularly listened to talk radio, and that two in three agreed with the proposition that government should do less, not more, seven points higher than the national average. Northern moderates may rebel against some of the priorities of a party with such strength in the South, but the electoral trends suggest that over time there will be more southerners within the congressional ranks, not fewer. On a sweltering day in the summer of 1995, George W. Bush sat in his office in the Texas capitol, reflecting on the implications of the changes in his party and the strength of its new foundation in the South. "Lesson 101 in politics," he said, "is never leave your base." That lesson was lost on Bush's father, who in

1992 struggled unsuccessfully to reassemble the conservative coalition that twice powered Ronald Reagan to victory. But the younger Bush's words stand as an article of faith among the members of the new Republican majority that emerged from the landslide of 1994.

In breaking the Democrats' historic hold on the South, the Republicans not only helped secure their own future but also bound themselves to issues and constituencies that now push them ever rightward. The South stands as the Republicans' protective shield against Democratic counterattacks in the North, and as migration continues to increase the population of the South and West at the expense of the North and Midwest, the advantage will only enlarge. But this reshaping also risks propelling the party far enough to the right to threaten losses at the center of the political spectrum. Those dangers remain prospective. For now, the GOP can look around the South as an enlarging electoral fortress. The speed and breadth of the transformation startled even many who have worked to advance it — and the impact on the party is equally surprising. Sitting one day in an Austin, Texas, office piled high with computer printouts and Texas paraphernalia, Bush strategist Karl Rove summed up the transformation with a Civil War analogy. "The party of northern aggression," he said, "has become the party of southern dominance."

★★★

6

The New Republican Agenda

D
URING THE LONG REIGN of the New Deal politi-
cal coalition, when new federal buildings sprouted in Washing-
ton like marble mushrooms after a rain, political scientists
described an iron triangle that created an apparently irre-
versible trend toward more public spending and an ever larger federal
government. This was the basic nexus of power in the capital: con-
gressional staff, lobbyists, and officials in the federal agencies them-
selves — three points on a triangle all looking to expand their empires
with new programs, new appropriations, new initiatives for favored
constituencies. The federal money was the solder hardening the tri-
angle and entrenching the position of all its players. For years, it ap-
peared unbreakable.

But now a kind of conservative iron triangle has developed to pur-
sue the retrenchment of federal power. At one point of the triangle is
the Republican majority in Congress. At the second point is the grow-
ing conservative presence in the states, where Republicans now
control thirty-one of the fifty governorships and nineteen state
legislatures, and where conservative experimentation was flourishing
long before 1994. The third point on the triangle is the Supreme
Court, where five Republican-appointed justices — Chief Justice
William H. Rehnquist, and Associate Justices Anthony M. Kennedy,
Clarence Thomas, Sandra Day O'Connor, and Antonin Scalia — are

coalescing into a potentially powerful, if still fragile, majority for limiting federal power and constraining programs of racial preference.

From the two other points on the triangle, conservatives in Congress are drawing both inspiration and fortification. The political success of Republican governors such as John Engler, William Weld, and Christine Todd Whitman in pursuing budget- and tax-cutting policies has encouraged congressional Republicans to sharpen their own knives; at the same time, the Republican gains in the state Houses have increased the willingness of congressional conservatives to shift control over social programs from Washington to the states. The push from Republican governors to cut state taxes has created the conditions for a period in which government spending may face downward pressure at the federal and state level simultaneously.

Operating on the third point, the Supreme Court strengthened the trend toward devolution of power away from Washington soon after the new majority took power. In April 1995, the Court's five-member conservative coalition struck down a federal law banning guns in schools and signaled a narrower interpretation of the Constitution's commerce clause that allows Congress to regulate interstate economic activity. While invalidating congressional term limits in a ruling issued the next month, four members of the conservative coalition — deserted only by Kennedy — issued a dissent stunning in the sweep of its assertion of state primacy over the federal government in setting domestic policy. That dissent and the decision in the school gun case suggest "the court is reaching the question at the heart of it all," Roger Pilon of the libertarian Cato Institute said. "Did we authorize all this government?"

Conservative Republicans routinely say they have reached for inspiration back beyond Bush to Ronald Reagan. But in fact, their ambitions now dwarf Reagan's. Reagan powerfully articulated the conservative case for reducing the federal government but, after the Democratic congressional gains in 1982, largely abandoned the effort. With Gingrich and his allies in the House leading the way, conservatives in the new iron triangle are now pursuing policies across the range of domestic concerns that exceed Reagan in the ferocity of their assault on liberal assumptions — particularly about the role of the federal government.

The plan approved in the House and Senate in 1995 to bring the federal budget into balance by the year 2002 envisions that over the next seven years the federal government will spend roughly $900 billion less than required to maintain current services — a reduction in the growth of government more than double the size of the cuts contained in Reagan's original budget package. Reagan and Bush both fulminated against affirmative-action programs that grant preferences to minorities in hiring and admission decisions, but neither lifted a finger to revoke the presidential executive order requiring federal contractors to undertake such programs. Now, Republicans in both chambers are pushing legislation to restrict or eliminate federal affirmative-action programs. On other issues of social policy — redesigning Medicare, limiting welfare, reducing regulation on business, requiring government to compensate property owners for rules that reduce the value of their land — the progression is the same.

This interconnected, self-reinforcing attempt to shrink the size and scope of the federal government constitutes a scale of possibility conservatives could not even have imagined during the Bush years. Indeed, when Clinton first arrived in Washington, the Republican Party appeared intellectually exhausted. In an anguished article written as Clinton marched toward the White House in the summer of 1992, Vin Weber declared, "In my fourteen years in national politics, I have never been so concerned about the future of conservative ideas." The Bush administration provided little inspiration for young conservative activists; nor had either Bob Dole or Bob Michel in Congress. In 1992, the Heritage Foundation's *Policy Review* asked Michel what agenda Republicans might pursue if they ever regained control of the House. Like a prisoner who cannot dream of the world beyond his cell, Michel's imagination could stretch no further than internal congressional reform: reducing the number of committees, applying to Congress the laws that it imposed on others. What Michel saw as victory's windfall, the House disposed of on the first day of the Gingrich era.

Bush, Michel, and Dole functioned like a cork, bottling up the militant elements in the party. Then, suddenly, after the 1992 election, the cork was removed. Bush went home to Texas. Michel deferred to Gingrich, en route to retiring after the 1994 election. Dole suppressed the deal-maker instincts he had displayed during the 1980s, and emerged as a cuttingly partisan opponent of Clinton. Perot's strong showing in 1992 demonstrated a constituency for bold changes in Washington.

The final ingredient in the new mixture was Clinton's own ambitious agenda. As Clinton moved to redefine the Democratic Party — and seize issues like welfare, crime, and deficit reduction that Republicans had long considered their own — he instilled a new sense of urgency behind the calls for new directions from conservative activists like Weber and Gingrich. Those efforts to rejuvenate the conservative agenda moved forward even as congressional Democrats resisted many of Clinton's initiatives. By forcing Republicans to reassess their assumptions — while many Democrats resisted reassessing their own — Clinton's attempt to redefine the terms of debate in American politics ironically may have inspired more new thinking in the GOP than in his own party.

THE PROPHET OF POLARIZATION

No one understood the challenge Clinton presented to the GOP more keenly than Bill Kristol, who had served as Dan Quayle's chief of staff in the Bush administration. During the dreary Bush years, Kristol had been cruelly celebrated as the administration's Edgar Bergen: the genius who could make even as wooden a prop as Quayle sit up and talk. Kristol had been singled out as a man to watch almost from the moment he arrived in Washington early in Reagan's second term as chief of staff for Bill Bennett, then bulling his way through the demure china shop of the academic world as Education secretary. Bennett said later he hired Kristol because he knew "his DNA pretty well," and in fact, in the world of conservative policy intellectuals, Kristol's blood lines were peerless. His mother was the historian Gertrude Himmelfarb. His father was the neoconservative intellectual Irving Kristol, a caustic essayist and indefatigable networker whose exertions had helped Bennett win his first Washington job as chairman of the National Endowment for the Humanities.

If Bill Kristol indulged any thoughts of youthful rebellion from his parents, he exorcised them early: As a Harvard undergraduate in the early 1970s he took perverse pleasure in defending Richard Nixon and the Vietnam War on a campus where opposition to both were more common than trust funds. After earning a Harvard Ph.D. in political science, Kristol pointed himself toward academia, eventually teaching at both his alma mater and the University of Pennsylvania. But when Bennett summoned him to Washington, Kristol found his métier. Compact and curly-haired, with a mischievous twinkle in his eyes, Kristol looked and acted less like a bureaucratic barracuda than a junior don. He was smart, quick-witted, and likable: a genial Machiavellian. As he ascended from the Education Department to the vice president's office, Kristol stood out as both a reliable advocate for conservative causes and a reliable source for reporters documenting Bush's failure to follow them. The only sour notes came from the occasional unnamed "White House aide" who groused that Kristol promoted himself and his boss at Bush's expense. But if self-promotion were a crime, Washington would be Alcatraz. After Clinton's victory, Kristol was one of the very few officials who left the Bush administration with his reputation enhanced.

For several months, Kristol pondered his options while surveying the state of the Right for the Milwaukee-based Bradley Foundation, among the leading bankrollers of conservative organizations. Then he convinced the Bradley executives and some politically connected conservative investors in New York that what the conservative movement really needed was a think tank under his direction. So was born the Project for the Republican Future.

In the era of the virtual corporation, Kristol created a virtual think tank, with a skeleton staff, a utilitarian office, and an emphatic absence of out-of-work cabinet officers collecting titles and six-figure salaries. Originally, he envisioned the project bridging the worlds of politics and ideas: publicly sponsoring the high-minded, eyelid-drooping seminars that inspire a run on the coffee machines at downtown Washington hotels every day, and privately advising Republican legislators on policy and strategy. But as they drafted their first (unsolicited) memo of advice for the GOP congressional leadership in the fall of 1993, Kristol and his confederates — two young political operatives named David Tell and Dan Casse — took an unanticipated turn. No strategic advice committed to paper was likely to stay private for long, they reasoned; why not just release it to the public?

Thus, on December 2, 1993, fax machines across Washington announced the arrival of a new political art form: the publicly distributed private strategy memo. Kristol expected only a modest response to the memo — an incitement for Republicans to undertake death-before-dishonor opposition to Clinton's health care plan. But it created an unexpected sensation and quickly sent the three youthful conspirators back to their fax machines. Eventually the Kristolgrams became an institution. The *Washington Times* routinely excerpted them on the day of their release; when Kristol moved to a new position on, say, term limits, it was often treated as news even in the major national newspapers. Convinced that Kristol had the ear of the Republican leadership, other conservative organizations lobbied him to embrace their causes, the way small companies lobby Wall Street columnists to tout their stocks.

These memos earned Kristol the reverent press notices that many conservatives assume are reserved only for liberals; reporters termed Kristol a "brilliant strategist" so often that it sometimes seemed he should print up business cards with that label. Not everyone was so enamored with him. The huge spotlight on the memos put their intended audience in an odd position because in publicizing the puppeteer they tended to reduce any Republicans following the advice to puppets. Echoing the criticism that emanated from Bush's White House, some conservatives grumbled that the memos seemed more about promoting Kristol than advancing the cause.

Kristol himself may have seen no conflict between those goals, and in fact his memos became signature documents in the Republican revival. From the start, Kristol's message placed him just behind Gingrich at the forefront of the GOP faction that argued for confrontation, not cooperation, with Clinton; Kristol became the living antithesis of the third way. On grounds of both principle and self-interest, he argued, Republicans should oppose Clinton root and branch. His memos had a St. Crispin's Day feel to them, a summoning of brothers to glorious battle. They were unabashedly and calculatingly political in that they viewed policy debates primarily in terms of their impact on the political fortunes of the two parties. Kristol considered the purpose of congressional deliberation not to narrow but to sharpen the divide between the parties, to frame differences for the voters in terms as stark as possible. In Kristol's vision, any concession to Clinton, any compromise that allowed him to advance his own agenda, impeded the ultimate Republican goal of regaining political power and implementing their own ideas. "The best that . . .

'cooperation' could produce is incoherent and ineffective legislation," he wrote, "and at worst it would weaken our chances to achieve truly principled conservative governance — through the election in 1996 of a Republican executive to join a Republican Congress."

To Democrats, this was only ornate gilding for a policy of crass, partisan self-interest. And there was in Kristol's thinking a reflexive quality that made it appear he applied to Clinton's policy proposals the same logic as the Queen in *Alice in Wonderland*: "Sentence first — verdict afterwards." Kristol's judgment remained the same whatever the issue: welfare reform, the crime bill, lobbying, and campaign finance reform. In each instance, he denounced Clinton's ideas as an unwarranted expansion of government and urged Republicans to kill them outright.

Kristol's martial exhortations had their greatest effect in the debate over health care reform. At a time when many Republicans still believed the party would be best served by making a deal with Clinton, Kristol argued in his first memo that the GOP should seek the "unqualified political defeat of the Clinton health care proposal." Kristol's counsel never wavered. At each step of the long legislative struggle over health care, as the Clinton plan clung for life on a crumbling ledge, Kristol urged Republicans to bring down the hammer again. Republicans, he said, should challenge Clinton at his premise and reject his proposition that there was a health care "crisis" that demanded a massive government response. They should understand the true stakes involved in the debate: Liberals saw government-guaranteed health care as the way to consolidate a middle-class majority for an activist state. Conservatives had to see the fight as "liberalism's Afghanistan — the overreaching that exposes liberalism's weakness and causes its collapse."

Many Republicans initially bridled at that message, fearing Kristol's approach would stamp the party as obstructionist — which was indeed the course of action he urged. Gingrich and Dole both publicly criticized Kristol for pushing the "no-crisis" line. ("He was sending exactly the wrong signal to the American people," Gingrich complained later. "The average American seeing a Republican say there is no crisis . . . thought we were saying there was no health care problem. . . . He coined a cute phrase which intellectually captured a moment but which reinforced a whole range of negatives about us. I thought it was very dangerous.") But as the NFIB and other groups in the antigovernment coalition turned up their efforts against the Clinton health care plan, as the weeks went by without Democrats reaching a consensus on how to proceed, as Daniel Patrick Moynihan reinforced Kristol's argument by declaring on national television that he also believed there was not a health care crisis, Republicans gradually moved toward the Kristol strategy of absolute opposition (if not necessarily his no-crisis justification for it). Each step toward greater resistance encouraged the next. "They would dip their toes in the no-crisis water and there would be yelping for about a month in D.C. and in the press and they'd get nervous about it," Kristol said later, "but it would turn out they would go home and no one was sort of blaming them for it. And, it's the way these things work: They kind of kept tiptoeing deeper and deeper and somehow kept being surprised that they were not drowning at all. They just kept going the next step."

Steadily that dynamic spilled over beyond health care and influenced all facets of the GOP agenda. As in Gingrich's decade-long campaign to paint the House as corrupt, Republicans found during Clinton's first two years that it was virtually impossible to overreach in attacking Washington or the federal government. In fact it was the opposite: The Republicans were continually prodded to greater militance by their conservative constituency. When they felt no backlash against their stiffening opposition to Clinton's health care plan in the first half of 1994, Republicans were encouraged to mount greater resistance to Clinton's crime proposals over the summer. The success at forcing Clinton to renegotiate the crime bill encouraged Republicans to put the last nail into the Democratic campaign finance and lobbying reform bills. The astonishing electoral reward that followed these victories emboldened Republicans in both chambers the next year to sign on to budget plans that only months earlier might have seemed to them a suicide pact.

This hardening of the Republican agenda reflected political calculations about deteriorating public support for Clinton and rising anger toward the federal government. But it also embodied less tangible changes in the intellectual climate. The breadth of the Republican assault against liberalism that emerged after 1992 would not have been possible without an intellectual realignment that has shaken both ends of the ideological spectrum.

On one side is a growing self-confidence among conservatives. This swagger is at the core of the generational shift within the party. Younger Republicans, like Gingrich, Weber, and Kristol, now commonly assume that given a clear choice, most Americans would prefer Republican ideas of limited government to liberal proposals to expand the state. There are limits to that confidence: To balance the budget, Republicans had to find massive savings in Medicare, but they tried to sell the changes as a plan simply to keep the system solvent.

But Republicans in the Gingrich wing of the party are usually comfortable — even enthusiastic — about polarizing debate in terms as sharp as possible. The liberal magazine *The American Prospect* hit the mark when it put on its cover a drawing of Gingrich (with other leading conservatives) glowering in a leather jacket on a street corner: In a way that liberals might have done a generation earlier, Gingrich seems to roll out of bed every morning eager to rumble with his ideological enemies. Bob Dole and Bob Michel were both born in 1923 and entered politics in the long shadow of the New Deal, at a time when Samuel Lubell memorably termed Republicans the "moon" to the Democrats' "sun"; in the eyes of many younger Republicans they never entirely unlearned those lessons. Conservatives like Gingrich and Kristol unreservedly consider the GOP the natural majority party.

Paralleling this rise in conservative confidence has been an erosion in the power of liberal ideas to control public debate. In some unquantifiable respect, the institutions that shape elite opinion and help to mold mass opinion — the major newspapers, the television networks, the leading universities — now have less faith in traditional liberal solutions than they did ten or fifteen years ago, notwithstanding the Republican belief that they reflexively trumpet liberal causes. Clinton's "New Democrat" agenda assumed a collapse in public support for centralization, redistribution, and entitlement. Even in left-of-center think tanks, no longer is there an automatic link between the identification of a problem and the assumption that a government program must be established to correct it. Conservatives still feel themselves under siege from the press and academia; but, in fact, conservative assumptions about the limits of federal action, the nature of poverty, and the balance between rights and responsibilities have gained intellectual respectability in direct proportion to the erosion of public faith in government.

That is why conservatives now dream of a counterrevolution more sweeping than Reagan's. But, as some of the party's most thoughtful analysts understand, the explosive momentum behind the antigovernment impulse in the GOP also exposes the Republicans to substantial risk. In American politics, no victory is ever final; history suggests a party can face its greatest danger in the euphoria that follows its greatest triumphs. As the guardrails that have limited the possibility of conservative change fall away, the most pertinent question for Republicans is straightforward: In reversing the growth of government that stretches back to the Progressive Era, how far is too far? What is the point that triggers a backlash in 1996 or 1998 or 2000? In this era of profound skepticism about government, does such a point exist at all? Or is the greater risk not reducing and reforming government dramatically enough?

Clinton's decision in 1995 to propose his own plan for balancing the budget over ten years underscores that conservative ideas about government's role now hold the upper hand in society; absent a severe economic reversal that increases demands for government-provided security, those ideas are likely to remain dominant at least until early in the next century. But the exact boundaries of that conservative victory must still be determined in innumerable political battles yet to come. And in that crucible, the GOP still faces the persistent risk of fracturing both its legislative and political coalition as it translates the general desire to reduce government into specific reductions in individual government programs, many of which are far more popular than Washington in the abstract.

The tension between these electoral calculations, the drive of the antigovernment grassroots coalition and their intellectual allies, and the substantive doubts among party moderates about aspects of the coalition's agenda are the forces shaping the policy decisions emerging from the Republican Congress. In the first year of Republican control, these competing factors played out in the repeated conflicts between Gingrich's brigades in the House and more cautious Republican moderates who held the balance of power in the Senate.

That struggle produced no clear winner. Republicans did coalesce behind their historic budget- and tax-reduction plan, which included unprecedented reductions in dozens of federal programs; did bar the federal government from imposing unfunded mandates on the states;

did reform the internal operations of Congress; and were poised to wipe out several of Clinton's signature initiatives, including his national service plan and proposal to fund one hundred thousand new police officers. But in other respects the record disappointed many of the revolutionaries. Only one item in the Contract failed in the House; but it was the term limit constitutional amendment avidly supported by the groups in the antigovernment coalition. More important, a lengthening list of proposals that did clear the House, often after great struggle, stalled in the Senate. With the moderate Republicans balking, the Senate rejected House plans to give the states complete control over programs like school lunches, drastically scaled back the House proposals to rewrite product liability laws, and untied the noose House Republicans designed for federal regulation. Oregon Senator Mark Hatfield's opposition doomed the Balanced Budget Amendment by a single vote. In both chambers, hesitation from moderates and some conservatives slowed the drive to derail affirmative action.

Did this record amount to progress or retreat for the conservative activists and their allies in the antigovernment coalition? The answer depended on the frame of reference. Viewed as a snapshot of a single moment in time, the results of 1995's legislative struggles show a conservative majority frequently frustrated in its ambitions. But that was probably the wrong way to look at the record. Seen instead as one stage in an evolving process — as one frame in an ongoing sequence — the picture showed continuing internal conflict in the context of a policy debate shifting inexorably to the right. No longer is anyone in Washington debating whether to increase government spending, or to expand government regulation, or to enlarge the social safety net for the poor; in each case, the debate is now confined to the question of how sharply to reduce the government role, and how the remaining resources should be distributed.

This evolution was perhaps most vividly apparent in the grueling Republican struggle over reforming the welfare system for the poor, one of the most emotional and polarizing issues in American politics. Criticism of welfare has been a staple of Republican campaign rhetoric since the 1960s. Yet historically proposals to reform the system from both parties were modest, operating within limits defined by the liberal vision of government's responsibility to the poor. As those limits eroded, a significant core of congressional Republicans aligned with a radical intellectual critique of government welfare programs that proposed more ambitious efforts to change the behavior of the poor than either Reagan or Bush ever contemplated. But translating that critique into law proved an extremely complex process — one that demonstrated not only the power of the drive to limit government, but the complex and overlapping fault lines that divide the new Republican majority, and the constraints those divisions impose on the party's ability to implement its agenda.

THE BATTLE OVER THE POOR

For all the controversy it generates, the welfare program for indigent families consumes a minimal portion of the national budget. The full menu of federal assistance to the needy — including food stamps, health care, housing and tax subsidies, and other programs — costs more than $230 billion a year, with health care accounting for about 40 percent of the total. But welfare itself — cash aid, that is — costs the federal government only $12.5 billion annually, about 1 percent of federal spending.

Yet in terms of social policy, the welfare program, known formally as Aid to Families with Dependent Children (or AFDC), has enormous impact. The welfare program is available to single parents, and in some limited instances to unemployed two-parent families, with children under eighteen; in practice, about 90 percent of welfare families are headed by women. The size of the welfare caseload has grown substantially in the past decade; as of 1994, welfare provided income for about five million poor families, or just over fourteen million people in all. That figure includes about 9.5 million children, which means that welfare is the principal source of cash aid for more than 13 percent of all children in America. Put another way, the number of children receiving welfare at any given point equals the number of children living in New York and Texas combined.

Much of the controversy surrounding welfare derives from the characteristics of those families. When the federal welfare program was initially established, as part of the Social Security Act of 1935, its sponsors primarily sold it as a means of supporting widows raising young children alone. From a political perspective, widows were ideal beneficiaries because no one could blame them for their condition. Welfare has become more controversial as the nature of the caseload has shifted to women whose distress could be seen as linked to their own decisions — to get divorced or, more recently, to bear children outside of marriage. Today, only about 2 percent of welfare families are headed by widows, and an absolute majority of children on welfare were born out of wedlock.

The other reason the program has become such a jagged political issue in the past quarter century is the racial composition of the families receiving aid. The number of whites and African-Americans receiving welfare is about equal, with each group comprising just under 40 percent of the welfare caseload; Hispanics account for almost all of the remainder. The balance has actually shifted away from blacks since the 1970s, when African-Americans constituted 45 percent of the caseload. But even so, blacks receive welfare at a rate triple their presence in the overall population, and are more likely to stay on welfare for long spells, making discussions about welfare always tense with racial implications.

That's true on both sides of the ideological spectrum. Many African-American legislators view virtually any discussion of reforming welfare as an attempt to appeal to white prejudices. For their part, conservatives have frequently validated those fears by using welfare as the symbol of government programs that take money from hard-working middle-class families and give it to the indolent and undeserving — a group that for many economically strapped white voters wears a black face. Ronald Reagan convincingly demonstrated the power of that imagery in his 1980 campaign when he denounced extravagant "welfare queens" who bilked the system and prospered by others' sweat.

Notwithstanding all the ferocious rhetoric surrounding welfare since the 1960s, the actual proposals for changing the system from politicians in both parties have been powerfully constrained by liberal assumptions about the public obligation to the poor. In the 1970s, both Richard Nixon and Jimmy Carter offered welfare reform plans that would have required more recipients to work, but also significantly expanded eligibility for public aid. (Both plans fell into a valley of disdain between liberals, who disliked the work requirement, and conservatives, who objected to expanding eligibility, and neither was enacted into law.) Reagan presented a harder edge, but he focused his energies on cutting spending and marginally reducing eligibility, rather than changing the program's fundamental structure.

In 1982, Reagan proposed a more sweeping change, suggesting a grand swap under which the federal government would assume the full cost of Medicaid and turn over to the states full responsibility for both AFDC and food stamps. But the idea met resistance both from local governments and the Democratic-controlled Congress, and Reagan let it die without much of a fuss. In his second term, as momentum gathered in Congress and the states for more fundamental reforms, Reagan's passivity belied his belligerent rhetoric. An internal task force charged with studying welfare emphasized how little was known, ruled out any new federal initiatives, and recommended mostly giving states greater flexibility to undertake experiments in reform. But under pressure from governors (including Arkansas's Bill Clinton) eager to redraw the system, Congress moved toward more ambitious change.

From the perspective of the mid-1990s, the debate that ensued seems remarkably decorous. Republicans (joined at points by Reagan) sought, modestly, to increase the number of families required to work in return for their benefits and to increase state flexibility. House Democrats sought to limit the work requirements to as few recipients as possible and initially attempted to increase benefits. Senate Democrats and the governors placed themselves in between. As in the 1970s efforts at reform, the principal focus in the debate was how to move people from welfare into work. In the end, Reagan signed a compromise that gave states increased money to spend on education and training but also established the expectation that more welfare recipients would be moved off the rolls into work. Reagan proclaimed the bill "would lead to lasting emancipation from welfare dependency." Several liberal lobbying groups denounced the package as punitive.

By the second half of the Bush administration, it was clear that the bill had failed to meet the expectations of its supporters or the fears of its critics. Partly because of bureaucratic inertia, partly because of the recession, and partly because states failed to put up the money needed to trigger the federal dollars, relatively few welfare recipients were placed in education and training programs, much less required to work for their grants. Meanwhile, under the spur of the recession, and a continually rising rate of out-of-wedlock births, the welfare rolls were growing rapidly.

Against that backdrop of failure, pressure began to build again for more fundamental reform. One source was the community of policy analysts who studied welfare. Led by David Ellwood, the Harvard professor who later became a key welfare policy maker in the Clinton administration, a range of experts across the ideological spectrum argued for directly attacking long-term dependency by limiting the length of time welfare recipients could receive benefits. The more liberal versions of these ideas, like Ellwood's, promised to provide public service jobs for those who could not find private sector employment after they hit the limit, and to offer the poor other boosts, including guaranteed health care and more generous tax benefits; the conservative versions of the time limit generally did not guarantee public jobs or other services. As disappointment grew over the 1988 reform, both the liberal and conservative version of the time limit attracted interest from innovative politicians. In 1992, Vin Weber and fellow Republican Representative Clay Shaw of Florida introduced a bill that imposed a four-year time limit without a guarantee of public employment. (Separately, though, Shaw joined with two other moderates in a 1992 manifesto on welfare reform that proposed experimenting with government-guaranteed jobs.) Most significant, Clinton early in his presidential campaign seized on the idea of time-limiting assistance. Clinton converted Ellwood's vision into his politically appealing promise to "end welfare as we know it" by requiring welfare recipients to work (in publicly provided jobs if necessary) after two years on the rolls.

The other source of pressure for reform came from governors moving forward with their own initiatives. Of these, the most important Republican was Wisconsin Governor Tommy Thompson. Thompson was a genial grocer's son from the tiny town of Elroy whose meaty handshake and Runyonesque diction effectively cloaked his smooth political skills. During two decades in the state assembly, Thompson had been frustrated by Democratic resistance to reforming welfare, and when he defeated a liberal Democrat for the governorship in 1986, he immediately set out to push the ideas he had been unable to advance in the legislative minority.

Using a uniquely powerful line-item veto that allows him to eliminate individual words in legislation, Thompson cut welfare benefits by 6 percent soon after taking office and put back much of the money into programs intended to move recipients to work. Then he undertook a path-breaking series of experiments intended to shape the behavior of those receiving aid. Children First toughened child-support collection and required men either to pay their obligation or perform public service work; Bridefare gave teenagers bonuses to marry and limited payments to women who had additional children while already on welfare; Learnfare, an idea that came to Thompson one day while driving between campaign appearances, docked part of the welfare payments for mothers whose children habitually skipped school. Later he won approval of a trial program to impose a two-year time limit on welfare recipients in two virtually all-white counties with low AFDC caseloads. Many of these programs were small experiments in only a few counties, and their impact was limited; but they all proved popular with voters. And, whether because of his own welfare-to-work initiatives, benefit reductions that made welfare less attractive, or an improving state economy, Thompson could point with pride to a state welfare caseload that fell while the national caseload rose rapidly.

From a national perspective, Thompson's flurry of innovations sent out two ripples. One was to encourage other Republican governors — like Michigan's John Engler and Massachusetts's William F. Weld, both elected in 1990 — to undertake reforms of their own state welfare systems. The other was to advance the idea that the goals of welfare reform should extend beyond demanding work toward encouraging personal responsibility in a variety of ways from those receiving aid. Thompson's reforms put Wisconsin in the position of offering financial incentives to shape the most intimate behavior of welfare recipients — how they supervised their children or whether they sought to have more children. Even centrist Democrats like Clinton found aspects of this "tough love" approach appealing, and eventually it would exert a far-reaching effect on the welfare debate.

To all of this Bush was almost entirely obtuse. Worried about Clinton's effective use of the welfare issue, activist Republicans throughout 1992 repeatedly urged the Bush administration to offer its own reforms. One sticky spring day, a delegation of House Republicans that included Gingrich laid out their reform ideas at a meeting with Bush's top domestic advisers, but could not shake them from their caution. "You go back to that White House and you tell those people, 'When in doubt, take risks!'" Gingrich finally cried, bolting up from the table. As he marched out of the room and down the hallway, those around the table could hear Gingrich still blustering, "Take risks! Take risks!" The advice went unheeded. When Bush finally unveiled his welfare plan at the end of July in 1992, it was limited to giving the states more flexibility to undertake their own experiments — roughly what Reagan had proposed six years earlier.

To the extent the Bush administration had anything to say about poverty, it came from the prolix and voraciously empathetic secretary of Housing and Urban Development, Jack Kemp. Kemp was a politician cut from his own mold. A former pro football quarterback for the Buffalo Bills of the old American Football League, he was elected to Congress from a blue-collar Buffalo, New York, district in 1970. Kemp became a hero of conservatives for his advocacy of the supply-side tax cuts that Reagan later enacted into law. But his passion for tax cuts was matched by his conviction that Republicans needed to reach out to minorities and uplift the poor; Kemp was equal parts Arthur Laffer and Dorothy Day.

When Bush appointed Kemp to run HUD, he saw an opportunity to implement his vision for simultaneously reviving the cities and breaking the Democratic hold on minority votes. Through the Bush years, Kemp's agenda enjoyed a powerful vogue among activist conservatives like Weber, Gingrich, and analysts at the Heritage Foundation who believed that Republicans had to establish credibility on the core domestic issues of poverty and dependency if they were ever to achieve majority status. Kemp's answer was what he often called "a conservative war on poverty": ideas such as empowerment zones that would eliminate capital gains taxes on businesses that set up shop in depressed inner-city neighborhoods; vouchers that would allow inner-city parents to send their children to private schools; and subsidies that would allow tenants at public housing projects first to manage, and then eventually purchase, their apartments. He wanted to attack welfare dependency by allowing recipients to accumulate more assets — so that they could, theoretically, save for college or start a business — and by eliminating all income taxes on low-income workers.

The spirit of Kemp's proposals was more important than their specifics. Kemp assumed two things: that Republicans were obligated to respond to the problems of the needy, and that if provided economic opportunity, the poor would seize it as eagerly as anyone else. To conservatives who complained that government programs like welfare provided incentives for dependency and indolence, Kemp asked, "Why can't the government do things right and cause better things to happen? Not perfect things to happen, but better things to happen."

Kemp proselytized for his agenda in places Republicans were rarely seen, like inner-city housing projects and soup kitchens, and he made converts from many who were initially skeptical of his motivations. But, apart from some second-tier aides, he made no converts where it counted most: in the White House. In part because of his hyperactive style, Kemp was never able to attract Bush's interest or overcome the virtuoso bureaucratic resistance of budget director Richard Darman. With some cause, Darman considered Kemp's agenda impractical and expensive. Many of Darman's criticisms were telling: The tab for rehabilitating public housing units to the point where they could be sold to their tenants might run as high as $100,000 — as much, Darman dryly noted, as it might cost to buy them new condominiums. Nor was there much evidence of success for enterprise zones. But the bigger hurdle for Kemp was Bush's disinterest. Under Kemp's relentless prodding, Bush nominally endorsed his agenda, but without a flicker of commitment.

After Bush's defeat, many Republicans initially expected Kemp to emerge as the conservatives' champion for 1996. But instead, he drifted away from the party, or perhaps allowed it to drift away from him. The new Republicans arriving in Congress displayed less and less interest in his agenda for "empowering" the poor. Kemp lobbied to include his proposals in the Contract With America but found no takers. "There was talk of an inner city–type package, but no one aggressively pushed for it," said Kerry Knott, who supervised development of the Contract as Dick Armey's chief of staff. No one, he said, thought it "would resonate that much in November."

For his part, Kemp recoiled from the ideas that had caught his party's imagination. At a forum sponsored by the *National Review* early in 1994, he sharply confronted former New York City Mayor Ed Koch after Koch declared that the nation's crime problem should properly be labeled a black problem. That fall, Kemp angered conservatives by joining with William Bennett to denounce Proposition 187, the California ballot initiative that hung out a huge "Not Welcome" sign for illegal immigrants. Campaigning for Republican candidates in the days before the party's most resounding victory since 1980, Kemp seemed lonely and frustrated — almost like Lear raging against the perfidy of his children, except that Kemp would never have had the discipline to confine himself to iambic pentameter. Republicans, Kemp complained as he toured the country that fall, were veering dangerously close to defining themselves as a party that wanted only "little government and big prisons."

On the winter afternoon a few weeks later when Kemp announced that he would not, after all, seek the GOP's 1996 presidential nomination, he merely ratified a verdict already delivered. After Bush's apostasy, the party had returned to Kemp's fervor for cutting taxes. But it had abandoned his view of how to combat the problems of the poor and expand its political coalition. He was a big-government conservative — Kemp opposed term limits and the Balanced Budget Amendment — at a time of small-government fervor on the Right. By the time Kemp took himself out of the race, said one longtime associate, the onetime lion of the Right represented "a party of one."*

The decline of Kemp and the empowerment agenda opened the way for a new conservative explanation for poverty, one that rejected Kemp's sunny optimism about the nature of the poor and his conviction that increasing economic opportunity was the surest way to reduce violence and disorder in the decaying inner cores of the nation's major cities. This new analysis focused less on the failings of society than on the failings of the poor themselves, and it led the debate over welfare and poverty down pathways that Reagan and Bush never considered within the boundaries of the possible.

---

*In 1995, a number of Republicans, led by House Speaker Gingrich, exhumed Kemp's empowerment rhetoric but in a manner that ironically underscored the extent to which the party had moved away from him. Gingrich and others talked about pursuing Kemp-style reforms, but as a "positive agenda" for minorities the party could use as a shield against critics of its efforts to restrict affirmative action — a drive that Kemp himself opposed as racially divisive.

THE RISE OF THE RETROCONS

In the 1980s, young conservatives concerned about poverty might have quoted Jack Kemp. In the 1990s, they invariably quoted Charles Murray. Murray is a balding, soft-spoken, sometimes prickly social scholar with a taste for fine wine and an unerring instinct for infuriating liberals. Given to both careful distinctions and Spenglerian generalizations, he presents explosive ideas in a peaceful, almost pained voice — as if enunciating bitter truth more in sorrow than anger. But much like the academic camp followers of the New Left in the 1960s, Murray takes an unmistakable outlaw pleasure in shocking intellectual propriety. In 1994 he veered down a road that many Republicans could not follow when he co-authored *The Bell Curve*, a nearly 850-page tome that linked race and intelligence. But while the GOP was reshaping its attitudes on welfare and poverty from the end of the Bush administration through the first half of Clinton's, Murray operated as a kind of magnetic pole, establishing a position that was admittedly outside the framework of the possible but that nonetheless drew many Republicans toward him.

In a series of books and articles that have catapulted him from obscurity over the past decade, Murray presented the Right's most radical critique of traditional liberal social welfare programs. In his 1984 book, *Losing Ground*, Murray argued that America was making progress on reducing poverty, increasing educational and employment opportunity for minorities, and reducing crime, until overly permissive government social policy launched in the 1960s interrupted or reversed the trends. Four years later, with his idiosyncratic and discursive meditation *In Pursuit of Happiness and Good Government*, Murray argued that government social programs preempted and debilitated the "little platoons" celebrated by Edmund Burke — the networks of voluntary and charitable organizations that provided the backbone of neighborhoods. In his 1984 book, he presented as a "thought experiment" the suggestion that government simply eliminate all income support programs for working-age people, and concluded that "the lives of large numbers of poor people would be radically changed for the better." Nearly ten years later, in a landmark October 1993 *Wall Street Journal* op-ed piece that changed the direction of the welfare reform debate, Murray dropped the pretense of merely thinking out loud. He flatly proposed that government eliminate all welfare payments for women who bear children outside of marriage.

Murray based these radical proposals on his belief that society was a self-regulating organism that tended to steer people toward the right behavior unless government interfered with the process. Murray, who was born in Iowa, worked as a Peace Corps volunteer in small Thai villages, and now lives in a pastoral town in rural Maryland, sometimes seemed to envision the world as a giant small town, where neighbors took in each other's laundry and helped keep the kids from down the block in line. "I don't think the human race is one bit different in 1994 than it was in 1954 or 1834 or 1734 on these issues," Murray told one interviewer. "The only thing that has changed is that government has deformed the way civil society functions."

Murray applied that logic most ambitiously to welfare. "Throughout human history," Murray argued in his *Wall Street Journal* article, illegitimacy had been kept in check because the mother-only family was not "a viable economic unit." But government had distorted that natural order with welfare payments that enabled single-parent families to survive. The purpose of welfare policy, Murray argued, should be to restore the natural economic barriers against illegitimacy. That meant welfare reform should focus not on encouraging welfare recipients to work — the principal goal for welfare critics since the 1960s — but on discouraging women from bearing children out of wedlock by denying them public assistance. Murray conceded that some women would not be able to support their children without government aid. For those cases, he coolly suggested loosening the laws governing adoption, and spending "lavishly on orphanages." All of that would cause suffering, he acknowledged, but over time that suffering would reduce misery by discouraging other women from unmarried pregnancies: "It will lead others," he wrote, "watching what happens to their sisters, to take steps not to get pregnant."

Perhaps looking to dampen the reaction against his inflammatory proposals, Murray centered his article on the rising illegitimacy rates among whites, which are still only about one-third the rates among blacks. (The piece was entitled "The Coming White Underclass.") But the storm came anyway. A who's who of left-of-center social scientists issued a statement declaring that the level of welfare benefits had, at most, a "small effect" on whether poor women had children outside of marriage. (Illegitimacy, they noted, had been rising even though the value of welfare benefits, adjusted for inflation, had fallen since the mid-1970s. And other scholars noted that illegitimacy was also rising among middle-class women who did not collect welfare.) But that was not precisely Murray's point; his argument was that welfare enabled illegitimacy by mitigating its consequences. "A girl is not necessarily saying to herself if I have a baby, I'll go on welfare," Murray maintained. "What's happening is that she has not had a lot of adults screaming at her for many, many years, don't, don't, don't get pregnant . . . [because] there has been a lifting of some of the short-term pain." That argument was inherently difficult to disprove, or, for that matter, to prove. But it instantly galvanized the imagination of conservatives, and drew a much more respectful response in the mainstream press than Murray's previous work.

With Murray's *Wall Street Journal* article, the conservative intellectual mantle on social policy clearly passed to a constellation of thinkers who rejected the economic focus of the Kemp empowerment agenda. The conservative columnist George Will once said the problem with Kemp's vision of poverty was that he assumed there was a level of economic growth that would reverse the rising rate of illegitimacy among the poor; none of the thinkers in the Murray circle shared Kemp's optimism on that point. Their view of human nature was less beneficent (or, as they would put it, more realistic). In their eyes, Kemp had it precisely backwards when he argued that upright behavior flowed from economic opportunity. Only by improving their behavior, they said, could the poor seize economic opportunity.

In this new group, there was no guiding figure, no organized division of responsibility, and differences of opinion around nuances. But the work of Murray, Myron Magnet, Marvin Olasky, James Q. Wilson, William J. Bennett, and Gertrude Himmelfarb — popularized by such activists as Robert Rector of the Heritage Foundation and Bill Kristol — created a critique of government and the culture that meshed as though written by a single hand. In the arena of social policy, they played the same role that Gingrich and his allies played in their attacks on the ethics of the Democratic Congress. By raising the case against federal social programs to an entirely new level, Murray and his fellow travelers furthered the fundamental delegitimation of the government in Washington.

Each of these thinkers — dubbed by one author the "retro-conservatives" for their belief that ancient virtues offered the solutions to modern problems — mined his or her own section of the quarry. Magnet, a journalist and fellow at the Manhattan Institute, argued in a 1993 book, *The Dream and The Nightmare*, that the violence and family breakdown among the underclass had its roots in the 1960s revolution in social and sexual mores. In his 1992 book, *The Tragedy of American Compassion* — a mix of careful historical research, religiously tinged idealism, and wholesale ideological assertion — University of Texas journalism professor Marvin Olasky contended that the poor were better served by the dense web of nineteenth-century private charities than the modern social welfare state. Wilson was a well-respected and prolific UCLA social scientist who wrote at a magisterial level about crime and the family; in *The Moral Sense*, he argued that nature endowed humans with an underlying predisposition toward virtuous behavior that modern culture has tried to efface. Bennett, a voluble and blunt former academic who served as Reagan's education secretary, touted the value of teaching exacting virtues to the young (and demonstrated that virtue is indeed sometimes its own reward by making a small fortune with the success of his modern McGuffey's reader, *The Book of Virtues*). Himmelfarb was a historian who celebrated the moral rigor of the English Victorians with nuanced and well-reviewed books such as *Poverty and Compassion* and *The De-Moralization of Society*.

At their most simplistic, the retrocons seemed to argue that all the poor needed to escape their predicament was a ruler across the knuckles. But the best of their work thoughtfully probed the limits of government-sponsored compassion and displayed genuine empathy in asserting the capacity of all people, regardless of circumstance, to uphold standards of honor and virtue, and insisting on the responsibilities of the comfortable to take personal interest in the lives of those without. Although the quality of their insights, and the subjects of their attention, varied, their conclusions converged. At the core of this new conservative canon were a series of sharply stated principles that attributed most of America's social problems to cultural permissiveness and counterproductive government programs.

Poverty, the retrocons generally agreed, was caused more by behavior than racial discrimination, an absence of economic opportunity, or an imbalance of resources. "[T]he key to the mystery of why, despite opportunity, the poorest poor don't work is that their poverty is less an economic matter than a cultural one," wrote Magnet, in direct dispute with Kemp and the empowerment conservatives. In particular, the retrocons argued that the most intractable problems facing society can be substantially traced back to the breakdown of the two-parent family and the rising rate of out-of-wedlock births, especially among the poor. Illegitimacy was "the single most important social problem of our time," wrote Murray in his *Wall Street Journal* article. "More important than crime, drugs, poverty, illiteracy, welfare or homelessness because it drives everything else."

Government social programs, the retrocons argued, compounded rather than alleviated these problems in several distinct respects. Murray emphasized misplaced incentives that enabled or cushioned self-destructive behavior — by "subsidizing illegitimacy" through welfare, or failing to impose sufficient penalties against law-breaking. Bennett spoke about "a habit of dependence" that weakened communities by encouraging them to look to Washington rather than attempting to solve their problems themselves. Olasky proclaimed the inferiority of bureaucratic government aid to private charities that provided true compassion by linking physical sustenance with moral uplift.

Government could improve the lives of the poor, the retrocons maintained, not by spending more on them, but by reorganizing social policy around the principles of personal and local responsibility. That meant rolling back government welfare programs, stiffening the penalties for crime, toughening educational standards, and ending affirmative-action programs that encourage minorities to perceive themselves as victims of an unjust society. In a supply-side vision of social policy, most of the retrocons argued that therapeutic charitable intervention in the lives of the poor would increase if government stepped out of the way.

Finally, the retrocons argued that to restore social order, society must publicly reaffirm moral standards, a project that meant unlearning the lessons of the 1960s. For the retrocons, the 1960s were the great departure — the decade that wrenched America from what it was and sent it off-course to what it has become. The counterculture enshrined by the "new class" in academia, the arts, and the media "sever[ed] welfare from shame" (Olasky); "withdrew respect from the behavior and attitudes that have traditionally boosted people up the economic ladder" (Magnet); and "waged an all-out assault on common sense and the common values of the American people" (Bennett).

To undo the damage, the retrocons insisted, public figures had to declare certain personal choices toxic — to unequivocally affirm the difference between right and wrong. Most of the retrocons, in fact, preferred (à la Bennett) to talk of virtues, which implied firm rules of conduct, rather than the traditional political construction of values, which carried to their ears a faint trill of relativism. Like the nineteenth-century Victorians, counseled Himmelfarb, America's leaders must "relegitimize morality as the basis of social policy and restore the language of virtue and vice."

Presented in stark and bristling language, these arguments marked a dramatic escalation of the antigovernment movement. In an intellectual process that paralleled the generational shift under way among Republican officeholders, the retrocon analysis built on, but greatly expanded, the work of the neoconservatives who provided the logic and vocabulary for conservative social policy in the Reagan era. The neoconservative critique, expressed by thinkers like Irving Kristol, Nathan Glazer, and Daniel Patrick Moynihan (who drifted to the Left through the 1980s even as the rest of the group moved Right), decried the Great Society for promising more than it could deliver, and declared the limits of social policy to steer and shape social reality. To the neoconservatives, the great lesson of the Great Society was the law of unintended consequences: the maxim, as adapted by Irving Kristol, that "the unanticipated consequences of social action are always more important, and usually less agreeable, than the intended consequences."

But at least into the 1980s, the neoconservatives still conceded the need for a social welfare state. Programs might be ineffective, they might waste money or disappoint the inflated expectations of their architects, but they did not inherently deepen the problems they intended to combat. A neoconservative analysis of social programs might have been entitled *Running in Place*, but not *Losing Ground*.

In declaring that government social programs exacerbated the problems they were intended to cure, Murray and his fellow travelers carried the argument a long next step, and allowed conservatives to contest the high ground of compassion. Like the neoconservatives, Reagan had emphasized the high cost and sometimes paltry return of social programs; he presented his cuts in such programs primarily in terms of fairness to taxpayers. That focus opened the door for Democrats to indict him as callous and unfair to the poor. Today many Democrats are exhuming those arguments against the Republican Congress. But the nature of the Republican defense has shifted. Reflecting the retrocon analysis, Republicans now portray welfare reform as an act of charity for those on the dole themselves. In the new telling, reducing welfare is less hard-eyed than softhearted. "This is not about a bigger welfare state or a cheaper welfare state," Gingrich declared. "This is about replacing a system that is killing our children." Republicans now routinely denounce Democratic compassion as a form of oppression, government aid as a "pathology," and public assistance as a narcotic that condemns the poor to lives of degraded dependency. "Liberalism is not only wrong," said Bennett, "but cruel." Democrats wanted to keep the poor in need, stranded on "the liberal plantation"; Republicans yearned to free their souls by emptying their pockets of the enslaving government lucre. So went the new conservative catechism.

Liberals and even many moderates found such argument Orwellian. It was one thing to agree that the behavior of the underclass often compounded their distress; it was another to assume that such behavior was a toxic form of trickle-down from the 1960s; and yet another to assert that denying government assistance to poor families would improve their condition. Sociologist Douglas Massey, the premier academic analyst of housing discrimination, said the retrocons' analysis ignored the role of racial segregation and economic deprivation in establishing the inner-city cultural patterns they condemned. John DiIulio, a rough-and-ready Princeton University criminologist whose work conservatives ordinarily revered, warned that ending welfare, while potentially carrying long-term benefits, would produce more desperation, violence, and crime along the way. The leaders of charitable organizations, like Catholic Charities USA, denounced as "sociological speculation fueled by ideological wishfulness", the suggestion that private giving could fill the gaps left by reducing government aid to the poor. Continuing the argument in exile, Kemp complained that the retrocon focus on reducing government aid brandished only sticks when carrots, "a massive effort to provide education and job training and hope," were a better way to change the behavior of the underclass.

From the start, those sentiments were strong enough to limit the retrocon agenda; no Republican endorsed Murray's call for the complete elimination of all welfare for unwed mothers, even on a prospective basis (as he later made clear he intended). Yet it was a measure of how far faith had eroded in government — how stygian was the despair over the chaos enveloping the underclass, and the inability of conventional liberal remedies to alleviate it — that Murray's ideas were not dismissed altogether, nor discredited, even after the controversy surrounding his book on race, genetics, and intelligence.

The clearest mark of Murray's ascent was the legitimization of public discussion about illegitimacy for the first time since 1965, when Daniel Patrick Moynihan, as a young assistant secretary of labor, wrote his famous report warning that rising illegitimacy rates threatened to submerge the lower-class black family in a "tangle of pathology." Moynihan was roundly denounced for blaming the victim in a backlash so intense that it shelved public discussion of illegitimacy for more than a quarter century.

Neither Nixon nor Carter addressed illegitimacy in the sweeping welfare reform plans they proposed during the 1970s. Even Reagan ducked the issue. At various points, conservatives in the administration suggested that Reagan address the rising tide of out-of-wedlock births, but the post-Moynihan taboo on the subject still held among the President's political advisers. "Even that recently it was still considered political dynamite to talk about illegitimacy because you sounded judgmental, and you appeared to be attacking women, which for Republicans is always dicey," recalled Gary L. Bauer, who ran the domestic policy operation in the last two years of the Reagan White House. Few others were bolder. The massive Family Support Act approved in 1988 did not directly tackle illegitimacy; the word never came up in the floor debate on the bill in the House. Nor did Kemp and the other empowerment conservatives feel comfortable discussing the issue.

The ice started to crack in 1992, when New Jersey approved a law denying the usual $64 monthly increase in benefits to women who had additional children while already on welfare. This so-called family cap legislation particularly turned heads because it was introduced by a black Democratic state legislator and signed into law by a Democratic governor. But the power of the taboo was still so strong that when Dan Quayle delivered a speech in May 1992 accusing the television show *Murphy Brown* of glamorizing illegitimacy with a plot line that had the main character giving birth but not getting married, he was widely derided as racist, sexist, or both. The tendency in the press to dismiss almost anything that came from Quayle's mouth as loony, and the awkwardness of the vice president of the United States entering into an argument with a fictional character — who, after all, did not exist — both provided fuel for the firestorm. But the trepidation in the White House over his speech reflected the larger belief that these ideas were still explosive. "The culture was sort of half ready," says Bill Kristol, "but the political system wasn't."

Yet this elite consensus denied two unavoidable truths that Murray's article crystallized and forced onto the political agenda. One was a growing body of social science data that pointed to the dangers in the inexorable rise in out-of-wedlock births. The numbers themselves were breathtaking. In 1960, 5.3 percent, or roughly one in twenty, American children were born out of wedlock. In 1991, nearly 30 percent of children were born out of wedlock — close to one in three. For African-Americans, the figures increased from roughly one in four in 1960 to more than two in three in 1991. Many of those parents made heroic efforts, and many of their families functioned well. But it became increasingly difficult to ignore the data showing that children born out of wedlock were more likely to perform poorly in school, to manifest emotional problems, to engage in crime, and to bear children out of wedlock themselves. Indeed, six months before Murray issued his manifesto in the *Wall Street Journal*, the *Atlantic Monthly*, the flagship journal of Left-leaning academia, summarized the solidifying sociological consensus about the impact on children of the breakup of the two-parent family under the provocative headline "Dan Quayle Was Right."

The other fact was the widespread public anxiety about eroding moral standards for which illegitimate births had become the most powerful symbol. Not only conservative intellectuals like Murray or religious conservatives like Pat Robertson and Ralph Reed feared the country's social framework was pulling apart. By the end of the 1980s pollsters from all points on the political spectrum regularly reported a widespread public sense that the social mechanisms for transmitting values from generation to generation were breaking down.

In the 1970s and 1980s neither party effectively addressed those concerns. Most Democrats rejected discussion of values as conservative ploys to distract attention from the economic issues they portrayed as the problems facing American families. Most Republicans responded by elevating proxy issues — like school prayer and limits on abortion — that symbolized support for conservative moral views and aroused intense passions in particular segments of the electorate, but had little practical effect on the cultural problems that concerned most Americans.

Even Quayle failed in 1992 partly because his critique was untethered. In his call for "family values" and denunciation of Murphy Brown, Quayle appeared to be rendering a negative moral judgment on single mothers themselves. Americans were uncomfortable with the growth of single-parent families, but they were equally uncomfortable with telling people how to live their lives. They had even less patience for lectures on morality from politicians. "Too much of the Republican 'family values' debate in 1992 seemed to be simply moralizing about values instead of explaining the human costs of the breakdown of certain value structures," Bill Kristol later acknowledged.

The retrocon analysis reconnected moral standards to public policy by highlighting the links between the decline of the two-parent family and real-world problems like welfare dependency, poor school performance, and above all, crime. It was possible to overstate the connection between crime and the change in family structure: Most children from single-parent families, of course, did not become criminals. But research found that father absence did increase the risk of criminal behavior. And the link between broken families and rising crime (particularly juvenile crime) had a powerful intuitive appeal for millions of Americans.

The shift of the values debate from abortion, prayer, and homosexuality — the preoccupations of the 1980s — toward illegitimacy, family structure, and crime reconfigured the calculus of cultural politics. The bitter experiences of 1992 (especially the turbulent GOP convention in Houston) convinced many Republican political strategists that

while cultural issues were necessary to mobilize religious conserva-
tives, they endangered the party with everyone else. The retrocon suc-
cess at linking moral decline with real-world problems pointed a way
out of that dilemma. Their analysis provided politicians with a way of
talking about values (or, as Bill Bennett put it, virtues) that spoke not
only to religious conservatives, but also to the daily concerns of subur-
ban families who might consider Pat Robertson one step from a faith
healer.

THE REVOLUTION OF RISING EXPECTATIONS

Sweeping, self-confident, and pointedly offensive to liberal sensibili-
ties, the retrocon analysis exerted a powerful appeal for Republican
politicians eager to style themselves as revolutionaries. Maybe few of
them read Murray's books or Magnet's or Olasky's; but more read the
op-ed pieces in the *Wall Street Journal* popularizing the arguments;
and more still read the memos from Kristol distilling them into polit-
ical terms; and yet still more heard Gingrich systematically introduce
these ideas into the Republican vocabulary. Gingrich quoted Olasky
and Himmelfarb so often it sometimes seemed he owned a share of
their royalties.

Murray's October 1993 *Wall Street Journal* article appeared just as
House Republicans were completing their own welfare reform pro-
posal. After Clinton's heavy emphasis on welfare reform in the 1992
campaign, the House Republicans had expected him to stress the
issue, and soon after the President took office Bob Michel appointed a
task force to prepare a party alternative. As chairman he tapped Rick
Santorum, an aggressive young conservative (he had been a member of
the Gang of Seven that beat the drums on the House banking scandal)
then serving his second term. Santorum was the ranking minority
member on the Human Resources Subcommittee of the Ways and
Means Committee, which had jurisdiction over welfare, and he drew
much of the task force from his colleagues there.

Though Santorum was a conservative in good standing, that placed
the task force to the left of the Republican caucus as a whole. In a
party increasingly defined by conservatives, the Human Resources
Subcommittee was one of the few places dominated by Republican
moderates — including Fred Grandy of Iowa, Clay Shaw of Florida,

and Dave Camp of Michigan. Ronald Haskins, the key Republican aide on the subcommittee, and probably the most knowledgeable Republican in Congress on welfare, was also a moderate. The prominence of the moderates testified to the low priority most Republicans placed on welfare. Apart from complaining about its cost, said Grandy, Republicans saw welfare as "the kind of thing that they don't even like to dip their toes in, let alone get their feet wet."

But despite the task force's relatively moderate cast, it produced a plan that could hardly be termed soft. The proposal followed Clinton's basic plan in providing more money for education and training and requiring welfare recipients to work after they had been on the rolls for two years; but it took a significant step to the right by then giving states the option to cut off aid completely after three more years, even to recipients willing to work. (Clinton's plan, when finally released, guaranteed jobs indefinitely to those affected by time limits who could not find work in the private sector.) Murray had been one of the first people Santorum met with when he took on the assignment, and the task force blueprint reflected Murray's effort to refocus the debate onto discouraging illegitimacy. The bill required states to deny additional benefits to women who have children while already on the rolls (the so-called family cap approved in New Jersey the previous year) and barred them from providing any cash assistance to unwed mothers under eighteen. But in each case, the task force plan allowed states to pass legislation exempting themselves from those provisions.

That escape clause reflected the task force's hesitation about fully embracing the Murray solution. Embedded in the Murray vision was what many of them considered a time bomb: If states completely denied aid to young women who had children out of wedlock, what would happen to those children? In his article, Murray had suggested that many of the young women would find other means to support their children; for those that didn't, he proposed that government should encourage adoption, or place the children in orphanages. From both a political and moral perspective (to say nothing of the high cost of constructing and operating orphanages), many of the task force Republicans considered it untenable to coerce large numbers of poor women into giving up their children. "Even in 1993 our judgment was this was a mistake and we should not go down that road," said one figure involved in drafting the report. "We thought we could solve the problem by requiring work."

Even so, the plan envisioned redesigning the welfare system to a much greater extent than Reagan or Bush had ever proposed. Compared even to where House Republicans had been just a year earlier, the plan constituted a rapid evolution in thinking. In 1992, Representatives Grandy, Shaw, and Nancy Johnson (a Connecticut moderate also on the Ways and Means Committee) had published a position paper largely written by Ron Haskins that lamented the rise in out-of-wedlock births, but concluded government could do nothing to reverse it. "The stark fact," they wrote, in a document issued by the House Wednesday Group, an internal GOP policy organization, "is that no known public policy will subdue or reduce these rates. . . . Huge and growing numbers of female-headed families are going to be a major part of the social environment for the foreseeable future." Now, all three, joined by other party moderates, had signed on to a plan to prod states toward unprecedented measures — measures most Democrats denounced as punitive and even racist — to discourage illegitimacy. The task force took its bill to the House Republican Conference and found broad support. One hundred sixty-two of the one hundred seventy-five House Republicans endorsed the Santorum task force bill when it was introduced in November 1993.

But as the aftershocks of Murray's article reverberated through conservative circles, a cry arose that the bill was neither tough enough nor focused sufficiently on discouraging illegitimacy. Beyond the appeal of its policy analysis, Murray's prescription pointed the Republicans out of what appeared a political dead end. For decades, Republicans had championed the cause of requiring welfare recipients to work. But now Clinton had seized that ground with his popular pledge to put welfare recipients to work after two years. Murray's arguments shifted the welfare debate onto terrain where Clinton would have great difficulty following. In declaring that illegitimacy was the issue, not work, many Republicans saw a chance to push the overall welfare debate to the right — and diminish Clinton's claim to the mantle of reform — even though that reduced the likelihood of Congress passing any legislation before the 1994 election.

Clinton gave Murray's arguments time to flower by delaying the introduction of his own welfare reform bill until the following June. To this day, moderates like Clay Shaw believe Clinton could have split the GOP and made a deal with Republican centrists if he had come forward quickly. But the President's failure to move — largely for fear of alienating House liberals he needed to pass his health care plan — gave time for the retrocons and their allies to yank the House Republicans to the right.

Over the winter, conservative agitation against the House Republican bill increased. Murray, who had endorsed a draft outline of the task force bill, jumped off the ship. "The Republican bill is way too close to what the Democrats want to do," he complained at the time. "I do not understand why these people think that getting poor women into the job market is going to solve the problem. You're still going to have communities where you don't have any fathers and that's the source of the problem."

Together with fellow retrocon James Q. Wilson, Murray argued for tougher measures against illegitimacy at an early December meeting with Gingrich. Wilson was in Washington for the annual policy conference of the American Enterprise Institute, and the two men were on their way to the group's gala banquet. So Murray had to make his case for reducing aid to the poor in a tuxedo. But mostly Murray, as was his style, stayed away from the daily fight; a self-described "wishy-washy libertarian" rather than a partisan Republican, he considered himself something of a political illiterate.

Others picked up his banner. Bennett, Kristol, and the Christian Coalition all pushed for legislation closer to Murray. Empower America, the think tank founded by Bennett, Kemp, and Weber, jumped on the pile with a memo that urged House Republicans to replace the task force bill with a "fundamentally different alternative" that married Murrayesque benefit cutoffs with Kemp's agenda to bring capitalism to the urban poor. Robert Rector of the Heritage Foundation burrowed away against the task force bill across Capitol Hill. Rector, a resolutely conservative policy analyst whose sometimes impenetrable monotone belied limitless confidence in his own ideas, was a polarizing figure even among Republicans. Clay Shaw, who played the lead role in steering the welfare bill to completion in 1995, eventually put out the word that he would not step into the same room with Rector.

But Rector had an audience among Congress conservatives, and he relentlessly lobbied them to scrap the task force bill.

Steadily, this barrage of outside criticism shifted the internal balance against the original bill. Gingrich asked Santorum to reconsider the legislation in light of Murray's criticisms. Representative Jan Meyers of Kansas introduced a Murray-flavored alternative bill in March. Finally, James Talent of Missouri and Tim Hutchinson of Arkansas, two House Republican freshmen, offered their own alternative to the task force plan.

Neither might have seemed a particularly formidable adversary. Talent was an imperially slim former Missouri state legislator with a cocky swagger and an eye on the clock; Hutchinson, whose congressional district included the Whitewater land development, had arrived in Congress as a close ally of the Christian Coalition. Their standing in the congressional hierarchy was suggested by their occupancy of offices on the ground floor of the Longworth office building, the low-rent district in the House; Talent's closet-sized personal office opened to a panoramic view of a wall in an interior courtyard.

But both proved adept legislative guerrillas. Like almost all young House Republicans, Talent and Hutchinson saw themselves as part of a conservative vanguard; the Ways and Means Republicans, in their eyes, were the "establishment" and therefore insufficiently "revolutionary . . . in their thinking." Talent took the lead in organizing their insurrection. His firsthand contact with the welfare system was minimal; there were few welfare recipients in his suburban St. Louis state legislative district. But he was an avid reader of Murray (he almost always included *Losing Ground* on a short list of books he recommended for his interns) and he had good antennae for ripening issues. Talent instructed one of his legislative aides to sound out opinions on the task force bill at some of Washington's conservative think tanks; that put him in touch with Rector. Rector was already working on an alternative bill with Republican Senator Lauch Faircloth of North Carolina, a Jesse Helms protégé serving his first term. After talking with Rector, Talent agreed to sponsor the measure in the House and enlisted Hutchinson.

The bill they produced was a monument to the retrocon analysis of poverty. Talent's statement introducing the bill quoted Olasky and

Murray and included a chart linking rising rates of illegitimacy and crime; Bennett joined Talent and Hutchinson at the press conference where they formally unveiled the measure. The bill differed from the task force blueprint primarily in proposing to deny benefits to a larger group of unwed mothers. Under their proposal, states would be required, without any option to exempt themselves, to deny additional benefits to women who had children while already receiving welfare — and to deny any welfare, food stamps, or housing assistance to unmarried mothers under twenty-one. By 1998, Talent and Hutchinson proposed, states would have to deny aid to any woman under twenty-five who had a child outside of marriage. States could use the money they saved to fund adoption, or group homes, or orphanages for the children of the women denied benefits.

The emergence of the Talent bill symbolized the House Republicans' enlarging sense of opportunity. The Santorum task force drafted its legislation at a time when Clinton looked strong — and many Republicans thought their survival depended on finding accommodation with a popular President enunciating centrist themes. That environment favored a blueprint for a compromise in which both parties could share credit. But Clinton's stumbles in 1994 strengthened the hand of the Republicans like Bill Kristol and Gingrich counseling confrontation and polarization. As health care and then the crime bill unraveled, reaching a deal with Clinton on any issue increasingly appeared less attractive to most Republicans than sharpening distinctions that could help the party gain control of Congress and impose its own agenda.

Santorum and his colleagues on the task force could never quite catch that curve. Looking back, Fred Grandy, a moderate who left the Congress after losing a race for the Iowa governorship in 1994, saw the rising clamor for a Murrayesque solution to welfare as an inevitable response to the larger dialectic between Clinton and the Republican Congress:

Why do sharks exhibit greater appetite tendencies when there is blood in the water? There was clearly a belief that a policy document, a kind of cold, calculating dull but well-meaning reconfiguration of the welfare laws was not as charismatic an opportunity as a welfare revolution. With the election of the Class of '92, which brought with it a more

conservative freshman body, coupled with a growing youthful conserv-
ative element in the Congress, the desire to make polemical statements
as opposed to writing policy documents increased. It was clear by
1993, with the health care debate struggling to get out of the gate, with
Clinton having misstepped so many times, with his popularity bounc-
ing up and down like an oscilloscope, that aligning with the President
for a centrist [welfare] policy was a crappy idea from a political point of
view. So there was this steeplechase to the right.

If not for the Contract With America, the dispute between the San-
torum task force and Talent and Hutchinson might have remained
academic. (As Democrats failed to move their own welfare bill, the
issue of a Republican alternative became largely theoretical.) But the
process of drafting the Contract forced the House leadership to
choose between the two approaches. Santorum and the other task
force members, citing their 162 sponsors, urged Armey to simply
write their bill into the Contract. But Gingrich and Armey had con-
verted to the view that the original bill was inadequately ambitious.
"That was a minority bill," Armey told the task force members dismis-
sively. "We need to come at it from the perspective of a majority."

Beyond the ideological sympathy of the party's leaders, Talent and
Hutchison had another important lever. Armey and Gingrich had de-
creed that the provisions in the Contract must excite the grassroots
antigovernment groups Republicans wanted to energize for the fall
campaign. After months of courting from Talent and Hutchinson, the
Christian Coalition and other social conservative organizations leaned
on the House leadership to include their provisions in the Contract.

Satisfying the concerns of the social conservatives on welfare re-
form became especially important because the Contract offered them
so little else. An anti-abortion amendment was off the table from the
start. Armey had lobbied intensively to include a plank on school
prayer, but Gingrich refused that too. Welfare thus became "one of
the few areas that the party leadership could signal to us that we were
of interest to them for something more than votes every two years,"
said Gary Bauer, the former Reagan policy director who had gone on
to head the Family Research Council, a social conservative organi-
zation.

Armey signaled the leadership's leaning early on by convening a meeting between Talent and Hutchinson, the drafters of the task force bill, and the grassroots social conservative groups. Sitting in the room, Hutchinson thought the task force Republicans seemed "almost offended" that Armey would invite in the groups to pressure them. But even in the face of a blunt message of support for Talent from the groups, the task force members, on both policy and political grounds, still resisted toughening the provisions denying benefits to unwed mothers. To Talent and Hutchison, the task force supporters waved the polling results that showed overwhelming public majorities against cutting off aid to young women. "From a political standpoint," said Hutchison, "they thought we were going to get beat to death on any kind of denial of benefits." Gingrich told Santorum that his bill had been revolutionary when it was introduced, but "the country has shifted and we have won the debate." Santorum shot back: "Newt, you know, a group of Washington folks who deal with this issue have moved, but that doesn't mean the country has moved."

Finally, with the deadline for completing the Contract approaching, Armey assembled Talent and Hutchinson, with Santorum, Mike Castle, and Nancy Johnson, and told them to work out a bill. Santorum's time had become consumed by his Senate campaign against Harris Wofford, so the mediator's role fell to Representative Dave Camp, a moderate former congressional aide from Michigan serving his second term. To Camp, Armey said flatly: "You resolve it, or I will." Armey never directly ordered Camp to steer the result more toward the Talent approach. But his intent was clear to everyone involved in the process. Why else would he direct them to negotiate with two freshman members who did not sit on the committee of jurisdiction, if not to move the product in their direction?

Throughout July, the two sides engaged in what Talent described as "very difficult" negotiations. The most intractable issue was whether to mandate the denial of benefits to underage unwed mothers. The moderates resolutely argued for maintaining the provisions in their bill that allowed states to continue providing aid; Talent demanded more. In the wilting steam of the Washington summer, the talks grew more heated. Some of the Ways and Means negotiators thought Talent's "very confrontational" approach displayed a lack of respect for the committee's position and expertise. But with the explicit support of the Christian Coalition and the other social groups, and the implicit backing of Gingrich and Armey, the two freshmen succeeded in steering the Contract language substantially in their direction.

In a triumph for the retrocon analysis, the Contract bill closed the escape hatches in the original bill: States would be mandated to deny benefits both to women who had additional children while on welfare and to unwed mothers under eighteen. During the negotiations, even the moderates moved to the right on some points. The original bill had *allowed* states to cut off all aid to welfare families after five years; the Ways and Means members pushed for, and won, a provision in the Contract bill that *required* states to terminate aid at that point.

Still, on the most emotional questions of how to fight illegitimacy, the moderates felt betrayed by the leadership's desire to placate the outside critics and grassroots social conservative groups. "Armey had to choose between the members who had worked on this and the outside groups, and he screwed us," said one negotiator on the moderate side.

In moving the bill closer to the retrocon agenda, the conservatives had outmuscled the moderates, not persuaded them. Their doubts about cutting off aid to unwed mothers under eighteen remained. But they conceded the argument because few of them thought the Republicans would win back the House — or that the leadership could force them to stand with the Contract bill if they did. On that they proved spectacularly mistaken. But the social conservatives were also surprised by what happened next. After the election, a new set of players emerged — and they moved the internal Republican battle over welfare reform in an entirely unanticipated direction.

THE TIDE ROLLS BACK

The electoral tide that carried Republicans to control over Congress also established the GOP as the dominant power in the states. In 1994, Republicans elected eleven new governors, raising their total to thirty. Of the nine largest states, Republican governors controlled all but Florida. With the added numbers, the governors sat down as a powerful new player in the roiling internal GOP debate over welfare reform.

Though Republicans rhetorically identified with the cause of transferring power from Washington to the states, contact between Republicans in Congress and the statehouses had historically been limited.

Some individual communication occurred — Bill Weld of Massachusetts and Gingrich, for instance, held several meetings about writing a book together — but even during the drafting of the Contract, governors had minimal input.

After the election, RNC chairman Haley Barbour encouraged the two sides to try again. His vehicle was the Republican Governors Association's post-election meeting scheduled for late November in Williamsburg, Virginia. Originally, the RGA planned to showcase the Republican presidential candidates at the meeting. But Barbour and Don Fierce, the RNC's director of strategic planning, urged them instead to invite the congressional leadership and shift the focus toward preparing a coordinated party line in the impending legislative struggle with Clinton and the Democrats. Barbour recruited Dole, Gingrich, and other congressional leaders, and just two weeks after the election, they traveled to Williamsburg for public and private meetings with the governors.

The session became a watershed in the welfare debate. With Republicans now holding Congress, the governors saw the opportunity to press their long-standing desire to convert more federal social programs, including welfare, into block grants that states would control. At a private breakfast, they found Dole and Gingrich a receptive audience. "When Gingrich came back from Williamsburg," said one House aide, "the message was block grants."

The push for block grants fit with the general Republican rhetoric about devolving power to the states. And it advanced the drive to balance the federal budget. To the congressional leadership, the governors offered an attractive bargain: Transform federal social programs into block grants, and we will accept less money to operate them. That prospect converted House Budget Committee chairman John Kasich into an enthusiastic advocate for the block grants, and gave the process almost irresistible momentum in the House.

Just as important, the move toward block grants fit the larger political vision of the RNC, which threw its weight behind the drive. Barbour and Fierce saw the drive to shift control over social policy to the states as an opportunity to solidify the GOP's identity as the anti-Washington party. "It reinforced a message of the campaign," said Fierce. "The symbolism of actually doing something and keeping your promise to move things away from Washington was so, so important."

In some respects, the governors envisioned change more radical than the Contract contemplated. The Contract did not eliminate welfare's status as an entitlement — a program, like Social Security or Medicare, that guaranteed aid to anyone who met the definition of need, no matter how much it cost the government every year. But under the block grant proposal the governors advanced, welfare would lose its entitlement status; once appropriations for the program ran out, even families who qualified for aid could be denied assistance. Ending the entitlement to welfare would constitute a major shift — a step that liberals termed a tear in the social safety net, and conservatives an overdue effort to reassert control over federal spending.

But conservatives also saw block grants as a threat to the measures they had won to shape the behavior of welfare recipients in the exhausting negotiations over the Contract. In their discussions with congressional leaders, Engler, Weld, and Tommy Thompson — who had taken the lead in negotiating the welfare package — insisted that Washington turn over the money without any strings. That position reflected the instinctive resistance of governors in both parties to mandates from Washington. But it also embodied quiet doubts among several Republican governors about the practical impact of the social experiments that appeared so attractive in Washington conference rooms. Some governors didn't like being told they had to deny aid to legal aliens; others didn't like the family cap; but, as always, the most controversial issue was the Murray-inspired requirement that they cut off aid to unwed mothers under eighteen. "They made it clear all the way through they didn't want to deal with teenage moms," said Shaw. The conservatives in Congress, who had long waved the banner of federalism to oppose Democratic social programs in Washington, now found the Republican governors raising that flag against their agenda. "Conservative micromanagement is just as bad as liberal micromanagement," Engler memorably declared.

For Talent and his supporters, these arguments endangered everything they had won the previous summer. Almost without exception, the social conservatives believed that unless the federal government required the governors to implement the retrocon measures on illegitimacy, the governors would not have the stomach to do so on their own. At the Heritage Foundation, Rector, with his characteristic intensity, came to see the governors as a kind of Fifth Column. "The governors, historically, have always been the biggest obstacles to re-form," he fumed. "They all have a propensity, with few exceptions, to end welfare by press release." In his meetings with the governors, Talent was more diplomatic, but not by much.

Adding to the anxiety of the social conservatives were their continued doubts about the commitment of the House moderates to the Contract measures, particularly the ban on aid to unwed women under eighteen. Immediately after the election, Gingrich had inflamed the entire issue by impetuously rushing into a public debate over placing poor children in orphanages. The Contract bill allowed states to apply the money saved from cutting off aid to women under eighteen to pay for orphanages, but that was only one of several options they could use to provide alternative forms of support. When Gingrich was challenged on the morality of separating poor children from their mothers, he insisted (in classic retrocon fashion) that some might be better off in orphanages. His combative remarks escalated the debate over orphanages and denying aid to underage mothers to the cover of the national newsweeklies — and quickly revived fears among moderate Republicans that the Murray solution to illegitimacy would be seen as callous and unfair.

But the moderates were themselves constrained by the intense pressure from the House leadership to support the Contract. In early December, Shaw, who had assumed the chairmanship of the Human Resources Subcommittee when Santorum won election to the Senate, told reporters that he did not feel bound to follow the Contract provisions, particularly those denying aid to underage mothers. After Elizabeth Shogren reported those comments in the *Los Angeles Times*, Bill Archer, the chairman of the Ways and Means Committee, called Shaw with a sharp message. Archer told Shaw he could lose his chairmanship if he broke from the Contract — and what was worse, that Gingrich might approve a committee reorganization that stripped Ways and Means of its jurisdiction over welfare. Shaw scrambled back into line. "We knew we were walking a thin line," said one of Shaw's allies.

These complex political calculations were all swirling in the background as the governors and congressional Republicans negotiated a new version of the Contract bill. For the congressional Republicans, the talks became a delicate balancing between the federalists and the moralists — the governors on one side, and the retrocons and social conservative groups on the other. In the euphoria of the Williamsburg meeting, Gingrich had promised the governors huge latitude in writing the bill, but that charter depreciated as the groups in the antigovernment coalition resisted its implications. "The most important players in the House are the outside right-wing groups, especially with Armey in charge," said one House negotiator. "The idea that the governors were going to write a bill that was acceptable to them is nuts. . . . The challenge was to see how far we could go in block grants, and still satisfy the right-wing groups here in Washington, and the Murray-Wilson perspective on [denying aid to unwed mothers] under eighteen."

The result of the talks confirmed both the surprising staying power of the Contract as a policy blueprint and the strength of the conservative grassroots groups in the Republican coalition. The legislation Shaw finally introduced in early February 1995 ended the entitlement to welfare and converted the program into a block grant as the governors sought. But, in a testament to the power of the Christian Coalition and their allies, all of the conservative national standards remained in the bill. States would be required to deny aid to unwed mothers under eighteen and their children, to impose a family cap, to cut off legal immigrants from assistance, and to terminate all aid after five years.

The agreement with the governors embodied in Shaw's proposal established the broad parameters of the welfare bill that the House approved some eight weeks later. But the ban on aid to single mothers under eighteen remained a bone in the throat for moderates. Just before the bill came to a subcommittee vote, Armey's office heard that the moderates were planning to drop the provision. Armey went to Shaw's office and dramatically appealed to the members to support the Contract provisions at least through the subcommittee. Republicans, he insisted, had to demonstrate faith to the social conservative groups that had supported them in the election. His appeal held the line; but not for long. Shaw still considered the lifetime ban "punitive" and at the full committee joined with moderates to significantly narrow it. The original provision made underage mothers and their children permanently ineligible for welfare; the moderates revised it to bar assistance only until the mothers turned eighteen. This time, Armey conceded defeat, recognizing that the lifetime ban probably could not survive on the floor. As a consolation to the social conservatives, the committee added a provision dreamed up by Rector giving states financial incentives to reduce illegitimacy without increasing abortion.

In the furor over illegitimacy, the issue that had dominated the debate for the previous twenty years — requiring welfare recipients to work for their checks — receded in importance. Eventually the House passed a provision requiring that by early in the next century half of all welfare recipients work for their assistance. But even those drafting that requirement acknowledged it was meaningless because the bill did not provide states with any money to cover the day care, transportation, and supervision costs associated with moving welfare recipients into work. The Congressional Budget Office later calculated that the costs were so prohibitive that only six states might meet the work requirement in the bill. Like Kemp's empowerment agenda, requiring work from welfare recipients no longer seemed revolutionary to many conservatives. They had raised their sights, from conditioning welfare on work, to cutting off welfare altogether, with the absolute time limit on assistance and ban on cash for underage single mothers.

Democrats howled that the Republican bill was weak on work and tough on children, and twisted by the desire to squeeze out large spending reductions to pay for the GOP tax cuts. But nothing they did slowed down the train. At the opening of the legislative session, the House leadership had privately listed welfare as one of the three top priorities in the Contract (along with the Balanced Budget Amendment and the tax cut), and Gingrich squeezed his troops to deliver on what he believed to be "a defining issue" between the parties. "There was a great deal of pressure," said Representative Mike Castle, a Republican moderate from Delaware, who remained queasy about the provisions to deny aid to underage mothers. At the last moment, the bill was nearly capsized when several anti-abortion groups convinced some pro-life Republican legislators that the benefit cutoffs would inspire an increase in abortions. Gingrich was so concerned about defection from pro-life conservatives that he drafted Bill Bennett, himself a Catholic opposed to abortion, to pitch for the legislation at a private Republican conference meeting the day before the vote. Fraying and strained, the Republican coalition still held. On March 24, after a bitter and racially raw floor debate, the House approved the most fundamental changes in the welfare program since its inception sixty years earlier. After months of internal struggle and acrimony, only five Republicans defected.

As soon as the bill passed the House, the argument between the governors and the social conservatives resumed in the Senate. At the Senate Finance Committee, where Republicans had not focused on the details of the welfare debate nearly as much as their counterparts in the House, the governors enjoyed great success in stripping out the conservative national standards they had failed to stop in the House. Under Chairman Bob Packwood, the committee followed the House model and converted welfare into a block grant. The states would still be required to place half their caseload into work programs by early in the next century, and to cut off aid to all recipients after five years; but the Senate committee eliminated all the House provisions on illegitimacy. This reflected some substantive qualms about the provisions, but many saw it as primarily an effort to push away the entire controversy. "A big portion of it," said Santorum, who had moved over to the Senate after defeating Harris Wofford the previous fall, "was [that Packwood] just decided that they didn't want to make decisions. And so [they decided to] punt."

After spending the previous year as the insider resisting more radical proposals for reform in the House, Santorum found himself in the opposite position in the Senate. He joined with a group of conservatives who threatened to oppose the Finance Committee bill unless it restored the House provisions aimed at discouraging illegitimacy; Faircloth, Talent's Senate ally, even threatened a filibuster if the provisions were not restored. From the other side, eight moderates wrote Dole threatening to oppose the bill if states were mandated to impose the provisions on illegitimacy. (Even more explicitly than in the House, the cause of "federalism" became a fig leaf for moderate Republicans opposed to the retrocon vision.) Adding to the confusion, the Senate became tangled in a complex dispute about how the proceeds from the block grant would be distributed — with rapidly growing southern and western states complaining that the allocation formula was tilted against them. Republican presidential politics further complicated the dispute when Phil Gramm assumed the leading role in pushing the retrocon-inspired conservative alternative to the Finance Committee bill.

Dole finally offered his own compromise bill that solved the money problem but failed to bridge the gaps over illegitimacy. Under intense pressure from Packwood and other moderates to oppose the retrocon provisions, Dole gave surprisingly little to the conservatives. His bill would have allowed states to cut off benefits to women under eighteen or impose a family cap, but not required them to do so. That balance misjudged the political market. With conservatives branding his illegitimacy proposals inadequate, moderates unhappy that the bill did not guarantee child care to women forced to work for their assistance, and Democrats united in opposition to all of the GOP welfare plans as punitive, no proposal — not Dole's, not Gramm's, not the Democrats' — could command a majority. In early August, in a scene reminiscent of the Democratic chaos from the previous summer, Dole was forced to pull his bill from the calendar just one day after he opened debate.

But, unlike the Democrats on health care or crime, Dole recouped his losses. Over the congressional recess in August, he cobbled together a new bill, moving left and right at the same time. Dole remained personally dubious about mandating the family cap. "My view all along was that if we are going to give the governors the options, let's give them the options," he said later. "It's hard to have a conservative constraint but we can't have these terrible liberal constraints on welfare." But to secure votes from conservative senators — and blunt Gramm's efforts to organize support from religious conservatives in the presidential race — Dole nonetheless added to his bill the requirement that states impose the family cap. That allowed him to win tacit consent from the Christian Coalition and other "pro-family" groups to exclude the House bill's benefit cutoff for underage mothers, which was anathema to the Senate Republican moderates. To further attract the Republican moderates, Dole added a provision requiring states to continue spending their own funds on the poor, and exempting from work requirements women with small children who could not find child care. After his stumbles earlier in August, Dole was back in his element: making deals, splitting the difference, testing, probing, simultaneously pushing "to the limit in both directions," as moderate Republican Senator James M. Jeffords of Vermont later put it.

Dole released his revised legislation in early September, and it broke the logjam. As it moved toward passage on the Senate floor, a coalition of Democrats and moderate Republicans (joined in some instances even by conservative Republicans) won a series of amendments that shouldered the bill further toward the center. The most dramatic moment came when the centrist coalition — over the bitter objections of Faircloth, Gramm, and other conservatives — won a two-to-one vote eliminating the requirement that states impose the family cap. Senator Pete Domenici of New Mexico, not always considered a moderate, led the uprising, which drew support from twenty Republicans and every Democrat. Domenici ridiculed the retrocon claims that denying welfare benefits would discourage illegitimacy: "If you believe that . . . you believe in the tooth fairy," he insisted on the floor. The fact that Domenici was ordinarily among Dole's closest Senate allies led some conservatives, especially in the House, to question whether Dole had arranged the entire sequence of events; a few days after the vote, one ranking House leadership aide said, "a lot of people do think it was choreographed" so that Dole could gain credit with conservatives for supporting the family cap, but not actually have to include it in the bill. No one could point to any hard evidence of such a deal, though, and Dole strongly denied it. A more obvious explanation for the revolt was the continued pressure of anti-abortion forces led by the Catholic Church against the family cap, which they feared would encourage abortion among the poor. "The bishops have a lot of stroke," Dole said with a laugh, "they have a lot of clout." For Domenici, who is Catholic himself, "it was a Catholic thing with the family cap," said one Senator involved in the discussions.

Dole's reversals on the floor actually advanced his cause. The cumulative effect of the bill's reshaping was to move it in a direction that most moderate Democrats felt uncomfortable opposing — even while retaining enough conservative provisions to hold support on the right. In the end, the bill passed with a stunning 87–12 vote, drawing opposition only from Faircloth and eleven liberals, including Daniel Patrick Moynihan, and Ted Kennedy, who denounced it as "legislative child abuse." ("I was afraid Kennedy would vote for it," Dole said wryly, "then I'd have to change my vote.") Even Clinton praised the final product and signaled he would sign a measure that followed its outline. Some conservatives grumbled about the retreats from the House legislation, but most understood they had cleared a major hurdle and that the process was not yet over. Dole moved quickly to send that message himself. Immediately after the vote, the senator called Ralph

Reed, the executive director of the Christian Coalition, and promised him that he would work to reinstate some version of the family cap in the House-Senate conference that would fashion the final legislation. Whatever Dole felt in his heart about the family cap, in his head he knew that he could not entirely deny the retrocon vision and still aspire to lead the GOP as its presidential nominee.

WHAT is the moral of this story? To many conservatives it suggests the Senate, with Republican moderates holding the balance of power, is out of step with the party and frustrating the revolution of 1994. To scholars it suggests the power of the legislative process to moderate the demand for change in any direction. Both conclusions have strong elements of truth. Yet to focus only on these disagreements obscures the extent to which the entire framework of debate within the GOP — and indeed the country as a whole — has shifted to the right.

The question, once again, is whether the internal Republican debate over welfare is viewed as a snapshot or just one frame in an ongoing sequence. Seen as a snapshot, the final result on welfare is likely to disappoint the retrocons and their allies. Even the House-passed bill, by significantly diluting the ban on cash assistance to unwed minors, frustrated the retrocons. "It shows you how thin we slice the bread in government," Bill Bennett sighed shortly after the House completed work. "It just shows you what a bad strainer the government is for a moral idea. It's the horse becoming a camel."

But viewed as a single point in an ongoing evolution of Republican thinking, the picture looks very different. Consider how much is now beyond dispute in the welfare debate: ending the individual entitlement to welfare; converting the program into a block grant that limits federal spending on the needy; requiring all welfare recipients to leave the rolls after five years of receiving aid, without providing them jobs; slashing overall spending on welfare programs. Even conservatives might have feared to broach all of these ideas not long ago. Now all had cleared both chambers and drawn signals of support even from President Clinton; nothing marked the shift more clearly than the anger the bill's advance provoked in liberals like Moynihan. Hearing such complaints, Clinton once again wavered, shifting toward opposition to the final welfare bill that the House and Senate negotiated late in 1995.

Even so, the GOP legislation fundamentally shifted the direction of the welfare debate the Republican Congress had inherited. The 1988 welfare reform law moved away modestly from the notion of unconditional entitlement toward a guiding principle of mutual obligation — with government putting more money into education and training but then theoretically requiring greater personal responsibility from those it helped. Clinton's original reform plan moved much further down that path, putting more bite in the call for personal responsibility by requiring work after two years, but retaining the idea that government was obligated to simultaneously increase its aid to the poor. All of the 1995 Republican welfare proposals rejected that vision of reciprocal responsibility. Instead, by imposing a time limit on welfare payments without guaranteeing jobs to those cut off, and by rejecting new funding for education or training, the GOP plans embodied the retrocon belief that the best way to encourage personal responsibility was to withdraw government assistance. (The one slight concession to the vision of reciprocal responsibility was the Senate provision providing limited new funding for child care.) If Clinton's original plan had called for a partnership between government and the poor to reduce dependency, the Republican plans placed the onus for escaping poverty squarely on the poor themselves.

Even on out-of-wedlock births, the retrocons could claim enormous success in reshaping the agenda. As recently as 1992, public officials still hesitated to declare childbearing outside of marriage wrong. Now hardly any leading figure in either party contests that characterization. The debate over welfare reform exposed limits to the measures the public would accept to enforce that judgment; even most Republicans viewed Gingrich's forceful advocacy of orphanages as a public relations disaster. Likewise, polls never showed much public support for denying benefits to unmarried mothers under eighteen. But those limits still allowed a measure of conservative reform greater than appeared possible under Bush, or to Shaw, Grandy, and Johnson in their 1992 manifesto. In 1992, the family cap was such a controversial idea that Bush only gingerly endorsed it; the House, with hardly any hesitation, imposed it on every state in the nation. Though the Senate rejected the mandatory family cap, the final legislation approved by House and Senate negotiators restored the provision in the original November 1993 House bill that imposed the family cap but allowed states to vote to exempt themselves from it. And whatever Congress decided, the idea was already spreading in the states; by mid-1995 fourteen states had either imposed the family cap on their own or were on the way to doing so.

As on welfare, resistance from party moderates diluted or derailed several other of the activist conservatives' most ambitious schemes in 1995. But, again, seen in the context of the party's shifting center of gravity, the ledger on 1995 looks very different. While important divisions remain on how far and how fast to move, on the basic questions of government's role in society even moderate Republicans are now accepting budget reductions and social policy changes that might have been considered irresponsible under Reagan. In early 1995, Hatfield inspired outrage from younger Republicans by opposing the Balanced Budget Amendment, but neither Hatfield nor any other Senate Republican voted against the GOP budget plan that plotted a path to a balanced budget by slashing nearly one trillion dollars in federal spending over the next seven years. And in the House, dissent from moderates proved much less an impediment to passage of the Contract than Gingrich and Armey initially expected; on the thirty-one key votes, an average of 98 percent of Republican House members voted for the Contract provisions. Only a single House Republican voted against the leadership's plan for balancing the budget.

"I would never define a moderate in the Republican Party as somebody who believes that the federal government programs should continue to exist at the present levels, that spending should continue to exist at the present levels, or that they're successful," says Representative Castle, a leading House moderate. "I think almost virtually all of us . . . feel that the size [and] scope of government have to be reduced. And we may differ as to which programs that should come from, but there is virtually nobody in that group who would be a fiscal moderate. There aren't too many fiscal moderates floating around in the Republican Party."

For all the resistance the Contract agenda faced in the Senate in 1995, the long-term trends in the GOP point toward an inexorable consolidation behind the conservative drive. One factor is generational. Over time, generational transition will narrow the gap between the Senate and the militant antigovernment ideology that is already dominant among House Republicans and certain to grow more so as

GOP gains extend in the South. Of the eleven Republican senators elected in 1994, only Olympia J. Snowe of Maine might qualify as a moderate. Of the seven Republican senators who routinely take moderate positions, just Snowe and James Jeffords of Vermont (the only congressional Republican who endorsed Clinton's health care plan) were elected after 1980. The Senate Republican caucus will never be uniformly conservative because the Northeast, as well as certain portions of the Midwest and the Northwest, are all more likely to elect moderate than conservative Republicans. Five of the seven Senate Republican moderates come from Oregon (Mark Hatfield), Maine (Snowe and William Cohen), or elsewhere in New England (John Chafee and Jeffords). But elsewhere, as Republican moderates leave office, they are being replaced by conservatives, many of them alumni from Gingrich's House. In 1994, conservative Republicans John Ashcroft of Missouri and Rod Grams of Minnesota both replaced retiring moderates; in Pennsylvania, Rick Santorum won back the seat that Democrat Harris Wofford claimed after the death of the Republican moderate John Heinz. (Heinz' widow underscored the extent of the ideological transition by denouncing Santorum during the campaign.) Both Santorum and Grams arrived after brief dips in the ideologically purifying waters of the House; Ashcroft was a governor with close ties to the religious conservative movement. "The Senate will never be the House, but it will be more like the House in its thinking in the future," Santorum says. "The revolution has not gotten here, but it will."

Intellectual change is reinforcing this generational change. For now, says Armey, even the House leadership recognizes that it has taken most Republicans "about as far as most of them have the tolerance to go" in rolling back government. But the likelihood is that within the GOP the boundaries of the possible will continue to shift to the Right. All the intellectual energy in the Republican Party is now focused on finding new ways to reduce the scope and reach of the federal government.

In think tanks, congressional offices, and the weekly meetings of the antigovernment coalition, conservatives already dream of new demolitions. Even as they struggle to complete the first steps toward converting federal social programs into block grants, many conservatives are already looking toward more fundamental reductions in the social safety net. One school proposes more radical devolution to the states. Governors like Tommy Thompson and like-minded conservatives on Capitol Hill say that after some interim period of block-granting money to the states, the federal government should simply withdraw funding for programs like welfare, use the savings to reduce federal taxes, and then allow states to raise their own taxes if they wish to continue providing the services. For many Republicans this approach has a powerful logic: Congressional Republicans eager to show results in reducing government are unlikely to remain enthusiastic for long about collecting taxes that allow state officials to expand their own bureaucratic empires. And the growing Republican control over state government gives conservatives confidence that if the federal government withdraws funds for social programs, most states would not fully replace the spending, thus advancing the goal of reducing government overall.

The competing school envisions pushing power over social programs out past government at any level, into the private and charitable sector. Marvin Olasky and his followers (including The Progress and Freedom Foundation, a think tank that amounts to an extension of Gingrich's brain) talk about capping or cutting government expenditures on the poor and using the savings to fund tax credits aimed at encouraging donations to private charities; the long-term goal is allowing those charities to supplant the government as the principal source of aid to the needy. "I believe in a social safety net," Gingrich has declared, "but I think that it's better done by churches and by synagogues and by volunteers."

There is hardly a federal agency so obscure, a policy so benign, that it has not aroused its own aspiring executioner in the GOP. Republicans in both Houses have prepared legislation to discard federal affirmative-action programs, and the brigades of Republican regulatory reformers in Congress are pointing their scythes at environmental laws like the Clean Water Act. Plans to wipe out the Federal Communications Commission pulse across the e-mail of the conservative Tofflerians. Dick Armey and Bill Archer, the chairman of the House Ways and Means Committee, are casting at a bigger fish: the progressive income tax. Armey wants to replace the progressive income tax with a flat tax that would eliminate all (or virtually all) deductions in return for an extremely low tax rate of 17 percent. Archer leads a competing faction that wants to replace the income tax with some sort of consumption tax, such as a national sales tax. Either option will almost certainly diminish (or even virtually eliminate) the progressivity of the tax code — the features that cause the affluent to pay a higher share of their income in taxes — and reduce federal revenues, increasing the pressure to further shrink government.

If provided sustained political control, how far would conservatives push this deconstruction of federal power? In some regards, the Republican rhetoric about repealing the welfare state or unwinding the New Deal is bombast. No one, for instance, is seriously contemplating eliminating Social Security or Medicare, the cornerstones of the American social welfare state. Though Republicans have proposed severe limits on federal environmental, occupational safety, and food purity laws, no one has seriously proposed their elimination. During the first years of the New Deal, federal government outlays equaled only 8 to 11 percent of the gross national product; today that figure has increased to about 22 percent of national output. Even the House and Senate budget plans would shrink government only to about 19 percent of GNP by 2002.

But arduous as it will be, the effort to balance the budget is clearly not the endpoint of the Republican plan to reshape the federal government. Just as Democrats did not cap the work of the New Deal until the Great Society three decades later, conservative Republicans now routinely talk about a decades-long march to dismantle the empire their rivals constructed through the heart of this century.

Even with the exceptions noted above, the sweep of this vision looks back beyond the Great Society and the New Deal, beyond even the Progressive Era that first installed a vigorous central government as a counterweight to the social and economic power of business. With the flat tax; severe cuts in spending programs that benefit the poor; retrenchment of affirmative action; and the reduction of regulation that places government in the position of forcing concessions from business, the activist core in the GOP would limit from almost every angle the authority that Washington has accumulated since the Progressive Era to challenge the distribution of income, opportunity, or power produced by the private economy. In its purest form, this agenda enshrines the social and economic results generated by the unfettered market as beyond the capacity, or right, of government to question:

"[T]here is no objectively meaningful standard on which to judge any market outcome as 'unfair,'" the Republican-controlled Joint Economic Committee wrote in an early 1995 report. Armey, characteristically, summarizes the case with less equivocation and more bluster: "The market is rational," he writes, "and the government is dumb."

Measured against the scale of those ambitions, the question of how far conservatives can push moderates in this Congress is a significant but secondary issue. The real question is whether the Republicans can sustain public support for their control of Congress and reinforce their position by retaking the White House. To extend the photographic metaphor, the issue is whether the accomplishments of this Congress represent the final image of the conservative revolution — or merely an early frame in a sequence that will unfold for years.

As during the 1980s, the Gingrich generation of Republican politicians and their allies in the antigovernment coalition are simultaneously fighting two battles, one internal, one external. Generational change will inexorably strengthen their hand in the internal battle against party moderates. But that victory will be meaningful only if they are also successful in the external battle — and win the lasting political control they need to continue their long march against the New Deal. In that quest, persuading the moderates in the Senate to accept all the specifics of their agenda is less important than persuading the country to accept its general direction. The most pressing threat to the Republican revolution is not resistance from a passing generation of moderate senators elected before Reagan; it is the real possibility that the breadth of the drive to reduce government will frighten voters as much as Clinton's effort to expand it.

★★★

III

Holding It Together

★★★

7

Big Tent

POLITICAL PARTIES owe their success to harmonizing disparate coalitions, and in the middle months of 1995, two events symbolized the precarious balancing act Republicans now face. The first came on May 17 in the Mansfield Room of the Capitol at a gathering called by the Christian Coalition. Fifteen television cameras lined the back wall, and at the front, a spindly lectern groaned under the weight of two dozen microphones. Ralph Reed, the group's executive director, acted as impresario for the event, and behind him stood a legion of Coalition state directors silently testifying to the organization's grassroots network. They had come to the Capitol to unveil a contract of their own, called the "Contract With the American Family," a knockoff of the GOP's campaign document, but tilted to the social and cultural issues that had been excluded from that original, one-hundred-days manifesto.

Two years earlier, many Republicans had shunned religious conservatives for contributing to George Bush's defeat, but the scene inside the Mansfield Room demonstrated the degree to which the party not only welcomed, but now felt beholden to, these activists. Reporters and other guests packed the room like a rush hour subway, all sweltering under the hot television lights. Republican elected officials milling behind Reed constituted a virtual who's who of the new GOP. House Speaker Newt Gingrich headed the list, but Phil Gramm, bidding for the support of religious conservatives in his presidential campaign, also had elbowed his way into the front row. Others included Senate Whip Trent Lott; House Whip Tom DeLay; House Budget Committee Chairman John Kasich; Senator Dan Coats, a longtime advocate of the religious conservatives' agenda; Senator Paul Coverdell, a pro-choice Republican whose 1992 victory in Georgia relied heavily on Christian Coalition support; and J. C. Watts, the former Oklahoma football star and one of only two black Republicans in the House. Bob Dole was the only big name missing from the ceremony, but in penance for a schedule conflict he had invited Reed and the Coalition leaders to his office for a private meeting immediately after the press conference. "We have finally gained what we have always sought," Reed said. "A place at the table, a sense of legitimacy and a voice in the conversation that we call democracy."

Three months later, the scene shifted to Dallas, as the political world paid court to Ross Perot's United We Stand America. Under a baking August sun, the Texas billionaire convened summer camp for political junkies and summoned the leaders of both political parties to participate. An exhibition hall at the Dallas Convention Center featured a political smorgasbord that traversed the ideological spectrum and beyond, ranging from mainline book publishers and mainstream political groups to one-world conspiracy kooks and anti-Trilateral Commission zealots. June Griffin of Dade, Tennessee, sold politically correct kitchenware for the conservative faith-and-freedom politics of the 1990s. Her "Bill of Rights" aprons came adorned with two pockets, a square one for a Bible, the other shaped like a holster to hold a pistol. Apart from the sideshow in the exhibition hall, most of the attendees were sober-minded, concerned citizens — representatives of what has become "the radical middle" of the American electorate. In the main arena, nearly four thousand people sat on folding chairs for hours on end and listened attentively to a parade of speakers that would have taxed the patience of all but the most committed of political activists. Mary Brenneman, an elderly California political activist, jotted notes as she listened. "I think this country is in a crisis," she said.

Democratic speakers gamely appealed to the audience. But theirs was a difficult sell, for this was a demonstrably anti-Clinton crowd. Ten Republican presidential candidates filled up most of one day's agenda, while on the other day, GOP leaders openly petitioned Perot's army to become permanent members of the new Republican coalition. Appealing to the audience's outsider instincts, Gingrich described the Republican Class of 1994 as "a third party" of its own that was pushing him and other Republican leaders "to be real revolutionaries." Haley Barbour, the last of eighteen speakers on the first day, pledged that the voices of the Perot movement would be heard by the party. "You need pass no litmus test to get involved," he said. "The party of the twenty-first century has an open door." But Perot resisted crossing the GOP threshold. Like Reed and the Christian Coalition, he too was peddling a "second Contract With America," which included far-reaching restrictions on lobbying and new rules for campaign financing that, like the Christian Coalition agenda, also had been excluded from the GOP's Contract With America. "I would like to go away," he said. "But if I go away, the odds we'll get these reforms are zero." A month later, underscoring his lack of confidence in the two parties, he announced his intention to form his own new political party.

In years past, Democratic candidates trooped the summer circuit of special interest constituency conventions, one week appearing before the barons of organized labor, another week before feminists, still another before civil rights leaders at the NAACP. Now the Republicans' time has come, as the gatherings in Washington and Dallas demonstrated. No two groups have done more to rearrange the contours of American politics in the past five years than religious conservatives and the army of voters massed under Ross Perot's outsider umbrella, and in any architectural rendering of the new Republican Party, the two represent load-bearing beams of the new coalition. Maintaining their allegiance is critical to the GOP's hopes of becoming the governing majority into the next century.

The growing political mobilization of religious conservatives reflects a realignment in voting patterns that offers long-term advantages for Republicans. But their increased power also creates enormous strains with the party's pro-choice, moderate bloc that, while shrinking, retains prominent spokesmen in governors like William Weld, Christine Todd Whitman, and Pete Wilson, and that was boosted by Colin Powell's decision to join the party with the expressed goal of trying to broaden its appeal. Religious conservatives and more secular moderates now agree on much of the GOP agenda. Economically there is little difference in their views, and of late they have found common ground on some social and cultural issues, like crime. But their debates over the details of welfare reform and seemingly irreconcilable differences over issues like abortion, school prayer, and homosexuality threaten a wider breach that not only could divide the party's coalitions but also drive less affiliated voters into a more permanent posture of independence. At the same time, the aggressiveness of religious and other conservatives in attempting to define what is acceptable Republican doctrine — symbolized by their effort to prevent Powell from running for President — threatens to narrow the appeal of the party at precisely the time the GOP needs to find ways to expand — if lasting realignment is the genuine goal of party leaders.

The size and strength of Perot's coalition, which has held close to the 19 percent of the vote he received in 1992, underscores the continuing drift toward dealignment from both parties within the electorate. The Perot movement's desire to disinfect the entire political system by remaining detached from both parties, an impulse that led Perot to begin organizing his new party, creates a huge impediment to GOP hopes of assembling a lasting majority coalition. In its rigidly unaffiliated state, the Perot movement may act as a block and tackle pulling apart the two-party structure — and some Republicans contribute to that process by characterizing the party along lines that are too sharply ideological.

Similarities in the two movements help to fortify the Republicans in the short run. Both embody the energy of the antigovernment, grassroots, populist forces driving the politics of the 1990s. Both draw their strength from citizens new to the political process — many of them initially unsophisticated about the intricacies of elections and campaigns but increasingly astute, even cold-blooded, in their capacity to manipulate the system toward their own ends. Both movements include many people deeply suspicious of power and political elites. And both have felt the sting of ridicule from both the media and the tight-knit community of political insiders.

But differences abound. Religious conservatives are most numerous in the South, while Perot's greatest strength comes in the angry West. The Christian Coalition attracts more women than men, while Perot appeals more to men. Religious conservatives have set their sights on dominating the Republican Party, while Perot voters want the two parties to reform themselves before casting their fate with one or the other. But even those differences are minimal compared to division along religious versus secular lines. Though the two movements share similar attitudes on many specific issues, the gulf between them on social and cultural issues remains significant. A poll of Christian Coalition members in the fall of 1995 found that 95 percent said they were neither members nor supporters of Perot's United We Stand. Similarly, Clinton pollster Stan Greenberg, in a 1993 survey for the Democratic Leadership Council, said, "The Perot voters are very secular and libertarian and extremely uncomfortable with the social conservatism and Christian right dominance of the Republican Party." Greenberg found that Perot and Clinton voters held "virtually identical views on abortion," and predicted that continued focus on abortion in the Republican Party would make it "difficult for Perot voters to turn back to the GOP." Another study concluded, "Perot voters attended church less regularly and were less involved religiously" than supporters of either Bush or Clinton.

Obviously, that did not prevent Perot voters from supporting Republicans in 1994, but in large part because Republicans emphasized economic and governmental reform issues like the Balanced Budget Amendment and term limits, not school prayer or abortion. The growing need to satisfy religious activists' desire for a socially conservative agenda while simultaneously catering to the reform-minded and even libertarian impulses of the Perot movement represents a challenge of coalition management that will test the dexterity of the Republican leadership. As bright stars in the new Republican constellation, the religious conservatives no longer will be satisfied by rhetorical bows or continued requests for patience. Nor will Perot voters, the most significant "freestanding" constituency in the electorate, easily be persuaded to trade in their outsider status for membership cards in the Republican club, especially now that Perot has committed to building a permanent third-party structure.

A RELIGIOUS REALIGNMENT

The turnout for the Christian Coalition press conference in May 1995 and the praise Republican leaders in Congress offered for the Coalition's agenda reflected the significance Republican leaders attached to the religious-based, pro-family movement. Arguably, religious conservatives now constitute the Republicans' largest and most loyal bloc of voters in terms of their mobilizing power — a Republican equivalent of organized labor in the Democratic Party; in loyalty, the equivalent of the black vote.

The 1992 and 1994 elections reinforced what appears to be a continuing shift in religious voting patterns. The blossoming army of white evangelical Christians, once a solid part of the New Deal coalition, has supplanted Mainline Protestants, for more than a century the heart of the GOP coalition, as the party's "senior partner." Add to that Protestant shift the growing identification with the Republican Party among many Roman Catholic voters — onetime Reagan Democrats who actually first tilted toward the GOP during Richard Nixon's presidency — and the depth of the GOP's dependence on religious conservatives becomes clear. These voting patterns alone affect the balance of power between the two parties. But what assures Christian conservatives the seat at the table that Reed talked about is the energy they now exhibit at the grassroots; they are the most potent political movement in the country today.

The realignment of religious conservatives to the Republican Party has been under way for two decades. As E. J. Dionne Jr. has pointed out, Richard Nixon won four-fifths of the vote in the most heavily Baptist counties in America in his 1972 campaign against George McGovern, while Ronald Reagan, running against born-again Christian Jimmy Carter in 1980, won nearly three-fifths of the vote in those same counties. George Bush captured about 70 percent of the vote of white evangelicals in his 1988 victory over Michael Dukakis. Through the 1980s, religious conservatives became increasingly prominent — and controversial — political players. Jerry Falwell's Moral Majority, the anti-abortion movement, and the 1988 presidential campaign of Marion G. (Pat) Robertson all highlighted the Republican Party's religious evolution. But Robertson's dismal showing in the Republican primaries, highly publicized scandals involving televangelists Jimmy Swaggart and Jim and Tammy Faye Bakker, the demise of Falwell's organization in 1989, and a backlash by abortion rights advocates after the 1989 Supreme Court decision allowing restrictions on abortion seemed to define the ceiling of conservative Christian political activism. Even in 1988, after more than a decade of growing attachment to the GOP among religious conservatives, Mainline Protestants were more likely to identify themselves as Republicans than evangelical Christians, although by then the two groups supported Republican House candidates in roughly the same percentages.

The symbolic low point for religious conservative involvement in the party came in Houston at the 1992 Republican convention, roundly criticized by the media, the Democrats, and many moderates as an exercise in political intolerance. Pat Buchanan warned conservatives to arm themselves for the coming religious and cultural war in America, Robertson sharply attacked Bill Clinton's values, Marilyn Quayle criticized Vietnam War protesters and dope smokers from her own baby boom generation, and the platform committee delivered forth a document widely described as conservative in the extreme. "I think if there was a cat that died in Houston that week, we were blamed for it," said Judy Haynes, who was a Christian Coalition organizer at the time. "Houston Republicans" soon joined "San Francisco Democrats" in the lexicon of political pejoratives, and if ever religious conservatives seemed like unwelcome house guests at a family reunion, it was in the weeks after the GOP convention, as the election slipped steadily away from Bush.

From a longer view, the contours of the 1992 presidential vote take on a different shape. A team of four scholars, John C. Green, Lyman A. Kellstedt, James L. Guth, and Corwin E. Smidt, has produced a series of revealing analyses that skillfully reinterpret the elections of 1992 and 1994. The four deftly mined a lode of data from exit polls, the University of Michigan's National Election Studies, and other survey research to illuminate the shape of the new Republican Party and the transformation of long-standing voting habits among the three major white religious denominations: evangelical Christians, Mainline Protestants, and Roman Catholics.

From this perspective, Bush's support from white evangelicals may have prevented his loss from being even larger than it was. Economic issues felled Bush in 1992, but social issues prevented many of his 1988 supporters from defecting to either Clinton or Perot, and also may have helped attract new voters to his column. White evangelicals made up Bush's strongest constituency, and among those who did not vote for Bush in 1988 but did in 1992, social issues appear to have been a compelling factor in their decision. Equally important, the post-election studies showed that Republican Party identification among white evangelicals increased during the campaign year. Beneath the surface of the Republican debacle lurked "the first rumblings of an electoral culture war" that would intensify in 1994.

These shifts certainly reflect broader societal trends, namely, the declining size of the population of Mainline Protestants in America, the rapid growth of the evangelical community, and the rising socio-economic status of both the evangelicals and Roman Catholics. Mainline Protestants, once the dominant religious group in the country, now account for only about one-fifth of the adult population, with the trend line pointing down. White evangelicals and Roman Catholics, in contrast, account for about a quarter each of the population.

The 1994 elections reinforced the trends of 1992, lending credence to the proposition that there has been a realignment in religious voting patterns. White evangelicals cast about one-third of all votes for Republican House candidates, and the overall community of religious conservatives (which also includes conservative Roman Catholics) provided two of every five GOP votes. This religious realignment offers another perspective for understanding the breakdown of the New Deal coalition of northern ethnic Catholics, southern white evangelicals, and African-Americans. Today, according to Kellstedt, Green, Guth, and Smidt, evangelicals stand firmly in the Republican camp, African-Americans and Jews side with the Democrats, and Mainline Protestants and Roman Catholics represent swing voters moving in opposite directions.

All these factors alone would be enough to give religious conservatives a seat at the Republican table. But other evidence demonstrates the degree to which religious conservatives now generate enthusiasm and vitality within the party. White evangelicals supported Republican candidates in much higher percentages than did other denominations, and a majority of them now identify themselves as Republicans, which is true for neither Mainline Protestants nor Roman Catholics, despite their voting patterns. And among the white evangelicals, there is no gender gap: Women supported Republicans in 1994 as enthusiastically as did men. Even more significant, the more these voters are mobilized, the more they respond by turning out and supporting Republican candidates. In general, evangelicals still vote at lower rates than Mainline Protestants, but among those who were directly encouraged to vote, participation rates rose dramatically — and those voters cast 94 percent of their votes for Republican candidates. Those percentages mirror the level of black support for Democratic candidates, which is one reason Republican leaders now pay so much attention to their religious constituency. Is it any wonder that religious conservatives expect so much of the Republican Party?

THE RELIGIOUS AWAKENING

The Christian Coalition succeeded where earlier groups failed by rejecting the "mailing list" politics of Christian conservative groups of the 1980s and emphasizing grassroots organizing. Relying initially on veterans of Robertson's 1988 presidential campaign and gradually widening their circle, Coalition organizers emphasized precinct politics, conservative issues, and tested techniques for influencing elections such as voter guides and scorecards — augmented by the technology of phone, fax, computer, and satellite dish — to reward and punish elected officials. "We saw an opportunity to make an impact where no one else was willing to go," said Judy Haynes, who began as the Coalition's southern regional organizer and ended up as Reed's deputy. "It was a precinct organization and nobody wants to do that because it's not a fun job and there's no glory in it. But if you keep doing it and you do it well, then you win."

The Christian Coalition emerged from the wreckage of the first efforts to enlist evangelical Christians in the modern conservative movement: Jerry Falwell's Moral Majority. Rising with Reagan in 1980, Falwell appeared to command hordes of inflamed born-again Christians determined to reclaim the ground they had lost since the Scopes trial half a century earlier. The Moral Majority's founding reflected a conscious effort by New Right strategists, including direct mail specialist Richard Viguerie, and Paul Weyrich, a conservative Catholic from Wisconsin with a knack for assembling alliances, to enlist the large audience of people who tuned in on Sunday mornings not to *Meet the Press* and *Face the Nation* but to the vociferous brotherhood of television preachers — Falwell, Pat Robertson, and Jim Bakker and Jimmy Swaggart. In these religiously conservative fundamentalists, Weyrich and Viguerie saw a potentially huge constituency for politically conservative messages on abortion, school prayer, busing, and pornography. Falwell, a preacher from Lynchburg, Virginia, whose own *Old-time Gospel Hour* was among the most successful of the Sunday televangelist offerings, agreed to lead the charge, and in June 1979 he formed the Moral Majority — a name whose strutting confidence symbolized the group's belligerent posture toward the Left. Over the next year, working through churches around the country it registered at least two million voters (the group claimed to have registered four or eight million) and gave Reagan a powerful boost in reclaiming the South from Jimmy Carter. The threat that a new political awakening among fundamentalists would reshape the electoral landscape appeared so imminent that liberal television producer Norman Lear, the father of *All in the Family*, was moved to start his own organization, People for the American Way, as a counterforce to the strength of the religious Right.

But Reagan's election in 1980 proved to be Falwell's high point. Like other groups in the so-called New Right of the 1980s, the Moral Majority subordinated grassroots organizing to direct mail fund-raising, which left it with a large mailing list but little muscle on the ground. An absence of political sophistication compounded the problems. Falwell inspired thousands of conservative Christians to enter the political arena. But he failed to train his recruits effectively, or to control his tongue; he had a weakness for inflammatory remarks that fit the portrait liberal caricaturists painted of him. Once he declared AIDS "a definite form of the judgment of God upon a society." On another occasion, Falwell said that if the United States entered into a nuclear war with the Soviet Union, "They could never touch us. God would miraculously protect America." Activists on the ground were even more prone to comments that betrayed extremism more than piety. One West Coast chapter leader publicly unburdened himself of the belief that homosexuals should be executed.

Eventually, all but the most conservative candidates thought twice about accepting Falwell's blessing. Even Paul Weyrich, the conservative strategist who had played perhaps the key role in launching the organization, eventually threw up his hands. "These were really people from the fundamentalist community and they had made the shift from arguing that it was a sin to be involved in politics to arguing that it was a sin not to be involved," Weyrich said. "That was as much of a shift as they could absorb. The actual mechanics of how to be involved was something that was sort of beyond them." Falwell finally accepted the inevitable and shuttered the Moral Majority in June 1989, ten years after its founding.

At that point, Robertson and the Christian Coalition stepped in. From its humble beginnings in late 1989, the Coalition grew steadily into an army of more than seventeen hundred local chapters in all fifty states and 1.7 million members by late 1995 — and was growing at the rate of a chapter a day. In the 1994 elections, the Coalition distributed forty million voter guides, including thirty-three million in the final weeks. The Christian Coalition involved itself in 120 House races and their candidates won an estimated 55 percent of them. Thirty of those contests were decided by five percentage points or less, which allowed religious conservatives to claim that their mobilization determined the outcome. Reed has boasted with some legitimacy that when it comes to political mobilization, the Coalition performs for the Republican Party the role organized labor long played for the Democrats, which is to provide a source of energized workers manning phone banks and walking precincts and in other ways mobilizing its community of voters to show up at the polls.

In the 1994 campaign, Coalition organizers tapped into a burgeoning network of churchgoers alarmed by the moral drift and decay they saw around them, from violent and profane rap lyrics to a diet of sexually suggestive prime-time television shows to widespread crime and illegitimacy in every major city in the country. Exit polls from 1994 found that 88 percent of churchgoing, white evangelicals cited "family values" as a major influence on their voting decisions (the highest percentage of any group in the electorate), and 90 percent said they were pro-life.

Although the anti-abortion movement provided many of the recruits in the religious conservative movement, many others were simply conservative parents whose first blush with political activism came through local schools that, to them, seemed determined to trample on their values. For these parents, it was bad enough that the courts had banned prayer in schools; now their children faced sex education classes that often emphasized condoms before abstinence or programs like New York's Rainbow Curriculum, which introduced first-graders to gay and lesbian lifestyles. Kathy Meixill, a young Minnesota mother newly involved in politics in 1994, told us she had put her three children in a private, religious school because she wanted an environment that taught "the six Rs: reading, writing, arithmetic, responsibility, respect, and religion."

The Christian Coalition found strong support among members of the home school movement and among a growing community of parents strongly opposed to the imposition of national education standards, even though President Bush and many conservative Republican governors had supported the development of these national guidelines. At political gatherings of religious conservatives, one obscure but impassioned rallying cry was to denounce OBE, or outcomes-based education, which the activists said encouraged New Age self-esteem rather than academic excellence.

The Christian Coalition's secret was to convert into a political movement the unease these families felt over the schools, the government, and the popular culture. Coalition organizers introduced these Christian conservatives to the nuts and bolts of politics. At training sessions, Coalition leaders explained precincts and state central committees, the structure of party politics, and the arcane rules that often determined victory or defeat in intraparty warfare. In the early stages of their existence, Coalition organizers targeted local school board elections, and with every success gained greater and greater confidence in their own political potential.

The first breakthrough came in San Diego in 1990, when candidates favored by Coalition organizers and their allies won sixty-six of eighty-eight targeted local races, including school board contests. Organizers quietly mobilized Christian conservatives by conducting voter registration drives in friendly churches, combing through church directories to develop phone lists, and distributing material in church parking lots on the eve of the elections. "The advantage we have," Reed said later, "is that liberals and feminists don't generally go to church. They don't gather in one place three days before the election." In those early days, Coalition organizers prided themselves on stealth tactics, which Reed later captured in a famous quotation he has been trying to live down ever since: "I paint my face and travel at night," he said. "You don't know it's over until you're in a body bag. You don't know until election night."

The movement's electoral successes, however, produced a vigorous backlash among those who feared the religious conservatives were attempting to legislate morality on their communities. In 1992, voters in

Vista, California, elected a school board with a three-to-two majority of religious conservatives. Board meetings turned into shouting matches over creationism and sex education. The new board jettisoned the seventh-grade sex education program for one that promoted abstinence while declaring birth control dangerous and premarital sex illegal. The new board members denied they were attempting to impose their values, but their agenda drew angry protests from other parents, and in 1994, the voters removed two of the Christian conservatives by recall and rejected five others running for open seats on the board.

Opponents looked for any opportunity to portray religious conservatives as extremists, and at times individual activists played directly into those caricatures. In Lake County, Florida, a school board dominated by religious conservatives ordered the faculty to teach students that American culture was "superior to other foreign or historic cultures" and sought to block a Head Start program as antifamily. In La Mesa, California, conservatives on the school board claimed a breakfast program for poor children represented government meddling in family life. A Texas Republican activist argued for the death penalty for homosexuals, based on his own interpretation of the Bible, while a local Missouri candidate labeled homosexuals "parasites" on society because they could not reproduce children.

Such examples notwithstanding, opponents of the religious conservatives overlooked the extent to which the Coalition's message spoke to a broad audience of ordinary Americans, people who worked in small businesses or in global corporations, coached Little League, attended church regularly, and even took an occasional glass of wine with dinner. Far from being social outcasts from some tiny religious sect, growing numbers of those in the religious conservative movement represented the mainstream of middle America. "They think we're right-wing fanatics," said Rob Iten, who worked in the commercial printing business and spoke to us while attending a Christian Coalition organizing meeting in St. Paul, Minnesota, in 1994. "We're not. We're normal people. We're being labeled." "We're family people," said George Plew of Coon Rapids, Minnesota. "We're not in some fringe."

Many of the new Christian activists populated the megachurches of suburban America, congregations of five thousand or ten thousand or more (congregations large and diverse enough even to include Clinton voters) whose Sunday services featured Christian rock bands, closed-circuit television, slick video presentations, and an up-tempo pace designed for the hurry-up lives of two-income families shuttling between soccer matches on Saturday, church on Sunday, and the orthodontist on Monday. Tom Kean, the former governor of New Jersey and one of the leading moderates in the party, attended the Iowa Republican convention in June 1994, in part to warn the GOP about religious intolerance. But he later admitted his surprise at discovering that many of those described as extremists were, in fact, the people next door. "I guess I expected zealots," he later said. "Instead I found decent, everyday people. . . . They shared a common belief that America was in the midst of a moral crisis. They deplored the rise in teenage pregnancy, abortions, AIDS, drug abuse, and violent crime. . . . Above all they wanted the family and its values respected once more."

CHRISTIAN Coalition leaders often insisted that they intended to remain independent from both political parties, but on the ground they made steady progress in taking over state Republican parties. In the summer of 1994, the magazine *Campaigns & Elections* estimated that the Christian conservatives then dominated eighteen state Republican parties, including Iowa, site of the first presidential caucuses; California; Florida; Texas; Oregon; and South Carolina; and that they exerted considerable influence on thirteen more — figures that the Christian Coalition and other groups in the movement never sought to dispute. Republican Party leaders saw the activism and influence of religious conservatives as a double-edged sword. The new recruits provided both energy and a vast new reservoir of votes for the party that, when combined with traditional Republicans more interested in economic issues, meant a bloc large enough to win most elections. But assimilating the religious conservatives sometimes proved difficult, and at times their growing power threatened to touch off an intraparty civil war with moderates who passionately objected to the newcomers' moral agenda.

Minnesota witnessed one of the fiercest battles of 1994. There, a grassroots army of religious conservatives (largely unaffiliated with the Christian Coalition), who were angry at Republican Governor Arne Carlson for his support of abortion and gay rights, overwhelmed the precinct and county caucuses of the Independent-Republican Party. At the state convention in June, they delivered the party's endorsement for governor to a little-known former state legislator named Allen Quist. A farmer, teacher, and father of ten children, Quist had an open and friendly manner, but he was unyielding in his opposition to abortion and gay rights, and could not escape the damage done to his candidacy by his statement that men had a "genetic predisposition" to head their households. Carlson never had been popular with many of the party's conservative activists, and the Quist-Carlson battle shaped up as a battle between pragmatism and ideology. Many moderates and even conservatives argued that Quist was unelectable and that his candidacy threatened other Republicans in the fall. But the "Quistian" conservatives, as they were dubbed, would not listen and drove many of those Republicans out of the convention process. "I'm pro-life, a fiscal conservative, pro-family, the whole gamut," said state Representative Gene Hugoson, who was denied a seat at the convention. "But in the words of some, I betrayed the cause because I didn't criticize Carlson."

Carlson aggressively counterattacked, accusing Quist of being "a cult leader with a Messianic complex," comparing his candidacy to the rise of Adolf Hitler and claiming Quist wanted to inject religion into state government. Quist claimed he was the victim of vicious stereotyping. The battle raged throughout the summer of 1994 until the September Republican primary, when an outpouring of nervous voters blunted Quist's candidacy and gave Carlson the nomination in a landslide. In the election's aftermath, Quist bitterly maintained he had been mugged by opponents, but even leaders of the conservative Christian movement criticized him for allowing himself to be caricatured. "There are certain minimal standards you have to meet as a statewide candidate and one of them is you have to be viewed as someone who believes women have the same potential as men," Ralph Reed said. "Some religious conservative candidates bring their private religious view of the institution of marriage into the broader arena of political debate about women's issues."

The Minnesota convention that endorsed Quist came during a three-week stretch in 1994 when religious conservatives flexed their muscles across the country. In Virginia, Christian conservatives provided the victory margins that nominated Oliver L. North, the central actor in the Iran-contra scandal, for Senate, and Michael Farris, a leader in the home-schooling movement, for lieutenant governor. (Both lost their elections, although Farris did far better than expected.) In Texas the following weekend, a state convention dominated by Christian conservatives elected Tom Pauken as state chairman and adopted a deeply conservative platform that described government-owned land as "socialism," called for the teaching of "creation science" in the schools, and sought to define the family as "persons related by blood, heterosexual marriage or adoption." An attempt to include a preamble that said, "It is inappropriate to require a certain type of religious expression for leaders, candidates, delegates," was withdrawn in the face of strong opposition from religious conservatives. One told the *New York Times*, "Right now the majority of the party is pro-life. And if people can't live within the Republican Party as it is, then they should move."

The triptych of state conventions sent fresh rumbles of dissatisfaction through a party that still had vivid memories of the 1992 Houston convention. As he circulated among contributors and other party regulars, Haley Barbour absorbed complaints that the party's hopes in November were threatened by a religious takeover. "The first thing out of people's mouths was abortion and the Christian Coalition," said Scott Reed, Barbour's chief of staff at the time. "He was getting hammered. Hammered!" But Barbour, like other party leaders, believed much of the criticism was off the mark. He also knew the religious conservatives were essential to a winning coalition. The publicity over Christian conservative dominance within the party might have damaged Republicans more had not the Democrats responded by attacking the movement as "the radical right" in a series of heavy-handed speeches that did far more to unify Republicans than they did to energize the Left. Religious conservatives, in particular, vowed not to be silenced by the criticism. "The religious right hasn't even touched the tip of the iceberg compared to the religious left," said Patricia Boyd, who attended the Minnesota convention. "Now it's our turn."

"A CHRISTIAN LEE ATWATER"

No one deserved more credit for the political success of the Christian Coalition and the self-described pro-family movement than Ralph

Reed. The most powerful sectarian leader in the country today, Reed, by his own account, never studied at a seminary, never commanded a congregation nor led a TV ministry, and never served as a deacon, elder, or lay minister of a church. He claims he never even taught a Sunday school class, and, at thirty-four, looks barely old enough to be excused from those classes to sit with the adults at morning worship. All Ralph Reed ever really wanted to be, he said, was "a Christian Lee Atwater," and in a few short years has far exceeded all expectations. Today on Capitol Hill, Republican staffers refer to him — not always charitably — as "God's LA" — short for "legislative assistant."

Reed has risen with amazing speed from the obscurity of Emory University's doctoral program to the cover of *Time* magazine, which in 1995 ran his photo under a headline reading "The Right Hand of God." He operates out of a nondescript office building in a low-rise industrial park just off Interstate 64 in Chesapeake, Virginia. But the Coalition's satellite uplink capabilities, his frenetic travel schedule, and an ever-present cellular phone all attest to his ubiquitous presence at the heart of the Republican revolution. His choir boy good looks and straight-arrow demeanor mesh perfectly with the throngs of people who attend Coalition functions or wait patiently for Reed to sign his book, *Politically Incorrect*. But his big belly laugh and displays of political cunning suggest a more complex personality, one equally at home in the sunny cathedrals of modern Christianity and the darker back rooms of contemporary, cutthroat politics. In his time at the Coalition, Reed has played multiple roles with equal agility: guerrilla warrior, obedient employee, long-range strategist, hard-nosed negotiator, and reassuring envoy to a skeptical, secular world. At times it is not clear whether he is a religious activist increasing the voice of conservative Christians within the Republican Party, or a Republican activist tightening the GOP's hold on the Christian conservative movement.

Born the son of a navy doctor and a mother who ran the Methodist Youth Fellowship program at church, Reed gravitated early to politics, drawn first by an endless stream of political biographies from the local library and later from a pre-teen adrenaline rush he felt watching the national political conventions in Miami, where he was living in 1972. Slightly built and short of stature, he ran for president of his junior high school class by adopting the moniker of Stephen A. Douglas in his 1858 Senate campaign against Abraham Lincoln. His posters read:

"Vote for Ralph Reed. The Little Giant." It was the last campaign where he cast himself in the mold of a moderate. Reed came to Washington with the Reagan youth brigades in 1981, working as a summer intern for a newly elected Georgia senator and later joining a cabal of young activists occupying lower-level jobs at the Republican National Committee. He became executive director of the College Republicans, where he worked closely with another operative with a taste for grassroots organizing, Grover G. Norquist, later to become president of Americans for Tax Reform. They read the works of Saul Alinsky and Tom Hayden and fancied themselves shock troops for the Right. "We viewed ourselves as the mirror image of the leaders of the New Left of the '60s," Reed said. "We saw ourselves as . . . entrepreneurs who were building a new generational consciousness that was pro-Reagan, conservative [and] very aggressive, very creative."

But the more time Reed spent in Washington, the more he felt his personal and professional lives out of sync. Raised in an environment that included regular attendance at church and Sunday school and summers at Methodist youth camp, Reed reveled in the fast-track world of national politics, but in observing his own behavior and the hypocrisy of politicians who preached family values by day and obliterated them by night, he felt a gnawing inadequacy. "I just made a decision that either I was going to change what I believed in or I was going to start living what I believed in," he said. "I did not want to go through life and have a disconnect between the life that I was living and the values that I was saying to the rest of society, 'This is what I think best.'" In 1983, Reed began attending an evangelical church in the Washington suburbs, and he gave up drinking and smoking — but not, as it would turn out, a life in politics. "I'm a political strategist," he said. "I just happen to be a committed Christian."

In 1985, Reed left Washington to begin graduate work in history at Emory in Atlanta, where he studied the rise and fall of social movements in America and wrote a dissertation on the history of evangelical higher education. He seemed on a new career path toward teaching and writing, but at a dinner during Bush's inaugural in 1989 he ended up at a table that included Pat Robertson. Robertson knew enough about Reed to share with him his desire to start a new organization that would keep the activists from his presidential campaign involved in politics. Falwell was preparing to disband the Moral Majority, by then just a paper tiger, and Robertson believed a new and different organization was needed to fill the void. Reed, who had supported Jack Kemp for President in 1988, agreed to help Robertson by writing a memo outlining how to structure the group. By the time Reed finished, he had decided that building a Christian-based political movement appealed to him far more than teaching history at a small, remote college.

In the beginning there was Reed, his wife Jo Anne, a few other staffers, and some seed money from Robertson. The nucleus in the states grew from the remnants of the 1988 Robertson network. Some of them had reconstituted local campaign teams into new organizations, but many others felt scarred and exhausted from their first taste of hardball politics. Reed coaxed them back to action, building a network of regional organizers. Early successes came in places like Iowa, where Ione Dilley had kept the Robertson team alive under the name "The Advance Group," and in South Carolina, where Roberta Combs built a powerhouse that quickly demanded the respect of Republican politicians in the state. But there were false starts as well. In Texas, the Coalition disbanded temporarily until Robertson's 1988 finance director, Dick Weinhold, seized the reins — and eventually the Coalition took control of the state party apparatus. By the end of 1990, the Coalition had 125 chapters and fifty-seven thousand members nationally. By 1995, the Texas chapter alone claimed sixty thousand members.

An emphasis on organization was one of Reed's two great contributions to his movement. The other was his ability to nudge the Christian conservative movement toward the mainstream without precipitating a break with his most conservative followers. After Bush's defeat, the Coalition, like other organizations of the pro-family movement, appeared radioactive to many Republicans. Marshall Wittmann, who went to work in the Coalition's Washington office in 1993, recalled the reaction of his colleagues in the Health and Human Services Department, all scrambling to find work after Clinton's victory, when he told them he had landed a job. "It was just sort of, 'Huh?'" he said. "They would pause and you sort of knew what was going through their minds." From the Coalition offices, Wittmann would send off letters to congressional offices and never receive a reply, and the temperature in the room seemed to drop whenever he joined meetings on Capitol Hill.

Sensing efforts within the party to marginalize the conservative Christian movement, Reed responded with an article in the summer 1993 issue of the Heritage Foundation's *Policy Review* entitled "Casting a Wider Net." The article marked a turning point for the movement. "The pro-family movement's political rhetoric has often been policy-thin and value-laden, leaving many voters tuned out," Reed wrote. He argued that religious conservatives would never reach their full potential by focusing principally on narrow issues like abortion or homosexuality, nor could they succeed by building their movement around a few dominant personalities (an ironic comment given Robertson's role in the Coalition). To gain influence and win elections, he counseled, "The pro-family movement must speak to the concerns of average voters in the areas of taxes, crime, government waste, health care and financial security." (Reed suffered a brief setback when, during a television interview at the opening of their annual convention that fall, Robertson publicly disagreed with Reed's pro-NAFTA stance, making clear that he, not his young assistant, would have the final say determining into which issues the Coalition would delve.) Reed also recommended that the movement decouple itself from the fortunes of individual candidates and no longer take its direction from even a sympathetic occupant of the White House. Religious conservatives, he said, should chart an independent course, build a grassroots following, focus on pro-family issues, and let the politicians come to them.

In writing the article, Reed had two goals: to exorcise the ghosts of the Houston convention and to demonstrate that the religious conservative movement was more broadly based than most people believed — including many of its leaders. "We commissioned a survey of our membership and we were stunned at what we got back," Reed said. "They looked like America. They weren't weird. They didn't have an agenda that was all that bizarre. It surprised me." To the public at large, Reed argued that religious conservatives cared as much about lower taxes and economic issues as anyone else; to his own constituency he argued that, with only 12 percent of the population in 1992 listing abortion as a key issue in their choice for President, the movement needed to expand its appeal.

Reed's prophecy about a "Field of Dreams" movement proved correct. After the 1994 elections, Republican presidential candidates, particularly Bob Dole, tacked right in hopes of winning the support of religious conservatives, and the candidates competed for bragging rights over who had snared the best of the Coalition's organizers. Congressional leaders eagerly sought the Coalition's blessing as they waded through the votes on their Contract With America, while the Coalition poured $1 million into a campaign to rally support for its contents. Dole negotiated directly with Reed over the outlines of a compromise on welfare reform, hoping that would bridge differences between Senate moderates and conservatives, while House leaders, seeking to head off a revolt within their ranks over their own welfare bill, sought to convince the Coalition to announce in advance that it would use the vote setting the terms for the floor debate as an item in its congressional scorecard, which is distributed by the millions. (The Coalition demurred, scoring instead the vote on final passage.) And Marshall Wittmann not only received responses to his letters, he found congressional staffers carefully analyzing their every word.

As the Coalition's profile rose, Reed sought to further soften its public image — and to smooth over lingering controversies created by Robertson. Robertson posed a special problem for the religious conservative movement. As the leader of a highly popular cable television program, *700 Club*, Robertson developed a cadre of loyalists throughout the country who were central to the Coalition's growth. But as a religious and political polemicist, he had developed an equally ardent corps of detractors, who believed that his political views and his interpretations of history represented extreme and bizarre theories.

One well-publicized fund-raising letter that went out over Robertson's signature said that the feminist agenda encouraged women "to leave their husbands, kill their children, practice witchcraft, destroy capitalism and become lesbians." In a bestselling book, *The New World Order*, published in 1991, Robertson espoused his theory that a "tightly knit cabal" of European and Wall Street bankers and other conspiracists had sought for generations "a new order for the human race under the domination of Lucifer and his followers." He also suggested that the United States had been forced into deep debt (which benefited these bankers) to fund a military establishment out of the misguided notion that the Soviet Union was a powerful adversary, when in fact it was barely a Third World nation economically. Robertson's critics charged that the book and other writings also reflected anti-Semitic leanings, in particular because of Robertson's attacks on liberal Jews, who he said were undermining Christianity in America. Robertson flatly rejected the charge of anti-Semitism in a television interview in April 1995, claiming he has been a strong supporter of Israel throughout his life. "What's happening," he said, "is these folks are using religion to undermine the political stand I take, which happens to be conservative."

Robertson remains a divisive figure, and some Republicans privately suggest that the Christian Coalition would find even greater acceptance among the electorate if it were to loosen its ties to Robertson, a course of action Reed rejects. "I think that the Christian Coalition as an organization is big enough [that] it transcends any single personality," Reed said. "That includes Pat, that includes me. But I do think that Pat was, and remains, critical. . . . He's absolutely invaluable."

Sensitive to charges of anti-Semitism against Robertson and criticism that some Christian conservatives were racially bigoted, Reed, however, has attempted to portray his movement as sympathetic to other religions and open-minded on issues of race and tolerance. He reached out to Jewish leaders in the spring of 1995, acknowledging in a speech that religious conservatives had been "insensitive" to the horrors of the Holocaust and that some in the Christian community bore some responsibility for what had happened. On questions of race, Reed tried to distance the religious conservative movement from other aspects of its past, in particular the role that some white southern ministers had played in the perpetuation of segregation. In his book, Reed chastised religious conservatives for "a legacy of racism" that they would have to overcome now that they sought to reenter the public arena. Reed's deft and nonthreatening communication skills brought religious conservatives a measure of credibility they had never enjoyed during the Falwell era, and he was generally careful not to overplay his hand. When he unveiled the Contract With the American Family, he emphasized that the Coalition was proposing "ten suggestions, not Ten Commandments," and that the document represented a political, not a theological, agenda. "We make no threats, we issue no ultimatums, and we make no demands on either party," he said. "There's a responsibility that comes with being a player," said Dick Weinhold, the chairman of the Texas chapter of the Coalition, noting that religious conservatives would need to tone down some of their rhetoric of the past. "I hate to use the word myself, but I guess the demagoguery that may have been there in the past needs to change."

But Reed walked a tightrope as he gently attempted to nudge his movement toward the political mainstream. It was in apparent response to those internal pressures that Reed, in a February 1995 speech to a conservative gathering in Washington, warned Republicans that a 1996 ticket that did not include pro-life nominees for President and vice president risked a revolt among religious conservatives and anti-abortion activists. Massachusetts Governor William Weld, a leading pro-choice Republican, dismissed the speech as the product of a naive and immature leader. "It was very ill-advised and very counterproductive," Weld said. "That's drawing a line in the sand with the tide coming in."

Reed's balancing act illustrated the Coalition's position as the leading, but hardly the only, voice in the burgeoning pro-family movement. Swimming alongside the Coalition were such groups as the Reverend James Dobson's Focus on the Family, which had an enormous following through Dobson's daily radio program; the Washington-based Family Research Council, a Dobson offshoot; the Traditional Values Coalition, headed by the Reverend Lou Sheldon, who has spoken out vociferously on the issue of homosexuality; Phyllis Schlafly's Eagle Forum; the American Family Association; the Christian Action Network; Concerned Women for America; and the National Right To Life Committee, the most effective pro-life organization in the country. While generally working in tandem on major issues, other elements of the pro-family movement sometimes chafed at Reed's prominence and rebelled against his strategic guidance to broaden the movement's agenda. Shortly after publication of *Casting a Wider Net*, Martin Mawyer, president of the Christian Action Network, wrote an op-ed article in the *Washington Post* taking Reed to task for seeming to abandon the abortion issue. "Our goal is not to increase our political power by deceiving the American public through talk of taxes, crime, health care or NAFTA," he wrote. "Our real concerns are abortion, school prayer and gay rights, and our mission is to present our case honestly to the American people and give them a chance to decide."

Reed's artful balancing act has done more to help the Republican Party than if he had remained within its camp as a GOP organizer. But just as there are strains between moderates and conservatives within the GOP, so too are there parallel differences among conservatives in the pro-family movement. Republican leaders expressed gratitude that the Coalition had crafted its Contract With the American Family carefully, with the most controversial element a religious liberties amendment that sought to restore voluntary prayer in schools and other aspects of public life. To pragmatic conservatives in the party, the contract reflected the growing maturity of the movement. "[Reed] knows what really matters out there with [religious conservatives] is not just values but the economic aspects," said Ed Gillespie, press secretary to Majority Leader Dick Armey. Added Marshall Wittmann, who had moved to the Heritage Foundation as a senior fellow: "The movement has been very fortunate to have Ralph Reed. . . . He has a very profound understanding of how a movement becomes mainstream within the framework of American politics and [becomes] long lasting." But to Pat Buchanan, Reed had taken a dive with the Contract, and other pro-family leaders warned that in his quest for respectability, Reed risked capitulating to the voices of moderation. "Ralph is going to have to be really careful to not end up a leader without a following," said Gary Bauer of the Family Research Council. "I don't think it is possible to come up with a substitute for the abortion issue."

THE ABORTION STRUGGLE

Of all the issues that threaten to divide the GOP coalition, none is more delicate or divisive than abortion, and yet no simple solution exists for the conundrum it presents as a political issue. Public opinion is now generally hardened into three camps: those unalterably opposed to abortion; those who favor it under almost any circumstances; and the broad, conflicted middle of the electorate who resist outlawing it, but who are uneasy about the number performed and unwilling to plant their feet firmly on either side of the great divide. The issue drives only a fraction of voters at either end of the spectrum, but any perceived change in the status quo can dramatically affect the balance between the two and the intensity it can inject into political campaigns. *Roe v. Wade*, the 1973 Supreme Court decision that legalized abortion, spawned the anti-abortion movement and ultimately drove many Democrats out of their party. The *Webster* decision in 1989 raised fears that the Supreme Court might overturn *Roe* and drove moderates, at least temporarily, away from the Republican Party. The reemergence of religious conservatives as a powerful voice within the GOP coalition threatens to upset the political equilibrium once again.

In a conversation one afternoon during his first year as chairman of the Republican National Committee, Lee Atwater agonized over the danger the abortion issue presented to his party. It was November 1989, a few weeks after Republicans had lost governor's races in Virginia and New Jersey; in both races the Democrats had emphasized support for preserving abortion rights, a powerful message in the aftermath of the *Webster* decision. Shaken by the losses, Atwater believed the party needed to find a new equilibrium on the issue. He was looking for a way to prod the party toward a new position more accommodating to suburban voters without totally offending the pro-life forces who remained essential to the party's growth. His reflections that afternoon offered a rough-draft look at what he later described as "The Big Tent," a vision of the GOP that would embrace both pro-choice and pro-life conservatives otherwise committed to limited government.

Atwater's Big Tent notion marked the first of a series of ongoing efforts by Republican leaders to caution anti-abortion activists against intolerance while simultaneously reassuring nervous moderates that the party required no litmus tests for membership — efforts that have met with only partial success among members of either group. Anti-abortion forces regard such talk as backsliding; moderates look at the anti-abortion language in the party platform and see the inclusionary rhetoric from the leadership as hollow. The most sharply worded warning came from Rich Bond in his outgoing speech as RNC chairman in January 1993. "Our job is to win elections, not to cling to intolerances that zealots call principles, not to be led or dominated by a vocal few who like to look good losing," he told the national committee. "That is a sure path to disaster." Bond urged the party to let the states deal with abortion "and return our national platform discussions to issues we as a party win and lose elections on — peace, prosperity, and national defense." Bond drew a standing ovation for that proposal, but Phyllis Schlafly, reflecting the position of the pro-life forces, snapped, "It's no wonder Bush lost with that kind of national chairman."

With the current Supreme Court unlikely to reverse *Roe*, efforts to restrict the availability of abortions must come through the legislative arena, and with the addition of roughly forty new pro-life votes in the House from the 1994 elections, Republicans returned to the debate with renewed energy. Emboldened by their new, slim majority in the House, anti-abortion forces sought to restrict federal funding of abortions for poor women; bar funding for abortions in the health care programs of federal workers; ban abortions in federal prisons and on military bases overseas; bar so-called partial-birth abortions performed at later stages of pregnancy; and ban family planning funds used in part for abortion counseling. None represented a frontal attack on the legality of abortion, but together they were enough to reinflame the debate, unsettle GOP moderates, and prompt abortion rights forces to claim that *Roe* was now in clear danger of extinction — which of course it was not.

Not surprisingly the House took the most extreme position, voting on several occasions to deny federal funding for abortion except when the mother's life was in danger and being the first to vote to outlaw a late-second- or early-third-term procedure called by opponents a "partial-birth abortion." In some cases, congressional actions restored policies that existed prior to the Clinton administration; in some cases they broke new ground. But the votes nonetheless shattered the unity Republicans had displayed on most other issues, as a bloc of forty to fifty-seven moderates in the House consistently defected from the majority to oppose the changes. Democrats and even some of the moderates voiced fears that the changes represented only the first stage of a bolder agenda to roll back abortion rights in America. "They are just giving Democrats food for political fodder," said Representative Steve Gunderson of Wisconsin.

Actions in Congress represent one front in the abortion war. The Republican platform represents the second large arena for conflict. In 1992, party moderates, partly out of deference to Bush, did not seek to remove the platform's starkly anti-abortion language on the floor of the Houston convention. But many of them have vowed not to duck again. Senator Arlen Specter of Pennsylvania based his brief presidential campaign largely on support for legalized abortion, and governors Wilson, Whitman, and Weld have expressed their intention to seek more moderate platform language in 1996. "I don't think it should say anything about abortion," Wilson said. The result, however, already may be decided. The resurgence of religious conservatives makes it unlikely that moderates can do much to change the language significantly, unless the pro-life forces capitulate.

Seeking to head off an embarrassing sideshow in San Diego, a number of Republicans sought to develop compromise language on a platform plank in 1994. George Weigel, president of the Ethics and Public Policy Center, and strategist William Kristol circulated a draft plank that, while strongly reaffirming the party's pro-life position, eliminated the call for a Human Life Amendment and urged Republicans to use the bully pulpit "to build a broad public consensus in favor of legal protection for the unborn." But the language neither mollified the moderates nor satisfied the conservatives and died on the vine, leaving the party farther from a compromise than before the effort began.

The debate erupted anew in the fall of 1995, this time largely within the pro-life community and sparked, ironically, by Colin Powell's emergence as a possible presidential candidate. The debate among pro-life conservatives hinged on the question of whether opponents of abortion could support someone like Powell, who is pro-choice but says he opposes abortion. The real point of dispute, however, centered around the question of what policies conservatives could pursue that would actually reduce the number of abortions performed each year. Many pro-life conservatives argued that it would be heresy to abandon the Human Life Amendment, but William Bennett and others forcefully asserted that, given the current climate of opinion, pursuit of the amendment represented an out-of-date strategy and that the current pro-life plank in the Republican platform had done nothing to reduce abortions. "Holding on to the chimera of a constitutional amendment to outlaw abortion (the means) has done nothing to reduce the number of abortions (which ought to be the end)," Bennett wrote in a pugnacious October 1995 letter to Paul Weyrich, who opposed jettisoning the plank. Someone like Powell, Bennett argued, could do more to reduce abortions by using the bully pulpit to promote abstinence, adoption, and individual responsibility than could many pro-life candidates who pay lip service to the issue but have neither the standing nor the desire to tackle it in office.

The elections of 1994 only served to highlight the gap between pro-life and pro-choice forces. Some pro-family leaders, buoyed by the turnout of their forces, stiffened in their opposition to change the platform language. Dobson and others sent Haley Barbour a threatening letter in the spring of 1995 warning him not to engage in efforts to dilute the platform. Buchanan, earlier, had encouraged anti-abortion activists to consider mounting a third-party movement if the Republicans shifted positions. But moderates like Weld are just as adamant about the need to modify the platform. "It's not a position that can persist over time as the position of the party unless you want to fracture the party and lose the election," he said. The pro-life forces command battalions of activists who are likely to control the platform process; the moderates, because of the prominence of their leaders, command more attention from a sympathetic media to reach a larger audience of independent voters outside the intraparty councils. Pragmatic pro-life forces represent a wild card. That is a recipe for trouble, no matter what the outcome of the debate, unless all sides approach the issue in a spirit of civility that has rarely been brought to the subject of abortion in the past.

Having built their new majority on the backs of social conservatives, Republican leaders risk at least as much by significantly altering the platform, and thus alienating their most energized and loyal constituents, as they might gain from a major bow to the moderates. The pro-life forces firmly in command of the party machinery understandably expect no backsliding in the GOP's commitment to its anti-abortion plank and will no doubt keep pushing forward on their agenda. But they risk jeopardizing the GOP's majority aspirations by overreaching in their attempts to restrict or outlaw abortions — and there is only so much party leaders can do to restrain them. On the most personal and explosive of all issues in the political arena, the Republicans find themselves trapped in a cage of their own creation.

THE PEROT CONSTITUENCY

If the Christian conservatives embody the emergence of religious believers as active participants in the political process, the Perot movement aptly symbolizes a growing body of nonbelievers in the system itself. No group better defines the disaffection with politics than those men and women who supported the idiosyncratic Texas billionaire in 1992 and who firmly continue to stand apart from the two parties today. With a fervor that faintly shimmers, they distrust politicians, parties, Washington lobbyists, the federal government, and especially Congress. Twice in two elections, these voters have dashed the hopes of the party in power by registering their dissatisfaction with the political status quo. Republicans now must convert that fickle record into more permanent allegiance to the GOP in order to create a stable, governing majority.

Sifting through the layers of the Perot movement requires the skills of a geologist. There is Perot himself, there are the activists in United We Stand America, there are the original Perot supporters, there are the newer Perot followers, there are the Perot dissidents, and then there is the large slab of independent-minded voters who fall somewhere between the Perot movement and the two political parties. The Perot constituency encompasses suburban reformers, economic conservatives, social moderates and libertarians, angry antigovernment rebels, and embattled workers struggling to stay afloat in the modern economy. Together this disparate group of voters has congealed into a semi-permanent bloc of outsiders unwilling to commit themselves to either party until they see genuine change both in Washington and in their own lives. What binds them is a loss of confidence that either party has the will to change the system or the answers to the country's problems — unless prodded constantly from afar. To these voters, America is governed not by two competing parties, but by a monolithic political elite, what Pat Muth, the United We Stand director in Florida, called "Depublicans."

Like religious conservatives, Perot supporters have been publicly praised and privately maligned by the inside-the-Beltway elites, who often have difficulty separating the motives and antics of the billionaire businessman from the aspirations of those described as his followers. But from the brigade of volunteers who mounted petition drives in suburban malls in 1992 to the organizers who painstakingly built United We Stand in the states in 1992–94 to the serious-minded activists who came to Dallas in the summer of 1995, the heart of the Perot constituency, at its best, always epitomized a political uprising on the part of people with no more of a special interest than the future of the country. As Irene Bragg told us in May 1992, as she helped organize the California Perot movement, "You're looking at a woman who has never worn a button, never put on a T-shirt and never put a bumper sticker on my car." Another Perot volunteer described the rebellion as "the Silent Majority clearing its throat." Explaining their own involvement in the movement, many Perot volunteers describe something akin to a religious conversion. David Goldman, a native New Yorker who later became a Perot coordinator in Florida, supported Paul Tsongas early in 1992 until Perot captured his loyalties. "Mr. Perot did awaken something inside of me about what it means to be an American and trying to give something back to the country," Goldman said.

Some politicians and political analysts mistakenly focus too much of their time and attention on Perot, assuming — or perhaps hoping — that his steep plunge in popularity after the NAFTA debate signaled the unraveling of his movement as a viable political force. But Perot's personal standing has always been subjected to significant swings. Pre-NAFTA, two-thirds of the America people said they had a favorable impression of Perot; post-NAFTA, a majority disapproved of him. But all the personal attention focused on Perot as a plausible or implausible presidential candidate obscured the underlying unrest that had conveniently attached itself to him. To most of these voters, Perot did not have all the answers, but at least he was asking the right questions. If nearly two-thirds of the public said they could never vote for him for President, almost one-third continued to say they could. If roughly a majority believed he did not have the temperament to be a good President, two-thirds or more believed he had good ideas about government, and a majority believed he had focused the political discussion on relevant issues that otherwise the two parties would have avoided. Americans may not have wanted to see him in the Oval Office; but they liked having him vex whoever was.

Others have seized on the chaos and discontent within Perot's own house as evidence that he had attracted a constituency of activists consumed by fringe agendas and personal ambitions. Perot's most significant organizational mistake was his decision, in building United We Stand nationally, to insist that the state organizations operate as freestanding entities, complete with their own charters, bylaws, fundraising requirements, and elected leadership, while still under control of the Dallas headquarters. The strains of building these chapters in 1993 and 1994 not only brought claims from a dissident corps of tyrannical rule by Perot and his Dallas aides, but also debilitated the organization with petty power struggles and political disputes. In creating their own network of organizations, Perot activists sometimes lost sight of their principal mission, which was to reform the system. "If you're worried about your by-laws and your nominating process and all these internal things, you're not out there getting campaign finance reform passed [or] getting the balanced budget passed," said Russell Verney, a former Democratic Party official in New Hampshire who became executive director of United We Stand.

Political pollsters, journalists, and academics have subjected the Perot movement to an extraordinary amount of scrutiny and analysis, hoping to understand what makes his supporters tick and whether they can be assimilated back into the two-party structure. Even after Perot's many problems, voters attracted to his ideas, loosely defined at least, encompassed somewhere between a fifth and a quarter of the entire electorate. Geographically, Perot has always been strongest in the West, weakest by far in the South. But his best showing in 1992 came in Maine, where he won 30.4 percent of the vote and nosed out Bush for second place, and he had strong pockets of support in states like Minnesota, the Dakotas, Kansas, Nebraska, and Texas. Demographically, Perot always has attracted more men than women, and more younger people than older people, although the bulk of the activist volunteers are retirees. What started out as a movement of middle- and upper-middle-class suburbanites has gradually evolved into a constituency that now contains a strong component of downscale voters without college degrees. Ideologically, Perot drew roughly equal support from liberals, conservatives, and moderates, but after 1992, like the rest of the country, his following began to tilt toward the right.

Republicans believe that eventually they will be able to woo a significant portion of the Perot movement into their coalition, and they have a much greater opportunity to do so than do the Democrats. In his survey of the Perot voters in 1993, Stan Greenberg found that a large majority had voted for Reagan or Bush in the 1980s, and the strong support Perot followers gave to Republican House candidates in 1994 only reinforced that profile. Both parties emerged from the 1992 election vowing to win over the Perot vote, but Republicans have made a more consistent and determined effort. Early in his tenure, Haley Barbour ordered state Republican leaders to make contact with the Perot organizations in their states and to make clear to these activists the GOP was interested in their ideas and suggestions. At the RNC meeting in Chicago in June 1993, Barbour even invited Perot's Illinois leadership to join the Republicans at a closed-door strategy session, all as a way of demonstrating good faith. In 1994, House Republican leaders constructed their Contract With America with a meticulous eye to the interests and passions of the Perot movement.

To an extraordinary degree, Republicans have allowed the sensibilities of the Perot movement to shape their own agenda, pushing the party farther and faster down certain policy tracks than it otherwise might have been willing to go. Term limits occupied one of the central planks in the Contract because Perot voters, not Republican incumbents, favored them, and Republican leaders enshrined the Balanced Budget Amendment at the top of the Contract to lure the Perotistas. The GOP's quest for a balanced budget by 2002 was fueled in large part by Perot's success in raising the issue in 1992.

It is unclear, however, whether Republicans can ever do enough to satisfy either Perot or his supporters. In part that reflects the contrary nature of the Perot movement and the mercurial personality of its leader. In Dallas in August 1995, many Perot activists appeared more annoyed by the failure of the Republican Congress to pass either the Balanced Budget Amendment or term limits than they were pleased by the actual steps the Republicans had taken to balance the budget. "We're not happy with the Republican Contract," David Goldman told us. And even those who applauded the GOP's courage in tackling the budget expressed disapproval over some of the specifics, particularly the inclusion of tax cuts while the country was still piling up mountains of debt. "This country's bankrupt," Russ Verney said. "You can't give away money you don't have. They're borrowing money to give tax breaks." Perot voters have shown consistent antipathy to the compromises or half steps so common to the political maneuvering of Washington, and Perot himself has demonstrated an uncanny ability never to be fully satisfied with either party's actions for very long.

But the broader hazard facing the Republicans in wooing the Perot movement is the disparate, fluid nature of the constituency, and of the Perot agenda. Republicans clearly have their best opportunity to make progress with the economic conservatives in the movement, those for whom the national debt and the recurring budget deficits stand as the greatest symbols of political irresponsibility. But in two other areas, political reform and the revitalization of the American economy, Republicans appear no better situated than Clinton and the Democrats to deliver progress sufficient enough to quell the forces of dissatisfaction.

Nothing stirs more resentment among Perot supporters than their perception that Washington remains in the grip of a political elite class, where special interest money lubricates a legislative machine hostile to the interests of ordinary citizens and finances a campaign system that has become increasingly negative over the past two decades. No news organization or political pollster who conducted a focus group with independent voters the past few years found anything but contempt for the way Washington works. Asked to state their impressions of the words "political party," a group of Perot supporters assembled by the *Washington Post* in 1992 fired back with a barrage of political buckshot that was stunning in its cynicism: "Corruption!" shouted one. "Liars," said another. Others in the group eagerly joined in the condemnation: "self-serving," "Old Boy networks," "special interests," "immorality." Democratic pollsters Peter D. Hart and Geoffrey D. Garin reported back on a series of focus groups they held in the summer of 1994. One Akron, Ohio, accountant expressed his frustration this way: "Everybody is out for themselves. They're not looking out for the good of everybody else. They just want to know, 'What am I going to get out of this? Am I going to be reelected?'"

But instead of moving to dampen this voter cynicism, Republicans went the other way once they took power, gobbling up money from PACs and corporate interests at a record pace in 1995. Walter Mischer, a legendary behind-the-scenes power broker in Texas politics in the 1970s and 1980s, always joked that in the world of political giving, "It's never too late to buy a seat on the train," and the Republicans preyed on the insecurities of a business community suddenly worried about its contacts with the new GOP majority. Bill Paxon, chairman of the National Republican Congressional Committee, issued a report on the four hundred largest PACs, showing how much each had given to Democrats and to Republicans in 1993–94 and identifying them under one of three headings: "friendly," "unfriendly," and "neutral." Common Cause reported that in the first two months of 1995, Republicans had raised $7.2 million in soft money, more than their entire haul in 1993. Michael Podhorzer, director of the liberal Citizen Action organization, said in a report analyzing contributions in 1994, "Contrary to their rhetoric, the House Republicans are conducting business as usual, except they are even cozier with the powerful special interests."

Republicans brazenly upbraided corporate contributors for not moving quickly enough to demonstrate their allegiance with the new majority. Freshman Representative Mark Souder refused to meet with the American Farm Bureau Federation until it hired more sympathetic lobbyists, and Republicans began to question the credentials and political leanings of much of the lobbying community in Washington. "They need to get the message in the PAC community that they need to hire staff people that represent the members' wishes and want to keep us in power," Souder told the *New York Times*. House Whip Tom DeLay sent a tart letter to PACs that had contributed to the Democratic opponent of one of the freshman Republicans, Randy Tate of Washington, in an effort to pry money out of them for Tate's next campaign. Warning the PACs that it was time "to work toward a positive future relationship" with the GOP, DeLay added, "I want you to know that your immediate support for Randy Tate is personally important to me and the House Republican leadership. I know I can speak for the majority of our conference in saying that we are anxious to have [the PAC] support the incumbent and not be idle until next year." Freshman Republicans, anticipating difficult reelection campaigns in 1996, interrupted their attacks on Washington business as usual long enough to muscle the interests that finance it: In the first half of 1995, nine freshman Republicans had raised at least $100,000 each from political action committees, prompting Ann McBride, president of Common Cause, to charge that the newcomers were "reaping huge sums of special-interest money from the very system they were elected to change."

Like Democrats in 1993–94, Republicans appeared to believe that by making progress on other aspects of the Perot movement's agenda, their turtlelike pace on campaign finance reform would go unnoticed. From a strategic standpoint, the Republican fund-raising drive made sense: They did not want to risk their fragile new majority in 1996 by fielding underfunded candidates. But they were uncharacteristically defensive about their failure to move more rapidly to reform the system and came under fire not only from the Perot movement but from two freshman Republicans in the House, Linda Smith of Washington and Sam Brownback of Kansas, who upbraided the leadership for failing to move quickly on their campaign finance legislation and became heroes to the Perotistas. In June 1995, Clinton and Gingrich shared a stage in New Hampshire, where they exchanged a handshake and pledges to appoint a commission to recommend changes in how campaigns are financed. Two months later, with no progress from the Republicans, Gingrich told the Perot activists the issue was "too serious [for] narrow, cheap political games," and instead of moving to appoint the commission, proposed to write an academic treatise on the even more amorphous topic of money's corrupting influence on society as a whole. This dodge did little to satisfy the Perotistas. Perot threw down the gauntlet by demanding that Congress pass a long list of strict reforms, and two weeks later, Verney issued an electronic newsletter to United We Stand members in which he said that "99 percent" of those who participated in the Dallas conference workshops "believe money and special interests have too much power in Washington — and they want that to change within one year." Later in the fall, Gingrich called for a commission and extended hearings to study the role of money in politics in what he called the beginning of a concerted Republican effort to reform the campaign finance system. Others, however, saw it as yet another attempt at delay, and Representative Linda Smith again challenged him publicly, warning that the public — and many of the members of the Class of 1994 — would resist the leadership's strategy and attempt to pass legislation over its opposition if this were merely another ploy to sustain the curent system.

The agenda of the Perot movement and the self-interest of the Republican Party may diverge sharply over the issue of money in politics, at least in the short run. But Republicans still have the power to take the steps necessary to begin reforming the system, if they choose. Perot's populist economic agenda, and the constituency behind it, represents a more daunting challenge to the GOP. Perot's opposition to NAFTA and the GATT agreements appeared to put him out of step with many of the suburban reformers who first formed his activist core. But the strength of his appeal among workers whose wages have declined steadily over the past two decades and who feel most threatened by changes in the global economy has been consistently understated. The Times Mirror Center for The People & The Press report on the electorate in the fall of 1994 concluded that these economically struggling "New Economy Independents," as they dubbed them, represented one of Perot's strongest groups of supporters and were among the most vigorous advocates of a third party. "Not anchored in either major party, these are the most important swing voters in the new electorate," the Times Mirror report said. "While most of them have jobs, their middle-class status seems precarious in the post-industrial economy and the future uncertain at best."

In fact, it was among those economically anxious Perot supporters that Republicans made their highest gains in 1994. Male Perot voters with high school educations cast 53 percent of their votes for Democratic House candidates in 1992, but only 28 percent in 1994. Male Perot voters with some time in college went from 49 percent Democratic support in 1992 to just 16 percent in 1994. Patterns among female Perot voters were similar: Among women with high school diplomas, support for Democratic candidates fell from 55 percent in 1992 to 25 percent in 1994; among women with some college, the percentage dropped from 49 percent to 38 percent.

Clearly the Republican antigovernment message resonated with these voters. But over time, Republican success at consolidating their support may turn less on bashing big government than on delivering economic security and prosperity. No group suffered greater wage loss than the people who supported Ross Perot in 1992, according to a study conducted by Ruy Teixeira of the Economic Policy Institute. His analysis concluded that while both Clinton and Perot supporters suffered wage declines between 1973 and 1992, the Perot voters fell behind the farthest. These voters are open to Republican efforts to blame their economic distress on affirmative action, immigration, and taxes. But these same voters share Patrick Buchanan's suspicious view of corporate America and foreign competition, not the free-market vision of Newt Gingrich or Bob Dole and the Republican establishment. To a degree that is underappreciated, many of Perot's most loyal followers rank job creation at the top of their list of issues. "In the inner cities, where you don't have jobs, there's a lot of turmoil and unrest," said Betty Montgomery, the South Carolina state director of United We Stand. "You've got to have entry-level jobs and those are the ones that are going out of the country." Raised a Democrat, Montgomery reflects the ambivalence many in the Perot movement now feel toward both parties. "There are a lot of people out there who are upset," she said. "People are not happy with the Democrats, but they're not sure they want to be Republicans." In future elections, Republicans may be able to win the votes of some of these disaffected Americans, but securing their lasting allegiance will be a far more difficult task.

Perot's decision in September 1995, after nearly a year of coy hints, to attempt to launch a third party further complicates the Republicans' hope of consolidating the Perot movement — as Republican leaders Gingrich and Barbour recognize. They see a Perot-driven third party for what it is: a clear threat to their need to win the White House to further their revolution. Up until the moment of his announcement, Perot appeared to be resisting calls within his own movement to create a new political party. On the eve of Perot's issues conference in Dallas in August 1995, Russ Verney of United We Stand offered clear reasons why the idea made no sense, citing everything from legal roadblocks to the potential for fringe candidates to hijack the party's nomination for congressional or state office to the huge financial obstacles any new party faced. A new party faced a Hobson's choice, he said: either raise money in the old-fashioned way that Perot long has denounced or face the reality of running permanently underfunded candidates for office. "If you don't have the money to be competitive, you've just gone through all that work to be the reiteration of the Libertarian Party," Verney said. "You exist nationally but you're irrelevant." But Verney cited an even more compelling reason not to plunge ahead with a new party. "The first time out, are we going to win one seat, two seats in the Senate? Ten seats, twenty, thirty seats in the House?" he asked. "Certainly not a majority of them, certainly not enough to force a major coalition. So you're talking time. And over a decade you would build up to the point where you held probably close to a third of the seats in both the House and the Senate if you remain a three-party structure. All this time that you're going towards that could be devoted to solving the problems today. We can solve a lot of these problems [long before that]. We can make great strides to solve them if we devote our energies to it."

Once he announced his intentions, Perot tried to finesse that problem by stating that, if his new party successfully secured ballot status across the country, it would run a candidate only for President in 1996, and would pick between Republican and Democratic candidates in other races. That approach could help the GOP in congressional races, but hurt it in the presidential race. If Perot's new party were to become a more permanent part of the political system, it could prove to be a far more destabilizing influence for both parties. Initially at least, any new party will attempt to convince a large swath of the electorate that both parties are captives of their extremes and that the polarization of politics only produces negative debates and legislative stalemates — the images that have typified Washington for a decade. Against such a head wind, the Republicans may find themselves repeatedly frustrated.

NEWT Gingrich often points to Franklin Roosevelt for inspiration when he describes the challenge Republicans now face in trying to hold together the fractious coalition assembled under Lee Atwater's Big Tent. Roosevelt, he points out, somehow managed to persuade southern segregationists and northern blacks that he and the Democrats were better for each of them than were Herbert Hoover and the Republicans. Surely, the argument goes, Republicans can do the same with their coalition of religious conservatives, economic conservatives, suburban moderates, western libertarians, economic nationalists, free-traders, and of course the less ideologically defined amalgam of Perot voters.

In some respects, the agendas of Perot voters and religious conservatives overlap, at least in their antigovernment sensibilities. Where they don't overlap, the Republicans may succeed in the short run by offering enough small bites to all sides, if only because these morsels will prove more satisfying than anything the Democrats are offering. But over time, the strains within the GOP coalition will become more difficult to manage, as all large institutions have discovered. The party needs both economic and social conservatives, but the balance of power has shifted. Long relegated to the back of the GOP bus, religious conservatives now demand to sit in the front rows with their more secular brethren. Ralph Reed scoffs at the notion that the Coalition has a secret agenda, but the growing influence of religious conservatives within the party nonetheless makes Republican moderates uneasy. As Weld said once, Republicans should "dance with the gal that brung" them, which is to say the issues of less government and lower taxes, not abortion or school prayer.

Republicans revived themselves after Bush's defeat by uniting economic and social conservatives, and just plain disaffected Americans under that banner of less government, and their success derived in part from their ability to enlarge the social issue agenda from abortion, prayer, and homosexuality to alternative issues like crime, illegitimacy, and the impact of Hollywood and popular culture on the sensibilities of children. But while morality is a powerful issue in American politics, religion continues to send ripples of uneasiness. The thin line between morality and religiosity may in truth represent a chasm that will hinder the party's efforts to build a governing coalition. At the same time, some GOP leaders have attempted to overinterpret the meaning of 1994 and to suggest that the party — and the country — are even more conservative and ideologically doctrinaire than reality permits. Unless Republican leaders maintain control of the extreme instincts and factions within their own party and find the formula for maintaining the conservative energy of 1994 while enlarging their appeal, the GOP's Big Tent may soon more resemble a three-ring circus.

Eventually Roosevelt's Democrats were forced to choose between the aspirations of African-Americans and the status quo of discrimination and segregation, and when they did what they had to do, their coalition began to dissolve. The Republicans do not face quite so difficult or stark a choice, but they do operate in a time of political instability where options do not always reduce to an either-or choice between the two parties. The more religious conservatives seek to dominate the inner workings of the Republican Party, the more conservative ideologues narrowly define the party's boundaries, the greater the danger that the broad middle of the electorate will see the GOP as outside the political mainstream, and seek a home if not permanently within the Democratic camp, at least temporarily outside the Big Tent.

These strains within the Republican coalition cannot be simply resolved or compromised away, particularly if Bill Clinton, the one common element in their dissatisfaction with politics today, no longer holds the White House. For much of 1995, Republican leaders maintained a remarkable degree of unity, but by the fall of the year, the shrinking corps of moderates once again began to assert themselves, and the emergence of Powell as a voice for moderation, either within the party or outside it, added weight to that part of the GOP spectrum that had been largely missing in the euphoria of the conservative takeover. "The Contract With America was certainly anchored on the right side of the Republican political spectrum," Powell told David Frost. "But there are a lot of other Republicans out there . . . who are a little bit more to the left of that point on the spectrum, and I think they will be heard in due course." Over time, clashes between conservatives and moderates threaten to enlarge into the kind of factional dispute that could either stifle progress on the GOP's conservative agenda or cripple their efforts to expand their coalition beyond their activist corps. In their own ways, religious conservatives and Perot voters resemble independent fiefdoms in American politics. One seeks to maneuver largely within the framework of the Republican Party, the other as an antidote to politics as usual. Both movements represent forces that are changing the existing order, but their energy pushes the political system in contradictory directions, one farther to the right, the other defining a radical center outside the parties. Republican pollster Fred Steeper has defined the different forces as populist cynicism and conservative cynicism, overlapping and reinforcing to some extent, but based on different impulses. Together they make the task of coalition management facing Republican leaders enormously complex — even if there were a modern FDR to lead them.

★★★

8

Waiting for Realignment

S TEVEN SPIELBERG at Spago's on Oscar night would not have generated more of a stir than Newt Gingrich did when he slipped through the door into Grover Norquist's crowded Capitol Hill town house precisely at eleven o'clock on the evening of April 7, 1995. From the living room to the small backyard to the rooftop patio that looked over the Capitol conservatives now claimed as their own, the house was filled with the best and the rightest — the cream of baby boom and Generation X conservatives, sipping beers, puffing on cigars, and slapping backs in expressions of congratulation. One man wore a button that read "Taxation is theft." Another wore an NRA baseball cap. The young Republican pollster Frank Luntz, as though displaying a trophy from a defeated enemy, came in a "Clinton '92" campaign jacket.

The party marked the exclamation point to a day of celebrations for Republicans. Earlier that morning, under bright sunshine that carried the hint of spring, the House Republicans had reassembled on the Capitol steps, where they had introduced the Contract With America almost seven months earlier, to cheer its completion: They had passed nine of the ten items (only term limits had failed) in six days fewer than the one hundred Gingrich had promised. Never mind that the Contract had already begun to languish in the Senate: In the exuberant din at Norquist's home that night, the sense of triumph was intoxicating. The room floated on self-assurance: the unshakable belief among these ambitious young men and women that their time had come. Norquist, the young conservative networker and strategist, a man who viewed politics as the conduct of war by other means, caught the mood with the cover to his invitation. He reprinted a quote not from the Contract, or any treasured conservative tome, but from the movie *Conan the Barbarian*, in which the great warrior is asked what is best in life, and replies, "To crush enemies, see them driven before you, and hear the lamentations of their women."

Many influences had shaped the political sensibility of the young conservatives who assembled that evening to commemorate the keening of the Democrats. Ronald Reagan had inspired them; Rush Limbaugh and P. J. O'Rourke had given them their cultural vocabulary — a jaunty anti-establishment impertinence that disdained liberalism as not only wrongheaded but uncool, an object not of fear but ridicule. (The final thought on Norquist's invitation read, "Non-transferable, non-refundable and certainly not recyclable.") But their view of the world was shaped above all by the man who stood alone in the doorway at eleven, looking vaguely uncomfortable as the room surged toward him and the inevitable chant erupted: "Newt, Newt, Newt."

THE gathering at Grover Norquist's home on that warm April evening was very much Newt Gingrich's party. In a much larger sense, the GOP itself is also becoming Gingrich's party. After the emotional high point of April 7, the House revolutionaries and their allies in the conservative populist movement suffered many frustrations through 1995 as the Senate rejected or diluted several key items in their Contract With America. But most understood that within the party, the tide was running toward them, that each passing election was likely to strengthen the position of the conservative voices in the GOP. "Every freshman class," marveled House Majority Leader Dick Armey, "seems to be more conservative."

These impatient young conservatives express an expansive vision. Like Reagan, who dreamed of defeating, not containing, the "evil empire" of communism, the Gingrich conservatives and their Senate allies dream not of limiting but humbling what former Education Secretary Lamar Alexander calls "the arrogant empire" in Washington. Revolution is an overused term in politics, promiscuously applied to almost every new President. But the goals of the dynamic forces in the GOP — represented by names like Gingrich and Armey, John Kasich and Bill Kristol, Phil Gramm and Tommy Thompson, Ralph Reed and Bill Bennett — justify the term.

To fulfill their policy ambitions — or even anything approximating them — the Republicans must first change the equation of contemporary electoral politics. Since 1968, America has settled into a pattern of fragmented political authority — with control of the White House and Congress routinely divided between the parties — incompatible with the extent of change Gingrich and his allies envision. To transform the government, the Republicans must first transform that pattern. They must construct a stable electoral majority that will provide them sustained control of both the White House and Congress.

Unified control of the executive and legislative branches does not guarantee a party success in driving the national agenda: Clinton, and Jimmy Carter before him, demonstrate that. But the opposite is true: It is almost impossible to fundamentally redirect the government without simultaneous control of the White House and both chambers in Congress. The three most intense bursts of legislative activity in this century — Woodrow Wilson's New Freedom; Franklin Roosevelt's New Deal; and Lyndon Johnson's Great Society — all came when the Democratic Party held the White House and both congressional chambers. The nearest exception, Ronald Reagan, also testifies to the rule. Reagan forced through his ambitious tax-and-spending reduction plan in 1981, when Republicans controlled the Senate and with the votes of a rump group of Southern Democratic House "Boll Weevils" effectively controlled the lower chamber as well. But after the Democrats regained working control of the House in the 1982 election, Reagan's conservative revolution quickly ran aground.

That history frames the political challenge facing the conservatives in the GOP and their allies in the antigovernment movement. It took the Democrats the generation from Franklin Roosevelt's election in 1932 to Lyndon Johnson's final year in 1968 (a period in which they simultaneously controlled the executive and legislative branches for twenty-six of those thirty-six years) to embed their vision of an activist government into the structure of American society. Even that project built on the outpouring of progressive legislation Woodrow Wilson and the Democratic Congress laid down during his first term. Today's ascendant Republicans cannot reverse the century-long Democratic expansion of federal power in a single congressional session, or, for that matter, over the four-year term that a Republican President will serve if the party can win back the White House in 1996. Only with sustained, unified control of government can these Republicans come close to inscribing their vision into law.

Spend and spend, tax and tax, elect and elect; so reportedly counseled Harry Hopkins as the Roosevelt Democrats assembled the sturdy New Deal political coalition. Now Republicans talk of their own durable majority united by reductions in spending, regulation, and taxes. Certainly that logic binds together the activist gun owners, small-business proprietors, conservative Christians, and property rights activists who constitute the grassroots antigovernment network. But these activists alone do not constitute an absolute electoral majority. And though the breadth and depth of the voter revolt in 1994 carried all the intensity of a realigning election — with results that underscored the intractability of the problems confronting the Democrats — the full meaning of 1994 will not be clear until the Republicans demonstrate whether they can solidify their gains in 1996 and beyond.

WAITING FOR REALIGNMENT

The 1994 election marks the third time in the past three decades that the prospect of realignment has glimmered before the Republicans. The first came when Richard Nixon's three-way victory in the 1968 election signaled the collapse of the Democratic New Deal coalition at the presidential level; the second, in 1980, when Ronald Reagan's landslide victory over Jimmy Carter carried into office a Republican majority in the Senate and clarified the partisan divisions that Nixon had blurred over the role of government.

But each time, Republicans failed to translate their success at the presidential level into a lasting shift in voter allegiances or control of Congress. Although Republicans held the White House for twenty of the twenty-four years after Nixon's election in 1968, they controlled the Senate for just the first six years of Reagan's presidency, and never came close to winning the House. Throughout, Democrats also dominated state and local offices. The result was institutionalized stalemate, an unprecedented division of power between Republican presidents and a Democratic Congress, with Democrats also controlling most of the largest state governments. The Republicans' inability to expand their presidential realignment down the ballot — at least potentially until 1994 — denied a succession of Republican presidents the power to define fully the national agenda.

The Republican failure to capture Congress while realigning the dynamics of presidential elections in 1968 was unprecedented. Since the modern party system solidified early in the nineteenth century, four earlier realignments had punctuated American political history. In each case, the party that won the White House also captured the Congress — and held both chambers of Congress and the presidency for at least the next twelve years, long enough to write its program into law. That was true in 1828 (when Andrew Jackson seized the White House by identifying the Democrats as the party of the common man); 1860 (when the new Republican Party, with Abraham Lincoln as its nominee, captured the White House on a platform of resisting the expansion of slavery and upholding the Union); 1896 (when Republican William McKinley consolidated the urban centers of the North and Midwest with a protectionist, pro-business message against a Democratic Party defined by the agrarian southern and western populism of William Jennings Bryan); and 1932 (when the Depression swept Franklin Roosevelt into power).

Why couldn't the Republicans match this record of congressional success after Nixon's victories in 1968 or 1972, or even after Reagan's victories in the 1980s? In each case, a reaction against GOP governance staggered their advance. In 1974, the Watergate scandal cost the GOP forty-seven House seats and reduced their numbers in the chamber to the lowest level since Johnson's landslide a decade earlier. With Reagan's victory in 1980, the Republicans climbed back to their pre-Watergate level in the House, and captured the Senate. But the recession of Reagan's first two years cost the GOP another twenty-six House seats in the 1982 elections, and placed control out of their reach again. Four years later, a surge of black voters in the South inspired by Jesse Jackson's 1984 presidential campaign and hostile to Reagan's agenda cost them control of the Senate.

There were, however, deeper factors that severed the historic link between the presidential and congressional vote. During the twenty-four years of Republican presidential dominance between Nixon's and

Clinton's elections, Democratic incumbents employed an arsenal of institutional weapons to resist the trend in national elections. Democratic-controlled state governments drew redistricting lines that favored their reelection. Congressional Democrats relentlessly exploited the ability to deliver pork barrel spending and deluge the district with free congressional mailings. And, especially during the 1980s, Democrats baldly marketed access to attract huge contributions from business interests ideologically more sympathetic to Republicans. When all of this wasn't enough, Democrats in competitive districts simply joined the hounds: On issues from school busing in the 1970s to Reagan's budget plan in 1981, Democrats with centrist constituencies freely deserted the national party to support conservative initiatives.

Most important, though, was the breakdown in party loyalty after World War II that diminished party-line voting. As partisan attachments weakened, and the percentage of voters defining themselves as true independents increased, a growing share of Americans routinely voted for one party in presidential elections and the other in congressional races. From 1900 through 1952, no more than 25 percent of congressional districts ever sent a representative to Congress from one party while giving a majority of its votes to a presidential candidate from the other; but at least that many congressional districts have split their ballots in each of the presidential elections since then — rising to a height of about 45 percent in both the Nixon and Reagan landslide reelections. Those figures (and the growing number of voters calling themselves independents) pointed toward a more fluid electorate that was increasingly skeptical about granting complete loyalty to either party. For many Americans, divided control of government became not an accident but a positive good, another way for voters dubious of both parties to hedge their bets. To the checks and balances that the founders wrote into the Constitution, Americans over the past generation seemed to have added their own innovation — a systematic division of power between the parties. Voters entrusted national security and the broad management of the economy to Republicans in the White House, but kept Democrats in Congress to look after the districts back home.

But the rising dissatisfaction with Congress finally overwhelmed the Democratic defenses. Initially the revolt manifested itself as a pox on incumbents from both parties: In 1990, both Republican and Democratic House incumbents saw their shares of the vote decline. But in 1992, the numbers continued to fall only for Democratic incumbents, and the party lost ten House seats despite Clinton's victory. Then the operational chaos and ideological miscalculations of Clinton's first two years merged anti-Washington and antiliberal streams into a single powerful current that swept the party from control of Congress.

Carried to the high ground on this tide, Republicans are now in a position to void the institutional advantages that fortified the Democratic congressional majority — or to exploit them themselves. But to achieve the unified political control that dominant parties exercised in earlier generations, the most pressing task for Republicans is to reverse the trend toward divided loyalties and lock in lasting allegiance up and down the ballot from the broad voter coalition that powered their 1994 gains.

That potential clearly exists. In some respects, the most dramatic aspect of the GOP success in 1994 was that it required no dramatic shifts in voter loyalties. One way of looking at the 1994 result was that the GOP did nothing more than finally re-create at the congressional level the voter coalition that drove the party's five presidential victories from 1968 through 1988. In fact, the GOP captured Congress with an electoral performance that matched only a lower peak on that twenty-year range of presidential successes. Without approaching the heights Nixon or Reagan reached in their landslide reelections, the 1994 Republican congressional vote closely followed the contours of George Bush's solid 1988 victory over Michael Dukakis. The Republicans used different issues in 1994 than 1988 to frame the differences between the parties, intensifying their antigovernment and anti-Washington message in the most recent race. Yet in both campaigns the GOP established an ideological division that separated the electorate in a remarkably similar fashion. Whether measured by race, gender, income, ideology, or education, exit polls show that the overall Republican share of the congressional vote in 1994 usually fell within a few percentage points of Bush's showing. In both cases, the GOP managed little support among minorities, but attracted almost three of every five white voters — including clear majorities of the white working class that once constituted the cornerstone of the Democratic political coalition.

What is most significant about these parallels is that they under-score the potential of the 1994 Republican voter coalition to dominate national elections and provide the GOP unified control of the executive and legislative branch into the next century. Both races show the potential for Republicans to align an insurmountable majority of white Americans behind a broadly conservative message on social values, taxes, and the role of government. With the 1994 results, Republicans have now demonstrated the existence of an ideologically coherent, demographically identifiable coalition that can produce a partisan majority in both congressional and presidential races — something Democrats simply cannot say.

But assembling such a coalition for one election is not the same as maintaining its allegiance while translating that broad ideological message into a specific policy agenda. Even Bush, whose own policy goals were minimal, proved unable to hold together his coalition in 1992 under pressure from a declining economy and internal divisions that set moderate voters against his activist conservative base. In seeking far more dramatic changes in policy — at a time when voters invest little confidence in politicians from either party — the current Republican leadership is imposing much greater stress on the fault lines in the GOP vote.

The internal divisions in the Republican coalition over such issues as gun control, abortion, and free trade are hardly unique. Every successful political coalition in American history has divided on some issues. As Clinton's first two years in office demonstrated, the differences among Democrats on issues such as free trade, gun control, affirmative action, welfare reform, taxes, and the death penalty are at least as great as the arguments among Republicans. The racial divisions in the Democratic coalition are even sharper than the tensions between religious and more secular elements of the Republican alliance.

To say that internal divisions run through both parties is merely to state a fact of political life. The United States is so large and diverse that by definition any coalition large enough to encompass an absolute national electoral majority is in some respects incoherent. The real question is not whether a political coalition can achieve unanimity on all issues but whether it can subsume its divisions beneath a unifying idea.

The Republican Party now has such a potential unifying idea: reduction in the size and responsibilities of the federal government. If Republicans can maintain voter support for the central goal of limiting federal power, these other divisions (with the possible exception of a Supreme Court or congressional vote eliminating the legal right to abortion) are unlikely to rupture its coalition. That reality frames one central question now facing the GOP: Will voters support the reduction of government as much in the specific as they do in the abstract?

On the subject of government, American public opinion is not so much divided as contradictory. Large percentages distrust government, oppose regulation, and want to balance the budget. But there is also overwhelming support for Medicare, environmental protection, spending on education, and an instinct to look toward government when things go wrong in society. Washington is blamed for doing too much, and then for not doing enough when planes crash or rivers choke on sludge. Clinton faced one side of this paradox: Though his election clearly signaled a public desire for greater attention to domestic problems, in office he collided with mountainous skepticism that the expansion of government was the route to progress. Republicans now face the opposite risk: that general public support for less government will not translate into endorsement of their specific reductions in spending, taxes, and regulation.

From any poll, suspicion and hostility toward the federal government roars like a primal scream. For the groups in the antigovernment coalition that hostility is an ideological proposition, but for most Americans it is not. In polling, far more people support the goal of reforming government than simply reducing it, and many specific government initiatives, like Medicare and environmental protection, are as popular as government itself is unpopular. Those attitudes caused public support to dwindle in late 1995 for the GOP plan to balance the budget over seven years — the centerpiece of the new conservative agenda.

Since at least the late 1980s, distrust of government has blotted out other populist suspicions. But those other attitudes remain a potential check on the fury focused at Washington. Almost three-fourths of Americans, for instance, still agree that too much power is concentrated in the hands of big business. Despite all the distrust of Washington, the idea of government as a counterweight to that corporate power retains substantial appeal. In a joint survey in 1995, Robert Teeter and Peter Hart, respectively, a prominent Republican and Democratic pollster, found that most Americans agreed with the general proposition that government overregulated business. But when asked whether business could be trusted "on its own" to control air and water pollution it creates, sell safe products, develop safe drugs, or provide safe working conditions for workers, majorities of 70 percent or more said no, that it was necessary for government "to keep an eye" on business. On each of those issues, even a majority of Republicans agreed that government oversight was necessary. "In the end," wrote Hart and Teeter, "Americans favor regulation over laissez-faire because their lack of trust in business exceeds their lack of trust in government." If the GOP revolution becomes seen not as shifting power from government to individuals, but merely freeing business from public oversight, the party is certain to suffer.

Yet these sentiments are only part of the story. The overall collapse of faith in the federal government looms over all these expressions of support for its individual functions. Support for individual regulatory initiatives can mask the extent to which voters have reached a general conclusion that government is too large, overreaching, and intrusive. The idea of shifting authority over social programs from Washington to state governments as most Republicans advocate also draws substantial support in survey after survey, and even the resistance evident in polls to cuts in individual spending programs looks different when viewed through a wider lens. Democrats are often mesmerized by poll numbers showing public support for greater spending on individual social programs. But most often the controlling dynamic is public skepticism that such programs would accomplish their intended goals.

Together, these closely balanced and contradictory opinions suggest a broad social consensus toward restraining the role of government — but with enormous differences remaining over the specifics of what that means. Absent a major economic downturn that overshadows all else, those differences are likely to be the central focus of the presidential and congressional campaigns in 1996 — and probably campaigns into the next century.

The Republican argument in this debate seems clear: All the trends in the party say it will further consolidate behind the agenda of the Gingrich generation and the antigovernment coalition. The Democratic position is much less certain. The New Democratic agenda that Clinton articulated in 1992 offered the potential to unify the party around a vision of reformed but reinvigorated government that focused on middle-class economic concerns, and sought to expand opportunity while demanding personal responsibility. But the mutual failures of Clinton and the Democratic Congress from 1993 to 1994 prevented the party from implementing that design. Now Democrats are as divided as at any point in the 1980s about where to go next.

Congressional Democrats, and the political consultants who work with them, have pinned their hopes primarily on the class-warfare and fairness arguments that the party wielded with limited success against Ronald Reagan in the early 1980s. Accusing the GOP of advancing tax cuts that benefit the affluent and business while slashing popular middle-class programs like Medicare and student loans, these congressional Democrats (especially in the House) hope to win back working- and middle-class white voters by inflaming lingering suspicions that Republicans care mostly about the rich.

As 1995 progressed, Clinton increasingly played those notes, too. But he recognized their limitations as a central organizing principle for the Democrats. Since the 1994 election, Clinton has conceded much more than the congressional Democrats to the drive to humble Washington, more even than he did with his promises in 1992 to "reinvent government." Looking toward 1996, Clinton is not campaigning to reverse the Republican revolution; rather he promises to resist its excesses on issues like the environment and Medicare and to protect an extremely limited number of targeted government investments in education and training. The most dramatic evidence of his shift came in June 1995, when, to the horror of congressional Democrats flaying the Republican budget-reduction plans, Clinton introduced his own proposal for balancing the budget over ten years.

The choices in Clinton's ten-year budget plan — protecting spending on education and job training while slashing many other social programs, like housing aid — envision a government that trims back its promises of economic security and concentrates its remaining energy on helping all Americans increase their opportunity to provide for themselves. "There will never be a time when government can do anything for people they won't do for themselves," Clinton said in a 1995 speech to the Democratic National Committee. "[But] I believe the role of government is to help people make the most of their own lives."

Clinton's release of a balanced budget plan marked the end of the robotic cooperation with congressional Democrats that undermined his first two years. The new approach was dictated largely by a secretive political consultant named Dick Morris. Morris, who had advised Clinton in Arkansas but worked mostly for Republicans in recent years, so preferred to remain in the shadows that he suggested White House Chief of Staff Leon Panetta call him Charlie — after the disembodied voice that delivered the instructions in the 1970s television hit *Charlie's Angels*. Energetic, glib, and unshakably self-confident, Morris emerged as a power in the weeks after the 1994 election, when Clinton — angry over the advice he had received, and characteristically prone to blame others for his misfortunes — downgraded or exiled entirely the political advisers who directed his 1992 campaign, including pollster Stan Greenberg and media consultant Mandy Grunwald.

Morris put forward a new organizing principle for Clinton's often chaotic presidency: a policy that he called "triangulation." Triangulation postulated Clinton as the referee between the two parties: the third point on the triangle between congressional Democrats and Republicans. At times, the theory went, he would work with the Republicans; at times he would join with Democrats to oppose the GOP. This approach ensured — even institutionalized — dissonance. One day Clinton reassured the Democratic base by issuing a ringing defense of affirmative action. The next he horrified congressional Democrats by announcing his own blueprint to balance the budget in ten years. One day he denounced Republican tax cuts as a giveaway to the rich, the next he stunned Democrats by declaring his own 1993 tax increase too large.

Through this sometimes confusing flurry of activity, Clinton's basic direction was back toward the New Democrat and economically populist themes he enunciated in 1992. On the one hand, he spoke more directly to anxious working-class voters by proposing a middle-class tax cut and a hike in the minimum wage, and aggressively confronting Japan to buy more American cars and auto parts. On the other, he unveiled several bold government-reform ideas — like sweeping consolidation of housing and job-training programs into new voucher systems that he probably never would have risked if Democrats still held Congress. On issue after issue — from spending reductions to permitting prayer in school to welfare reform — he spoke relentlessly about "common ground" and positioned himself as the point of reason between extremists in both parties. When he issued his budget plan, Clinton talked about congressional Democrats as if describing the members of another party: "I'm sympathetic with the *Democratic position*" that urged scorched-earth opposition to the GOP budget proposals, he said, "but I don't believe that's the appropriate position for the President." (Emphasis added.)

By the fall, Clinton shifted toward resolute opposition to the GOP budget — while still calling for bipartisan compromise. The conflicting signals were themselves the point. As 1996 approached, Clinton was virtually levitating himself out of the Democratic Party and crafting a centrist appeal based on autonomy from both parties. Amid growing talk of potential independent presidential candidacies — and Perot's announcement that he would form a third party — Clinton was methodically working to shed his partisan identity and sprout new wings as something like an independent himself. "Bill Clinton," observed Floyd Ciruli, a sharp-eyed Democratic pollster in Colorado, "is becoming an unaffiliated candidate."

WHETHER that will be enough to ensure his survival is an open question. More often than not, a party that suffers as large a midterm election loss as Democrats did in 1994 surrenders the White House two years later. Congressional blowouts in 1890, 1894, 1910, 1930, 1958, 1966, and 1974 all foreshadowed switches in White House control. One election that broke the pattern was 1946. Halfway through Harry Truman's first term, Republicans surged into control of both the House and Senate. But in 1948, Truman stunned the political world by winning reelection over Republican Thomas E. Dewey and carrying the Democrats back to majorities in both chambers with a full-throated attack against the "do-nothing" Republican Congress. Gingrich, for one, thinks that experience offers a clear lesson for the GOP in 1996. "What we don't want is Tom Dewey," he said. "We don't want a guy who doesn't get it. If Dewey had understood the [Republican] Congress, he would have beaten Truman. Any nominee who understands where we are going and what the transformation is, is a great nominee. The only nominee you have to worry about is a nominee who is repudiating what we are doing as a party."

Yet the balance, and the history, are more complex than Gingrich suggests. Truman based his campaign largely on convincing the country that Dewey and the Republican Congress intended to reverse the gains of the New Deal. A Republican nominee that year who promised to join the conservative Congress in an all-out assault on Roosevelt's legacy might have stirred more enthusiasm than Dewey, who offered only a bland centrism, but could also have provoked a greater backlash. The country's underlying attitude toward government tilts much more toward the Republicans in 1996 than it did in 1948. But the GOP still faces the challenge of finding a nominee who can motivate the ascendant revolutionary elements in the party without frightening the centrist voters Republicans also need to win the White House.

The explosion of energy on the Right — the sense among all the groups in the antigovernment coalition that their time is at hand after the disappointments of Reagan and Bush — both propels and complicates the Republican drive toward the White House. With the right candidate, Republicans can expect to benefit from a huge mobilization from groups such as the NRA and Christian Coalition eager to dislodge President Clinton. But in their eagerness to activate those groups, the Republicans risk forgetting most voters mistrust ideologues of any sort. No party can thrive while denying the most militant elements within its coalition; but as the Democrats learned with George McGovern in 1972, surrendering to them can be even more disastrous.

So powerful is the conservative surge that it could scramble the usual calculus of presidential politics. Historically, presidential elections have turned primarily on assessments of the incumbent's performance. Yet the extent to which Gingrich and his allies have dominated the agenda since 1994 could make the 1996 presidential election a referendum on the Republican Congress as well. Clinton has never established a durable majority of support, but Republicans face the burden of persuading the country to give them a free hand to accelerate the changes they began in 1995. Clinton's strongest argument is likely to be negative: that Americans need him in the White House to prevent the congressional Republicans from going too far. In the few elections at stake in 1995, Democrats drew some blood — particularly while winning the Kentucky gubernatorial race — by denouncing congressional Republicans as reckless extremists. Even some Republicans worry that argument could strike a chord again in 1996: "My concern, as a Republican," says Jack Kemp, "is if we lurch the country too far [to the right] . . . the American people would say, 'Well, I don't particularly like the President . . . but I'm glad he's there to keep us from a lurch.'" Dole expressed similar concerns as Republicans struggled to resolve their legislative differences in the fall of 1995. "I think we have to be very careful that we're not perceived as just caring about business and people with money and people who are healthy and people that don't have disabilities and people that are white as opposed to people of color, ethnicity," he said.

What seems most certain is that the general election debate in both the presidential and congressional races will occur within a framework determined more by Republican than Democratic conceptions of government's role. Of all the electoral possibilities that can be imagined for the next few years, the least likely is Democrats receiving a mandate to enlarge the scope of federal intervention in American life. Indeed, the momentum behind the drive to limit government is so powerful that it is unlikely to entirely stall no matter which party is in power. Many specifics remain to be fought out and election results in the next few years will slow or accelerate the process, alter the balance between tax cuts and spending cuts, change the lists of programs favored and condemned, and establish the outer boundaries of the change. But in the near term, nothing is likely to entirely reverse the course set in 1994 toward a smaller government.

THE CONSERVATIVE LEAP OF FAITH

Newt Gingrich *thinks* 1994 was different from 1980 or 1968, the last two times Republicans felt realignment at hand. But even he is not sure. Sitting in his office one steamy summer afternoon in 1995, chomping on a sandwich, glowing in the success of his book *To Renew America*, he looked over the horizon with cautious confidence. "I do think there is a potential that literally enough different things finally came together in 1994 that you are really entering a different [political] era," he said between bites. "[But] we will find out next year whether it is an aberration."

In fact, it will take more than the election of 1996 to settle whether Republicans have brought the nation to the new political era that Gingrich needs to implement his designs; the party needs several successful elections to consolidate the level of control Democrats enjoyed in the decades after Roosevelt. As they face that challenge, Republicans now hold a perceptible advantage over the Democrats. But the imbalance is not as large as the Democratic advantage in the heyday of the New Deal coalition, nor is it insurmountable. It is not difficult, for instance, to imagine Clinton holding the White House in 1996 — or, less likely, Democrats retaking the House in the next few years — in a backlash against Republicans moving too far or too fast to eliminate government programs and regulatory protections that most Americans support.

Still, the GOP's central mission of limiting government is large enough to occupy its imagination and unify its core supporters. In contrast, continued ideological and racial divisions among the Democrats inhibit their ability to present a clear and compelling alternative to the GOP vision. While the Democrats flounder, several distinct groups of voters are clearly realigning into a lasting attachment with the GOP: born-again Christians, small-business owners, and white southerners most important among them. Despite all of Clinton's efforts to change his party's image on questions of values, millions of Americans still identify Democrats with the forces of cultural dissolution and permissiveness, while associating Republicans with standards, order, and individual responsibility. Meanwhile, after each census, population shifts carry more congressional seats and electoral votes to the southern and western states, where Republicans are strongest, while diminishing the count in northeastern and midwestern states, where Democrats remain most competitive. For each of these reasons, Republicans have cause to join Gingrich in hoping that 1994 marked a realigning election that will open a sustained era of conservative political control.

But building a stable political order atop the underlying current of dissatisfaction with American life may be like constructing a fortress in the sand. The persistent alienation that voters now express about the political system is a force inimical to electoral stability of any sort. In such an environment voters may simply not trust either party enough to provide it with undivided control of government for any length of time. The long-awaited political realignment may be contingent on conditions that no longer exist: a willingness by a majority of voters to identify their interests firmly with one party. The basic trend toward political independence — which implied neutrality between the parties when it first accelerated during the 1960s — now appears to be taking on a harder edge as more Americans feel themselves affirmatively hostile to both of the established choices. "The electorate is still controlled by voters who hate both parties," says Democratic pollster Geoff Garin, "and what matters is which party do they hate more at a given moment in time."

That discontent is now the greatest threat to Republican political dominance — indeed, it is the greatest threat looming over both parties. Over the short term, Republicans can attract many disaffected voters just by keeping their promises to reform government programs. But if Republicans are to extend their control into a lasting realignment, ultimately those reforms must deliver tangible results that diminish the anxiety about the nation's future that corrodes confidence in the political system.

Republicans ironically now find themselves in the same position as Democrats during the 1960s. The Great Society was a great leap of faith — that the expansion of government could solve social problems festering in American life. Though the Great Society made progress on some fronts, troubling trends in education, crime, and family structure all continued, and several even accelerated after the 1960s. Whether, as Charles Murray argues, that was because government intervention compounded the problems — or rather because government failed to intervene forcefully enough — government was blamed and Democrats discredited.

The current GOP agenda represents at least as great a leap of faith. This time the gamble is that removing government will solve problems left unsolved by government's intervention. Like the liberals who devised the Great Society, Gingrich and his allies today may be seeding disappointment by promising far more than changes in government policy — in any direction — can deliver. "The mistake of the Democratic majority was believing it could create the good society by merely building government up," argues Don E. Eberly, president of the Commonwealth Foundation, a conservative think tank. "The danger for the Republican majority may be believing it can re-create the good society by merely tearing government down."

In the sweep of their ambitions, Republicans now find themselves colliding with one of their most penetrating critiques of liberalism. If the conservative criticism of the Great Society provides any overriding lesson, it is the law of unanticipated consequences — the maxim that any change in policy usually carries with it unintended and unpredictable side effects. Indeed perverse consequences occur so frequently in public policy they should no longer be considered unanticipated. For the past quarter century, keen-eyed conservatives have shown how the law of unintended consequences defeated liberal hopes of solving problems by expanding government. Now the law of unintended consequences looms over conservative hopes of solving problems by reducing government. There is no reason to believe it is easier to predict the consequences of retrenching government than enlarging it. As John DiIulio writes: "Big government is a raging bull in a china shop of a social system; it breaks things on the way in, while inside, and on the way out."

Consider social policy. The retrocons and the Republican allies have blamed the welfare system for crime, family breakdown, and urban chaos. But there is no guarantee that limiting welfare will improve any of those conditions; it could easily cause further deterioration on each of those fronts. No state has ever put to work anywhere near the number of welfare recipients the Republican plan would require them to place in jobs. When the five-year time limit on welfare in the GOP plan is fully phased in, as much as 40 percent of the existing welfare caseload — some two million families — will be cut off from assistance. Who can say with certainty what will happen when so many welfare recipients, many of them without high school diplomas or meaningful experience in the workplace, flood the low-wage labor market?

The same can be said for the breakdown in the family. Charles Murray's argument that welfare makes it easier for women to bear children outside of marriage is difficult to refute. But in many inner-city neighborhoods, illegitimacy has become such a commanding social norm that merely reducing welfare benefits may not be powerful

enough to reverse it. In fact, no program from any point along the ideo-
logical spectrum has been found to significantly discourage out-of-
wedlock births. "I do not know of a silver bullet program that I could
use and say that we can reduce illegitimacy," concedes Wisconsin
Governor Tommy Thompson, perhaps the leading Republican wel-
fare reformer.

Economic issues pose similar questions. It is possible, as conserva-
tives suggest, that cutting taxes, reducing regulation, and balancing
the federal budget will spur a new era of growth and productivity that
reignites a rise in living standards. But it is by no means certain.

There are many valid reasons to balance the federal budget. Mil-
lions of Americans consider it morally wrong to pass on debt to future
generations of taxpayers. Eliminating the deficit would reduce future
interest payments on the national debt and free more funds, either for
new spending or tax cuts. Most economists believe that balancing the
budget would cause long-term interest rates to drop from one to two
percentage points. Lower interest rates would provide tangible savings
to homeowners and borrowers of all kinds. And the reduction in bor-
rowing costs should increase business investment and help the econ-
omy to grow faster over the long term — though the magnitude of the
effect is very much in dispute. Some private economists expect dra-
matic results, but the Congressional Budget Office forecasts that a bal-
anced budget would only "allow the economy to grow modestly
faster" and could exert such a mild impact on the nation's long-term
prospects that "a few years down the road, it may be impossible to
disentangle the effects of balancing the budget from other forces oper-
ating at the same time in the U.S. economy." Other economists
warn that rapidly reducing the deficit could slow the economy in the
near term.

Even if a balanced budget improves long-term growth, that won't
necessarily solve the income problems of average families. More
growth is better than less. But without changes in the forces that are
depressing incomes for less well educated workers, even more robust
growth could simply channel greater gains to upper-income families,
without lifting the pressure on those closer to the middle. The econ-
omy grew by more than 50 percent from 1973 through 1993, but the
median income still fell for all families except those with two earners

(who enjoyed only modest growth themselves), and hourly wages declined for men without college educations. By themselves, reductions in the size of government may not be enough to overcome the other forces economists indict for this sluggish progress in living standards, particularly technological advances and international competition that have diminished the value of less-skilled labor.

Even reducing taxes offers no guarantee of quelling unrest. Though many Americans instinctively blame taxes for their distress, the federal tax burden on average families slightly declined through the 1980s. Tax cuts can temporarily ease the sting of stagnating wages. But it is not possible to cut taxes fast enough to restore families to the level of income growth that their counterparts experienced in the 1950s and 1960s; for a typical family with two children and one parent in the workforce, the income "lost" from slower growth than in the postwar years quickly exceeds the benefits even from the $500 per child tax credit that Republicans support.

The Democratic responses to the strains on living standards, based primarily on increasing access to education and training, may be just as inadequate to the challenge. Existing federal job-training programs have had only mixed success in increasing the long-term earnings of participants. Helping more young people attend college, as Clinton has proposed by expanding student loans and allowing college tuition to be deducted from income taxes, should increase overall earnings because workers with college degrees earn more than those without them. But Bureau of Labor Statistics projections of job growth for the next decade estimate very small increases in the share of jobs requiring a college education. Unless the economy increases its demand for skilled workers, increasing the supply of college graduates could merely create a glut that lowers their wages — particularly as more employers shift white-collar jobs, like software design, to contractors abroad.

On both the economic and cultural fronts, the magnitude of these problems is sobering. This is not to say society is helpless against them. On even the most entrenched problems, the right mix of public policies and social changes can move the rock forward. Crime is a good example. For most of the past three decades, the growth of crime appeared inexorable; yet the crime rate has dropped over the past few years. But these declines in the crime rate are moderate dips from very high levels. The experience of a generation or more ago, when people left doors unlocked and strolled at night unafraid, remains very distant. The violent crime rate has dropped 1.7 percent from its high point in 1991; but this lower level is still 360 percent greater than the violent crime rate in 1960. And most leading criminologists believe the crime rate will rise again in the next few years as the wheel of demographic change again increases the number of teenage boys.

In that regard, crime is typical of the most troubling problems we face. Each of the basic trends roiling American life — income stagnation, family breakup, crime — is a powerful force beyond the reach of any government to command. These problems, in fact, are now common to all major nations across the industrialized world, driven by basic changes in technology and the global economy and by the loosening of traditional moral strictures on behavior.

These conditions need not be permanent. But dramatic progress, if it comes at all, will almost certainly come from large social and economic changes that government might modestly encourage but cannot hope to summon or dictate. Eventually, as some economists argue, increased application of computer technology could produce a twenty-first-century productivity boom that again lifts sagging incomes. Over time, America could experience a revolution in cultural mores and morals similar to the social reformation that allowed Victorian England to reduce crime and illegitimacy rates in the last half of the nineteenth century. Some intriguing signs, in fact, already point toward such a shift in contemporary attitudes: a stabilization in the divorce rate, the backlash against sexually degrading advertising and music, the rapid growth of Promise Keepers, a movement that encourages men to remain attached to their families.

But while waiting for such fundamental economic and social transformations to arrive — if they ever do — government will be stretched merely to prevent further deterioration in the trends in family structure, crime, and economic security for the less educated. In each instance, the regression from thirty years ago is so large that it is difficult to imagine any set of policies now under consideration re-creating the earlier experience. For politicians of either party, success might be stabilizing these problems at a level most Americans still find unacceptable. Whether that will be enough progress to satisfy the public may be the largest question in American politics today.

THE THIRD WAY

Most often in our history the nation has entrusted one party to lead by providing it unified authority over both the executive and legislative branches. In their days, the Federalists, the Democrat-Republicans of Thomas Jefferson and James Madison, the Democrats of Andrew Jackson, and the Republicans of Abraham Lincoln all enjoyed sustained control of both Congress and the White House. The apex of unified control came from 1896 through 1954, when first the Republicans from McKinley to Herbert Hoover and then the Democrats of Franklin Roosevelt and Harry Truman each dominated government for a generation: Overall one party or the other simultaneously controlled both chambers of Congress and the White House for fifty of those fifty-eight years. Then during the 1960s, Democrats unified control of Congress and the White House for the eight years John F. Kennedy and Lyndon Johnson served in the White House.

This pattern of consolidated authority for one party has broken down only when the government appears incapable of coping with the nation's problems. Then the political system fragments, neither party establishes lasting allegiances with the voters, and the nation drifts without a firm course. The first such period came in the antebellum years leading into the Civil War. As both the Democrats and the Whigs, the dominant parties of the age, failed to confront the challenge of slavery, political upheaval became commonplace. From 1836 until 1860, six consecutive one-term Presidents passed through the White House, while over that period, control of the House switched hands seven times and of the Senate twice. Four of the five Presidents elected from 1844 through 1860 could not amass a popular majority of the vote; except for one vigorous term from Democrat James K. Polk, the nation drifted until Abraham Lincoln won the 1860 presidential election for the Republicans (in a race that splintered the country between four choices) and forced the resolution of the conflict.

Order crumbled again in the last quarter of the nineteenth century. Lacking both will and imagination, and riven by internal divisions, both the Democrats and Republicans proved incapable of responding to the problems of a Gilded Age America wracked by powerful, disquieting forces; industrialization, urbanization, massive immigration, and the centralization of economic power into the hands of financial magnates, giant corporations, and the trusts. Democratic President Grover Cleveland expressed the stunted credo of both parties when he declared that government's functions "do not include the support of the people." Against that indifference, large groups of Americans — farmers groaning under tight money policies that raised their debts and flattened their prices; urban laborers struggling against a new economic system that denied them control of their work or a secure wage — came to view the government as corrupt and irrelevant, if not positively hostile. "Never had so many citizens held their government in such low regard," wrote Robert Wiebe in *The Search for Order*, his classic history of the period.

The restiveness destabilized political life for two decades. By the mid-1870s, the partisan alignment imposed by the Civil War and its aftermath had lost much of its meaning; but no new pattern of loyalty replaced it. From 1876 through 1896, the nation briskly turned the page on five consecutive one-term Presidents, only one of whom could attract a majority of the popular vote. Control of the White House flipped between the parties three times in those five elections. Over the same twenty-year period, the parties traded control of the House five times, and the Senate four times. Frequently control of both chambers was narrowly divided between the parties (including the only tie in Senate history). For only four of those twenty years did one party control both houses of Congress and the White House. When a sharp economic downturn in the 1890s intensified the anger at the paralyzed political system, the country whipsawed with breathtaking speed and intensity: Republicans lost 85 House seats in the election of 1890 (nearly half their total) and surrendered the White House to Democrat Grover Cleveland in 1892. Only two years later, dissatisfaction with the new Democratic President propelled a Republican gain of 120 House seats in the midterm elections of 1894 — the largest one-year swing in congressional control, before or since. In this stormy climate, Washington accomplished little: These decades witnessed a "government of intricate partisan maneuver and token legislation," as Wiebe put it. Not until Republicans imposed a new political order with McKinley's realigning victory in 1896 was the nation able to move forward again into the Progressive Era.

The political era that began with the presidential election in 1968 — another time marked by economic anxiety, social dislocation, and alienation from government — stands as the third sustained period of fragmented political authority in the nation's history. Since Nixon took office in 1969, one party has held all the levers of government for just six years — the four years of the Carter administration and the first two years of Bill Clinton's. That is a record of divided control comparable to the late nineteenth century. And as in the late 1800s, the inability of one party to establish clear national leadership has resulted in indecision, alienation, and intensifying discontent.

Compared to the nineteenth century, the political disorder of the past twenty-eight years has been mild; indeed, there has been a relatively stable stalemate between Republicans who held the White House for most of the period and Democrats who controlled Congress. But the explosive reversals of the early 1990s — which saw voters rout the Democrats from Congress just two years after they abandoned George Bush in near-record numbers — suggest that, just as in the 1890s, mounting frustration with Washington is accelerating political instability. If disenchantment continues to mount, the nineteenth-century precedents suggest greater turbulence could lie ahead.

One manifestation of that potentially greater turmoil is the steadily growing interest in alternatives to the two parties. Historically, the emergence of new parties has been one of the clearest signs of dissatisfaction with government and the political system. During both periods of sustained political instability in the nineteenth century, third parties proliferated.

As in the nineteenth century, discontent with the two major parties is again increasing agitation for a new choice. In surveys, as many as three in five Americans say they would like to see a third party formed, up from about only one in five during the 1960s and roughly two in five during the 1980s. The nearly twenty million votes cast for Perot in 1992 — despite behavior that had millions of other Americans questioning his stability — underscored the willingness of Americans to look beyond the two parties. Now, with his announcement that he intends to build his own third party, Perot could create a permanent institutional vehicle to reinforce that inclination.

Usually third parties have emerged from an ideological extreme. In the nineteenth century, third parties found an opening because the major parties converged and blurred their differences, leaving room on their flanks. Today, the situation is the opposite: The opportunity for a new alternative arises from a continuing polarization that is opening space between the parties. "The middle is not being occupied," says political scientist Martin P. Wattenberg, "and that's where most of the people are."

Both parties are ossifying in a manner that limits their reach to voters in the center. For years, Democratic interest groups have enforced liberal orthodoxy; they greatly complicated Clinton's efforts to reach out to moderate voters. Now a similar process is taking place within the Republican party, as the grassroots conservative groups exert enormous unifying force behind positions such as opposition to gun control and abortion. Adding to this centrifugal pressure is the impact of the realignment in the South. As conservative Republicans replace moderate Democrats across the South, the center of the House is being systematically obliterated.

These structural forces merely encourage key leaders in both parties in the direction they already want to go. In particular, the leadership on both sides in the House — Gingrich and Armey on the one hand, Democrats Richard Gephardt and David Bonior on the other — believe their electoral prospects are improved by framing the sharpest possible ideological choice between the parties. That impulse is less powerful in the Senate, but the stark choices that emerge from the House have limited the opportunity for compromise even in the upper chamber. Though Senate moderates have forced changes in several House Republican initiatives, the polarized nature of debate has left many of them feeling disenchanted and powerless. New Jersey Democratic Senator Bill Bradley struck a chord in the summer of 1995 when he declared that he would not seek reelection because "politics is broken" and public debate "has settled into two familiar ruts" between Democrats "who distrust the market [and] preach government as the answer to our problems" and Republicans who are "infatuated with the 'magic' of the private sector and reflexively criticize government as the enemy of freedom." Only a few weeks later, former New Jersey Governor Thomas H. Kean, a Republican, said he would not run to succeed Bradley because the "radical Right" had seized control of the GOP agenda and left little room for moderates such as himself.

In each party, the advocates of polarization believe that moderate voters will snap in their direction if they are forced into the starkest choice possible. That approach makes sense only so long as the parties can maintain a zero-sum game in which a loss for one is a gain for the other. But this deliberate destruction of the middle ground — combined with continuing anxiety about the nation's future and unrelieved distrust of the political system — is creating an almost irresistible environment for political entrepreneurs to explore insurgencies that exploit unhappiness with both parties. Perot is now just one face in that crowd. At various points in 1995, the list of political figures talking about (or being touted for) an independent presidential campaign rivaled the list of contenders for the Republican presidential nomination. The names circling around this third track included Jesse Jackson, Paul Tsongas, Bradley, former Republican Senator Lowell P. Weicker (who was elected governor of Connecticut as an independent), former Joint Chiefs of Staff Chairman Colin Powell, Perot, and Patrick J. Buchanan.

The names on that list suggest how the discussion of alternatives to the two parties is feeding on itself. Once the idea was mostly the province of political gadflies like Perot. Now the claim that the two parties are no longer serving the nation is coming from figures closer to the heart of the political establishment. For Perot to indict both parties is like a small-town grocer complaining about the new Safeway; but when a leading Democratic senator like Bradley says that "we live in a time when, on a basic level, politics is broken," he invests the argument with a different kind of credibility. As more established voices join the chorus urging alternatives to the two parties, the idea is bound to seem less radical and risky. And as the prospect of new alternatives becomes less forbidding to voters, more established political leaders may see an advantage in aligning themselves with it — further increasing the idea's credibility. The explosive surge of interest in Powell surrounding the publication of his autobiography in the fall of 1995 demonstrated not only his personal appeal, but the continued attraction millions of Americans feel to the idea of selecting a President from outside the normal channels of the political system.

Though the list of politicians talking about potential independent presidential candidacies covers every meaningful point on the ideological spectrum, most analysts believe the core constituency for such a challenge would be moderate voters who share the frustrations of

Bradley and Kean about choosing between extremes. Each potential candidate would add his or her own flavors to the mixture, but an agenda aimed at those voters would inevitably include some combination of fiscal discipline, political reform, a cultural message that blended tolerance with insistence on personal responsibility, and a plea for national unity based on surmounting ideological, racial, and partisan divisions. (Though he ultimately decided not to seek the presidency as a Republican or an independent, Powell demonstrated the appeal of that combination during his triumphant fall 1995 book tour.) With a candidate personally credible as President, all evidence suggests such a message could prove tremendously appealing against the backdrop of intensely polarized debate between the two parties in Washington.

One difficulty for any independent candidate would be keeping the agenda centered on those consensus issues. In American politics, the center is a very elastic term; it includes socially liberal, political reform–oriented, pro–free trade college graduates, and culturally conservative voters without college degrees attracted to economic nationalist themes of protectionism and nativism. These groups can be united in their dissatisfaction with the nation's direction and the two major parties, but if an independent candidate moved close to the White House — much less won it — these divergent interests would place as much strain on his coalition as the Democrats and Republicans face.

Traditionally the two parties have defused third-party insurgencies by absorbing their issues. With William Jennings Bryan as their presidential nominee, the Democrats engulfed the populist agenda in the 1890s; in the 1970s, Nixon diluted but still co-opted George Wallace's message of racial backlash. That process could repeat itself. The GOP's unwavering antigovernment message, and hostility toward Clinton and the Democrats, attracted two-thirds of 1992 Perot voters back into the Republican camp in 1994. But the continuing signs of support in surveys for alternatives to the two parties suggest the difficulty of cementing those bonds. As much as anything else, it is hostility toward politicians that inspires the interest in a third party and independent presidential candidates; almost by definition, neither party can serve as an entirely acceptable outlet for that emotion.

Cultural impulse, historical tradition, and practical impediment still encourage Americans to resolve their political conflicts through the two parties. But the longer majorities of Americans continue to distrust Washington and view politicians as controlled by special interests, the greater the opportunity will grow for a credible independent presidential candidate to make the case that both parties serve themselves and not the nation. The two major parties are now in a position similar to the big three American auto companies in the late 1970s: engaged in a ritualistic battle for a declining share of the market. The question is whether any political entrepreneur can organize that discontent by offering an appealing alternative to the existing choices — the way the Japanese auto manufacturers exploited the consumer discontent with Detroit. The procedural barriers to providing such a new political choice are formidable. But there is no question that the market for it exists.

THE TWO-FRONT WAR

The last elections of the twentieth century find the two great national parties engaged in two competitions. One pits them against each other; the second finds them jointly struggling against the gusts of discontent that are billowing the demands for new political alternatives.

The rules of the first contest now require the Democrats and Republicans to maximize their differences — to raise almost every issue into a confrontation between incompatible world views, darkness and light. It is a battle in which Newt Gingrich spends a decade portraying the Democratic-controlled House as corrupt and then is cudgeled by Democratic attacks on his own ethics the moment he takes power; where talk radio hosts systematically work to dehumanize their opponents and collapse the middle ground; where Republican Senate filibusters block Clinton's initiatives, and Democratic Senate filibusters entangle the Republican revolution; where Clinton produces a purist health care reform proposal that loses public confidence and congressional Republicans replicate the mistake with an overly ideological plan to balance the federal budget; in which both sides resist the clamor for true political reform because they believe they can manipulate the existing system to their advantage; where interest groups in both parties equate compromise with betrayal. It is democracy at twenty paces.

For the two major parties, the struggle in the second contest demands the opposite behavior. The underlying economic and cultural trends in American life are likely to continue breeding dissatisfaction with the nation's direction, especially among voters without college educations, the group facing the most severe strain on their living standards. Against that backdrop, rebuilding trust in the political system will not be easy. If the parties have any chance to restore public confidence and tamp down the agitation for new alternatives, it is to cultivate common ground in Washington that returns to Americans a sense that their government is conducting the public business in a reasoned and reassuring manner and responding to the demands for reform. A politics aimed at quelling alienation would begin in the spirit of Reinhold Niebuhr: recognizing that while it may not be in our capacity to cure through public policy the nation's underlying economic and cultural dilemmas, we remain obligated to seek improvements wherever we can — "to push hard against an age that is pushing very hard against us," as Bill Bennett has written.

Here the tools are plowshares, not swords. American opinion on government is divided and inconsistent, but beneath their conflicting impulses, most Americans recognize that neither unbounded government nor the unshackled market offers the best hope of progress against the complex problems we face. Just as the public recoiled against Democratic efforts to expand and enlarge government during Clinton's first two years, polls showed Americans increasingly wary of Republican efforts to shrink government in 1995. Voters may already be ahead of the political world in recognizing the need for a blend of public and private responses. In 1995, the pollsters Robert Teeter and Peter Hart asked a national survey whether they placed primary responsibility with the government, businesses, community leaders, or individuals to solve a lengthy list of social problems, from providing income assistance to the needy to improving education and moral values and controlling crime and pollution. In almost every instance a substantial number of those polled looked to government for solutions, but in only two instances did an absolute majority look to government. In most cases, a majority divided responsibility between government and the other elements of society — individuals, community groups, and businesses.

That instinctively moderate response points toward the road not taken in the cacophonous struggle between the two parties — toward a political debate that neither demonizes nor lionizes government, but recognizes it as a tool, a means for Americans to work collectively against problems too large for them to master alone. Major reform in the federal government is now inevitable: The revolution in information technology that has undermined centralized bureaucracies in business is equally irresistible in the public sector. No matter which party holds power, the federal government in ten years will be smaller relative to the economy; more streamlined; and searching for new means to fulfill its mandates. "There is only one direction things can go," one White House aide said the day after Clinton introduced his own plan to balance the budget.

Conservatives are right that, in the future, Americans will be less likely to look to Washington for answers. But liberals are surely correct that Americans will not want their federal government to simply throw up its hands and abandon the task of building a good society to the whims of the market. Both parties have acted with misplaced certitude — as if a single key could unlock these doors. But more than either side will admit, each is perplexed by the economic and cultural changes transforming American life, and groping for new directions. "We don't have an overall, overarching, compelling thesis for the future of the country," admits Jeffrey Eisenach, the president of the Gingrich-inspired think tank, the Progress and Freedom Foundation. Indeed, the events of 1995 have made clear that, even within the antigovernment coalition, several distinct visions of conservatism are now contending for dominance.

The truth is that *neither* party can say it knows how to reverse the rising rate of illegitimacy, or to integrate the isolated urban poor into the economic and social mainstream, or to restore economic security for working families. The limits of their knowledge should encourage humility, compromise, and the willingness to experiment with many alternatives. And yet all indications suggest that neither party is eager to find common ground. Both sides appear more comfortable shouting from across the room than sitting down at the kitchen table to work out their differences. This approach exposes both parties to more risk than they appear to realize. The reflexive resistance of many Democrats to any reforms in the federal government risks entombing their party in the past — as the voice of those forces committed to resisting irresistible change. The mechanical tendency of many Republicans to blame all problems on the federal government threatens to widen the disconnect between Americans and their leaders to an extent that disables both parties.

Republicans now define the terms of debate in American politics. But by sowing the wind of anger at Washington and the political system, Republicans may ultimately reap the whirlwind of radical political change that endangers them as much as the Democrats. As a political project, the Republican agenda has been an enormous success, for it has encouraged many Americans to believe that the economic and cultural trends unsettling national life are rooted in misguided government policies pursued by an insular political class. But in fact, while government may have exacerbated, or failed to solve, problems such as stagnant incomes and the eroding family structure, these are complex phenomena rooted in global forces, and unlikely to be reversed simply by terminating government programs.

Many of the underlying changes in political habits and attitudes point toward the Republicans as a new majority party. But these changes still lack the glue that bound together earlier majority coalitions: public faith that political change will produce a brighter, more prosperous future. Discontent is a powerful solvent; but the only proven adhesive in American politics is a vision of national progress that enlarges the circle of opportunity and reconnects Americans to their leaders. If the Republican Party acquires no broader mission than retrenching government for its own sake, it has little chance of resolving the full range of economic and cultural concerns that brought it to power — and thus little chance of maintaining sustained allegiance from the swing voters who decide national elections.

Ideas matter in American politics, but results matter more. Clinton won the White House in 1992 because Americans concluded that the Bush Republicans had failed. Republicans captured Congress two years later because voters decided that Democrats had failed. If the public concludes, either in 1996 or beyond, that the Gingrich Republicans have indulged ideological extremes while failing to renew American life, the years ahead may look less like the relatively ordered division of power over the past generation and more like the chaos of the late nineteenth century — an environment in which an increasingly frustrated public turns from one party to another to choices we cannot yet imagine. Since the rise of Franklin Roosevelt, Republicans have struggled without success to regain the dominant position in American politics. They are closer now than at any point in the last sixty years. But the very forces of discontent that have carried them to this high ground may yet sweep the prize from their reach.

Acknowledgments

WE ARE INDEBTED to scores of people who have contributed directly and indirectly to our understanding of American politics and the two political parties in transition and we will not attempt to name all of them here. But some played especially important roles in the conception and execution of this book and we are particularly grateful to them.

The idea for this book came from David S. Broder of the *Washington Post*, who months before the 1994 election said there would be a need early in 1996 for a book examining the transformation of the Republican Party, and he encouraged us to undertake it. He bears no responsibility for what came after that, but for his inspiration at the beginning of this project, we are truly grateful.

We also would like to thank our researcher, Christine Egy, who kept us knee deep in background material and provided clear thinking as we scrambled to meet our deadlines.

More than two hundred elected officials, administration aides, political operatives, and political scientists made time for our questions, often more than once, and we are indebted to them all.

The editors of our respective newspapers have been generous to us, both in granting us time off to complete the manuscript during one of the busiest and liveliest political years in recent memory and in accommodating the demands of reporting and writing the book before the leave began. At the *Washington Post*, we would like to thank Leonard Downie, Bob Kaiser, Karen DeYoung, and Bill Hamilton. Political editors Bob Barnes and Maralee Schwartz helped us juggle competing demands on our time and went beyond the bounds of friendship in making this project possible. At the *Los Angeles Times*, Mike Miller, Jack Nelson, and Dick Cooper arranged for the leave that it made it possible to complete this book on a tight schedule. Richard Schlosberg and Shelby Coffey provided a supportive and encouraging environment throughout.

Other colleagues at our newspapers and elsewhere have provided insights, information, or encouragement, and while we cannot name them all, we would like to thank: Ann Devroy, Tom Edsall, E. J. Dionne Jr., Howard Kurtz, David Maraniss, Kevin Merida, Ken Cooper, Eric Pianin, Helen Dewar, Michael Weisskopf, Richard Morin, Ruth Marcus, Paul Taylor, Lou Cannon, Bob Woodward, Mary McGrory, Steve Barr, Al Kamen, Sharon Warden, Ann O'Hanlon, John Harris, Bill Booth, Bill Claiborne, Ed Walsh, Tom Kenworthy, John Yang, Marilyn Thompson, Sharon LaFraniere, Roger Simon, Marcia Kramer, Colette T. Rhoney, Bob Hillman, Joe Klein, Carin Pratt, Bob Shogan, and Bob Schieffer. Special thanks to Dale Russakoff, Charles Babcock, and Serge Kovaleski of the *Washington Post* for their exceptional reporting on Newt Gingrich.

At the *Los Angeles Times*, John Broder, Elizabeth Shogren, and Janet Hook shared information on questions that arose while writing this book. Maloy Moore helped to ferret out fugitive facts throughout. John Brennan, Susan Pinkus, and Claudia Vaughn provided detailed information and creative analysis of many public opinion surveys. Pat Luevano and Santa Traugott of the Center for Political Studies at the University of Michigan provided data graciously and expeditiously. Bruce Blakeman of The Wirthlin Group provided historical polling data at a critical moment. Ruy Teixeira shared his own insightful analysis of exit polls from the past several elections. Lawrence Mishel and Gary Burtless patiently explained income trends to reporters who specialize in politics. Lee C. Smith, Kathleen Frankovic, Peter Hart, Geoff Garin, Ed Goeas, Mike Baselice, and George Shipley also provided polling data and analysis, while Kim Brace of Election Data Services gave us a wealth of 1992 national data. Cheryl Rubin opened the archives at the Heritage Foundation to help us track the evolution of conservative thought on social policy.

Many friends and colleagues took the time to review chapters. None of them bear responsibility for any mistakes that remain, but all improved the product: John King, Charlie Cook, Stuart Rothenberg, Vin Weber, Richard Cohen of National Journal, Paul Burka, Earl Black, Lee Bandy, Pete Wehner, David Whitman, David Lauter, Michael Duffy, and Mark Halperin.

Olwen Price transcribed hours of tapes skillfully and quickly.

Our editor, Fredi Friedman, guided us through the project with a firm hand and a wealth of insights. Jacquie Miller at Little, Brown kept us on schedule.

Our agent, Robert Barnett, was enthusiastic from the moment we first approached him with the idea of the book and has been both friend and adviser at every step of the process.

Throughout the writing of this book, our families sustained — and survived — this collaboration. Ronald Brownstein benefited from the encouragement of his mother, his brother, and his sister — and the patience and affection of his wife, Nina Easton, who not only accepted in good humor the burden of becoming a single parent for the better part of a year and losing her own office, but also shared her own research, interviews, and insights on the conservative movement. Taylor and Daniel Brownstein managed to keep themselves out of their dad's office — even when they were sure something much more fun than whatever they were doing was going on within. One of the greatest satisfactions in finishing this book comes in being able to resume with them the basement baseball season that its writing interrupted.

Dan Balz thanks his mother for her enthusiastic support throughout the project, as well as the encouragement of his brother, and regrets that his father did not live to see this book produced. He is even more indebted to his wife, Nancy Balz, for love and long friendship, and for encouragement throughout this project in spite of the disruptions that came with it. She has been through this with other authors, but never in quite so intimate a way. Her office and dining room may now return to normal. She is truly special. John Balz accepted with good humor the presence of his father around the house all summer, which is probably not a teenager's first wish, and contributed more than he knows to the finished product.

Finally, we thank all of the American families who have over the last decade shared their thoughts with us on doorsteps, in shopping malls, at county fairs, and at campaign rallies. It is from these conversations that we have learned the most about hopes and fears shaping the ongoing and unfinished revolution in American politics.

Notes and Sources

UNLESS OTHERWISE NOTED, the direct quotations in this book come from interviews by the authors with the person quoted; a few otherwise uncited quotations come from someone who attended the meeting where the quote was made.

INTRODUCTION

The quote from Bob Dole comes from the Sept. 20, 1995, issue of the *Washington Post*. The description of Gibbons's tirade comes from the *Washington Post* and the *New York Times* of Sept. 21, 1995, while the events in the House Commerce Committee and the protests on the Capitol grounds are described in the Sept. 23, 1995, editions of the *Washington Post*.

Walter Dean Burnham reported that George Bush suffered the fourth-largest election-to-election decline in his article "The Politics of Repudiation," in *The American Prospect*, winter 1993, p. 25. Burnham is also the source for the simultaneous decline of incumbent vote shares in both parties in 1990; see *The Clinton Presidency: First Appraisals*, edited by Colin Campbell and Bert A. Rockman (Chatham, N.J.: Chatham House, 1995), p. 369. The observation that Americans have viewed the nation as on the wrong track for most of the past ten years is based on polling data provided by the Wirthlin Group. For American attitudes toward generational advance and doubts about the future, see "The American Dream: Renewing the Promise," by Frank Luntz, released by the Hudson Institute on Dec. 8, 1994, pp. 21–22.

The discussion of the basic trends underlying political turmoil draws partially

377

on material included in Ronald Brownstein's article in the *Los Angeles Times Magazine* of May 5, 1994, entitled "The New Age of Anxiety."

On living standards, many sources were valuable. Lawrence Mishel and Jared Bernstein, *The State of Working America, 1994–95* (Armonk, N.Y.: M. E. Sharpe, 1994), is an invaluable resource; see pp. 140–146 for analysis of the wage experience of workers at different education levels. See p. 34 for the table showing that the two-earner couple was the only form of family whose median income increased in the twenty years after 1973. For the U.S. position as the nation with the widest income gap between rich and poor, see Gary Burtless and Timothy Smeeding, "America's Tide: Lifting the Yachts, Swamping the Rowboats," the *Washington Post*, dated June 15, 1995. A paper by Burtless, a senior fellow at the Brookings Institution, and Lynn A. Karoly of Rand Corp., entitled "Demographic Change, Rising Earnings Inequality and the Distribution of Personal Well-Being, 1959–1989," shows that per-person income for the families clustered around the center of the income ladder annually increased only half as fast in the 1980s as it did in the 1970s, and just one-quarter as rapidly as it did during the 1960s. Similar findings of middle-class income stagnation are contained in a Congressional Budget Office study of income trends included in the 1993 *Green Book*, published by the House Committee on Ways and Means; see, particularly, p. 1405. Also see testimony by Karoly to the House Committee on Ways and Means Subcommittee on Human Resources on Oct. 26, 1993, for detailed analysis of wage trends. The observation that the median family income would not double again for centuries is included in the 1994 "Economic Report of the President," p. 115.

Data on the earnings experience of workers in their prime years is taken from Stephen J. Rose, "On Shaky Ground: Rising Fears About Incomes and Earnings" (Washington, D.C.: National Commission for Employment Policy, 1994). See, particularly, tables on pp. 20 and 31. For Carnevale's observation about enhanced job insecurity, see p. viii. Also see Rose's article "Declining Family Incomes in the 1980s: New Evidence from Longitudinal Data," in *Challenge* magazine, Nov.–Dec. 1993. For data on the changing composition of displaced workers, see Bureau of Labor Statistics report "Displaced Workers, 1991–92" (July 1995). For more optimistic views on the income picture, see Karl Zinsmeister, "Payday Mayday," in *The American Enterprise*, Sept.–Oct. 1995; Alan Reynolds's essay in *The New Promise of American Life*, edited by Lamar Alexander and Chester E. Finn Jr. (Indianapolis: The Hudson Institute, 1995); Marvin H. Kosters's testimony to the House Ways and Means Subcommittee on Human Resources, dated Oct. 26, 1993; and "It Just Seems Like We're Worse Off," by Paul Richter, in the *Los Angeles Times* of Jan. 26, 1995.

On family structure, the best source is the Census Bureau. See "Household and Family Characteristics: March 1993," by Steve W. Rawlings (June 1994), p. xv, for the rising share of children under eighteen living with only one parent. On divorce rates, see Census report "Marriage, Divorce, and Remarriage in the 1990s," by Arthur J. Norton and Louisa F. Miller (Oct. 1992). On divorce and out-of-

wedlock birthrates, a useful compendium is William J. Bennett, *The Index of Leading Cultural Indicators: Facts and Figures on the State of American Society* (New York: Touchstone, 1994); see p. 48 for National Center for Health Statistics data on out-of-wedlock birthrates in major cities and p. 46 for the overall rate. Sociologist Lee Rainwater projected an out-of-wedlock birthrate of 40 percent in testimony to the Senate Finance Committee on Oct. 19, 1993.

The best source of public attitudes toward government over time is the National Election Study conducted by the University of Michigan Center for Political Studies; it is the source of all the poll data in this section. Fred Steeper's intriguing analysis about the two forms of public discontent with government appears in "Who Will Reconnect with the People: Republicans, Democrats, or . . . None of the Above," published by *Americans Talk Issues* in Aug. 1995; see pp. 4–10.

Bill Clinton's quotes are taken from his announcement address on Oct. 3, 1991, and from an address at Georgetown University on Nov. 20, 1991.

1. THE WHIRLWIND

Information about the Second Congressional District in Kentucky comes from Michael Barone and Grant Ujifusa's *The Almanac of American Politics 1996* (Washington: National Journal, 1995), pp. 549–551; from Philip D. Duncan and Christine C. Lawrence's *Politics in America, 1996* (Washington, D.C.: Congressional Quarterly, 1995), pp. 532–533; and from an article, "Kentucky Derby," by Al Cross, in the July 1994 issue of *Campaigns & Elections* magazine. Some of the information about the special election in Oklahoma comes from David Beiler's "Return of the Plainsman" in the same issue of *Campaigns & Elections*. Information about the role of independent, conservative groups in the special elections comes in part from an article by Al Cross in the June 5, 1994, *Louisville Courier-Journal* and from a complaint filed with the Federal Election Commission by the Democratic Congressional Campaign Committee. The Gingrich and Greenberg quotations about the Kentucky election come from an article in the *Washington Post* on May 26, 1995.

Background on the political landscape comes both from interviews and a number of polls. Particularly helpful were David S. Broder and Richard Morin's report on a survey of attitudes about Congress in the July 3, 1994, issue of the *Washington Post*, as well as the Times Mirror Center for The People & The Press survey, *The New Political Landscape*, issued in Sept. 1994, and a report on focus groups conducted by Democratic pollsters Peter Hart and Geoff Garin. "The only certainty" line comes from John Reilly, a veteran of many Democratic campaigns. Haley Barbour's comments about where the party went astray come from the text of the speech he delivered to the Republican Governors' Association on Nov. 16, 1992. Don Fierce of the Republican National Committee provided descriptions of the RNC's efforts to reach out to religious conservatives and other grassroots antigovernment groups. Albert Mitchler of the Republican National

Committee provided copies of the committee's direct mail pieces, from which several quotations are drawn.

In the section dealing with the role of Newt Gingrich, quotations from Gingrich come from a number of interviews we conducted, beginning in July 1993 and running through July 1995. Descriptions of Joe Gaylord's battle plan come directly from the document, a copy of which was made available to us. A number of Republican officials provided information about the development of the Contract With America; the information included videotapes of the Raleigh and Denver focus groups, memoranda by Ed Goeas and Frank Luntz summarizing their research, copies of the mock-ups of the *TV Guide* ad for the Contract, internal memos from the staff of Representative Dick Armey, strategy memos from Barry Jackson and Chuck Greener outlining to Republican candidates how to counter Democratic attacks against the Contract, and documents prepared for Republican candidates. The interview with Dianne Feinstein took place on Sept. 25, 1994. Background on the GOP message comes from scripts of the television commercials or from our own reporting at the time. Conclusions about the impact of Clinton's health care plan on the electorate comes from a post-election survey entitled "The Revolt Against Politics," conducted Nov. 8–9, 1994, by Stanley B. Greenberg for the Democratic Leadership Council and released Nov. 17, 1994.

Information about Republican fund-raising comes from interviews with several of the principals involved, as well as from official reports and analyses. Haley Barbour, Scott Reed, and Bill Paxon were particularly helpful in describing the GOP plans and the financial plight of the National Republican Congressional Committee. Gingrich's fund-raising letter to his House colleagues was made available to us by a GOP official. Gingrich's comments to PAC directors come from an interview on Oct. 13, 1994, while his warning of the "two coldest years in Washington" comes from a report by Glenn R. Simpson in the weekly newspaper *Roll Call,* dated Oct. 6, 1994. Reports by the Federal Election Commission and a series of excellent studies by Common Cause show the extent to which the GOP plan succeeded. Gary Jacobson's "The 1994 House Elections in Perspective," a paper delivered at the Midwest Political Science Association meeting, Apr. 6–8, 1995, contains an excellent analysis of the impact of money on House campaigns. Also helpful is Larry Makinson's article in the June 15, 1995, issue of "Capital Eye," a publication of the Center for Responsive Politics, and Joshua Goldstein's "PACs in Profile," also published by the Center.

The description of Gingrich's anger over Bill Paxon's projection comes from interviews with Paxon, John Morgan, and another official who did not want to be identified. The description of the discussion about Gingrich's becoming Speaker comes from Gingrich's *To Renew America* (New York: HarperCollins, 1995), pp. 116–117, and from the recollections of Joe Gaylord. The interview with Leon Panetta took place Oct. 13, 1994. Gingrich's comments about the Contract and the Democrats come from an interview on Oct. 17, 1994. The quotation from

Bill McInturff about Clinton's overseas trip was made to Ann Devroy of the *Washington Post* and was published Oct. 20, 1994.

The section about Election Day and the aftermath relies heavily on exit poll data from VNS-NES and Mitofsky International, the two principal exit polling organizations in 1994. One of the most helpful sources of information after the election was *Congressional Quarterly* magazine and, in particular, the reporting of Rhodes Cook. Figures about the surge in GOP votes come from Cook's article "Rare Combination of Forces May Make History of '94," in the Apr. 15, 1995, issue. Several other studies helped illuminate the results of the 1994 elections. Among them are Fred Steeper's "This Surge Is Different," published in the *Cook Political Report*, Feb. 8, 1995; Stanley B. Greenberg's "The Conservative Republican Surge and the Democratic Reaction," a monograph published in July 1995; "How the Republicans Captured the House," by David W. Brady, John F. Cogan, and Douglas Rivers, published in the *Cook Political Report*, Feb. 8, 1995; and "The Republican Tidal Wave of 1994: Testing Hypotheses About Realignment, Restructuring, and Rebellion," by Alfred J. Tuchfarber, Stephen E. Bennett, Andrew E. Smith, and Eric W. Rademacher, a paper presented at the American Political Association meeting, Sept. 1, 1995. Gary Jacobson's "1994 House Elections," cited above, also provides useful insights into the dynamics of the 1994 vote.

The description of Gingrich on the morning after the election comes from the notes and recollections of Dale Russakoff of the *Washington Post*.

2. THE CLINTON IMPASSE

President Clinton's comments in the opening section are taken from an interview we conducted with him in San Francisco on Sunday, Nov. 6, 1994. Stanley B. Greenberg's acknowledgment that voters "revolted against Democratic-dominated national politics" comes from "The Third Force: Why Independents Turned Against Democrats — and How to Win Them Back" (Washington, D.C.: Democratic Leadership Council, 1994), p. 1.

Useful sources on the decline of the Democratic presidential coalition that began in 1968 include James L. Sundquist, *Dynamics of the Party System: Alignment and Realignment of Political Parties in the United States* (Washington, D.C.: The Brookings Institution, 1983); Stephen E. Ambrose, *Nixon: The Triumph of a Politician, 1962–1972* (New York: Simon & Schuster, 1989), p. 557; Stanley B. Greenberg, *Middle Class Dreams: The Politics and Power of the New American Majority* (New York: Times Books, 1995); Thomas Byrne Edsall and Mary D. Edsall, *Chain Reaction: The Impact of Race, Rights, and Taxes on American Politics* (New York: W. W. Norton, 1991); E. J. Dionne Jr., *Why Americans Hate Politics* (New York: Simon & Schuster, 1991); and Kevin P. Phillips, *The Emerging Republican Majority* (New Rochelle, N.Y.: Arlington House, 1969). Lionel Trilling's observation on the dominance of liberalism is reprinted in Dionne, p. 56. Nixon's intention to frame the 1972 election as a choice between "square America and radical America" is noted in Ambrose, p. 557. Sundquist (p. 394) reports that 80 percent of Wallace 1968 voters backed Nixon in 1972.

Randall Rothenberg's *The Neoliberals: Creating the New American Politics* (New York: Simon & Schuster, 1984) provides a good overview on neoliberal thought, particularly its economic focus. The most useful texts for tracing the similarities and divergence between neoliberals and the Democratic Leadership Council are speeches and policy statements from the period. For the DLC, see, particularly, Chuck Robb's speeches at Hofstra University (Apr. 12, 1986) and George Mason University (Mar. 27, 1987), as well as at the National Press Club (Apr. 3, 1986), the Commonwealth Club (July 22, 1986), and the Federal City Council (Sept. 9, 1986). The seminal DLC document on electoral politics is William A. Galston and Elaine Kamarck, "The Politics of Evasion" (Washington, D.C.: Progressive Policy Institute, 1989). For neoliberals, Gary Hart's campaign speeches were useful, particularly his remarks to the Democratic National Convention (July 18, 1984); at the University of Texas (May 24, 1986); to the DLC itself (Oct. 10, 1985); and, on family, at Trinity University (Feb. 2, 1986).

Ruy Teixeira's analysis of exit poll data from 1988 yielded the information that Bush carried a majority of white men at every income level. Key works that track the evolution of Stan Greenberg's thinking include "Report on Democratic Defection" (The Analysis Group, 1985); "From Crisis to Working Majority," *The American Prospect* (fall 1991); and "Liberalism: Beyond the Great Society and New Deal" (The Analysis Group, 1989).

Clinton's thoughts poured forth in a torrent of interviews, television appearances, and speeches during the 1992 campaign. To list all of those would rival this book at length. Particularly important statements were his speech to the DLC on May 6, 1991; his announcement address on Oct. 3, 1991; and the three "New Covenant" speeches that he delivered at Georgetown University in the fall of 1991. Also see "Putting People First: A National Economic Strategy for America" (June 21, 1992). We also relied heavily on interviews we conducted with Clinton before and during his candidacy and after his election.

On Clinton in office, both Bob Woodward's *The Agenda: Inside the Clinton White House* (New York: Simon & Schuster, 1994) and Elizabeth Drew's *On the Edge* (New York: Simon & Schuster, 1994) are energetic, thoroughly reported works (though we reach different conclusions about the causes of Clinton's problems). The suggestion from Galston and Kamarck that Clinton appoint a bipartisan government is contained in Will Marshall and Martin Schram, *Mandate for Change* (New York: Berkley Books, 1993), p. 325. David Obey's denunciation of Clinton was reported in the *Washington Post* on Jan. 1, 1992. Fred Wertheimer recounted the internal congressional politics that derailed campaign finance reform in "How Money Beat Change" in the *Washington Post*, Oct. 10, 1994.

For Clinton's handling of welfare and crime, we have relied mostly on our own interviews with principals while the events were unfolding. *Congressional Quarterly* was an invaluable resource on both the budget and health care fights, as was the reporting in the *Los Angeles Times* of Ed Chen and David Lauter. The *Los*

Angeles Times on Nov. 11, 1993, reported the conciliatory signals over health care from Bob Dole and Haley Barbour. In a recap of the health care fight, the *New York Times* on Aug. 29, 1994, showed opposition to the plan crossing support in early 1994.

The figure on the share of Democrats that had never served with a President from their own party comes from "Leadership Test" by Richard E. Cohen in the *National Journal* on Mar. 13, 1993; Cohen's reporting on Congress was an indispensable asset for us in all areas we examined. Our analysis of the Democrats' contracting base in the 1994 election is based on exit polls conducted by Voter News Service. Two other analyses of the results were especially helpful: Greenberg, "The Conservative Surge and the Democratic Reaction" (1995); and Ruy Teixeira, "What Kind of New Democrat Should Bill Clinton Be?" (Washington, D.C.: Economic Policy Institute, 1994).

3. THE LONG MARCH

This chapter draws considerably from a four-part series published in the *Washington Post*, Dec. 18–21, 1994, written by Dale Russakoff, Charles Babcock, Serge Kovaleski, and Dan Balz. Descriptions of the opening day of the 104th Congress come from our own reporting and from various newspaper reports. The quotation from radio talk show host Bill Cunningham comes from an article by Howard Kurtz in the *Washington Post*, Jan. 5, 1995. Gingrich made the comment about his rise to power in an interview on Dec. 16, 1994.

In the section describing the formation of the Conservative Opportunity Society, all quotations unless otherwise noted come from interviews with the authors. Particularly helpful were Vin Weber, Bob Walker, Connie Mack, Steve Gunderson, Nancy Johnson, Tom Tauke, and Gingrich. Some of the quotations previously appeared in the *Washington Post* series on Gingrich. Judd Gregg was helpful in providing some of the early COS memos and documents. The dispute over the Indiana election in 1985 draws on our reporting from the time, but the quotation by Gingrich about possible disruptions to the House comes from an article he wrote in the *Cedartown (Ga.) Standard* on May 14, 1985. Background on Fernand St Germain's ethical problems comes from Michael Barone and Grant Ujifusa's *The Almanac of American Politics 1988* (Washington, D.C.: National Journal, 1987). John M. Barry's *The Ambition and the Power* (New York: Viking, 1989), a book about the speakership of James C. Wright of Texas, is a particularly helpful source in understanding the fight between Gingrich and Wright. Gingrich's quote about having led "a human life" comes from an interview with Dale Russakoff on Dec. 16, 1994. Gingrich's quotation about using the press to force an investigation of Wright comes from John Barry's book. Wright's quote likening his feelings about Gingrich to a dog and a hydrant was widely published during the investigation into his finances, while his quote about Gingrich as a nihilist comes from a newspaper column he wrote shortly after the 1994 elections. It was quoted in the *Washington Post* on Dec. 20, 1994. Descriptions of Wright's resignation come from articles by Tom Kenworthy and Don Phillips published in the *Washington Post*, June 1–3, 1989.

In the section about Gingrich's battles with Republicans in the 1980s, the quotes from Bob Dole about supply-side economics come from an article by Hobart Rowen in the *Washington Post*, Sept. 5, 1982. Quotes from Barber Conable and Dole during the Senate debate over taxes in 1982 come from an article in the *New York Times*, Aug. 8, 1982, and from the Congressional Record of July 19, 1982, p. 16907. Gingrich's criticism of the bill is contained in a release from his office dated Aug. 13, 1982. Praise for Dole's role and Dole's defense of the bill comes from articles by Rudolph Penner in the *New York Times* dated Sept. 12, 1982, and from a profile of Dole by Haynes Johnson of the *Washington Post* dated Aug. 23, 1982. The "tax collector for the welfare state" has been widely quoted. The fight over the 1984 Republican platform draws from a number of newspaper reports the week of the convention, including the *Washington Post*, the *New York Times*, and *Human Events*. Dole's comment about the "young hypocrites" was quoted in the *New York Times* on Sept. 9, 1984. The 1985 budget fight draws from material in the 1985 *Congressional Quarterly Almanac* (Washington, D.C.: Congressional Quarterly, 1986), p. 456.

The section about the 1990 budget fight draws on our own reporting at the time, subsequent interviews, and on several interviews conducted by Bob Woodward that were used in the *Washington Post* series on Gingrich. The quotation from Dick Armey about Bush comes from Armey's book, *The Freedom Revolution* (Washington, D.C.: Regnery Publishing, 1995), pp. 86–87. Gingrich's whip race draws from a number of interviews with participants. Particularly helpful were Steve Gunderson, Vin Weber, Bob Walker, Ed Rollins, and Jerry Lewis. Gingrich's quotation describing how he "changed the party" comes from an interview on July 28, 1993. Tom DeLay's criticism of the Bush White House was during an interview on July 13, 1995. Descriptions of Bush's decision to renounce his no-new-taxes pledge come from our reporting at the time with the major participants, but some of Gingrich's recollections are from an interview on July 12, 1995. Walter F. Mondale's praise for Bush comes from an article in the *New York Times* dated July 3, 1990. Richard Darman's quotation indicating that Gingrich had not indicated he would oppose the budget plan in 1990 was published in the *Washington Post* on Dec. 21, 1994. Some of the background on the package comes from the 1990 *Congressional Quarterly Almanac* (Washington, D.C.: Congressional Quarterly, 1991), p. 132, while Dole's quotes critical of Gingrich and others were made on NBC's *Meet the Press* on Sept. 16, 1990. Republican criticism of the plan as "the fiscal equivalent of Yalta" comes from the *Washington Post*, Oct. 1, 1990.

In the section describing Gingrich's expanding circle of power, the initial quotation comes from the *Washington Post* of Dec. 21, 1994. The polling cited as an example of the slight increase in support for Washington "to take action" is a *Washington Post*–ABC News poll in 1988 showing that 45 percent of Americans favored a larger government, 49 percent a smaller government. Weber's quotation about the lack of domestic initiatives in the Bush administration comes from an interview on June 7, 1995. Gingrich's quotation about capturing "seventy or eighty percent of the incoming freshman class" comes from his Dec. 16, 1994, interview. His quote about shifting "the entire planet" is cited in the *Washington Post* series on Dec. 20, 1994. The "transformational figure" self-description was made in an Oct. 17, 1994, interview. Gingrich's letters about GOPAC's goals comes from the *Washington Post* of Oct. 2, 1995. The description of Armey as a "one-man think tank" comes from "Conservatives, Ahoy!," by Vin Weber in the Feb. 15, 1993, issue of the *National Review*. Armey described his note to Dick Darman during an interview on July 1, 1995. The quote describing conservative ambitions comes from Armey's *The Freedom Revolution*, pp. 285–286. Descriptions of the unrest among conservative backbenchers in the early 1990s come from interviews with a number of the participants, including Jim Nussle, John Boehner, Frank Luntz, and Tom Tauke. The quote from Mark Foley about the Class of 1994 comes from an article by Francis X Clines in the *New York Times* dated Aug. 6, 1994.

The final section of the chapter comes from interviews with a number of the participants in the budget deliberations, including Bob Dole, Dick Armey, Newt Gingrich, John Kasich, and Don Fierce. Dole's decision to sign the tax pledge and the description of his meeting with Grover G. Norquist come from an interview with Norquist.

4. LEAVE US ALONE

The description of the National Rifle Association annual convention is based on our notes from the event. The demographic interlinks between small-business proprietors, conservative Christians, and gun owners are taken from a poll conducted by Frank Luntz immediately after the 1994 election. Kellyanne Fitzpatrick provided special cross-tabs central to the analysis.

On talk radio generally, see Murray B. Levin, *Talk Radio and the American Dream* (Lexington, Mass.: D. C. Heath & Co., 1987). Also helpful is *Congressional Quarterly Researcher*, "Talk Show Democracy," Apr. 29, 1994. The Association of Talk Radio Hosts and Michael Harrison, editor and publisher of *Talkers* magazine, provided information on the growth of talk radio; *Talkers* is an important resource for anyone following the medium's growth. Bob Dornan's comments about his opponents were recounted in Michael Barone and Grant Ujifusa, *The Almanac of American Politics 1988* (Washington, D.C.: National Journal, 1987), p. 164. For the mobilization of New Jersey talk radio against Jim Florio, see the *New York Times* of July 17, 1990, "Anti-Tax Station Turns FM into Florio Mashing." On Limbaugh's career and thought, a good place to start are his two books, *The Way Things Ought to Be* (New York: Pocket Books, 1992), and *See, I Told You So* (New York: Pocket Books, 1993). His lengthy articulation of the classic conservative populist argument is taken from *See*, p. 19. Especially useful magazine articles on Limbaugh include "Bull Rush" by Peter Boyer in the May 1992 *Vanity Fair*, and James Bowman's "The Leader of the Opposition" in the Sept. 6, 1993, *National*

Review; Boyer also reported on the *Frontline* documentary on Limbaugh that aired Feb. 28, 1995. John Fund's article "The Power of Talk" in the spring 1995 issue of *Forbes Media Critic* looks at Limbaugh within the context of the broader conservative mobilization of talk radio. Richard Berke's Mar. 12, 1995, piece in the *New York Times*, entitled "The Legman for Limbaugh," underscored his impact in Republican circles. See the *Washington Times* of Mar. 12, 1995, for the result when Limbaugh urged his listeners to criticize media reporting of the school lunch controversy.

For the controversy over Limbaugh's accuracy, see FAIR, *The Way Things Aren't: Rush Limbaugh's Reign of Error* (New York: New Press, 1995) and Limbaugh's responses: his article "Voice of America" in the fall 1994 issue of the Heritage Foundation's *Policy Review* and his undated paper "Responding to FAIR'S Charges Printed by Major Print Media Outlets." For public opinion about talk radio in general and Limbaugh in particular, we relied heavily on "The Vocal Minority in American Politics," released by the Times Mirror Center for The People & The Press on July 16, 1993, and an unreleased memo from Kim Parker at the center entitled "Men, Women, and Rush Limbaugh" (Dec. 1994). Clinton's frustration at Limbaugh is recounted in the *Los Angeles Times* of June 25, 1994 (and was also repeated during our conversation with him on Nov. 6, 1994).

On conservative populism generally, one good recent source is Michael Kazin, *The Populist Persuasion: An American History* (New York: Basic Books, 1995). Kazin recounts the populist use of the term "plain people" (p. 28) and Wallace's denunciation of the professor who "can't park his bicycle straight" (p. 236). Americans for Limited Terms' undated direct mail letter, fall 1994, provides the quote on "career politicians." Two helpful general articles are "The New Populism," in the Mar. 13, 1995, issue of *Business Week*, and "Today's GOP: The Party's Over for Big Business," in the Feb. 6, 1995, issue of *Forbes*. The remarks from Jack Faris, Wayne LaPierre, and Ralph Reed are drawn from Jack Faris, *Small Business Under Siege* (Nashville: Hammock Publishing, 1994), p. 3; the *San Diego Union-Tribune* of Apr. 3, 1994, for LaPierre; and Ralph Reed, *Politically Incorrect: The Emerging Faith Factor in American Politics* (Dallas: Word Publishing, 1994), p. 83.

On term limits generally, see Gerald Benjamin and Michael J. Malbin, *Limiting Legislative Terms* (Washington, D.C.: Congressional Quarterly, 1992); *Congressional Quarterly Researcher*, "Testing Term Limits," Nov. 18, 1994; and Patrick B. McGuigan, "Better Sooner than Later: How the Oklahoma Term Limitation Initiative Came to Pass" (paper delivered to the Western Political Science Association, Mar. 21–23, 1991). U.S. Term Limits provided the figures on the margin of victory for term limit initiatives. Ed Crane's comments on officeholders are taken from Edward H. Crane and Roger Pilon, *The Politics and Law of Term Limits* (Washington, D.C.: Cato Institute, 1994), p. 12.

Osha Gray Davidson, *Under Fire: The NRA and the Battle for Gun Control* (New York: Henry Holt, 1993), provides an excellent overview of the NRA's relationship with George Bush and of the organization's political role in general. The decline in Bush's share of the vote among evangelical voters is taken from the exit poll data presented in the *New York Times* of Nov. 5, 1992.

For background on Grover Norquist, see "Meet the Antitax Man" by Jeff Shear in *National Journal,* dated June 25, 1994. Norquist's political column in *The American Spectator* is a good window to his thinking, as is his article "Prelude to a Landslide: How Republicans Will Sweep the Congress" in the fall 1993 issue of *Policy Review.* (He predicted the triumph would come in 1996.) For the small-business and conservative attack against Bill Archey, see "Deal Us In" by Kirk Victor in the Apr. 3, 1993, *National Journal.*

The National Rifle Association has drawn extensive journalistic and academic attention. Among the most useful sources for NRA thinking are Davidson, *Under Fire*; Wayne LaPierre, *Guns, Crime, and Freedom* (Washington, D.C.: Regnery Publishing, 1994); as well as back issues of the NRA's magazine, *American Rifleman.* Helpful newspaper and magazine articles include "Recoil from the NRA's Two Top Guns" by Kim Masters in the *Washington Post* of Apr. 29, 1995; "The Fight to Bear Arms" in the May 22, 1995, issue of *U.S. News & World Report*; "Why They Shoot" by Philip Weiss in the *New York Times Magazine,* dated Sept. 11, 1994; and "Firepower" by Charles Mahtesian in the Mar. 1994 issue of *Governing.* Celinda Lake graciously provided detailed analysis of polling conducted for *U.S. News* on gun owners. John Brennan also provided data from the *Los Angeles Times* poll on gun owners. Tanya Metaksa's clash with Warren Cassidy was recounted in "She's Gunning at Legislation" by Peter H. Stone in the *National Journal,* dated June 25, 1994; Stone has written several helpful articles on the NRA. Neal Knox suggested a conspiracy in the assassinations of the Kennedys and King in a column entitled "Another Coincidence," reprinted in the *Shotgun News.* The *Washington Post* of Apr. 29, 1995, revealed that someone posted a bomb recipe on an NRA bulletin board. LaPierre's description of gun ownership as "the ultimate safeguard" against tyranny comes from *Guns,* p. 167.

Figures on the voting behavior of groups in the conservative populist coalition come from the VNS exit poll and Frank Luntz' post-election survey. LaPierre's description of "jack-booted thugs" was contained in an Apr. 1995 fund-raising letter reprinted in the *Washington Post* on Apr. 28, 1995.

5. DIXIE RISING

The description of the Republicans as "scarcely a party" comes from *Southern Politics in State and Nation,* by V. O. Key Jr. (Knoxville: University of Tennessee Press, 1984), p. 277. The Alexander Heard quote is taken from *The Republican Establishment: The Present and Future of the G.O.P.* (New York: Harper & Row, 1967), by Stephen Hess and David S. Broder, p. 329. The story of the east Texas votes comes from Paul Burka of *Texas Monthly.* The predictions of the Republican takeover of the South come from *The Emerging Republican Majority* (New Rochelle, N.Y.: Arlington House, 1969), by Kevin Phillips, pp. 187–208 and 286–289. Blease Graham's quote about Republican sheriffs is taken from an arti-

cle by William Booth published in the *Washington Post* on Feb. 19, 1995. Rhodes
Cook's "Dixie Voters Look Away: South Shifts to the GOP" was published in
Congressional Quarterly on Nov. 12, 1994. The figures on how many of the south-
ern congressional districts won handily by George Bush and now held by Repub-
licans come from comments provided by Earl Black of Rice University. Figures
on percentages of white men and women supporting Republican House candi-
dates come from VNS-NES exit polls.

Many of the figures in the section describing the South's economic and demo-
graphic transformation come from the Census Bureau. Median family income
figures are quoted from *U.S. News & World Report*, dated Oct. 17, 1994. The
analysis of the fastest-growing congressional districts comes from the Census Bu-
reau and was reported in the 1992 *Congressional Quarterly Almanac* (Washington,
D.C.: Congressional Quarterly). The description of southern conservatism
comes from *Politics and Society in the South* (Cambridge, Mass.: Harvard Univer-
sity Press, 1987) by Earl Black and Merle Black, p. 213. The section on the pres-
idential transformation of the South draws heavily from Earl Black and Merle
Black's *Vital South* (Cambridge, Mass.: Harvard University Press, 1992), with spe-
cific material on Eisenhower's elections from p. 189 and on the 1964 Goldwater
campaign from p. 210. The reference to Theodore H. White's *The Making of the
President 1960* (New York: Atheneum, 1961) uses material from p. 360. The ref-
erences to polls on racial perceptions of the parties comes from Thomas Byrne
Edsall and Mary D. Edsall's *Chain Reaction: The Impact of Race, Rights, and Taxes on
American Politics* (New York: W. W. Norton, 1991), p. 36. Phillips's description of
the 1968 election comes from *The Emerging Republican Majority*, pp. 35 and
286–287. Lee Atwater's study of southern politics, "The South in 1984," is a type-
script dated Apr. 1983.

The section on South Carolina and Texas relies heavily on interviews with
many of the participants, including Carroll Campbell, Warren Tompkins, Don
Fowler, David Wilkins, John Morgan, Lindsey Graham, Mark Sanford, Bob In-
glis, George W. Bush, John Sharp, Karl Rove, Karen Hughes, George Shipley,
Jack Martin, Matthew Dowd, Tom Pauken, Dick Weinhold, and many others.
Background on Strom Thurmond's role in building the Republican Party in
South Carolina comes from *Strom Thurmond and the Politics of Southern Change*
(New York: Simon & Schuster, 1993), pp. 359–360, by Nadine Cohodas. De-
scriptions of the 1986 South Carolina gubernatorial race come from a number of
newspapers. The quotation by Mike Daniel comes from an article by David
Shribman in the *Wall Street Journal*, dated Oct. 15, 1986. Figures showing the
growth in Republican voting in Texas House races come from Curtis Gans's re-
port for the Center for the Study of the American Electorate, dated June 23,
1995. Statistics showing the movement of conservative Texans out of the Dem-
ocratic Party and into the Republican Party come from analyses supplied by the
Tarrance Group and Shipley and Associates as well as from exit poll data from
CBS News and VNS-NES. Ben Ginsberg, a former official at the Republican
National Committee, helped to provide background information on the Republi-

cans' redistricting strategy. Mark Gersh of the National Committee for an Effective Congress also offered data and insights into the changing political balance in the South.

6. THE NEW REPUBLICAN AGENDA

The Supreme Court decision striking down the federal law banning guns in schools was reported in the *Los Angeles Times* on Apr. 27, 1995. The term limits case in which four Justices filed the extraordinarily sweeping dissent was *U.S. Term Limits Inc. v. Thornton*, decided on May 22, 1995. Roger Pilon's quote appeared in the *New York Times* on May 24, 1995. The fact that contemporary Republican budget cuts are more than twice the size of Reagan's efforts to reduce the growth of federal spending is based on a Congressional Budget Office estimate that Reagan's 1981 budget would have reduced federal spending by $381 billion over the next seven years. (See CBO, "The Economic and Budget Outlook: Fiscal Years 1986–1990, Feb. 1985, p. 153.) Vin Weber's lament about the future of conservative ideas appeared in his article "No Mandate for Leadership" in *Policy Review*, summer 1992. Bob Michel's limited agenda was cited in "An Offer Too Good to Refuse" by Adam Meyerson, also in *Policy Review*, winter 1995.

On Bill Kristol, several profiles were useful in addition to our own interviews. Jon Meacham's "The GOP's Master Strategist" in the Sept. 1994 issue of *Washington Monthly* was the source of Bill Bennett's remark about Kristol's DNA. Also extremely valuable was Nina Easton's "Merchants of Virtue" in the *Los Angeles Times Magazine* of Aug. 21, 1994; that article coined the term "retrocon" and explored the links between Kristol, Bennett, and Charles Murray. On the Bradley Foundation, see "Banker with a Cause" by James A. Barnes in the *National Journal* of Mar. 6, 1993. A good overview of Kristol's thinking is found in "Kristol Ball: William Kristol Looks at the Future of the GOP," an interview by Adam Meyerson in *Policy Review*, winter 1994; that is the source of his description of health care as "liberalism's Afghanistan." The best source on the thinking of Kristol and his confederates is the series of memos from the Project for the Republican Future; his denunciation of cooperation with Clinton is taken from his Sept. 26, 1994, memo. *The American Prospect* depicted Gingrich (along with Bob Dole, Phil Gramm, and Rush Limbaugh) in a black leather jacket on the cover of its spring 1995 issue.

The basic background on the cost and scope of the federal welfare program comes from several sources. Figures on the size of the welfare caseload were provided by the Department of Health and Human Services. Total government spending on the needy, and the share that is devoted to health care, is taken from "America's Failed $5.4 Trillion War on Poverty" by Robert Rector and William F. Lauber, the Heritage Foundation, June 1995. The fact that only 2 percent of welfare recipients are now widows comes from the 1993 *Green Book*, published by the House Ways and Means Committee, p. 697; information on the racial composition of the welfare caseload and the share of children born out of wedlock is contained in "Facts Related to Welfare Reform," published by Health and Human Services, Jan. 1995. That document also is the source for the $12.5 billion federal cost of welfare.

For a brief summary of Nixon's and Carter's welfare reform proposals, see "Clinton's Welfare Reforms Shaped by Predecessors' Frustrated Efforts," *Los Angeles Times*, dated June 14, 1994. For Reagan's New Federalism, see his State of the Union Address, Jan. 26, 1982. The results of the Reagan administration's internal task force were reported in Michael Novak et al., *The New Consensus on Family and Welfare* (Milwaukee: Marquette University Press, 1987), p. 80. For Bush's welfare thinking, see the White House transcript of his remarks at the Riverside Convention Center, July 31, 1992, and the media briefing the same day by Gail Wilensky. The *1988 Congressional Quarterly Almanac*, pp. 349–364, is a valuable source on the debate over the Family Support Act. The growth in the welfare rolls thereafter is reported in the *Green Book*, p. 637. Clay Shaw expressed his interest in welfare reform that guaranteed government jobs in "Moving Ahead: How America Can Reduce Poverty Through Work," a paper Shaw, Nancy L. Johnson, and Fred Grandy released in June 1992; see pp. 35–36.

The description and analysis of Tommy Thompson's welfare reform initiatives are based principally on an interview with the governor and two detailed studies: "The New Paternalism in Action," by Lawrence Mead, published by the Wisconsin Policy Research Institute in Jan. 1995; and "State Strategies for Welfare Reform: The Wisconsin Story" by Michael Wiseman, published by the Institute for Research on Poverty at the University of Wisconsin (Madison), in June 1995. The fall in the Wisconsin welfare caseload under Thompson is reported in Mead, "New Paternalism," p. 7. Other useful pieces on Thompson include "The Captains of Conservatism" by Charles Mahtesian in *Governing*, dated Feb. 1995; "Fighting Tommy Thompson" by Charles Sykes in the *National Review*, dated Aug. 12, 1991; and "Governor Get-a-Job" by Norman Atkins in the *New York Times Magazine*, dated Jan. 15, 1995.

On Jack Kemp's experience in the Bush administration, a valuable source is Jason DeParle, "How Jack Kemp Lost the War on Poverty," in the *New York Times Magazine*, Feb. 28, 1993. Other reflections on Kemp's thinking include his articles, "GOP Victory in 1988," in *Policy Review*, summer 1988; "A New Agenda for Ending Poverty," in the *Washington Post* of May 3, 1992; "Tackling Poverty," in *Policy Review*, winter 1990; and "GOP Contract — My Amendments," in the *Wall Street Journal* of Sept. 23, 1994. For Kemp's clash with Ed Koch, see the *National Review*, May 15, 1994. For his break with the party over Proposition 187, see his joint Empower America release with Bill Bennett: "A Statement on Immigration" (Oct. 19, 1995).

On the retrocons, the best source is their own voluminous writings, but several magazine pieces were helpful, including Nina Easton's "Merchants of Virtue" and Jason DeParle's profile of Murray in the *New York Times Magazine*, dated Oct. 9, 1994, entitled "Daring Research or 'Social Science Pornography?'" Murray's "thought experiment" on eliminating welfare is contained in his book *Losing*

Ground: American Social Policy, 1950–1980 (New York: Basic Books, 1984), p. 229. His proposal to eliminate welfare payments to unmarried mothers is contained in his article "The Coming White Underclass," which appeared in the *Wall Street Journal* of Oct. 29, 1993. His observation that "government has deformed the way civil society functions" was made in an interview with Nina Easton. All the quotes in his extension of that logic to welfare are taken from "The Coming White Underclass." The statement disputing Murray's arguments about illegitimacy and welfare was signed by seventy-six social scholars and released by the Center on Budget and Policy Priorities in June 1994. Clinton made his remark in an interview with Tom Brokaw on NBC, Dec. 3, 1993, that Murray had done "the country a great service."

George Will's complaint about Jack Kemp was quoted in David Frum, *Dead Right* (New York: New Republic Books, 1994), pp. 87–88. Magnet's assertion that poverty is more an economic and cultural problem is contained in his book *The Dream and The Nightmare: The Sixties' Legacy to the Underclass* (New York: Quill, 1993), pp. 15–16. Murray's anointment of illegitimacy as "the single more important" social problem is taken from "The Coming White Underclass." Bennett's analysis of "a habit of dependence" comes from Easton's article "Merchants of Virtue." For Olasky's elevation of charity over government bureaucracy, see his book *The Tragedy of American Compassion* (Washington, D.C.: Regnery Publishing, 1992), particularly p. 233. The quotes on the 1960s are taken from Olasky (p. 175), Magnet (p. 19), and Bennett's book *The De-Valuing of America: The Fight for Our Culture and Our Children* (New York: Touchstone, 1992), p. 13. Himmelfarb made her call for American leaders to "relegitimize morality" in her article "Re-Moralizing America" in the *Wall Street Journal* of Feb. 7, 1995.

For neoconservative thinking, two valuable sources are Peter Steinfels, *The Neoconservatives: The Men Who Are Changing America's Politics* (New York: Simon & Schuster, 1979), and John Ehrman, *The Rise of Neoconservatism: Intellectuals and Foreign Affairs, 1945–1994* (New Haven: Yale University Press, 1995); as the title suggests, Ehrman's work focuses mostly on foreign policy. Steinfels (p. 99) quotes Irving Kristol on the law of unintended consequences.

Gingrich made his remark about "replacing a system that is killing our children" in a speech to the Republican National Committee on Jan. 20, 1995. The dissents from the retrocon vision are found in a variety of forums. See Douglas S. Massey and Nancy A. Denton, *American Apartheid: Segregation and the Making of the Underclass* (Cambridge, Mass.: Harvard University Press, 1993), and John J. DiIulio Jr., "White Lies About Black Crime," *The Public Interest*, winter 1995. For criticism from charitable leaders, see *Los Angeles Times*, dated June 19, 1995. Kemp made his comments in an interview on Oct. 12, 1994.

For the growth in out-of-wedlock births, see William J. Bennett, *The Index of Leading Cultural Indicators: Facts and Figures on the State of American Society* (New York: Touchstone, 1994), p. 46. The article "Dan Quayle Was Right" by Barbara Dafoe Whitehead appeared in *The Atlantic Monthly*, dated Apr. 1993. For growing public anxiety about values during the late 1980s, see "American Family Values: Results of Focus Groups and Survey Research," Aug. 29, 1989, by the Democratic polling firm Mellman & Lazarus. Kristol criticized the 1992 convention in his *Policy Review* interview, winter 1994. A voluminous literature now surrounds family structure and crime; a good summary is "Family Life, Delinquency, and Crime: A Policymaker's Guide," published by the Office of Juvenile Justice and Delinquency Prevention in the Justice Department in May 1994.

The discussion of the evolution of the House Republican welfare reform plan is based almost entirely on interviews with the principals. Reporting from Elizabeth Shogren in the *Los Angeles Times* and David Whitman in *U.S. News & World Report* provides valuable background. Grandy, Johnson, and Shaw made their remark that "no known public policy will subdue" rising rates of illegitimacy in "Moving Ahead," executive summary p. ii. Bennett, Kemp, and Weber criticized the GOP welfare plan in an Empower America memo dated Apr. 13, 1994. Engler's denunciation of "conservative micromanagement" came in testimony to the House Ways and Means Committee, Jan. 13, 1995. Gingrich defended orphanages on *Meet the Press* on Dec. 4, 1994. Shogren reported Shaw's comments on the Contract in the *Los Angeles Times* on Dec. 2, 1994. The CBO calculation that only six states might meet the work requirement in the House bill was reported in *Congressional Quarterly*, dated May 27, 1995. Jeffords made his remark that Dole pushed "to the limit in both directions" in the *Washington Post* of Sept. 25, 1995. Domenici's disparagement of the family cap was reported in the *Washington Post* on Sept. 14, 1995. Gingrich expressed his preference for a private social safety net on *Meet the Press*, Dec. 4, 1994. The Congressional Budget Office provided the calculation that the Republican budget plans would reduce federal spending to about 19 percent of gross national product.

On the deference of the GOP agenda to the market, several sources are valuable. See "The Mirage of Economic Equality," released by the Joint Economic Committee on May 2, 1995; also note Bill Kristol's essay in *The New Promise of American Life*, edited by Lamar Alexander and Chester E. Finn Jr. (Indianapolis: The Hudson Institute, 1995), particularly p. 124. Useful also is Michael Barone's introductory essay in *The Almanac of American Politics 1996* (Washington, D.C.: National Journal, 1995), in which he projects that government in the twenty-first century will gradually revert to the limited role it played in the nineteenth century: "establishing an ordered environment in which consensus economic transactions can take place" but not questioning the outcomes or social impacts of those transactions. In his book, *The Freedom Revolution* (Washington, D.C.: Regnery Publishing, 1995), Armey summarizes the case with characteristic bluster: "The market is rational," he writes, "and government is dumb" (see p. 316).

7. BIG TENT

The opening section of chapter 7 contains several references to surveys of or about the Christian Coalition. Frank Luntz conducted the poll for the Christian Coalition in Sept. 1995. Stanley B. Greenberg's poll of Perot voters, "The Road to Realignment: The Democrats and the Perot Voters," was commissioned by the Democratic Leadership Council and was released July 1, 1993. The findings about church attendance of Perot voters come from "Religious Voting Blocs in the 1992 Election: The Year of the Evangelical?" by Lyman A. Kellstedt, John C. Green, James L. Guth, and Corwin E. Smidt, published in the *Sociology of Religion 1994*.

We draw heavily from the work of Kellstedt, Green, Guth, and Smidt in the section describing the changing patterns of religious voting in America. The quartet of scholars produced three articles that were especially useful, in addition to the one cited above: "Murphy Brown Revisited: The Social Issues in the 1992 Election," published in *Disciples and Democracy: Religious Conservatives and the Future of American Democracy* (Washington, D.C.: Ethics and Public Policy Center, 1994), edited by Michael Cromartie; "Has Godot Finally Arrived?," in *The Public Perspective*, June/July 1995; and "Evangelical Realignment: The Political Power of the Christian Right," published in *Christian Century*, July 5–12, 1995. The reference to Richard Nixon's support among Baptists comes from *Why Americans Hate Politics* (New York: Simon & Schuster, 1991) by E. J. Dionne Jr.

Background material on the failures of the Moral Majority and other activities of religious conservatives in the 1980s come from a number of sources, including A. James Reichley's *Religion in American Public Life* (Washington, D.C.: The Brookings Institution, 1985), and Jeffrey K. Hadden and Anson Shupe's *Televangelism: Power and Politics on God's Frontier* (New York: Henry Holt, 1988). Falwell's quote about AIDS comes from an article in the *Los Angeles Times*, dated Sept. 29, 1985, while his decision to close the organization was described in a *New York Times* article dated June 12, 1989. Reports about the political success of religious conservatives in local elections and the backlash those victories triggered come from several different sources: Erin Saberi's "From Moral Majority to Organized Minority: Tactics of the Religious Right," in *Christian Century*, dated Aug. 11–18, 1993; background materials prepared by People for the American Way; articles by Seth Mydans in the *New York Times* of Nov. 28, 1994, and by William Hamilton in the *Washington Post* of May 12, 1994; *Mother Jones*, Mar./Apr. 1994; and "An Army of the Faithful," by Robert Sullivan in the *New York Times Magazine* of Apr. 25, 1993. We interviewed Kathy Meixill, George Plew, and Rob Iten in Minnesota in June 1994. The quotes by Tom Kean come from the *Bergen Record*, dated July 3, 1994. *Campaigns & Elections* published its analysis of the Christian Coalition's influence on state Republican parties, "Has the Christian Right Taken Over the Republican Party?" by John F. Persinos, in the Sept. 1994 issue. The Minnesota fight comes from our own reporting at the time, although Arne Carlson's quote about Allen Quist as "a cult leader" was made to a weekly newspaper in Minnesota. The Texas state Republican convention received extensive coverage in the press, and we have drawn from a number of articles, including Richard L. Berke's in the June 12, 1994, issue of the *New York Times*, and an op-ed piece by Molly Ivins in the *Washington Post* on June 16, 1994, as well as from the party platform itself.

Two interviews with Ralph Reed, Reed's book *Politically Incorrect: The Emerg-*

ing Faith Factor in American Politics (Dallas: Word Publishing, 1994), along with considerable background material in other periodicals and newspapers helped us in profiling Reed's rise to power. Other articles we drew from included "The Gospel According to Ralph" by Jeffrey H. Birnbaum in the May 15, 1995, issue of *Time*; a series in the *Washington Post* by David Von Drehle, Thomas B. Edsall, and R. H. Melton, dated Aug. 14–15, 1994; and "Life Beyond God" by Leslie Kaufman in the Oct. 16, 1994, issue of the *New York Times Magazine*. Others interviewed who provided helpful information on the growth of the Coalition include Marshall Wittmann, Brian Lopina, Dick Weinhold, Ione Dilley, and Judy Haynes. Pat Robertson's book *The New World Order* (Dallas: Word Publishing, 1991) drew a harsh critique from Michael Lind in the Feb. 2, 1995, issue of the *New York Review of Books*. Robertson answered back on several television interviews, most specifically on CNN's *Evans and Novak* on Apr. 15, 1995. Reed's quotation that Robertson is "absolutely invaluable" to the Coalition comes from an interview on Aug. 22, 1995. His comments about the Holocaust are from the prepared text of his speech to the Anti-Defamation League of B'nai B'rith on Apr. 3, 1995. His quotes about "a legacy of racism" are contained in his book *Politically Incorrect*. His comments that the Christian Coalition contract contained "ten suggestions, not Ten Commandments" come from his press conference on May 17, 1995. Weld's criticism of Reed comes from an interview on Mar. 20, 1995. Martin Mawyer's criticism is in an op-ed article in the *Washington Post* on Sept. 26, 1993. Gary Bauer's criticism is from an interview with the authors.

The description of Lee Atwater's concerns about abortion are from an interview at the time. Rich Bond's attack on single-issue politics and Phyllis Schlafly's rejoinder come from an article by David S. Broder and Thomas B. Edsall in the Jan. 30, 1993, editions of the *Washington Post*. Steve Gunderson's comments about abortion are from an interview on July 21, 1995. Weld, Wilson, and Whitman were interviewed about abortion on NBC's *Meet the Press* on Nov. 20, 1994. George Weigel and William Kristol outlined their proposal for rewriting the platform plank on abortion in an article in the *National Review*, dated Aug. 15, 1994. Bennett's letter to Weyrich is dated Oct. 13, 1995, and was widely released to the press.

In the section about the Perot movement, the quotations from Perot followers come from our own reporting during the past four years. We also draw on a number of polls that focused on Perot and his supporters, including a *U.S. News & World Report* poll conducted in May 1993 by Ed Goeas and Celinda Lake; the Stan Greenberg poll for the Democratic Leadership Council previously cited; a *Washington Post*–ABC News poll in Aug. 1995; and a CBS News–*New York Times* poll that same month. The *Washington Post* conducted three focus groups with a handful of Perot supporters in Phoenix between 1992 and 1994, and those sessions helped to illuminate the anger toward politicians and the two parties. Similar findings come from focus groups conducted by Peter Hart and Geoff Garin in the summer of 1994. The information about fund-raising by Republicans in 1995 comes from a variety of sources, including an article by John Moore in the Mar. 25, 1995, issue of *National Journal;* an Apr. 6, 1995, report by Common Cause, and another on Aug. 15, 1995; and an Apr. 6, 1995, report by Citizen Action. Richard L. Berke of the *New York Times* had two good articles describing the GOP's heavy-handed tactics in soliciting funds; one ran on Mar. 20, 1995; the other on June 16, 1995. Verney's assertion that "99 percent" of the Dallas conference attendees wanted to curb the power of money in Washington is contained in UWSA Legislative Update no. 26 posted on the Internet on Aug. 29, 1995. Information about the economic status of Perot supporters comes from the Times Mirror Center for The People & The Press study entitled "The New American Landscape," released in Sept. 1994, as well as from an analysis of exit poll data from 1992 and 1994 provided by CBS News. Another helpful study was done by Ruy Teixeira of the Economic Policy Institute, entitled "The Politics of the High-Wage Path: The Challenge Facing Democrats," dated Oct. 1994. The interview with Russ Verney took place on Aug. 9, 1995, about six weeks before Perot decided to form a third party, and gives some insight into how quickly the thinking changed in the Perot camp during the late summer of 1995.

8. WAITING FOR REALIGNMENT

For the electoral results in this chapter, we have relied upon the indispensable *Vital Statistics on American Politics,* by Harold W. Stanley and Richard G. Neimi (Washington, D.C.: Congressional Quarterly, 1994), and also on Congressional Quarterly's "Guide to Congress." Figures on the rise in split-ticket voting are reported on p. 147 of *Vital Statistics.* Also useful was the Walter Dean Burnham essay on the 1994 election in *The Clinton Presidency: First Appraisals,* edited by Colin Campbell and Bert A. Rockman (Chatham, N.J.: Chatham House Publishers, 1995). Burnham's essay (p. 369) is the source for the fact that both Democratic and Republican incumbent House members saw their vote decline in 1990, and that only Democratic incumbents continued to decline in 1992.

Comparisons of the 1988 Bush vote and 1994 Republican congressional vote are based on analyses of the 1988 CBS–*New York Times* exit poll and the 1994 VNS exit poll. Ruy Teixeira was gracious in performing some specialized calculations that deepened the analysis.

Many polls pinpoint the paradoxical public attitudes about government. One particularly valuable work was the joint survey by Robert Teeter and Peter Hart for the Council for Excellence in Government released in March 1995. It is the source of the information that far more people support reforming government than reducing it (p. 21). That poll also revealed the doubts that business could be trusted to behave on its own (pp. 14–16). Also valuable was the Times Mirror Center for The People & The Press study "The New Political Landscape," released in Oct. 1994, which is the source for the figure that three-fourths of the public still believe too much power is concentrated in big business. It also contains representative findings on the extent to which the public believes government programs are inefficient and wasteful (see p. 24).

Most of the discussion of Democratic responses to the Republican advance is based on our interviews with administration and congressional figures. Clinton's statement of government's role is from a speech to the Democratic National Committee on June 28, 1995. His declaration that he was sympathetic to the "Democratic position" on the budget was quoted in the *Washington Times*, dated June 15, 1995.

Don Eberly's quote on the dangers of overpromising in the Republican revolution is taken from his article "Even Newt Can't Save Us" in the *Wall Street Journal* on Mar. 2, 1995; Bill Bennett has frequently made the same point in his speeches and writings. John DiIulio's observation that "big government is a raging bull" comes from his article in the winter 1994 issue of *The Public Interest*. The figure on the number of families who will be cut off welfare when the GOP time limit is fully phased in is taken from the Urban Institute's *Welfare Reform Briefs, Number Five*, dated May 1995. For disappointing results of the family cap welfare reform, see the Rutgers University study reported in the *Washington Post* of June 21, 1995; for the disappointing results of liberal programs to discourage teen pregnancy, see the report "Lives of Promise, Lives of Pain: Young Mothers After New Chance" by Janet C. Quint and Judith S. Musick (New York: Manpower Demonstration Research Corp., 1994).

The Congressional Budget Office's study — "An Analysis of the President's Budgetary Proposals for Fiscal Year 1996" — reports (p. 55) that most economists believe a balanced budget would reduce interest rates one or two percentage points. For expectations of dramatic economic benefits from a balanced budget, see *Business Week* of July 24, 1995; for the CBO's projection, see the 1996 report, pp. 54 and 58. The stability of the federal tax burden on middle-income families is recounted in a CBO study included in the 1993 edition of the *Green Book*, published by the House Committee on Ways and Means (p. 1497). Lawrence Mishel performed calculations showing that even with a tax cut, families gaining ground at the speed the median income is increasing today would still not match the advance of families gaining ground at the rate the median income increased during the 1950s and 1960s. The Bureau of Labor Statistics' projections on job growth for the next decade are contained in its publication *Monthly Labor Review*, dated Nov. 1993. On the mixed success of federal job-training programs, see James J. Heckman, "Is Job Training Oversold?," in *The Public Interest*, spring 1994.

Figures on crime are from the Federal Bureau of Investigation. Expectations that demographic change will again cause crime rates to increase in the next few years are common among criminologists; see James Q. Wilson, "What to Do About Crime," in *Commentary*, Sept. 1994, for a representative analysis. The global nature of trends in family breakup, crime, and income stagnation are covered in a variety of sources. On crime, see Wilson, "What to Do," p. 25. On rising illegitimacy rates across the Western world, see Sara McLanahan and Gary

Sandefur, *Growing Up with a Single Parent: What Hurts, What Helps* (Cambridge, Mass.: Harvard University Press, 1994), pp. 138–142. On income stagnation (and the tradeoff with unemployment), see Richard B. Freeman, *Working Under Different Rules* (New York: Russell Sage Foundation, 1994), and Lawrence F. Katz in *Widening Earnings Inequality: Why and Why Now*, edited by Janet L. Norwood (Washington, D.C.: Urban Institute, 1994). For expectations of a productivity boom, see Michael Rothschild in *The New Democrat*, July–Aug. 1995; anticipation of a coming productivity boom is also a regular theme in *Business Week*. For expectations of a cultural revival, see Gertude Himmelfarb, *The De-Moralization of Society: From Victorian Virtues to Modern Values* (New York: Alfred A. Knopf, 1995), pp. 229–232.

Several works helped our analysis of the late nineteenth century. The most valuable was Robert H. Wiebe, *The Search for Order: 1877–1920* (New York: Hill & Wang, 1967); his observation that "never had so many citizens" distrusted their government is quoted on p. 5. James MacGregor Burns, *The Workshop of Democracy* (New York: Alfred A. Knopf, 1985), is the source (p. 226) for Grover Cleveland's definition of government's role.

Polling figures on interest in a third party are taken from *USA Today* of Aug. 11, 1995, for the contemporary numbers; the historical figures are found in Gordon S. Black and Benjamin D. Black, *The Politics of American Discontent: How a New Party Can Make Democracy Work Again* (New York: John Wiley & Sons, 1994), pp. 23–24. For Bill Bradley's denunciation of the party, see his retirement statement, dated Aug. 16, 1995. For Thomas H. Kean's similar remarks, see the *Washington Post* of Sept. 1, 1995. Bill Bennett's call for Americans to "push hard against an age that is pushing very hard against us" is contained in his introduction to Don Eberly's essay, *Restoring the Good Society: A New Vision for Politics and Culture* (Grand Rapids, Mich.: Baker Books, 1994).

Bibliography

Alexander, Lamar, and Chester E. Finn Jr. *The New Promise of American Life*. Indianapolis: The Hudson Institute, 1995.

Ambrose, Stephen E. *Nixon: The Education of a Politician 1913–1962*. New York: Simon & Schuster, 1987.

———. *Nixon: The Triumph of a Politician 1962–72*. New York: Simon & Schuster, 1989.

Armey, Dick. *The Freedom Revolution*. Washington, D.C.: Regnery Publishing, 1995.

Armor, John. *Why Term Limits?* Ottawa, Ill.: Jameson Books, 1994.

Barone, Michael. *The Almanac of American Politics 1996*. Washington, D.C.: National Journal, 1995.

Barry, John M. *The Ambition and the Power*. New York: Viking Press, 1989.

Barta, Carolyn. *Perot and His People: Disrupting the Balance of Political Power*. Fort Worth, Tex.: The Summit Group, 1993.

Benjamin, Gerald, and Michael J. Malbin. *Limiting Legislative Terms*. Washington, D.C.: Congressional Quarterly, 1992.

Bennett, William J. *The De-Valuing of America: The Fight for Our Culture and Our Children*. New York: Touchstone, 1992.

———. *The Index of Leading Cultural Indicators: Facts and Figures on the State of American Society*. New York: Touchstone, 1994.

Black, Earl, and Merle Black. *Politics and Society in the South*. Cambridge, Mass.: Harvard University Press, 1987.

———. *The Vital South*. Cambridge, Mass.: Harvard University Press, 1992.

Black, Gordon S., and Benjamin D. Black. *The Politics of American Discontent: How a New Party Can Make Democracy Work Again.* New York: John Wiley & Sons, 1994.

Blumenthal, Sidney. *The Rise of the Counter-Establishment: From Conservative Ideology to Political Power.* New York: Times Books, 1986.

Blumenthal, Sidney, and Thomas Byrne Edsall. *The Reagan Legacy.* New York: Pantheon, 1988.

Broder, David S. *The Changing of the Guard: Power and Leadership in America.* New York: Simon & Schuster, 1980.

Bruce, Steve. *The Rise and Fall of the New Christian Right.* Oxford University Press, 1990.

Butler, Stuart, and Anna Kondratas. *Out of the Poverty Trap: A Conservative Strategy for Welfare Reform.* New York: Free Press, 1987.

Cannon, Lou. *President Reagan: The Role of a Lifetime.* New York: Simon & Schuster, 1991.

Caro, Robert A. *The Years of Lyndon Johnson: Means of Ascent.* New York: Alfred A. Knopf, 1982.

———. *The Years of Lyndon Johnson: The Path to Power.* New York: Alfred A. Knopf, 1990.

Cohodas, Nadine. *Strom Thurmond and the Politics of Southern Change.* New York: Simon & Schuster, 1993.

Connelly, William F. Jr., and John J. Pitney Jr. *Congress' Permanent Minority?: Republicans in the U.S. House.* Lanham, Md.: Littlefield, Adams, 1994.

Cramer, Richard Ben. *What It Takes: The Way to the White House.* New York: Random House, 1992.

Crane, Edward H., and Roger Pilon. *The Politics and Law of Term Limits.* Washington D.C.: The Cato Institute, 1994.

Davidson, Osha Gray. *Under Fire: The NRA and the Battle for Gun Control.* New York: Henry Holt, 1993.

Dionne, E. J. Jr. *Why Americans Hate Politics.* New York: Simon & Schuster, 1991.

Drew, Elizabeth. *On the Edge.* New York: Simon & Schuster, 1994.

Duffy, Michael, and Dan Goodgame. *Marching in Place: The Status Quo Presidency of George Bush.* New York: Simon & Schuster, 1992.

Dugger, Ronnie. *On Reagan: The Man and His Presidency.* New York: McGraw-Hill, 1983.

Duncan, Philip D., and Christine C. Lawrence. *Politics in America 1996: The 104th Congress.* Washington, D.C.: Congressional Quarterly, 1995.

Eberly, Don E. *Restoring the Good Society: A New Vision for Politics and Culture.* Grand Rapids, Mich.: Baker Books, 1994.

Echeverria, John, and Raymond Booth Eby. *Let the People Judge: Wise Use and the Property Rights Movement.* Washington, D.C.: Island Press, 1995.

Edsall, Thomas Byrne, and Mary D. Edsall. *Chain Reaction: The Impact of Race, Rights, and Taxes on American Politics.* New York: W. W. Norton, 1991.

Ehrman, John. *The Rise of Neoconservatism: Intellectuals and Foreign Affairs, 1945–1994.* New Haven: Yale University Press, 1995.

Foner, Eric. *Free Soil, Free Labor, Free Men: The Ideology of the Republican Party Before the Civil War.* London: Oxford University Press, 1970.

Fox, Richard. *Reinhold Niebuhr.* San Francisco: Harper & Row, 1987.

Freeman, Richard B. *Working Under Different Rules.* New York: Russell Sage Foundation, 1994.

Frum, David. *Dead Right.* New York: New Republic Books, 1994.

Gingrich, Newt. *To Renew America.* New York: HarperCollins, 1995.

Glazer, Nathan. *The Limits of Social Policy.* Cambridge, Mass.: Harvard University Press, 1988.

Gold, Steven D. *The Fiscal Crisis of the States.* Washington, D.C.: Georgetown University Press, 1995.

Goldman, Peter, et al. *Quest for the Presidency 1992.* College Station, Tex.: Texas A&M University Press, 1994.

Greenberg, Stanley B. *Middle Class Dreams: The Politics and Power of the New American Majority.* New York: Times Books, 1995.

Greider, William. *Who Will Tell the People: The Betrayal of American Democracy.* New York: Simon & Schuster, 1992.

Hadden, Jeffrey K., and Anson Shupe. *Televangelism: Power and Politics on God's Frontier.* New York: Henry Holt, 1988.

Hardeman, D. B., and Donald C. Bacon. *Rayburn: A Biography.* Austin, Tex.: Texas Monthly Press, 1987.

Hess, Stephen, and David S. Broder. *The Republican Establishment: The Present and Future of the G.O.P.* New York: Harper & Row, 1967.

Himmelfarb, Gertrude. *The De-Moralization of Society: From Victorian Virtues to Modern Values.* New York: Alfred A. Knopf, 1995.

Judis, John. *Grand Illusion.* New York: Farrar, Straus & Giroux, 1992.

Kazin, Michael. *The Populist Persuasion: An American History.* New York: Basic Books, 1995.

Key, V. O. Jr. *Southern Politics in State and Nation.* Knoxville: University of Tennessee Press, 1984.

Knaggs, John. *Two-Party Texas: The Years of John Tower, 1961–1984.* Austin, Tex.: Eakin Press, 1985.

Kohl, Lawrence Frederick. *The Politics of Individualism: Parties and the American Character in the Jacksonian Era.* New York: Oxford University Press, 1989.

LaPierre, Wayne. *Guns, Crime, and Freedom.* Washington, D.C.: Regnery Publishing, 1994.

Limbaugh, Rush H. III. *See, I Told You So.* New York: Pocket Books, 1993.

——. *The Way Things Ought to Be.* New York: Pocket Books, 1992.

Lipset, Seymour Martin, and William Schneider. *The Confidence Gap: Business, Labor, and Government in the Public Mind.* New York: Free Press, 1983.

Magnet, Myron. *The Dream and The Nightmare: The Sixties' Legacy to the Underclass.* New York: Quill, 1993.

Maraniss, David. *First in His Class: A Biography of Bill Clinton.* New York: Simon & Schuster, 1995.

Massey, Douglas S., and Nancy A. Denton. *American Apartheid: Segregation and the Making of the Underclass*. Cambridge, Mass.: Harvard University Press, 1993.

McCullough, David. *Truman*. New York: Simon & Schuster, 1992.

McLanahan, Sara, and Gary Sandefur. *Growing Up with a Single Parent: What Hurts, What Helps*. Cambridge, Mass.: Harvard University Press, 1994.

Mishel, Lawrence, and Jared Bernstein. *The State of Working America, 1994–95*. Armonk, N.Y.: M. E. Sharpe, 1994.

Moore, Stephen. *Restoring the Dream: The Bold New Plan by House Republicans*. New York: Times Books, 1995.

Murray, Charles. *In Pursuit of Happiness and Good Government*. New York: Simon & Schuster, 1988.

———. *Losing Ground: American Social Policy, 1950–1980*. New York: Basic Books, 1984.

Murray, Charles, and Richard J. Herrnstein. *The Bell Curve: Intelligence and Class Structure in American Life*. New York: Free Press, 1994.

Norwood, Janet. *Widening Earnings Inequality: Why and Why Now*. Washington, D.C.: The Urban Institute, 1994.

Novak, Michael, et al. *The New Consensus on Family and Welfare*. Milwaukee: Marquette University Press, 1987.

Olasky, Marvin. *The Tragedy of American Compassion*. Washington, D.C.: Regnery Publishing, 1992.

Phillips, Kevin P. *Arrogant Capital*. Boston: Little, Brown, 1994.

———. *The Emerging Republican Majority*. New Rochelle, N.Y.: Arlington House, 1969.

———. *Post-Conservative America*. New York: Random House, 1982.

Podhoretz, John. *Hell of a Ride*. New York: Simon & Schuster, 1993.

Quayle, Dan. *Standing Firm: A Vice Presidential Memoir*. New York: Harper-Collins, 1994.

Ranney, Austin. *The American Elections of 1984*. Durham, N.C.: Duke University Press, 1985.

Reed, Ralph. *Politically Incorrect: The Emerging Faith Factor in American Politics*. Dallas: Word Publishing, 1994.

Reichley, A. James. *Religion in American Public Life*. Washington, D.C.: The Brookings Institution, 1985.

Renberg, Dan, ed. *A House of Ill Repute*. Princeton, N.J.: Princeton University Press, 1987.

Reston, James B. Jr. *Lone Star: The Life of John Connally*. New York: Harper & Row, 1989.

Rothenberg, Randall. *The Neoliberals: Creating the New American Politics*. New York: Simon & Schuster, 1984.

Simon, Roger. *Road Show*. New York: Farrar, Straus & Giroux, 1990.

Smith, Richard Norton. *Thomas E. Dewey and His Times*. New York: Touchstone, 1982.

Stanley, Harold W., and Richard G. Niemi. *Vital Statistics on American Politics.* Washington, D.C.: Congressional Quarterly, 1994.

Steinfels, Peter. *The Neoconservatives: The Men Who Are Changing America's Politics.* New York: Simon & Schuster, 1979.

Sundquist, James L. *Dynamics of the Party System: Alignment and Realignment of Political Parties in the United States.* Washington, D.C.: The Brookings Institution, 1983.

Taylor, Paul. *See How They Run.* New York: Alfred A. Knopf, 1990.

Thompson, Jake H. *Bob Dole: The Republicans' Man for all Seasons.* New York: Donald I. Fine, 1994.

White, Theodore H. *The Making of the President 1960.* New York: Atheneum, 1961.

Wiebe, Robert H. *The Search for Order: 1877–1920.* New York: Hill & Wang, 1967.

———. *Self-Rule: A Cultural History of American Democracy.* Chicago: University of Chicago Press, 1995.

Wilson, James Q. *The Moral Sense.* New York: Free Press, 1993.

Witcover, Jules. *Marathon: The Pursuit of the Presidency 1972–1976.* New York: Viking Press, 1977.

Woodward, Bob. *The Agenda: Inside the Clinton White House.* New York: Simon & Schuster, 1994.

Index

and gun control, 160, 161
and health care plan, 183, 253
and 1994 elections, 51, 55, 56, 57
and NRA, 192
and Perot voters, 304
populism of, 175, 179
and Reagan, 216
and retrocons, 270
in the South, 212, 229, 244
and talk radio, 167, 194
and taxes, 171
and term limits, 256
and third party, 367
and welfare reform, 281
See also government, federal
Appropriations Committee, House, 48, 148, 151, 204
Archer, Bill, 49, 204, 286, 296
Archey, William T., 182, 387
Armed Services Committee, Senate, 102
Armey, Dick, 148, 149, 151, 204, 324, 380, 384, 385, 392
on balanced budget, 154
on Bush, 131
on Clinton, 106
and Contract With America, 38–40, 263, 281–283, 287, 294
and Gingrich, 37, 343, 365
and Limbaugh, 185
and Norquist, 181
on Republicans, 295, 342
on role of government, 298
on taxes, 137, 200, 296
Ashcroft, John, 295
assault weapons, ban on, 61, 103, 178, 197, 199, 201
in crime bill, 91, 196
NRA on, 94, 160, 188, 193–195
Atwater, Lee, 216, 316, 317, 338, 388
on abortion, 325, 394
and Campbell, 221–223
and Dukakis, 70, 177
Ayres, Whit, 225

Baird, Zoe, 60
Baker, James A., 128, 177, 228
Bakker, Jim and Tammy Faye, 306, 309

Barbour, Haley, 22, 98, 157, 207, 328, 379, 380, 383
on Clinton, 31, 32, 105, 107
and Contract With America, 52
and crime bill, 196
and fund-raising, 46, 47
and Gingrich, 39, 40
and GOP, 29, 30, 34
and governors, 284
and Kentucky election, 24, 26
and Limbaugh, 185
and Perot, 303, 332, 337
and religious conservatives, 33, 316
Barry, John, 123, 124, 383
Base Closing Commission, 149
Bauer, Gary L., 272, 281, 324, 394
Beasley, David, 219, 227
Begala, Paul, 68, 84, 86, 89, 95, 171
Bell Curve, The (Murray & Wilson), 265
Bennett, William J., 275, 343, 369, 379, 390, 396, 397
on abortion, 327, 328, 394
and antigovernment coalition, 15, 267
and Kristol, 249, 250, 389
and Limbaugh, 169, 170
on Proposition 187, 264
on welfare reform, 268–271, 278, 280, 288, 292, 391, 392
Bentsen, Lloyd, 98, 228, 232, 236
Berkowitz, Herb, 189
bipartisanship, 34, 104–106
Black, Earl, 211
Black, Merle, 211, 240, 243, 388
Black Caucus, 92, 93, 195
blacks. *See* African-Americans
Bliley, Thomas, 48
Bliss, Ray, 30
block grants, 284, 285, 287, 289, 292, 295, 296
Bob Jones University, 225
Boehner, John, 40, 48, 146, 147, 199, 385
Bond, Rich, 325, 326, 394
Bonior, David, 365
Book of Virtues, The (Bennett), 268
Boren, David, 22
Bosnia, 74, 81
Boyd, Patricia, 316
Bradley, Bill, 365–367, 397